International Debt Statistics 2020

International Debt Statistics 2020

WORLD BANK GROUP

1818 H Street NW, Washington DC 20433
Telephone: 202-473-1000; Internet: www.worldbank.org

1 2 3 4 22 21 20 19

ISBN (paper): 978-1-4648-1461-7
ISBN (electronic): 978-1-4648-1462-4
DOI: 10.1596/978-1-4648-1461-7

Cover design: Jomo Tariku, World Bank Group

The Library of Congress Cataloging-in-Publication Data has been requested.

Table of Contents

Foreword

Today's landscape of development finance is marked by the growing debt vulnerabilities of low- and middle-income countries. The post-2008 financial crisis era is characterized by a rapid rise in lending to them, fueled by factors including buoyant commodity prices, quantitative easing, and low interest rates in high-income countries. With increased access to international capital markets, many low- and middle-income countries shifted away from traditional sources of financing and experienced a sharp rise in external debt, raising new concerns about sustainability.

Among the low- and middle-income countries, several IDA-only countries have been recording the highest increases in external debt since the 2008 crisis. By the end of 2018, IDA-only countries had accumulated a total of $387 billion external debt stock, more than double the level of a decade earlier. External debt among Sub-Saharan African countries grew faster than in other regions: Over half of the countries in the region have seen their external debt stocks double. The increase in external debt stock over the same period is more pronounced for some countries: 885 percent for Ethiopia, 521 percent for Zambia, 437 percent for Uganda, and 395 percent for Ghana.

Ghana's sovereign Eurobond, issued in 2007, marked the entry of African countries into the international capital markets. Since then, 12 other IDA-only countries have gained market access with bond issuance and other private sources of financing. The sovereign borrowers in Sub-Saharan Africa have accumulated $116 billion in bonds, and 89 percent of those bonds were issued by IDA-only countries.

Sustainable borrowing is an important tool for economic growth and poverty eradication. It boosts countries' capacity for long-term financing to invest in infrastructure, education, employment, and health. However, the rapid rise in debt accumulation and the shifts in debt composition pose new challenges for managing it. For both borrowers and creditors to safeguard debt sustainability, and for governments to design effective macroeconomic policies, debt transparency is critical.

Accurate and comprehensive information on the levels of debt, as well as its composition, is more necessary than ever.

This year's *International Debt Statistics* (IDS) presents the freshest data on trends in external debt in low- and middle-income countries. IDS now provides the clearest picture yet of government borrowing and sources of lending by type of creditor, with increased perspicuity on data availability and improved data comparability. For the first time, IDS features detailed data on borrowing by public corporations and guarantees provided by governments, which sheds light on their contingent liabilities.

IDS 2020 provides a select set of indicators, with an expanded data set available online. The World Bank is committed to continue working with governments and partners to improve data coverage, quality, and timeliness and to promote greater debt transparency and sustainability.

David Malpass
President
The World Bank Group

Acknowledgments

This volume was prepared by the Debt Data Team of the Development Data Group (DECDG) at the World Bank, led by Evis Rucaj under the management of Haishan Fu, Director, and comprising Parul Agarwal, Arzu Aytekin Balibek, Allen Charles Church Jr., Wendy Ven-dee Huang, Daniella Kathyuska Bolanos Misas, Malvina Pollock, Rubena Sukaj, and Rasiel Vellos, who worked closely with other teams in DECDG. The team was assisted by Christelle Kouame. The overview of current developments was prepared by the Debt Data Team of DECDG; country economists reviewed the data tables. The work was carried out under the direction of Haishan Fu. Valuable input was provided by the Office of the Senior Vice President, and by the Chief Economist, Development Economics.

International Debt Statistics electronic products were prepared by a team led by Malarvizhi Veerappan and comprising Ramgopal Erabelly, Rajesh Kumar Danda, Karthik Krishnamoorthy, and Ugendran Machakkalai. The cover was designed by Jomo Tariku and Parul Agarwal. Jewel McFadden from DEC Knowledge and Strategy and Susan Graham and Orlando Mota from Global Corporate Solutions, Design and Publications, coordinated the publication and dissemination of the book.

PART I
Overview

Executive Summary

Financial flows to low- and middle-income countries came under pressure in 2018 due to a combination of factors impacting the global economy, including rising U.S. interest rates and dollar appreciation, trade tensions, and general concerns about a slowdown in growth. These pressures were exacerbated by idiosyncratic country factors, including acute external financial vulnerabilities (for example, high external debt combined with low foreign exchange reserves), worsening domestic economic and political risk, or exposure to mounting trade tensions. Overall financial inflows to low- and middle-income countries (debt and equity) fell 19 percent relative to the 2017 level. Central to this picture was China, which received over 42 percent of the net financial flows to low- and middle-income countries in 2017–18, a reflection, in part, of China's efforts to open its domestic bond and stock markets, and of the Morgan Stanley Capital Investment's (MSCI's) decision to include Chinese stocks in its benchmark indexes. Net financial inflows to China fell by a modest 4 percent in 2018, compared to a 29 percent decline to other low- and middle-income countries. The volume of financial flows to China and the level of its external debt stock are not large relative to the size of the domestic economy— Chinese debt as a share of GNI was 14 percent in 2018—but they are significant relative to other low- and middle-income countries, and they dominate the aggregate trends. To assist in the interpretation of the data, this report looks beyond the headline numbers to outcomes and trends at the regional and country-specific level and for some sub-groups, including those eligible for IDA resources.

Net financial (debt and equity) flows to low- and middle-income countries totaled $1 trillion in 2018, but this was 19 percent below the 2017 level

Driving the downturn was a 28 percent fall in net debt inflows, to $529 billion, and a 49 percent reduction in portfolio equity inflows, to $35 billion. FDI inflows of $469 billion did not change much from 2017. The volume, and direction, of net financial flows in 2018, both debt and equity, were propelled by outcomes in China. It accounted for 49 percent of the combined net debt flows and 43 percent of the combined net equity flows to low- and middle-income countries in 2018. Net financial flows to China fell 4 percent in 2018, with an 18 percent decline in net debt flows largely offset by higher equity inflows. This contrasted sharply with other low- and middle-income countries where the net financial flows were, on average, 29 percent lower than in 2017.

External debt stocks at the end of 2018 approached $8 trillion, but the overall pace of accumulation was much slower than in 2017

On average, the external debt stock of low- and middle-income countries rose 5.2 percent in 2018, about half the rate of accumulation (10.4 percent) in 2017. China's external debt stock rose 15 percent, to $2 trillion—one quarter of the combined end-2018 external debt stocks of low- and middle-income countries. The average increase in 2018 external debt stocks in low- and middle-income countries other than China was 2 percent, but in some countries the increase was much larger. Conversely, for several of the largest borrowers, including the Russian Federation, South Africa, and Turkey, external debt stocks declined.

With debt stocks on the incline, debt burdens of low- and middle- income countries were broadly in line with those of 2017

The ratio of external debt to GNI averaged 26 percent, while the debt to export ratio averaged 101 percent— only moderately lower than the prior year of 105 percent. About 45 percent of those countries' debt to export ratio record over 150 percent, with the Sub-Saharan Africa region dominating.

Net debt inflows to low- and middle-income countries fell 28 percent in 2018, to $529 billion, driven by downturns in both long-term and short-term debt inflows.

Net long-term debt inflows fell to $304 billion ($409 billion in 2017) due to a sharp reduction in net inflows from bondholders. These fell 47 percent, to $157 billion. The 86 percent rise in net inflows from multilateral creditors reflected the International Monetary Fund's (IMF's) support for Argentina, which was the key factor in the 86 percent rise in net inflows from multilateral creditors in 2018. They rose to $61 billion, of which half went to Argentina. Net inflows from multilateral creditors to other low- and middle-income countries were unchanged from the 2017 level. Short-term debt flows to low- and middle-income countries, other than China, contracted 62 percent in 2018, to $37 billion ($97 billion in 2017).

Bond issuance by low- and middle-income countries fell sharply 2018

On average, bondholders accounted for half of net long-term debt inflows to low- and middle-income countries in 2018, and for many countries, including some the world's poorest, they were the primary source of external financing. Low- and middle-income countries issued $302 billion in international bonds in 2018. This was 26 percent lower than in 2017, when issuance hit an all-time high of $405 billion. Global economic uncertainties, the tightening of capital markets, and for some countries, credit rating downgrades, drove the downturn. But 2018 was a banner year for sovereign borrowers in Sub-Saharan Africa. New issuance by countries in the region, excluding South Africa, more than doubled, to a new high of $17 billion, and were characterized by longer maturities; all issues included a 30-year tranche, and all of them were oversubscribed.

Aggregate Financial Flows to Low- and Middle-Income Countries

International financial flows to low- and middle-income countries in 2018, debt and equity combined, totaled a little over $1 trillion. This was close to 20 percent lower than the comparable figure for 2017. Measured relative to GNI, aggregate financial flows were equivalent to 3.4 percent, a marked decrease from 2017 (4.4 percent), and well short of the 6.9 percent recorded in 2010.

Table O.1 Aggregate Net Financial Flows to Low- and Middle-income Countries, 2009–2018
US$ (billion)

	2009	2010	2011	2012	2013	2014	2015	2016	2017	2018
Net financial flows, debt and equity	655.6	1,373.3	1,323.4	1,212.7	1,446.1	1,117.5	209.4	725.5	1,274.9	1,032.2
Percent of GNI (%)	4.0	6.9	5.7	4.9	5.5	4.1	0.8	2.8	4.4	3.4
Net Debt Inflows	170.8	719.8	715.2	580.0	804.6	525.3	-318.2	210.6	734.4	528.7
Long-term	137.9	290.5	406.1	459.2	439.8	383.1	162.3	247.4	408.6	303.8
Official creditors	81.5	74.8	35.6	31.7	28.3	46.2	47.9	62.4	56.4	78.5
World Bank (IBRD and IDA)	17.5	22.5	6.5	12.0	14.0	14.9	17.3	13.6	12.9	14.8
IMF	26.4	13.4	0.5	-8.4	-17.7	-7.2	4.8	5.0	3.6	30.9
Private creditors	56.4	215.6	370.4	427.5	411.5	337.0	114.5	184.9	352.2	225.4
Bonds	47.3	104.5	150.6	213.4	166.8	171.6	70.8	121.2	295.5	157.2
Banks and other private	9.1	111.2	219.8	214.1	244.6	165.4	43.7	63.7	56.7	68.1
Short-term	32.9	429.3	309.2	120.8	364.9	142.1	-480.5	-36.8	325.8	224.9
Net equity flows	484.8	653.5	608.1	632.7	641.4	592.3	527.6	514.9	540.4	503.5
Net FDI inflows	360.8	527.3	604.4	538.9	570.9	508.4	506.0	470.3	471.5	468.6
Net portfolio equity inflows	124.0	126.2	3.8	93.8	70.6	83.9	21.6	44.6	68.9	34.9
Change in reserves (- = increase)	-622.8	-692.7	-454.8	-283.7	-519.1	96.9	607.6	277.4	-313.3	93.3
Memorandum item										
Workers remittances	270.9	299.8	337.9	364.2	384.4	412.9	426.1	415.4	446.7	481.5

Sources: World Bank Debtor Reporting System, International Monetary Fund, and Bank for International Settlements.

Uncertainties in global financial markets deterred investment in low- and middle-income countries. The decline in net financial flows was the result of a 27 percent drop in net debt inflows (gross disbursements minus principal payments) and a sharp contraction in portfolio equity flows. Net debt inflows fell to $529 billion in 2018, from $734 billion in 2017, and portfolio equity inflows fell 49 percent, to $35 billion. FDI equity inflows, long considered the most stable and resilient component of otherwise volatile financial flows, were $469 billion, unchanged from their 2016 and 2017 levels.

The headline numbers mask an important divergence in the volume and directional trend of international financial flows in 2018. Foremost is the dominance of international financial flows to China, which absorbed almost 49 percent of the combined net debt inflows, and 43 percent of the combined net equity flows to low- and middle-income countries in 2018.

Aggregate financial flows to China fell 4 percent in 2018, with an 18 percent reduction in net debt flows largely offset by a corresponding 22 percent rise in net equity flows (box O.1). This was in marked contrast to aggregate net financial flows to low- and middle-income countries, other than to China: These fell 29 percent in 2018, with debt inflows 35 percent, and net equity inflows 21 percent, lower than the comparable figures for 2017.

Figure O.1 Debt and Equity Flows to Low- and Middle-Income Countries, 2009–18

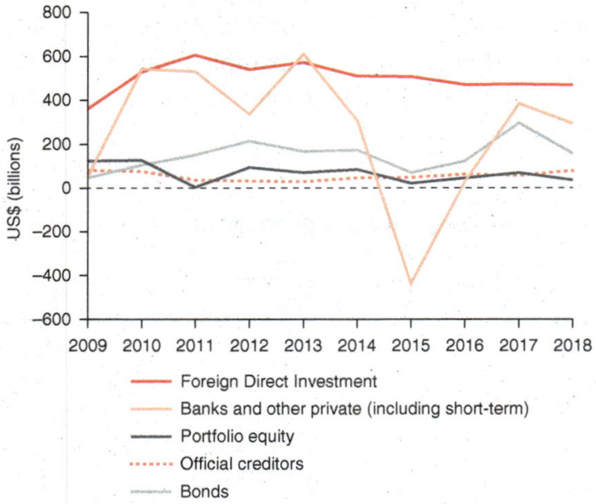

Sources: World Bank Debtor Reporting System; International Monetary Fund; and Bank for International Settlements.

Figure O.2 Aggregate Net Financial Flows to Low- and Middle-Income Countries, excluding China, 2009–18

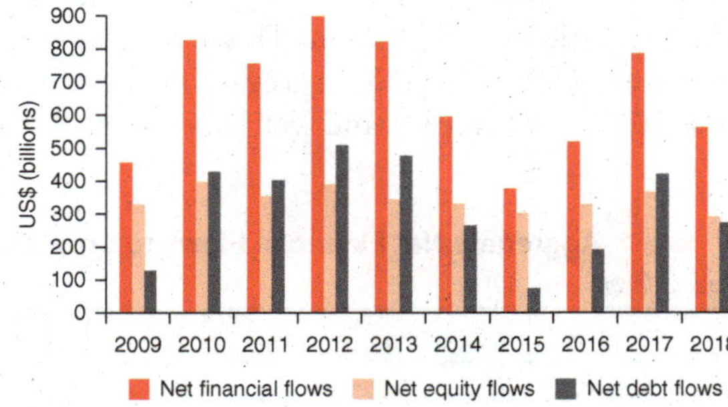

Sources: World Bank Debtor Reporting System; International Monetary Fund; and Bank for International Settlements.

Box O.1 China Debt Increases in Response to Further Capital Liberalization Reforms

Throughout the past decade, China has been far and away the largest recipient of financial flows, debt and equity, to the low- and middle-income countries. Net financial inflows to China from 2009 to the end of 2018 totaled $3.8 trillion—37 percent of net financial flows to all low- and middle-income countries. The net financial flows to China were 54 percent debt and 46 percent equity, primarily FDI. Two-thirds of the $257 billion in debt inflows was short-term debt. Regarding long-term debt, the largest share, 63 percent, constituted public and publicly guaranteed debt inflows. Nonguaranteed inflows to Chinese private-sector entities accounted for only 37 percent of long-term debt inflows, and 10 percent of overall debt inflows.

China's external debt stock at the end of 2018 was $1.96 trillion, 15 percent higher than the comparable debt stock at the end 2017 with short-term debt stock rising 18 percent, twice as fast as long-term debt. Most of the increase in debt stocks in 2018 is attributable to local currency (renminbi) debt owed to nonresidents and directly linked to China's measures to increasingly liberalize the current and capital account, to reform its foreign exchange administration, and to liberalize its financial market. The direct connection of the Shanghai stock market to those in Hong Kong SAR, China and Shenzhen is a prelude to connecting to London in 2019 and the MSCI's decision to include Chinese stocks in its benchmark indexes; these actions raised investor demand for renminbi-denominated bonds and stocks, currency and deposits, and trade credit. Portfolio equity inflows increased 68 percent in 2018, and of the $38 billion in bonds issued by the public sector in 2018, 56 percent were purchased by nonresidents in domestic currency.

Figure BO.1.1 Aggregate Net Financial Flows to China, 2009–18

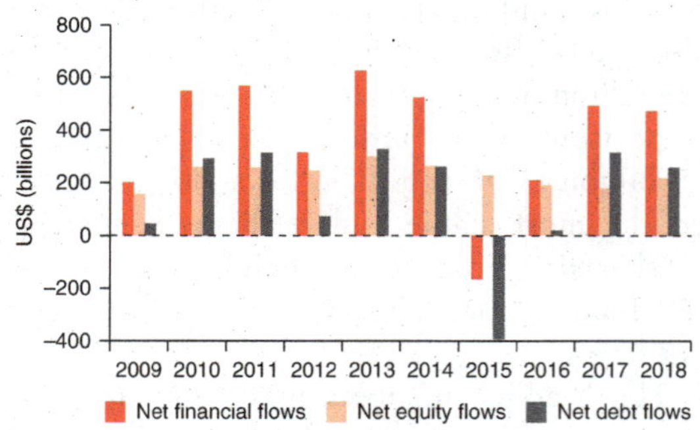

Sources: World Bank Debtor Reporting System; International Monetary Fund; and Bank for International Settlements.

External Debt Stocks in 2018

External debt stocks approached $8 trillion at the end of 2018 but, on average, the pace of accumulation was much slower than in 2017

The total external debt of low- and middle-income countries rose 5.2 percent in 2018, to $7.8 trillion, almost half the rate of accumulation (10.4 percent) recorded in 2017. The increase in debt stocks was the outcome of net debt inflows of $529 billion and valuation changes in year-on-year exchange rates in relation to the U.S. dollar (around half the external debt of low- and middle-income countries is denominated in currencies other than the U.S. dollar). Short-term debt was the fastest growing component of external debt stocks in 2018. It rose 12 percent, to $2.2 trillion, equivalent to 28 percent of total external debt stock. Long-term external debt stocks rose 3 percent, to $5.7 trillion, at the end of 2018.

The increase in external debt stocks was dominated by China, which accounted for one- quarter of the combined end-2018 external debt stocks of low- and middle-income countries. China's external debt stock rose 15 percent in 2018; short-term debt increased by 18 percent, and long-term debt by 9 percent. Outcomes in the remaining top ten largest borrowers (based on the end-of-2018 debt stocks) were significantly different. For this group of countries, external stocks at the end 2018 were, on average, unchanged from the end-of-2017 level, and in some cases were lower. Russia's external debt stock contracted 12 percent in 2018, and South Africa and Turkey reported a moderate decline. The outlier was Argentina where external debt stocks rose 19 percent in 2018, attributable in large part to the IMF economic support package and increased short-term borrowing. For the remaining low- and middle-income countries, (excluding China and the other top ten borrowers) external debt stock rose, on average, 4 percent in 2018, but for some countries it was much larger.

Outcomes at the regional and country levels were divergent. Countries in the Middle East and North Africa region recorded the fastest accumulation in external debt stock, on average 6 percent, propelled by Egypt, which posted a 17 percent increase. At the opposite end of the spectrum, countries in Europe and Central Asia reported a 5.5 percent reduction in external debt stocks from the 2017 level.

Viewed from the perspective of maturity structure and distribution by type of borrower: 28 percent of the combined end-2018 external debt stocks of low- and middle-income countries were short-term; 38 percent were long-term obligations of public and publicly guaranteed borrowers; and 33 percent were nonguaranteed long-term obligations of private entities. If China is excluded, the picture changes significantly: the share of short-term debt falls to 16 percent, and the share of long-term debt owed by public and publicly guaranteed borrowers rises to 46 percent.

The composition of China's external debt stock— 62 percent short-term debt, and 12 percent the long-term obligations of public sector borrowers at the end of 2018—is atypical for low- and middle-income countries.

Figure O.3 External Debt Stocks of Low- and Middle-Income Countries, 2009–18

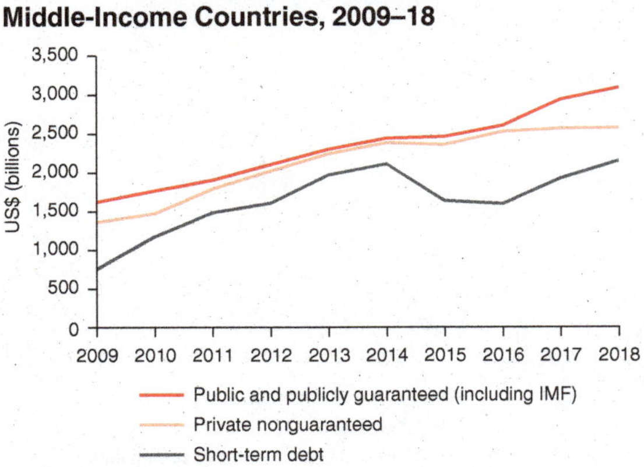

Source: World Bank Debtor Reporting System.

Figure O.4 Top Ten Borrowers, Change in External Debt Stock, 2017–18

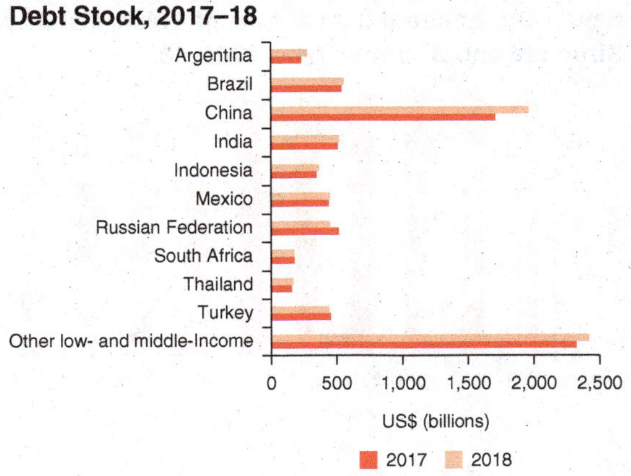

Source: World Bank Debtor Reporting System.

Figure O.5 External Debt Stocks of Low- and Middle-Income Countries, Regional Trends, 2009–18

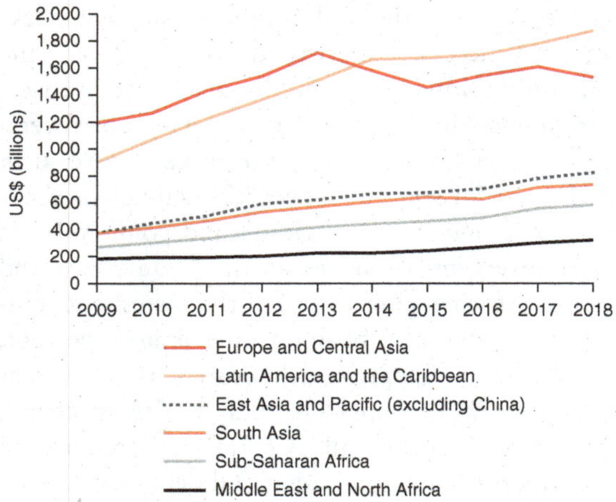

Source: World Bank Debtor Reporting System.

Figure O.6 External Debt Stock of Low- and Middle-Income Countries, excluding China, Maturity Structure and Borrower Type, 2009–18

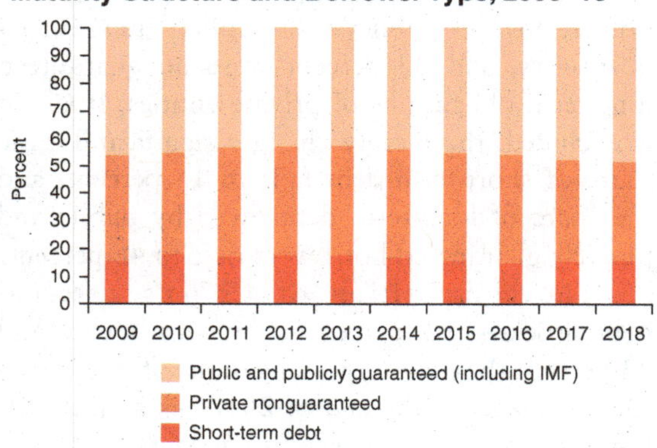

Source: World Bank Debtor Reporting System.

Figure O.7 External Debt Stocks of China, Maturity Structure and Borrower Type, 2009–18

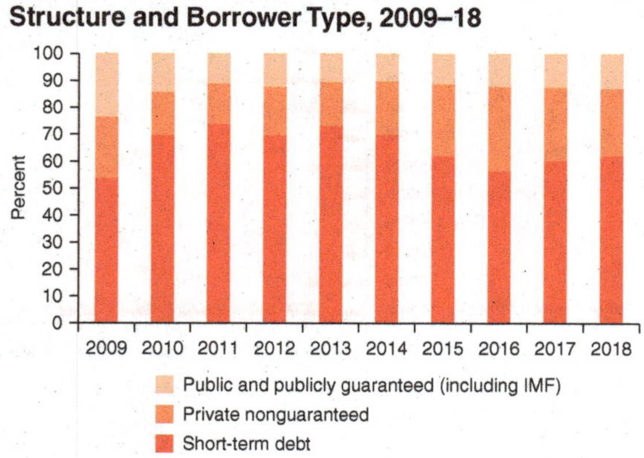

Source: World Bank Debtor Reporting System.

External Debt Flows in 2018

Net debt inflows to low- and middle-income countries fell 28 percent in 2018, to $529 billion, driven by downturns in both long-term and short-term debt inflows. Short-term debt flows to low- and middle-income countries, other than China, contracted 62 percent in 2018, to $37 billion ($97 billion in 2017). China accounted for 84 percent of the $225 billion in net short-term debt inflows to all low- and middle-income countries in 2018. Net long-term debt inflows fell to $304 billion in 2018 ($409 billion in 2017). The primary factor was the 47 percent drop in net inflows from bondholders, to $157 billion; this was partially offset by increased inflows from commercial banks and other private entities, which rose 20 percent, to $68 billion.

Net inflows from official creditors rose 39 percent, due to the 86 percent rise in net inflows from multilateral creditors. They climbed to $61 billion, but this was the outcome of IMF financing for Argentina—an IMF $57 billion bailout package agreed in 2018; it accounted for half of net inflows to low- and middle-income countries from all multilateral institutions in 2018. Excluding this transaction, net inflows from multilateral creditors to other low- and middle-income countries were unchanged from the 2017 level.

Net long-term debt inflows to public and publicly guaranteed borrowers fell by one-third in 2018, to $190 billion (from $285 billion). Net long-term debt inflows to private non-guaranteed borrowers also declined in 2018, falling by 8 percent, to $113 billion ($124 billion in 2017). As a result,

Figure O.8 Creditor Composition of Net Long-Term External Debt Flows, 2009–18

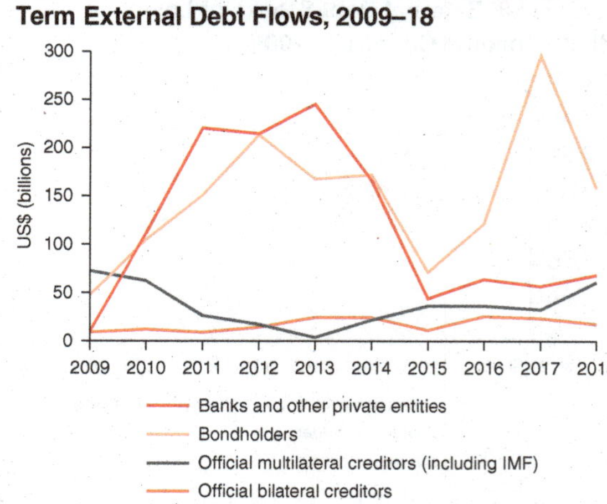

Source: World Bank Debtor Reporting System.

Table O.2 Bond Issuance by Low- and Middle-Income Countries, 2017–18
US$ (billion)

	Public issuers		Corporate issuers		All issuers	
	2017	2018	2017	2018	2017	2018
East Asia and Pacific	66.5	68.0	71.1	59.4	137.6	127.4
of which: China	33.3	38.1	61.1	50.4	94.4	88.5
Europe and Central Asia	41.9	30.9	20.5	11.4	62.4	42.3
Latin America and the Caribbean	87.1	69.2	34.3	21.3	121.3	90.5
Middle East and North Africa	15.7	12.7	0.3	0.3	16.0	13.0
South Asia	33.3	5.4	5.5	0.9	38.7	6.3
Sub-Saharan Africa	26.9	20.6	2.4	1.7	29.3	22.2
Low- and middle-Income countries	**271.2**	**206.7**	**134.0**	**95.0**	**405.2**	**301.7**

Source: World Bank Debtor Reporting System.

public and publicly guaranteed borrowers' share of net long-term debt inflows dropped to 63 percent, down from 70 percent in 2017.

Bond issuance by low- and middle-income countries fell sharply in 2018

Bond issuance by the 122 countries reporting to the World Bank Debtor Reporting System (DRS) totaled $302 billion in 2018, 26 percent below the record high issuance in 2017 ($405 billion), but still well above the comparable figure for 2016. Tighter capital market conditions, global economic uncertainties, and for some, credit-rating downgrades, deterred both public-sector and private-sector borrowers. New issuance by sovereign and other public-sector entities fell 24 percent in 2018, to $207 billion, while new issuance by private sector entities was down 29 percent from its prior year level, to $95 billion.

China accounted for 30 percent of bond issuance by low- and middle-income countries in 2018. Public and private sector entities in China issued $89 billion in 2018, 6 percent lower than the comparable figure for 2017, and characterized by offsetting trends. Bond issuance by public sector entities in China rose to $38 billion, an increase of 14 percent from the prior year level, while issuance by private- sector entities contracted by 18 percent over the same period, to $50 billion. In contrast to China, bond issuance by other top ten borrowers was down 39 percent in 2018, to $141 billion, with a notably sharp reduction by India, Russia, and South Africa. Issuance by other low- and middle-income countries fell a moderate 8 percent, to $72 billion.

For sovereign borrowers in Sub-Saharan Africa, 2018 was a banner year for issuance

Sovereign bond issuance by Sub-Saharan countries continued apace in 2018 to reach a new record high of $17.4 billion (excluding South Africa)—well over double the $9 billion issued in 2017. Major oil exporters, Angola and Nigeria, led the way, issuing $3.5 billion and $5.4 billion, respectively. Cote d'Ivoire, Ghana, Kenya, and Senegal each tapped the markets for around $2 billion. Proceeds from these issuances were used for infra-

Figure O.9 Net Long-Term External Debt Flows, Borrower Composition, 2009–18

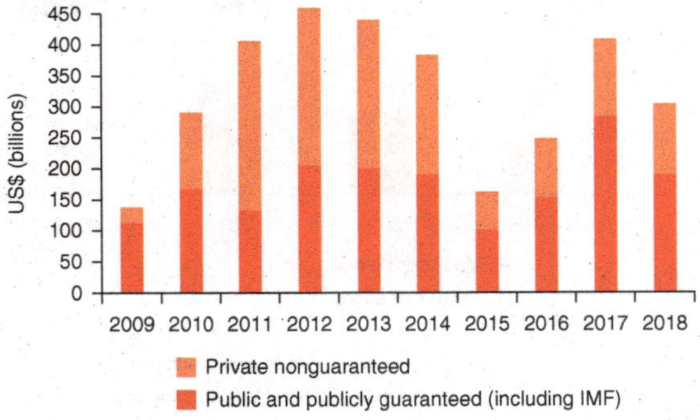

Source: World Bank Debtor Reporting System.

Figure O.10 Bond Issuance by China and Other Top Ten Borrowers, 2017–18

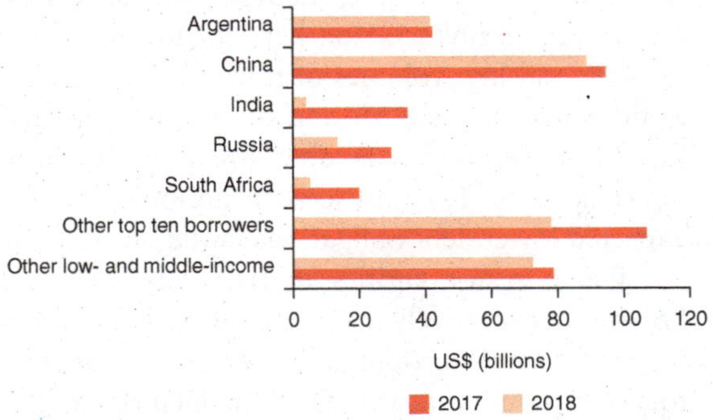

Source: World Bank Debtor Reporting System.

structure financing, balance-of-payments support, and refinancing of prior operations. All issues were heavily oversubscribed, a reflection of investor confidence in the region and attractive yields. The 2018 sovereign issues were characterized by longer maturities, and all included a 30-year tranche. Between 2009 and 2018, sovereign borrowers in Sub-Saharan Africa active in international markets (excluding South Africa) issued around $46 billion; countries eligible for IDA resources accounted for 85 percent of those bond issues.

Borrowing Activities of IDA-Only Countries

The combined external debt stock of countries classified as IDA-only almost doubled levels of 2009

Net debt flows to IDA-only countries reached $25 billion in 2018, 32 percent higher than the previous year, bringing external debt levels to $388 billion at end of the year. This marked a 6 percent increase from the comparable figure for end-2017, and close to double the 2009 levels. Over 90 percent of this debt was long-term. Net long-term inflows of public and publicly guaranteed debt to IDA-only countries rose 17 percent in 2018, to $25.2 billion. This increase was mainly led by a rise in net disbursements, which continued an upward trajectory in 2018 with an 19 percent increase, reaching 37.4 billion. Notably, this increase was not matched by an increase in new external loan commitments by public sector entities. New gross commitments in all IDA-only countries totaled $45.8 billion, a 4 percent decrease from 2017. The slowdown in new borrowing underscores investors' concerns about debt sustainability in IDA-only countries, uncertainty in financial market, sluggish economic growth, and low volumes of trade, because of the trade wars that have slowed down the non-Paris Club creditors into a lending stream to developing economies. This can serve as an indication for expected lower debt obligations in the future.

Public sector entities in IDA-only countries borrowed exclusively from multilateral creditors in 2018, which accounted for 46 percent of their total new commitments. IDA remained the largest creditor in the region with a 26 percent share on its own. A substantial decrease was noted in the borrowing from non-Paris Club bilateral creditors, amounting to 17 percent of the total share of new borrowing (a continued decline from the 43 percent share held in 2010), while Paris Club bilateral creditors have maintained the same share of 12 percent in 2018 to financing developing economies. Bonds pushed new commitments in the IDA-only group to $6.5 billion, equivalent to a 14 percent share during the year.

Concerns that external debt in some IDA-only countries may be at or approaching levels that pose a high risk of debt distress had a minimal impact on the new borrowing. In 2018, public sector borrowers contracted $46 billion in new external gross loan commitments, just 4 percent below the comparable figure for 2017, and brought total gross loan commitments for the past decade, 2009–18, to $381 billion—of which, bilateral creditors accounted for 44 percent, multilateral creditors for 40 percent, and private creditors (bondholders, commercial banks and other private creditors) 16 percent. For subsets of IDA-only countries, borrowing patterns differ sharply. In Sub-Saharan Africa, several countries have regularly accessed international capital markets in recent years, and/or borrowed from commercial banks, raising their share of new external gross loan commitments from 2009 to 2018, to 25 percent. The outcome was an increase in private creditors' share of outstanding public long-term debt to 41 percent at the end of 2018, compared to 17 percent at the end of 2009.

Figure O.11 Long-Term Commitments to IDA-Only Countries, 2015–18

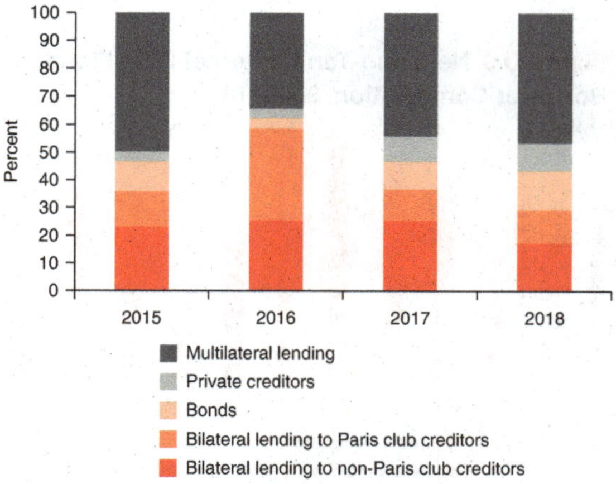

Source: World Bank Debtor Reporting System.

In contrast, IDA-only countries in other regions have continued to rely primarily on concessional financing from official creditors, with 58 percent of their new gross commitments coming from multilateral creditors—an 18 percent increase from 2017. Bilateral creditors accounted for a 39 percent share, with 21 percent being attributed to non-Paris Club member countries, and 18 percent to Paris Club ones. Bangladesh remained the largest IDA-only borrower with an external debt stock of $52 billion in 2018, with 33 percent of its new gross loan commitments coming from IDA.

Private creditors accounted for just 3 percent of external gross loan commitments over the same period. The divergent borrowing patterns are reflected in debt indicators. The debt-to-GNI ratio for IDA-only countries combined averaged 32 percent at the end of 2018; for countries in Sub-Saharan Africa, it averaged 30 percent, and for those located elsewhere, it averaged 20 percent.

Debt Indicators, 2009–18

Debt indicators confirm that debt burdens have contributed to economic vulnerabilities

On average, the external debt burden of low- and middle-income countries remains moderate. The ratio of external debt to GNI averaged 26 percent at the end of 2018, unchanged from the prior year average, and the ratio of external debt-to-export earnings improved slightly, falling to an average of 101 percent, from 105 percent in 2017. The low level of China's external debt, relative to GNI, 14 percent, and to exports, 68 percent, at end-2018 weighs heavily on these averages. The ratio of external debt to GNI in other low- and middle-income countries, excluding China, averaged almost 35 percent at the end of 2018, and the external debt-to-exports ratio was 120 percent.

Country-specific indicators vary widely, and for many low- and middle-income countries, they are on a deteriorating trajectory, giving credence to concerns about unsustainable debt burdens and the heightened risk of debt crises in some countries. The percentage of low- and middle-income countries with a debt-to-GNI ratio below 30 percent fell from 42 percent in 2009 to 25 percent at the end of 2018. Thirty percent of low- and middle-income countries had an external debt-to-GNI ratio above 60 percent at the end of 2018, and in 9 percent of countries, the ratio surpassed 100 percent.

The debt-to-export ratio shows a parallel trend. At the end of 2018, 45 percent of low- and middle-income countries had an external debt-to-export ratio of over 150 percent, compared to 25 percent in 2009, and in 25 countries, the ratio exceeded 200 percent— double the number in 2009.

Outcomes for countries in Sub-Saharan Africa are illustrative. About half of the countries in the region have seen external debt stocks double, and in some instances more than triple, since 2009. At the end of 2018, the average debt-to-GNI and debt-to-export ratios of countries in the region,

Figure O.12 External Debt-to-GNI Ratio, Low- and Middle-Income Country Distribution, 2009 and 2018

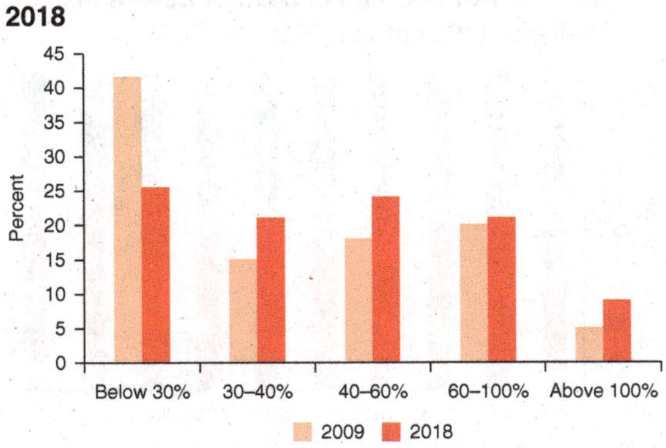

Sources: World Bank Debtor Reporting System; and International Monetary Fund.

Figure O.13 External Debt-to-Export Ratio, Low- and Middle-Income Country Distribution, 2009 and 2018

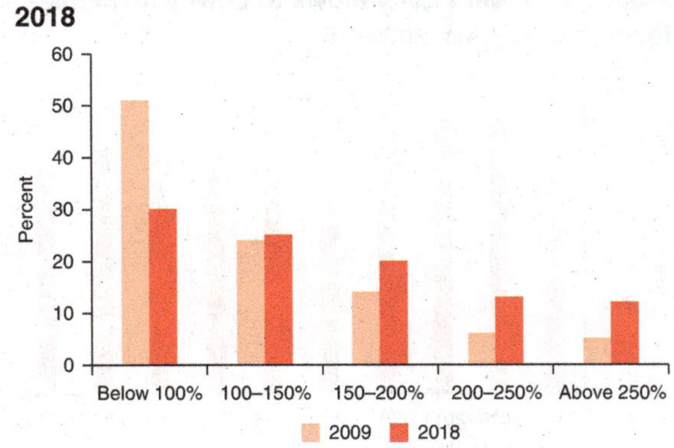

Sources: World Bank Debtor Reporting System; and International Monetary Fund.

excluding South Africa, was 32 percent and 127 percent, respectively; the comparable ratios for 2009 were 24 percent and 87 percent, respectively.

Equity Flows in 2018

Equity flows have been a key element of financial flows to low- and middle-income countries throughout the past decade, averaging $570 billion per annum and accounting for 49 percent of aggregate flows (debt and equity combined). Most equity inflows, 93 percent, comprised FDI.

FDI equity inflows in 2018 were unchanged from 2017, but with wide divergence at the regional and country level

FDI inflows to low- and middle-income countries remained stable in 2018, totaling $469 billion, virtually the same as in 2017. Inflows to China, the world's second largest FDI recipient, after the United States, are worth noting: They rose 10 percent in 2018, to $154 billion. Excluding China, net FDI inflows to other low- and middle-income countries fell, on average 5 percent in 2018; but the major factors of the downturn were FDI flows to Russia, which dropped by almost $17 billion in response to geopolitical concerns, sluggish GDP growth, and divestments (sale of foreign affiliates to Russian investors). When China and Russia are excluded, FDI inflows to other low- and middle-income countries were $304 billion in 2018, about the same as the prior year. At the regional and country-specific level there was wide divergence.

FDI inflows to China over the past decade totaled $2 trillion, well over twice the combined inflows to the next largest recipients, Brazil and India, with inflows of $541 billion and $336 billion, respectively over the same period. There was some lessening of the concentration in FDI inflows to low- and middle-income countries in recent years, with diversification to a wider pool of recipients. In 2018 China accounted for one- third of FDI inflows to low- and middle-income countries; but its share of these flows has softened (in 2013 its share was 50 percent).

Countries in Sub-Saharan Africa recorded the largest rise in FDI inflows in 2018, up 17 percent from the prior year to $24 billion, but this was attributable to the rebound of inflows to South Africa to $1.3 billion, from an outflow of $0.3 billion in 2017, and a slowing of repatriation of earnings in Angola with concomitant reduction in outflows to $5.9 billion ($7.3 billion in 2017). FDI inflows to other countries in the region were, on average, marginally higher in 2018 but with large divergence across countries. Heightened risk perceptions reduced inflows to Nigeria by 43 percent, to $2 billion. Inflows to Ghana fell 8 percent, to $3 billion, but those to the oil and gas sector remained strong. In Kenya inflows rose from negligible levels to a record $1.6 billion across diverse industries, in response to measures to facilitate private investment and improve Doing Business rankings. In Uganda, FDI inflows were up 79 percent, to $1.3 billion, mostly in the oil and gas sector. Inflows to Ethiopia, the largest FDI recipient in East Africa, were resilient, despite an 18 percent fall to $3.3 billion.

Figure O.14 Net Equity Flows to Low- and Middle-Income Countries, 2009–18

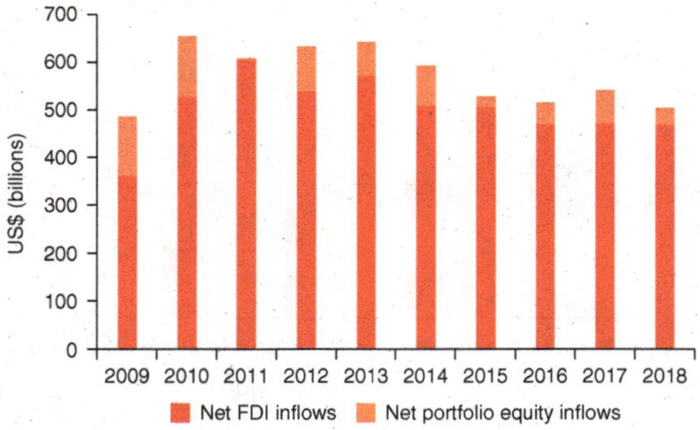

Source: International Monetary Fund.

Figure O.15 FDI to China and Other Low- and Middle-Income Countries, 2009–18

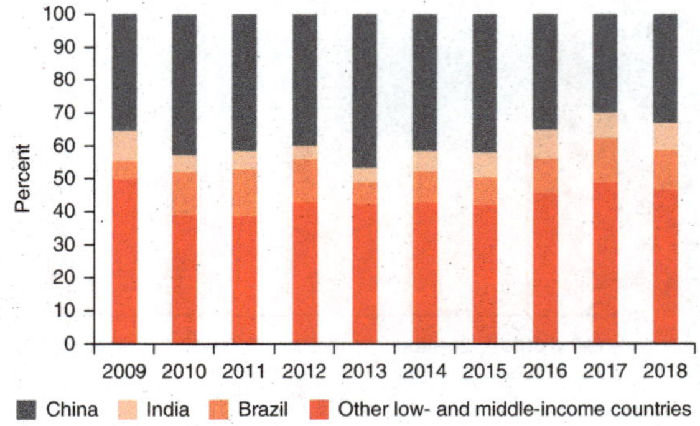

Source: International Monetary Fund.

FDI inflows to countries in the East and Pacific region, other than China, rose 11 percent in 2018, driven primarily by a 50 percent rise in flows to Thailand, to $13.3 billion. These came mostly from Asia investors, and they included new ventures and reinvestment by multinational corporations with a long-time presence in the country. FDI inflows to countries in South Asia increased 6 percent, to $45 billion. Inflows to India rose 6 percent, to $39.4 billion, reflecting new investment in the manufacturing and services sectors and cross-border mergers and acquisitions, including Walmart (United States) and India's biggest e-commerce platform, FlipKart. Inflows to Bangladesh climbed 40 percent, to $2.1 billion, due to large-scale investment in power generation and the $1.5 billion acquisition of United Dhaka Tobacco by Japan Tobacco. Inflows to countries in Europe and Central Asia, other than Russia (at $37.3 billion), were unchanged from the 2017 level, but for individual countries the picture was mixed. Inflows to Turkey were up 18 percent, to $12 billion, and in Serbia they rose 88 percent, to $3.1 billion, facilitated by the country's strategic location, diverse economy, and skilled labor force. In contrast, Azerbaijan and Kazakhstan saw inflows halved, due to sharp contraction in investments into the oil and gas sectors.

Countries in Latin America and the Caribbean record a 9 percent fall in FDI inflows in 2018, to $118 billion, due mostly to downturns in inflows to Brazil and Colombia. In Brazil, challenging economic conditions and a sharp reduction in mergers and acquisitions, from record levels in 2017, reduced FDI inflows 13 percent, to $56 billion. Inflows to Colombia fell 19 percent, notably in the oil sector. Flows to Argentina were resilient; despite economic turbulence, they rose 15 percent, to $10.4 billion, buoyed by investments in shale gas production. Net FDI inflows to countries in the Middle East and North Africa region fell 6 percent because of lower inflows to the Arab Republic of Egypt, Jordan, and Iran. Despite an 8 percent fall, inflows to Egypt remained strong, $6.8 billion, directed largely at the oil and gas sector. Morocco reaped the benefit of stable economic performance: inflows rose 54 percent, to $3 billion, directly to the infrastructure and automotive sectors.

Portfolio equity flows in 2018 retreated from most emerging market countries except China

Portfolio equity inflows are the most concentrated element of financial flows to low- and middle-income countries, and throughout the past decade only a few countries have benefited to any significant degree from such inflows in any given year. Cumulative portfolio equity inflows from 2009 to the end of 2018 totaled $672 billion, of which 83 percent went to three countries: China, $315 billion (47 percent); Brazil, $131 billion (19 percent); and India, $112 billion (17 percent).

Long recognized as the most capricious element of financial flows, portfolio equity flows

Figure O.16 Regional Distribution of Foreign Direct Investment, 2016–18

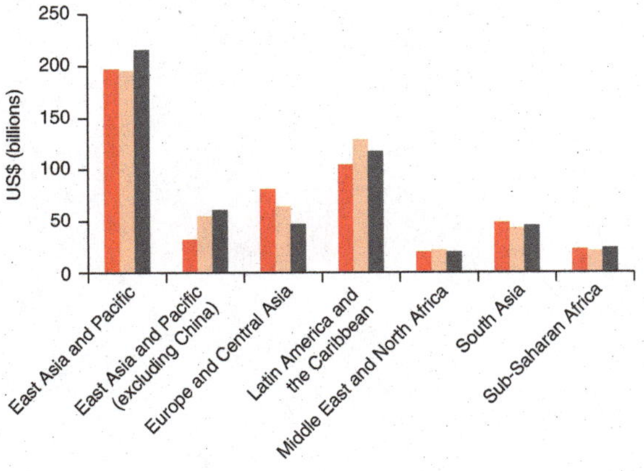

Source: International Monetary Fund.

Figure O.17 Portfolio Equity Flows to Select Countries, 2016–18

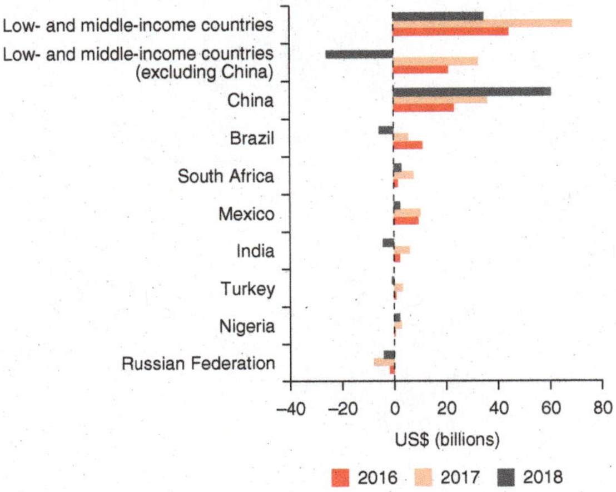

Source: International Monetary Fund.

lived up to their reputation in 2018, a year characterized by a widespread retreat from most emerging markets over concerns that centered on both domestic and global economic conditions. The exception was China where inflows soared 68 percent, to $61 billion, in response to actions by the Chinese government to liberalize the current and capital account, reform the foreign exchange administration, and liberalize the financial market.

A special attraction for investors was implementation of a direct automated connection from the Shanghai stock market to markets in Hong Kong SAR, China, and Shenzhen (a prelude to a similar connection to the London stock market in June 2019), and the MSCI's decision to include Chinese stocks in its benchmark indexes, raising overseas investor demand for renminbi-denominated stocks. Portfolio equity inflows rose 68 percent, to $61 billion ($36 billion in 2017) and served to contain the aggregate decline in portfolio equity inflows to low- and middle-income countries. These fell 50 percent, to $35 billion.

Excluding China, portfolio equity flows to low- and middle-income countries were negative in 2018—an outflow of $26 billion compared to an inflow of $33 billion in 2017. Uncertainty over political and economic outcomes weighed heavily on investor sentiment in Brazil, and led to an outflow of $5.6 billion in 2018, resulting in a net outflow of $10 billion. Similar concerns prompted investors to reduce exposure in India by $10 billion, resulting in a net outflow of $4.4 billion. Trade-related and political tensions with the United States reduced inflows to Mexico but they remained positive. Attractive valuations encouraged bargain hunting by global investors, which resulted in moderate inflows to Nigeria and South Africa.

PART II
Aggregate and Country Tables

ALL LOW- AND MIDDLE-INCOME COUNTRIES

(US$ billion, unless otherwise indicated)

	2008	2014	2015	2016	2017	2018
Summary external debt data by debtor type						
Total External debt stocks	**3,462**	**6,939**	**6,452**	**6,726**	**7,424**	**7,810**
Use of IMF Credit	49	112	112	113	124	151
Long-term external debt	2,691	4,712	4,706	5,013	5,377	5,505
Public and publicly guaranteed sector	1,372	2,329	2,347	2,489	2,815	2,935
Public Sector	1,368	2,323	2,343	2,485	2,811	2,933
of which: General Government	1,008	1,622	1,681	1,790	2,036	2,112
Private sector guaranteed by Public Sector	5	6	4	4	3	3
Private sector not guaranteed	1,318	2,384	2,358	2,524	2,562	2,570
Short-term external debt	722	2,115	1,635	1,599	1,924	2,154
Disbursements (long-term)	**601**	**973**	**790**	**974**	**1,144**	**1,028**
Public and publicly guaranteed sector	182	380	310	346	485	417
Public Sector	181	379	309	346	484	416
of which: General Government	113	257	211	231	319	254
Private sector guaranteed by Public Sector	1	1	0	0	0	0
Private sector not guaranteed	419	593	480	628	659	612
Principal repayments (long-term)	**389**	**583**	**632**	**732**	**739**	**756**
Public and publicly guaranteed sector	151	182	213	198	204	257
Public Sector	150	181	211	196	203	256
of which: General Government	104	116	104	104	111	134
Private sector guaranteed by Public Sector	1	1	1	1	1	1
Private sector not guaranteed	239	401	420	534	535	498
Interest payments (long-term)	**113**	**155**	**165**	**180**	**195**	**213**
Public and publicly guaranteed sector	57	73	80	90	104	112
Public Sector	57	72	80	90	104	112
of which: General Government	45	56	61	68	78	83
Private sector guaranteed by Public Sector	0	0	0	0	0	0
Private sector not guaranteed	56	82	85	90	92	101
Summary external debt stock by creditor type						
Long-term External debt stocks	**2,691**	**4,712**	**4,706**	**5,013**	**5,377**	**5,505**
Public and publicly guaranteed debt from:	1,372	2,329	2,347	2,489	2,815	2,935
Official creditors	704	917	923	983	1,070	1,103
Multilateral	391	559	572	596	647	667
of which: World Bank	207	275	283	292	316	325
Bilateral	313	358	351	387	423	437
Private creditors	668	1,412	1,424	1,506	1,745	1,832
Bondholders	433	934	988	1,076	1,301	1,393
Commercial banks and others	235	479	436	430	444	439
Private nonguaranteed debt from:	1,318	2,384	2,358	2,524	2,562	2,570
Bondholders	167	411	365	395	476	484
Commercial banks and others	1,152	1,973	1,993	2,129	2,085	2,086
Use of IMF Credit	49	112	112	113	124	151
Net financial inflows						
Net debt inflows						
Use of IMF Credit	10	-7	5	5	4	31
Long-term	212	390	158	242	405	273
Official creditors	18	53	43	57	53	48
Multilateral	20	29	32	32	29	30
of which: World Bank	7	15	17	14	13	15
Bilateral	-2	24	11	26	24	17
Private creditors	193	337	114	185	352	225
Bondholders	-14	172	71	121	295	157
Banks and other private	207	165	44	64	57	68
Short-term	-26	142	-481	-37	326	225
Net equity inflows						
Foreign direct investment	503	508	506	470	472	469
Portfolio equity	-50	84	22	45	69	35
Debt ratios						
External debt stocks to exports (%)	64	95	100	108	105	101
External debt stocks to GNI (%)	21	25	25	26	26	26
Debt service to exports (%)	10	11	13	15	14	14
Short-term to external debt stocks (%)	21	30	25	24	26	28
Multilateral to external debt stocks (%)	11	8	9	9	9	9
Reserves to external debt stocks (%)	114	92	90	82	79	74
Gross national income (GNI)	16,680	27,556	26,219	26,345	28,889	30,565

EAST ASIA AND PACIFIC

(US$ billion, unless otherwise indicated)

	2008	2014	2015	2016	2017	2018
Summary external debt data by debtor type						
Total External debt stocks	**711**	**2,435**	**1,998**	**2,117**	**2,487**	**2,784**
Use of IMF Credit	2	17	16	16	17	17
Long-term external debt	469	1,040	1,036	1,173	1,285	1,392
Public and publicly guaranteed sector	267	453	438	479	554	629
Public Sector	267	452	437	479	553	629
of which: General Government	198	312	336	360	400	421
Private sector guaranteed by Public Sector	0	0	0	0	0	0
Private sector not guaranteed	202	587	598	694	732	763
Short-term external debt	241	1,377	946	929	1,185	1,375
Disbursements (long-term)	**85**	**264**	**222**	**285**	**365**	**365**
Public and publicly guaranteed sector	22	84	68	66	99	112
Public Sector	22	84	68	66	99	112
of which: General Government	18	52	46	48	49	41
Private sector guaranteed by Public Sector	0	0	0	0	0	0
Private sector not guaranteed	63	180	154	218	265	253
Principal repayments (long-term)	**65**	**128**	**162**	**219**	**239**	**216**
Public and publicly guaranteed sector	20	43	48	33	33	31
Public Sector	20	43	48	32	32	31
of which: General Government	14	32	14	21	15	16
Private sector guaranteed by Public Sector	0	0	0	0	0	0
Private sector not guaranteed	45	85	114	187	206	185
Interest payments (long-term)	**14**	**24**	**26**	**29**	**35**	**46**
Public and publicly guaranteed sector	9	10	12	12	14	19
Public Sector	9	10	12	12	14	19
of which: General Government	7	7	8	9	10	14
Private sector guaranteed by Public Sector	0	0	0	0	0	0
Private sector not guaranteed	5	14	15	17	21	27
Summary external debt stock by creditor type						
Long-term External debt stocks	**469**	**1,040**	**1,036**	**1,173**	**1,285**	**1,392**
Public and publicly guaranteed debt from:	267	453	438	479	554	629
Official creditors	190	195	187	201	210	214
Multilateral	74	93	97	100	106	110
of which: World Bank	42	52	54	55	59	60
Bilateral	117	102	90	101	104	103
Private creditors	77	258	251	278	344	416
Bondholders	54	182	205	221	283	345
Commercial banks and others	23	76	45	57	61	70
Private nonguaranteed debt from:	202	587	598	694	732	763
Bondholders	19	122	115	132	184	216
Commercial banks and others	183	465	484	562	547	547
Use of IMF Credit	2	17	16	16	17	17
Net financial inflows						
Net debt inflows						
Use of IMF Credit	0	0	0	0	0	0
Long-term	19	136	60	66	126	149
Official creditors	1	4	2	3	3	5
Multilateral	3	3	6	4	4	5
of which: World Bank	1	2	3	2	2	2
Bilateral	-3	2	-3	-1	0	0
Private creditors	19	132	58	63	123	144
Bondholders	3	61	25	38	113	101
Banks and other private	16	71	33	24	10	42
Short-term	-13	159	-432	-17	256	187
Net equity inflows						
Foreign direct investment	175	259	261	197	195	215
Portfolio equity	-2	51	4	24	35	49
Debt ratios						
External debt stocks to exports (%)	33	70	60	66	69	72
External debt stocks to GNI (%)	12	20	16	16	17	18
Debt service to exports (%)	4	5	7	9	9	8
Short-term to external debt stocks (%)	34	57	47	44	48	49
Multilateral to external debt stocks (%)	10	4	5	5	4	4
Reserves to external debt stocks (%)	306	174	186	162	146	128
Gross national income (GNI)	5,769	12,358	12,855	13,088	14,261	15,832

EUROPE AND CENTRAL ASIA

(US$ billion, unless otherwise indicated)

	2008	2014	2015	2016	2017	2018
Summary external debt data by debtor type						
Total External debt stocks	**1,170**	**1,576**	**1,452**	**1,539**	**1,602**	**1,525**
Use of IMF Credit	29	28	30	30	32	30
Long-term external debt	919	1,268	1,203	1,291	1,321	1,251
Public and publicly guaranteed sector	284	499	468	479	538	504
Public Sector	283	498	467	478	538	504
of which: General Government	156	270	262	279	320	314
Private sector guaranteed by Public Sector	0	1	1	1	1	0
Private sector not guaranteed	636	769	735	812	783	747
Short-term external debt	221	280	219	219	249	243
Disbursements (long-term)	**293**	**186**	**149**	**252**	**272**	**197**
Public and publicly guaranteed sector	51	45	55	57	93	55
Public Sector	51	45	55	57	93	55
of which: General Government	21	38	42	35	50	38
Private sector guaranteed by Public Sector	0	0	0	0	0	0
Private sector not guaranteed	242	141	94	195	179	141
Principal repayments (long-term)	**173**	**189**	**222**	**181**	**207**	**242**
Public and publicly guaranteed sector	43	62	73	45	47	84
Public Sector	43	62	72	45	47	83
of which: General Government	23	34	39	15	21	39
Private sector guaranteed by Public Sector	0	0	0	0	0	0
Private sector not guaranteed	130	126	149	136	160	158
Interest payments (long-term)	**41**	**45**	**45**	**45**	**45**	**45**
Public and publicly guaranteed sector	12	14	14	16	18	21
Public Sector	12	14	14	16	18	21
of which: General Government	9	12	11	10	12	13
Private sector guaranteed by Public Sector	0	0	0	0	0	0
Private sector not guaranteed	28	30	32	29	27	24
Summary external debt stock by creditor type						
Long-term External debt stocks	**919**	**1,268**	**1,203**	**1,291**	**1,321**	**1,251**
Public and publicly guaranteed debt from:	284	499	468	479	538	504
Official creditors	77	127	126	130	144	142
Multilateral	49	93	91	93	102	99
of which: World Bank	30	41	41	41	45	45
Bilateral	28	34	35	37	41	43
Private creditors	206	372	342	349	395	362
Bondholders	78	166	164	183	220	221
Commercial banks and others	128	205	178	166	174	141
Private nonguaranteed debt from:	636	769	735	812	783	747
Bondholders	47	66	56	67	78	78
Commercial banks and others	589	703	679	745	705	670
Use of IMF Credit	29	28	30	30	32	30
Net financial inflows						
Net debt inflows						
Use of IMF Credit	6	-7	3	1	0	-1
Long-term	119	-3	-73	72	65	-45
Official creditors	5	11	6	6	6	2
Multilateral	3	6	3	4	2	0
of which: World Bank	1	2	2	1	1	1
Bilateral	2	5	2	2	3	2
Private creditors	114	-14	-79	66	59	-47
Bondholders	-22	4	-7	27	38	3
Banks and other private	136	-18	-72	39	22	-50
Short-term	-18	-39	-61	-2	29	-6
Net equity inflows						
Foreign direct investment	133	61	55	81	64	47
Portfolio equity	-16	-10	-7	-1	-5	-7
Debt ratios						
External debt stocks to exports (%)	100	122	148	169	149	122
External debt stocks to GNI (%)	36	40	48	53	50	46
Debt service to exports (%)	19	20	28	26	24	24
Short-term to external debt stocks (%)	19	18	15	14	16	16
Multilateral to external debt stocks (%)	4	6	6	6	6	7
Reserves to external debt stocks (%)	53	38	38	36	38	41
Gross national income (GNI)	3,223	3,929	3,019	2,891	3,232	3,305

LATIN AMERICA AND THE CARIBBEAN

(US$ billion, unless otherwise indicated)

	2008	2014	2015	2016	2017	2018
Summary external debt data by debtor type						
Total External debt stocks	**851**	**1,657**	**1,669**	**1,693**	**1,774**	**1,868**
Use of IMF Credit	4	21	20	20	21	48
Long-term external debt	716	1,384	1,389	1,442	1,512	1,534
Public and publicly guaranteed sector	419	736	761	816	882	914
Public Sector	416	733	758	814	880	912
of which: General Government	309	512	519	559	604	626
Private sector guaranteed by Public Sector	3	3	3	2	2	2
Private sector not guaranteed	298	648	628	626	630	620
Short-term external debt	131	252	261	231	241	286
Disbursements (long-term)	**148**	**280**	**242**	**279**	**276**	**261**
Public and publicly guaranteed sector	62	131	92	129	141	127
Public Sector	61	131	92	129	141	127
of which: General Government	36	76	52	80	88	80
Private sector guaranteed by Public Sector	1	1	0	0	0	0
Private sector not guaranteed	86	148	150	150	135	134
Principal repayments (long-term)	**93**	**127**	**163**	**208**	**190**	**175**
Public and publicly guaranteed sector	47	34	55	67	77	77
Public Sector	47	34	54	66	77	77
of which: General Government	35	25	29	34	45	31
Private sector guaranteed by Public Sector	0	1	1	1	1	1
Private sector not guaranteed	46	93	108	141	113	98
Interest payments (long-term)	**42**	**59**	**65**	**74**	**81**	**77**
Public and publicly guaranteed sector	25	34	40	44	53	47
Public Sector	25	34	40	44	53	47
of which: General Government	20	26	30	35	41	36
Private sector guaranteed by Public Sector	0	0	0	0	0	0
Private sector not guaranteed	17	25	25	30	28	30
Summary external debt stock by creditor type						
Long-term External debt stocks	**716**	**1,384**	**1,389**	**1,442**	**1,512**	**1,534**
Public and publicly guaranteed debt from:	419	736	761	816	882	914
Official creditors	126	198	201	204	213	218
Multilateral	97	144	151	156	159	168
of which: World Bank	34	54	56	57	57	58
Bilateral	29	54	49	48	53	50
Private creditors	293	538	560	612	670	696
Bondholders	251	414	426	478	534	548
Commercial banks and others	41	124	135	134	135	148
Private nonguaranteed debt from:	298	648	628	626	630	620
Bondholders	76	200	170	170	181	158
Commercial banks and others	221	447	458	456	449	462
Use of IMF Credit	4	21	20	20	21	48
Net financial inflows						
Net debt inflows						
Use of IMF Credit	0	-1	0	0	0	29
Long-term	55	152	80	71	86	86
Official creditors	6	12	6	4	7	6
Multilateral	5	6	8	6	3	8
of which: World Bank	2	2	2	2	-1	2
Bilateral	1	5	-2	-1	4	-2
Private creditors	49	140	73	67	79	80
Bondholders	8	64	26	52	71	36
Banks and other private	41	76	47	15	8	43
Short-term	-3	26	8	-29	12	45
Net equity inflows						
Foreign direct investment	87	107	106	104	129	118
Portfolio equity	-11	19	14	21	20	-5
Debt ratios						
External debt stocks to exports (%)	92	149	173	177	165	160
External debt stocks to GNI (%)	21	29	35	36	34	38
Debt service to exports (%)	15	17	24	30	26	22
Short-term to external debt stocks (%)	15	15	16	14	14	15
Multilateral to external debt stocks (%)	11	9	9	9	9	9
Reserves to external debt stocks (%)	53	45	43	44	43	42
Gross national income (GNI)	4,043	5,666	4,795	4,653	5,184	4,972

MIDDLE EAST AND NORTH AFRICA

(US$ billion, unless otherwise indicated)

	2008	2014	2015	2016	2017	2018
Summary external debt data by debtor type						
Total External debt stocks	**169**	**226**	**239**	**268**	**299**	**321**
Use of IMF Credit	1	10	11	13	17	18
Long-term external debt	138	175	187	202	229	252
Public and publicly guaranteed sector	111	134	144	156	180	196
Public Sector	110	134	143	155	180	196
of which: General Government	86	101	108	115	133	146
Private sector guaranteed by Public Sector	1	1	0	0	0	0
Private sector not guaranteed	27	41	43	47	49	56
Short-term external debt	30	40	41	52	53	50
Disbursements (long-term)	**12**	**27**	**38**	**41**	**43**	**48**
Public and publicly guaranteed sector	10	15	25	28	31	31
Public Sector	10	15	25	28	31	31
of which: General Government	7	10	19	18	23	22
Private sector guaranteed by Public Sector	0	0	0	0	0	0
Private sector not guaranteed	2	12	13	13	12	17
Principal repayments (long-term)	**16**	**22**	**21**	**24**	**24**	**23**
Public and publicly guaranteed sector	14	12	11	15	13	12
Public Sector	14	12	11	15	13	12
of which: General Government	10	10	8	10	9	7
Private sector guaranteed by Public Sector	0	0	0	0	0	0
Private sector not guaranteed	2	10	10	10	11	11
Interest payments (long-term)	**5**	**6**	**6**	**7**	**8**	**9**
Public and publicly guaranteed sector	5	4	4	5	5	7
Public Sector	4	4	4	5	5	7
of which: General Government	3	4	3	4	4	5
Private sector guaranteed by Public Sector	0	0	0	0	0	0
Private sector not guaranteed	0	2	2	2	2	3
Summary external debt stock by creditor type						
Long-term External debt stocks	**138**	**175**	**187**	**202**	**229**	**252**
Public and publicly guaranteed debt from:	111	134	144	156	180	196
Official creditors	75	88	91	103	114	116
Multilateral	32	43	43	49	57	58
of which: World Bank	11	15	16	18	22	24
Bilateral	44	45	48	54	58	59
Private creditors	36	47	53	53	66	80
Bondholders	24	39	44	46	58	68
Commercial banks and others	12	7	9	7	8	12
Private nonguaranteed debt from:	27	41	43	47	49	56
Bondholders	0	1	1	1	0	1
Commercial banks and others	27	40	43	46	49	55
Use of IMF Credit	1	10	11	13	17	18
Net financial inflows						
Net debt inflows						
Use of IMF Credit	0	2	1	3	3	2
Long-term	-4	5	17	16	19	26
Official creditors	-2	1	7	13	6	4
Multilateral	1	1	3	7	5	2
of which: World Bank	0	1	2	2	2	2
Bilateral	-3	0	5	6	2	2
Private creditors	-3	4	10	3	13	22
Bondholders	-1	0	6	1	11	11
Banks and other private	-2	3	5	2	1	11
Short-term	-2	4	1	11	1	-3
Net equity inflows						
Foreign direct investment	28	17	16	19	21	20
Portfolio equity	0	1	-1	1	-1	0
Debt ratios						
External debt stocks to exports (%)	45	65	83	107	102	94
External debt stocks to GNI (%)	17	17	20	22	25	..
Debt service to exports (%)	6	8	10	13	11	10
Short-term to external debt stocks (%)	17	18	17	19	18	16
Multilateral to external debt stocks (%)	19	19	18	18	19	18
Reserves to external debt stocks (%)	154	121	101	83	..	..
Gross national income (GNI)	1,007	1,289	1,209	1,236	1,181	..

SOUTH ASIA

(US$ billion, unless otherwise indicated)

	2008	2014	2015	2016	2017	2018
Summary external debt data by debtor type						
Total External debt stocks	**324**	**605**	**636**	**624**	**707**	**730**
Use of IMF Credit	7	15	15	16	17	16
Long-term external debt	267	487	517	502	564	583
Public and publicly guaranteed sector	156	258	272	271	318	327
Public Sector	156	258	272	271	318	327
of which: General Government	138	210	222	225	274	279
Private sector guaranteed by Public Sector	0	0	0	0	0	0
Private sector not guaranteed	110	229	245	231	246	256
Short-term external debt	50	103	103	107	126	131
Disbursements (long-term)	**46**	**150**	**80**	**60**	**104**	**80**
Public and publicly guaranteed sector	25	62	35	26	61	40
Public Sector	25	62	35	26	61	40
of which: General Government	22	47	25	20	54	28
Private sector guaranteed by Public Sector	0	0	0	0	0	0
Private sector not guaranteed	21	88	45	34	43	40
Principal repayments (long-term)	**27**	**90**	**45**	**72**	**48**	**57**
Public and publicly guaranteed sector	16	18	17	25	20	29
Public Sector	16	18	17	25	20	29
of which: General Government	15	7	8	16	11	21
Private sector guaranteed by Public Sector	0	0	0	0	0	0
Private sector not guaranteed	11	72	28	47	28	29
Interest payments (long-term)	**7**	**13**	**12**	**12**	**13**	**19**
Public and publicly guaranteed sector	3	4	4	4	5	6
Public Sector	3	4	4	4	5	6
of which: General Government	2	2	2	3	4	5
Private sector guaranteed by Public Sector	0	0	0	0	0	0
Private sector not guaranteed	4	9	8	8	9	12
Summary external debt stock by creditor type						
Long-term External debt stocks	**267**	**487**	**517**	**502**	**564**	**583**
Public and publicly guaranteed debt from:	156	258	272	271	318	327
Official creditors	138	163	165	171	189	204
Multilateral	89	106	107	109	118	121
of which: World Bank	59	67	67	68	72	72
Bilateral	49	56	57	62	71	82
Private creditors	18	95	107	100	129	124
Bondholders	8	62	73	69	101	94
Commercial banks and others	11	33	34	31	28	30
Private nonguaranteed debt from:	110	229	245	231	246	256
Bondholders	16	7	8	10	15	14
Commercial banks and others	95	222	237	220	231	242
Use of IMF Credit	7	15	15	16	17	16
Net financial inflows						
Net debt inflows						
Use of IMF Credit	3	0	1	1	0	0
Long-term	19	60	35	-13	56	23
Official creditors	6	7	6	8	11	16
Multilateral	5	4	4	4	4	5
of which: World Bank	1	2	2	2	1	2
Bilateral	1	3	2	4	7	11
Private creditors	13	53	29	-21	44	6
Bondholders	2	32	13	-2	36	-7
Banks and other private	11	20	17	-19	8	13
Short-term	9	-5	0	4	19	4
Net equity inflows						
Foreign direct investment	50	37	45	48	43	45
Portfolio equity	-16	14	2	2	6	-5
Debt ratios						
External debt stocks to exports (%)	85	103	119	116	117	110
External debt stocks to GNI (%)	21	23	24	21	21	21
Debt service to exports (%)	10	18	11	16	11	12
Short-term to external debt stocks (%)	16	17	16	17	18	18
Multilateral to external debt stocks (%)	27	18	17	18	17	17
Reserves to external debt stocks (%)	83	59	63	66	65	59
Gross national income (GNI)	1,530	2,581	2,699	2,921	3,344	3,456

SUB-SAHARAN AFRICA

(US$ billion, unless otherwise indicated)

	2008	2014	2015	2016	2017	2018
Summary external debt data by debtor type						
Total External debt stocks	**236**	**441**	**457**	**484**	**555**	**583**
Use of IMF Credit	6	20	19	19	21	22
Long-term external debt	181	358	373	404	464	493
Public and publicly guaranteed sector	135	249	265	288	342	365
Public Sector	135	249	265	288	342	365
of which: General Government	120	218	233	251	304	326
Private sector guaranteed by Public Sector	0	0	0	0	0	0
Private sector not guaranteed	46	109	108	116	122	128
Short-term external debt	49	62	65	61	70	68
Disbursements (long-term)	**18**	**67**	**58**	**57**	**85**	**78**
Public and publicly guaranteed sector	13	43	33	40	60	51
Public Sector	13	43	33	40	60	51
of which: General Government	9	33	27	29	55	46
Private sector guaranteed by Public Sector	0	0	0	0	0	0
Private sector not guaranteed	5	24	25	18	25	27
Principal repayments (long-term)	**14**	**27**	**20**	**27**	**31**	**43**
Public and publicly guaranteed sector	9	12	9	13	13	24
Public Sector	9	12	9	13	13	24
of which: General Government	7	7	5	7	9	19
Private sector guaranteed by Public Sector	0	0	0	0	0	0
Private sector not guaranteed	4	15	11	14	18	19
Interest payments (long-term)	**5**	**8**	**11**	**13**	**13**	**17**
Public and publicly guaranteed sector	3	6	7	8	9	12
Public Sector	3	6	7	8	9	12
of which: General Government	3	5	6	7	7	10
Private sector guaranteed by Public Sector	0	..	..	..	..	..
Private sector not guaranteed	1	2	4	4	4	5
Summary external debt stock by creditor type						
Long-term External debt stocks	**181**	**358**	**373**	**404**	**464**	**493**
Public and publicly guaranteed debt from:	135	249	265	288	342	365
Official creditors	97	146	154	174	200	210
Multilateral	50	78	82	88	104	110
of which: World Bank	30	46	48	52	61	66
Bilateral	47	67	72	86	96	99
Private creditors	38	103	111	114	142	155
Bondholders	18	69	75	79	104	117
Commercial banks and others	21	34	36	35	38	38
Private nonguaranteed debt from:	46	109	108	116	122	128
Bondholders	8	15	16	16	17	17
Commercial banks and others	37	94	92	100	105	111
Use of IMF Credit	6	20	19	19	21	22
Net financial inflows						
Net debt inflows						
Use of IMF Credit	1	0	0	0	1	2
Long-term	4	40	38	30	54	35
Official creditors	3	17	15	23	19	14
Multilateral	3	8	8	8	12	10
of which: World Bank	2	6	6	5	6	6
Bilateral	0	9	7	15	8	5
Private creditors	1	22	22	7	34	21
Bondholders	-2	10	8	4	26	13
Banks and other private	4	12	14	3	8	8
Short-term	1	-2	3	-4	8	-2
Net equity inflows						
Foreign direct investment	30	26	24	22	20	24
Portfolio equity	-6	10	9	-2	14	2
Debt ratios						
External debt stocks to exports (%)	59	96	128	145	144	134
External debt stocks to GNI (%)	21	26	29	33	35	36
Debt service to exports (%)	5	8	9	13	12	14
Short-term to external debt stocks (%)	21	14	14	13	13	12
Multilateral to external debt stocks (%)	21	18	18	18	19	19
Reserves to external debt stocks (%)	64	41	35	30	29	28
Gross national income (GNI)	1,110	1,715	1,574	1,475	1,597	1,611

AFGHANISTAN

(US$ million, unless otherwise indicated)

	2008	2014	2015	2016	2017	2018
Summary external debt data by debtor type						
Total External debt stocks	**2,144**	**2,613**	**2,637**	**2,597**	**2,717**	**2,605**
Use of IMF Credit	131	335	300	277	285	275
Long-term external debt	1,995	2,021	2,009	1,965	1,998	1,966
Public and publicly guaranteed sector	1,995	2,021	1,990	1,950	1,982	1,949
Public Sector	1,995	2,021	1,990	1,950	1,982	1,949
of which: General Government	1,994	2,021	1,990	1,950	1,982	1,949
Private sector guaranteed by Public Sector	..	..	..	..	..	..
Private sector not guaranteed	..	..	19	15	16	17
Short-term external debt	18	257	328	355	435	364
Disbursements (long-term)	**96**	**32**	**26**	**12**	**3**	**16**
Public and publicly guaranteed sector	96	32	26	12	3	16
Public Sector	96	32	26	12	3	16
of which: General Government	96	32	26	12	3	16
Private sector guaranteed by Public Sector	..	..	..	..	..	..
Private sector not guaranteed	..	..	..	..	..	..
Principal repayments (long-term)	**1**	**12**	**24**	**27**	**27**	**29**
Public and publicly guaranteed sector	1	12	19	23	23	24
Public Sector	1	12	19	23	23	24
of which: General Government	1	12	19	23	23	24
Private sector guaranteed by Public Sector	..	..	..	..	..	..
Private sector not guaranteed	..	..	5	4	4	5
Interest payments (long-term)	**6**	**9**	**10**	**8**	**9**	**9**
Public and publicly guaranteed sector	6	9	9	8	8	8
Public Sector	6	9	9	8	8	8
of which: General Government	6	9	9	8	8	8
Private sector guaranteed by Public Sector	..	..	..	..	..	..
Private sector not guaranteed	..	..	1	1	1	1
Summary external debt stock by creditor type						
Long-term External debt stocks	**1,995**	**2,021**	**2,009**	**1,965**	**1,998**	**1,966**
Public and publicly guaranteed debt from:	1,995	2,021	1,990	1,950	1,982	1,949
Official creditors	1,994	2,021	1,990	1,950	1,982	1,949
Multilateral	904	1,086	1,030	991	1,023	984
of which: World Bank	438	395	370	351	364	348
Bilateral	1,091	934	960	958	959	965
Private creditors	0	..	..	..	..	..
Bondholders	..	..	..	..	..	..
Commercial banks and others	0	..	..	..	..	..
Private nonguaranteed debt from:	..	..	19	15	16	17
Bondholders	..	..	..	..	..	..
Commercial banks and others	..	..	19	15	16	17
Use of IMF Credit	131	335	300	277	285	275
Net financial inflows						
Net debt inflows						
Use of IMF Credit	36	-19	-20	-15	-8	-4
Long-term	95	20	2	-15	-24	-12
Official creditors	95	20	7	-11	-19	-8
Multilateral	95	11	-8	-9	-19	-15
of which: World Bank	43	-6	-8	-8	-8	-8
Bilateral	1	8	16	-2	0	7
Private creditors	..	..	-5	-4	-4	-5
Bondholders	..	..	..	..	..	..
Banks and other private	..	..	-5	-4	-4	-5
Short-term	..	33	88	26	80	-70
Net equity inflows						
Foreign direct investment	40	43	169	94	52	139
Portfolio equity	0	0	0	0	0	..
Debt ratios						
External debt stocks to exports (%)	108	120	155	202	210	..
External debt stocks to GNI (%)	21	13	13	13	13	13
Debt service to exports (%)	0	2	3	5	5	..
Short-term to external debt stocks (%)	1	10	12	14	16	14
Multilateral to external debt stocks (%)	42	42	39	38	38	38
Reserves to external debt stocks (%)	113	256	236	249	264	280
Gross national income (GNI)	10,234	20,483	20,087	19,459	20,291	19,485

ALBANIA

(US$ million, unless otherwise indicated)

	2008	2014	2015	2016	2017	2018
Summary external debt data by debtor type						
Total External debt stocks	**4,261**	**8,640**	**8,657**	**8,741**	**10,062**	**10,122**
Use of IMF Credit	152	151	244	387	489	470
Long-term external debt	2,960	6,614	6,619	6,485	7,424	7,487
Public and publicly guaranteed sector	2,298	3,666	3,846	3,763	4,339	4,563
Public Sector	2,298	3,666	3,846	3,763	4,339	4,563
of which: General Government	1,961	3,322	3,552	3,491	4,055	4,250
Private sector guaranteed by Public Sector	..	..	..	..	..	..
Private sector not guaranteed	661	2,949	2,773	2,722	3,085	2,924
Short-term external debt	1,150	1,875	1,795	1,869	2,149	2,165
Disbursements (long-term)	**870**	**634**	**1,321**	**450**	**777**	**1,269**
Public and publicly guaranteed sector	650	443	956	205	422	931
Public Sector	650	443	956	205	422	931
of which: General Government	530	443	952	189	420	792
Private sector guaranteed by Public Sector	..	..	..	..	..	..
Private sector not guaranteed	220	191	365	245	355	338
Principal repayments (long-term)	**144**	**539**	**1,072**	**487**	**407**	**921**
Public and publicly guaranteed sector	58	178	499	191	221	554
Public Sector	58	178	499	191	221	554
of which: General Government	40	151	478	160	198	456
Private sector guaranteed by Public Sector	..	..	..	..	..	..
Private sector not guaranteed	86	361	573	297	185	368
Interest payments (long-term)	**65**	**185**	**98**	**95**	**96**	**147**
Public and publicly guaranteed sector	44	79	90	84	83	120
Public Sector	44	79	90	84	83	120
of which: General Government	35	75	86	82	80	114
Private sector guaranteed by Public Sector	..	..	..	..	..	..
Private sector not guaranteed	21	105	9	11	12	28
Summary external debt stock by creditor type						
Long-term External debt stocks	**2,960**	**6,614**	**6,619**	**6,485**	**7,424**	**7,487**
Public and publicly guaranteed debt from:	2,298	3,666	3,846	3,763	4,339	4,563
Official creditors	1,877	2,744	2,584	2,531	2,983	3,037
Multilateral	1,294	2,091	1,943	1,889	2,279	2,362
of which: World Bank	835	1,086	1,020	991	1,300	1,301
Bilateral	584	653	641	642	705	675
Private creditors	421	921	1,262	1,232	1,355	1,526
Bondholders	79	522	631	611	696	942
Commercial banks and others	341	399	630	621	660	584
Private nonguaranteed debt from:	661	2,949	2,773	2,722	3,085	2,924
Bondholders	23	244	133	148	192	245
Commercial banks and others	638	2,705	2,640	2,573	2,894	2,679
Use of IMF Credit	152	151	244	387	489	470
Net financial inflows						
Net debt inflows						
Use of IMF Credit	-8	63	100	156	77	-7
Long-term	727	94	250	-37	370	348
Official creditors	160	284	14	3	244	138
Multilateral	144	253	-19	-11	241	149
of which: World Bank	32	227	-3	2	226	40
Bilateral	16	31	33	14	3	-11
Private creditors	566	-190	236	-40	126	210
Bondholders	34	-22	56	15	43	340
Banks and other private	532	-168	180	-56	83	-130
Short-term	640	-128	-80	74	280	16
Net equity inflows						
Foreign direct investment	893	933	877	1,048	1,073	1,274
Portfolio equity	23	34	9	-15	-12	-4
Debt ratios						
External debt stocks to exports (%)	113	207	246	225	219	193
External debt stocks to GNI (%)	33	65	75	73	77	67
Debt service to exports (%)	7	18	33	15	11	21
Short-term to external debt stocks (%)	27	22	21	21	21	21
Multilateral to external debt stocks (%)	30	24	22	22	23	23
Reserves to external debt stocks (%)	54	30	36	35	35	38
Gross national income (GNI)	12,946	13,350	11,522	12,054	13,057	15,052

ALGERIA

(US$ million, unless otherwise indicated)

	2008	2014	2015	2016	2017	2018
Summary external debt data by debtor type						
Total External debt stocks	**6,246**	**5,521**	**4,671**	**5,463**	**5,707**	**5,710**
Use of IMF Credit	198	1,736	1,660	1,611	1,706	1,666
Long-term external debt	4,745	1,810	1,188	1,866	1,904	1,725
Public and publicly guaranteed sector	3,301	1,125	870	1,653	1,716	1,523
Public Sector	3,114	1,120	867	1,650	1,713	1,521
of which: General Government	925	428	350	1,247	1,365	1,268
Private sector guaranteed by Public Sector	186	5	3	3	3	2
Private sector not guaranteed	1,444	685	318	214	188	202
Short-term external debt	1,304	1,975	1,823	1,986	2,096	2,319
Disbursements (long-term)	**675**	**43**	**47**	**1,033**	**11**	**44**
Public and publicly guaranteed sector	268	4	0	984	1	0
Public Sector	268	4	0	984	1	0
of which: General Government	121	4	0	984	0	0
Private sector guaranteed by Public Sector	0	0	0	0	0	0
Private sector not guaranteed	407	39	47	49	11	44
Principal repayments (long-term)	**1,058**	**235**	**582**	**302**	**176**	**151**
Public and publicly guaranteed sector	914	211	167	149	140	121
Public Sector	892	199	166	148	139	121
of which: General Government	229	51	47	45	41	40
Private sector guaranteed by Public Sector	22	11	1	0	1	1
Private sector not guaranteed	144	24	415	153	36	29
Interest payments (long-term)	**161**	**37**	**79**	**22**	**31**	**29**
Public and publicly guaranteed sector	113	28	21	17	26	26
Public Sector	110	28	21	17	26	26
of which: General Government	24	9	8	6	20	21
Private sector guaranteed by Public Sector	3	0	0	0	0	0
Private sector not guaranteed	48	9	59	5	4	3
Summary external debt stock by creditor type						
Long-term External debt stocks	**4,745**	**1,810**	**1,188**	**1,866**	**1,904**	**1,725**
Public and publicly guaranteed debt from:	3,301	1,125	870	1,653	1,716	1,523
Official creditors	2,223	950	752	1,580	1,682	1,512
Multilateral	13	2	1	949	1,079	1,031
of which: World Bank	11	2	1	1	0	..
Bilateral	2,210	949	751	630	603	481
Private creditors	1,078	175	118	73	34	11
Bondholders	..	..	..	..	..	..
Commercial banks and others	1,078	175	118	73	34	11
Private nonguaranteed debt from:	1,444	685	318	214	188	202
Bondholders	..	..	..	..	..	..
Commercial banks and others	1,444	685	318	214	188	202
Use of IMF Credit	198	1,736	1,660	1,611	1,706	1,666
Net financial inflows						
Net debt inflows						
Use of IMF Credit	..	0	..	..	..	..
Long-term	-383	-192	-535	731	-165	-107
Official creditors	-173	-142	-117	880	-97	-99
Multilateral	-122	0	0	983	-1	0
of which: World Bank	-102	0	0	0	-1	..
Bilateral	-51	-141	-117	-104	-97	-99
Private creditors	-210	-50	-418	-149	-68	-8
Bondholders	..	..	..	..	..	..
Banks and other private	-210	-50	-418	-149	-68	-8
Short-term	554	647	-152	163	110	223
Net equity inflows						
Foreign direct investment	2,520	1,465	-396	1,650	1,202	1,506
Portfolio equity	0	..	..	..	..	..
Debt ratios						
External debt stocks to exports (%)	7	8	12	16	14	12
External debt stocks to GNI (%)	4	3	3	3	3	3
Debt service to exports (%)	1	0	2	1	1	0
Short-term to external debt stocks (%)	21	36	39	36	37	41
Multilateral to external debt stocks (%)	0	0	0	17	19	18
Reserves to external debt stocks (%)	2,293	3,253	3,097	2,094	1,711	1,405
Gross national income (GNI)	169,770	209,164	161,526	158,560	164,955	177,548

ANGOLA

(US$ million, unless otherwise indicated)

	2008	2014	2015	2016	2017	2018
Summary external debt data by debtor type						
Total External debt stocks	**15,502**	**56,936**	**56,272**	**57,167**	**52,618**	**54,563**
Use of IMF Credit	421	914	532	396	389	1,374
Long-term external debt	12,690	48,362	47,574	52,391	48,534	50,878
Public and publicly guaranteed sector	12,690	27,826	27,304	34,815	35,599	38,208
Public Sector	12,690	27,826	27,304	34,815	35,599	38,208
of which: General Government	5,528	12,582	14,857	18,764	20,781	24,288
Private sector guaranteed by Public Sector	1	..	..	..	..	..
Private sector not guaranteed	..	20,535	20,270	17,577	12,934	12,669
Short-term external debt	2,391	7,660	8,166	4,380	3,695	2,312
Disbursements (long-term)	**4,622**	**13,294**	**5,380**	**13,189**	**5,086**	**9,192**
Public and publicly guaranteed sector	4,622	9,649	3,592	13,189	5,086	8,164
Public Sector	4,622	9,649	3,592	13,189	5,086	8,164
of which: General Government	1,562	3,857	3,592	5,189	3,810	6,364
Private sector guaranteed by Public Sector	0	..	..	..	..	..
Private sector not guaranteed	..	3,645	1,788	..	..	1,028
Principal repayments (long-term)	**1,130**	**6,770**	**6,017**	**7,666**	**7,997**	**6,783**
Public and publicly guaranteed sector	1,130	4,893	3,964	5,639	4,481	5,489
Public Sector	1,129	4,893	3,964	5,639	4,481	5,489
of which: General Government	688	1,148	1,176	1,245	1,965	2,793
Private sector guaranteed by Public Sector	1	..	..	..	..	..
Private sector not guaranteed	..	1,877	2,054	2,027	3,515	1,293
Interest payments (long-term)	**443**	**1,294**	**1,379**	**1,760**	**1,071**	**2,318**
Public and publicly guaranteed sector	443	1,021	1,078	1,398	751	1,876
Public Sector	443	1,021	1,078	1,398	751	1,876
of which: General Government	241	482	563	975	380	1,108
Private sector guaranteed by Public Sector	0	..	..	..	..	..
Private sector not guaranteed	..	273	301	362	320	442
Summary external debt stock by creditor type						
Long-term External debt stocks	**12,690**	**48,362**	**47,574**	**52,391**	**48,534**	**50,878**
Public and publicly guaranteed debt from:	12,690	27,826	27,304	34,815	35,599	38,208
Official creditors	4,003	13,725	13,404	22,518	24,400	23,820
Multilateral	429	1,147	1,602	2,018	2,239	2,268
of which: World Bank	369	478	929	940	1,025	1,042
Bilateral	3,575	12,577	11,802	20,499	22,161	21,552
Private creditors	8,687	14,102	13,899	12,297	11,200	14,388
Bondholders	..	1,000	2,500	2,500	2,500	6,000
Commercial banks and others	8,687	13,102	11,399	9,797	8,700	8,388
Private nonguaranteed debt from:	..	20,535	20,270	17,577	12,934	12,669
Bondholders	..	..	..	..	..	..
Commercial banks and others	..	20,535	20,270	17,577	12,934	12,669
Use of IMF Credit	421	914	532	396	389	1,374
Net financial inflows						
Net debt inflows						
Use of IMF Credit	..	-500	-345	-124	-30	1,012
Long-term	3,492	6,524	-637	5,523	-2,910	2,409
Official creditors	825	2,016	-285	9,122	1,827	-566
Multilateral	8	670	479	432	184	44
of which: World Bank	6	40	472	26	55	31
Bilateral	817	1,345	-763	8,691	1,643	-610
Private creditors	2,667	4,509	-352	-3,599	-4,738	2,975
Bondholders	..	..	1,500	0	..	3,500
Banks and other private	2,667	4,509	-1,852	-3,599	-4,738	-525
Short-term	140	-3,680	514	-3,785	-660	-1,362
Net equity inflows						
Foreign direct investment	5,266	4,185	4,974	-122	-7,293	-5,918
Portfolio equity	0	0	0	0	0	0
Debt ratios						
External debt stocks to exports (%)	24	93	163	200	147	130
External debt stocks to GNI (%)	21	42	51	60	44	54
Debt service to exports (%)	3	14	23	34	26	22
Short-term to external debt stocks (%)	15	13	15	8	7	4
Multilateral to external debt stocks (%)	3	2	3	4	4	4
Reserves to external debt stocks (%)	115	47	42	41	33	28
Gross national income (GNI)	74,821	136,862	110,286	95,864	118,386	101,047

ARGENTINA

(US$ million, unless otherwise indicated)

	2008	2014	2015	2016	2017	2018
Summary external debt data by debtor type						
Total External debt stocks	**129,752**	**153,182**	**176,575**	**188,758**	**236,471**	**280,516**
Use of IMF Credit	490	2,927	2,799	2,716	2,877	30,923
Long-term external debt	109,822	116,365	114,341	145,025	178,133	182,011
Public and publicly guaranteed sector	70,924	75,661	72,211	105,334	127,059	131,182
Public Sector	70,766	75,660	72,211	105,334	127,059	131,182
of which: General Government	68,016	75,194	71,911	105,193	126,958	131,112
Private sector guaranteed by Public Sector	158	1	0	..	..	..
Private sector not guaranteed	38,899	40,703	42,130	39,691	51,074	50,828
Short-term external debt	19,440	33,891	59,434	41,017	55,461	67,583
Disbursements (long-term)	**7,036**	**19,533**	**16,414**	**54,737**	**58,919**	**53,887**
Public and publicly guaranteed sector	4,046	13,439	8,493	40,188	41,045	43,889
Public Sector	4,046	13,420	8,493	40,188	41,045	43,889
of which: General Government	4,039	12,171	8,272	40,089	41,045	43,889
Private sector guaranteed by Public Sector	..	18	0	..	..	..
Private sector not guaranteed	2,990	6,095	7,920	14,549	17,873	9,998
Principal repayments (long-term)	**5,664**	**9,755**	**10,821**	**11,677**	**24,110**	**21,494**
Public and publicly guaranteed sector	3,396	4,747	6,365	5,363	17,762	15,728
Public Sector	3,387	4,693	6,364	5,363	17,762	15,728
of which: General Government	3,260	4,518	5,977	5,106	17,722	15,698
Private sector guaranteed by Public Sector	9	54	1	..	..	..
Private sector not guaranteed	2,268	5,008	4,455	6,313	6,348	5,766
Interest payments (long-term)	**3,684**	**6,757**	**6,076**	**13,389**	**14,787**	**14,311**
Public and publicly guaranteed sector	2,478	5,361	5,145	12,289	12,400	10,963
Public Sector	2,478	5,361	5,145	12,289	12,400	10,963
of which: General Government	2,436	5,323	5,110	12,269	12,392	10,959
Private sector guaranteed by Public Sector	1	0	0	..	..	..
Private sector not guaranteed	1,206	1,396	931	1,100	2,387	3,348
Summary external debt stock by creditor type						
Long-term External debt stocks	**109,822**	**116,365**	**114,341**	**145,025**	**178,133**	**182,011**
Public and publicly guaranteed debt from:	70,924	75,661	72,211	105,334	127,059	131,182
Official creditors	20,785	28,989	28,999	28,052	29,588	29,897
Multilateral	14,903	19,870	19,778	20,237	21,342	23,005
of which: World Bank	5,069	6,007	5,852	6,048	6,327	6,879
Bilateral	5,882	9,119	9,221	7,816	8,246	6,891
Private creditors	50,139	46,672	43,212	77,282	97,471	101,285
Bondholders	49,175	46,039	42,709	76,838	97,400	101,228
Commercial banks and others	964	634	503	444	71	57
Private nonguaranteed debt from:	38,899	40,703	42,130	39,691	51,074	50,828
Bondholders	7,921	7,199	8,516	11,703	16,405	15,508
Commercial banks and others	30,978	33,504	33,614	27,988	34,669	35,320
Use of IMF Credit	490	2,927	2,799	2,716	2,877	30,923
Net financial inflows						
Net debt inflows						
Use of IMF Credit	..	0	..	..	..	28,623
Long-term	1,372	9,778	5,593	43,060	34,809	32,393
Official creditors	-360	3,522	450	-931	1,088	390
Multilateral	-268	461	-78	462	1,066	1,669
of which: World Bank	-605	-94	-142	198	239	557
Bilateral	-92	3,061	528	-1,394	22	-1,279
Private creditors	1,732	6,256	5,143	43,992	33,721	32,003
Bondholders	-998	5,254	3,123	39,002	27,274	26,887
Banks and other private	2,730	1,002	2,020	4,990	6,447	5,117
Short-term	164	-1,749	25,341	-18,073	17,471	12,149
Net equity inflows						
Foreign direct investment	4,949	6,010	9,377	7,992	9,095	10,449
Portfolio equity	-531	218	239	985	3,013	-508
Debt ratios						
External debt stocks to exports (%)	149	181	244	254	306	339
External debt stocks to GNI (%)	37	30	30	35	38	56
Debt service to exports (%)	11	20	25	35	52	45
Short-term to external debt stocks (%)	15	22	34	22	23	24
Multilateral to external debt stocks (%)	11	13	11	11	9	8
Reserves to external debt stocks (%)	35	19	13	19	22	23
Gross national income (GNI)	352,615	515,532	583,615	545,339	626,304	499,735

ARMENIA

(US$ million, unless otherwise indicated)

	2008	2014	2015	2016	2017	2018
Summary external debt data by debtor type						
Total External debt stocks	**3,612**	**8,556**	**8,931**	**9,956**	**10,329**	**11,019**
Use of IMF Credit	270	570	536	528	530	451
Long-term external debt	2,821	7,078	7,731	8,356	8,910	9,434
Public and publicly guaranteed sector	1,449	3,380	3,998	4,472	5,228	5,371
Public Sector	1,449	3,380	3,998	4,472	5,228	5,371
of which: General Government	1,439	3,349	3,899	4,351	5,015	5,151
Private sector guaranteed by Public Sector	..	..	..	..	..	..
Private sector not guaranteed	1,373	3,698	3,733	3,884	3,683	4,063
Short-term external debt	521	908	664	1,072	889	1,134
Disbursements (long-term)	**776**	**2,082**	**2,067**	**1,855**	**1,501**	**1,871**
Public and publicly guaranteed sector	164	285	984	603	676	347
Public Sector	164	285	984	603	676	347
of which: General Government	159	266	911	575	588	321
Private sector guaranteed by Public Sector	..	..	..	..	..	..
Private sector not guaranteed	612	1,797	1,084	1,252	824	1,524
Principal repayments (long-term)	**253**	**1,077**	**1,308**	**1,173**	**1,117**	**1,282**
Public and publicly guaranteed sector	15	42	260	73	91	138
Public Sector	15	42	260	73	91	138
of which: General Government	15	42	257	69	85	125
Private sector guaranteed by Public Sector	..	..	..	..	..	..
Private sector not guaranteed	238	1,035	1,048	1,101	1,026	1,144
Interest payments (long-term)	**70**	**176**	**199**	**236**	**250**	**281**
Public and publicly guaranteed sector	11	71	100	123	140	162
Public Sector	11	71	100	123	140	162
of which: General Government	11	71	99	120	136	156
Private sector guaranteed by Public Sector	..	..	..	..	..	..
Private sector not guaranteed	58	105	99	113	110	119
Summary external debt stock by creditor type						
Long-term External debt stocks	**2,821**	**7,078**	**7,731**	**8,356**	**8,910**	**9,434**
Public and publicly guaranteed debt from:	1,449	3,380	3,998	4,472	5,228	5,371
Official creditors	1,444	2,661	2,972	3,447	4,193	4,338
Multilateral	1,111	2,162	2,466	2,824	3,237	3,278
of which: World Bank	1,030	1,609	1,652	1,742	1,810	1,798
Bilateral	333	499	506	623	956	1,060
Private creditors	4	719	1,026	1,025	1,035	1,034
Bondholders	..	700	1,000	1,000	1,000	1,000
Commercial banks and others	4	19	26	25	35	33
Private nonguaranteed debt from:	1,373	3,698	3,733	3,884	3,683	4,063
Bondholders	..	..	100	100	100	100
Commercial banks and others	1,373	3,698	3,633	3,784	3,583	3,963
Use of IMF Credit	270	570	536	528	530	451
Net financial inflows						
Net debt inflows						
Use of IMF Credit	-20	-113	-9	8	-29	-68
Long-term	523	1,005	760	681	384	589
Official creditors	149	241	415	530	580	208
Multilateral	80	221	385	410	301	87
of which: World Bank	68	96	92	123	5	14
Bilateral	70	21	30	120	279	122
Private creditors	374	764	344	151	-196	381
Bondholders	..	..	400	0	0	0
Banks and other private	374	764	-56	151	-196	381
Short-term	20	-242	-245	408	-183	245
Net equity inflows						
Foreign direct investment	1,036	334	154	219	70	302
Portfolio equity	3	1	4	4	-3	0
Debt ratios						
External debt stocks to exports (%)	117	189	222	229	194	196
External debt stocks to GNI (%)	29	70	81	92	86	87
Debt service to exports (%)	12	32	38	34	27	30
Short-term to external debt stocks (%)	14	11	7	11	9	10
Multilateral to external debt stocks (%)	31	25	28	28	31	30
Reserves to external debt stocks (%)	39	17	20	22	22	21
Gross national income (GNI)	12,353	12,151	10,996	10,770	11,991	12,595

AZERBAIJAN

(US$ million, unless otherwise indicated)

	2008	2014	2015	2016	2017	2018
Summary external debt data by debtor type						
Total External debt stocks	**4,497**	**12,101**	**13,450**	**14,769**	**15,468**	**16,212**
Use of IMF Credit	316	224	213	206	219	214
Long-term external debt	3,045	9,856	11,690	13,167	14,574	15,429
Public and publicly guaranteed sector	2,718	8,408	8,843	10,804	12,637	13,957
Public Sector	2,718	8,408	8,843	10,804	12,637	13,957
of which: General Government	1,683	6,437	6,805	7,518	8,219	7,540
Private sector guaranteed by Public Sector	..	..	..	..	..	..
Private sector not guaranteed	327	1,448	2,847	2,363	1,937	1,471
Short-term external debt	1,136	2,021	1,548	1,396	675	570
Disbursements (long-term)	**741**	**3,049**	**3,628**	**2,862**	**2,913**	**3,269**
Public and publicly guaranteed sector	526	2,730	1,216	2,751	2,849	3,250
Public Sector	526	2,730	1,216	2,751	2,849	3,250
of which: General Government	279	2,614	866	1,227	1,131	902
Private sector guaranteed by Public Sector	..	..	..	..	..	..
Private sector not guaranteed	216	319	2,412	111	64	19
Principal repayments (long-term)	**173**	**1,565**	**1,585**	**1,330**	**1,811**	**2,288**
Public and publicly guaranteed sector	150	570	584	736	1,302	1,805
Public Sector	150	570	584	736	1,302	1,805
of which: General Government	49	374	386	488	548	1,550
Private sector guaranteed by Public Sector	..	..	..	..	..	..
Private sector not guaranteed	23	995	1,001	594	509	483
Interest payments (long-term)	**90**	**277**	**294**	**403**	**447**	**547**
Public and publicly guaranteed sector	78	123	208	259	330	455
Public Sector	78	123	208	259	330	455
of which: General Government	30	65	149	165	206	261
Private sector guaranteed by Public Sector	..	..	..	..	..	..
Private sector not guaranteed	11	154	86	144	117	91
Summary external debt stock by creditor type						
Long-term External debt stocks	**3,045**	**9,856**	**11,690**	**13,167**	**14,574**	**15,429**
Public and publicly guaranteed debt from:	2,718	8,408	8,843	10,804	12,637	13,957
Official creditors	1,889	4,471	4,731	5,595	6,628	6,868
Multilateral	1,137	3,387	3,708	4,572	5,552	5,775
of which: World Bank	775	1,920	2,096	2,203	2,665	2,538
Bilateral	752	1,084	1,023	1,023	1,076	1,094
Private creditors	829	3,937	4,112	5,208	6,009	7,089
Bondholders	..	2,250	2,250	3,250	3,750	3,750
Commercial banks and others	829	1,687	1,862	1,958	2,259	3,339
Private nonguaranteed debt from:	327	1,448	2,847	2,363	1,937	1,471
Bondholders	..	..	..	..	..	..
Commercial banks and others	327	1,448	2,847	2,363	1,937	1,471
Use of IMF Credit	316	224	213	206	219	214
Net financial inflows						
Net debt inflows						
Use of IMF Credit	-22	-4	-2	..	..	..
Long-term	568	1,483	2,043	1,531	1,102	982
Official creditors	213	488	355	881	918	262
Multilateral	184	457	384	890	914	247
of which: World Bank	98	314	200	122	435	-116
Bilateral	29	31	-29	-9	4	15
Private creditors	355	995	1,688	651	184	720
Bondholders	..	1,750	..	1,000	500	..
Banks and other private	355	-755	1,688	-349	-316	720
Short-term	4	416	-473	-152	-721	-105
Net equity inflows						
Foreign direct investment	3,521	4,430	4,048	4,500	2,867	1,403
Portfolio equity	0	10	24	0	0	0
Debt ratios						
External debt stocks to exports (%)	14	35	63	80	73	60
External debt stocks to GNI (%)	10	17	26	42	40	36
Debt service to exports (%)	1	5	9	10	11	11
Short-term to external debt stocks (%)	25	17	12	9	4	4
Multilateral to external debt stocks (%)	25	28	28	31	36	36
Reserves to external debt stocks (%)	144	121	47	40	43	41
Gross national income (GNI)	43,832	73,087	51,047	35,395	39,106	44,480

BANGLADESH

(US$ million, unless otherwise indicated)

	2008	2014	2015	2016	2017	2018
Summary external debt data by debtor type						
Total External debt stocks	**23,408**	**33,008**	**36,309**	**38,823**	**47,158**	**52,124**
Use of IMF Credit	758	1,470	1,613	1,546	1,625	1,536
Long-term external debt	20,755	27,385	28,064	29,440	34,766	41,557
Public and publicly guaranteed sector	20,333	24,276	24,718	26,348	31,371	36,664
Public Sector	20,333	24,276	24,718	26,348	31,371	36,664
of which: General Government	20,275	23,702	24,144	25,769	30,779	36,081
Private sector guaranteed by Public Sector	..	..	..	..	..	..
Private sector not guaranteed	422	3,109	3,346	3,093	3,395	4,892
Short-term external debt	1,894	4,153	6,633	7,836	10,767	9,031
Disbursements (long-term)	**2,044**	**3,789**	**2,806**	**3,279**	**5,530**	**8,984**
Public and publicly guaranteed sector	1,729	2,591	2,267	3,099	4,752	6,997
Public Sector	1,729	2,591	2,267	3,099	4,752	6,997
of which: General Government	1,703	2,358	2,242	3,068	4,728	6,953
Private sector guaranteed by Public Sector	..	..	..	..	..	..
Private sector not guaranteed	314	1,198	538	180	778	1,986
Principal repayments (long-term)	**669**	**1,572**	**1,290**	**1,348**	**1,491**	**1,694**
Public and publicly guaranteed sector	631	1,292	989	915	1,015	1,195
Public Sector	631	1,292	989	915	1,015	1,195
of which: General Government	620	1,282	979	906	988	1,156
Private sector guaranteed by Public Sector	..	..	..	..	..	..
Private sector not guaranteed	38	280	301	433	475	498
Interest payments (long-term)	**217**	**280**	**237**	**272**	**421**	**762**
Public and publicly guaranteed sector	203	262	212	232	362	628
Public Sector	203	262	212	232	362	628
of which: General Government	201	258	200	220	350	615
Private sector guaranteed by Public Sector	..	..	..	..	..	..
Private sector not guaranteed	14	18	25	40	59	134
Summary external debt stock by creditor type						
Long-term External debt stocks	**20,755**	**27,385**	**28,064**	**29,440**	**34,766**	**41,557**
Public and publicly guaranteed debt from:	20,333	24,276	24,718	26,348	31,371	36,664
Official creditors	20,277	24,227	24,678	26,314	31,338	36,638
Multilateral	17,301	19,765	20,019	20,849	23,521	24,971
of which: World Bank	10,613	11,417	11,534	11,890	13,621	14,501
Bilateral	2,977	4,461	4,658	5,465	7,817	11,667
Private creditors	56	49	40	34	33	26
Bondholders	..	..	..	..	..	..
Commercial banks and others	56	49	40	34	33	26
Private nonguaranteed debt from:	422	3,109	3,346	3,093	3,395	4,892
Bondholders	..	..	..	..	..	..
Commercial banks and others	422	3,109	3,346	3,093	3,395	4,892
Use of IMF Credit	758	1,470	1,613	1,546	1,625	1,536
Net financial inflows						
Net debt inflows						
Use of IMF Credit	203	65	209	-19	-13	-52
Long-term	1,374	2,217	1,516	1,931	4,039	7,290
Official creditors	1,118	1,279	1,284	2,189	3,741	5,808
Multilateral	1,017	720	1,021	1,388	1,578	1,952
of which: World Bank	607	522	599	716	1,020	1,219
Bilateral	101	559	263	801	2,163	3,855
Private creditors	257	938	232	-258	298	1,483
Bondholders	..	..	..	..	..	..
Banks and other private	257	938	232	-258	298	1,483
Short-term	527	418	2,480	1,204	2,930	-1,736
Net equity inflows						
Foreign direct investment	1,055	2,257	2,437	2,127	1,477	2,075
Portfolio equity	-130	358	-105	114	258	-38
Debt ratios						
External debt stocks to exports (%)	132	100	103	103	120	118
External debt stocks to GNI (%)	24	18	17	17	18	18
Debt service to exports (%)	5	6	5	5	6	6
Short-term to external debt stocks (%)	8	13	18	20	23	17
Multilateral to external debt stocks (%)	74	60	55	54	50	48
Reserves to external debt stocks (%)	24	66	74	82	70	60
Gross national income (GNI)	98,684	184,407	207,743	234,168	260,455	286,521

BELARUS

(US$ million, unless otherwise indicated)

	2008	2014	2015	2016	2017	2018
Summary external debt data by debtor type						
Total External debt stocks	**15,153**	**40,014**	**38,258**	**37,516**	**39,584**	**38,844**
Use of IMF Credit	568	613	511	496	525	513
Long-term external debt	7,027	26,573	26,273	26,398	29,335	28,729
Public and publicly guaranteed sector	5,439	15,636	15,837	18,142	20,988	19,988
Public Sector	5,419	15,593	15,800	18,142	20,988	19,988
of which: General Government	3,416	12,468	12,444	13,642	16,727	16,894
Private sector guaranteed by Public Sector	19	42	37	0	..	..
Private sector not guaranteed	1,589	10,937	10,436	8,257	8,346	8,741
Short-term external debt	7,558	12,827	11,474	10,622	9,725	9,602
Disbursements (long-term)	**3,309**	**5,267**	**3,778**	**2,615**	**5,811**	**7,204**
Public and publicly guaranteed sector	2,168	3,695	2,992	2,143	4,349	2,673
Public Sector	2,168	3,695	2,992	2,143	4,349	2,673
of which: General Government	1,521	3,264	2,173	1,935	4,039	2,367
Private sector guaranteed by Public Sector	..	0	0	0	..	..
Private sector not guaranteed	1,141	1,572	786	472	1,462	4,531
Principal repayments (long-term)	**858**	**2,976**	**3,710**	**5,014**	**3,030**	**4,130**
Public and publicly guaranteed sector	183	2,099	2,483	2,314	1,680	3,455
Public Sector	182	2,090	2,478	2,277	1,680	3,455
of which: General Government	127	1,270	1,926	893	1,029	1,998
Private sector guaranteed by Public Sector	1	9	5	37	..	..
Private sector not guaranteed	675	877	1,228	2,701	1,350	675
Interest payments (long-term)	**238**	**885**	**980**	**964**	**1,109**	**1,288**
Public and publicly guaranteed sector	182	704	781	745	868	1,022
Public Sector	180	698	777	743	868	1,022
of which: General Government	158	482	593	559	688	789
Private sector guaranteed by Public Sector	1	6	4	2	..	..
Private sector not guaranteed	56	181	199	219	241	265
Summary external debt stock by creditor type						
Long-term External debt stocks	**7,027**	**26,573**	**26,273**	**26,398**	**29,335**	**28,729**
Public and publicly guaranteed debt from:	5,439	15,636	15,837	18,142	20,988	19,988
Official creditors	3,547	11,940	13,005	14,071	15,968	16,423
Multilateral	50	3,145	2,838	3,360	3,942	3,810
of which: World Bank	42	590	642	725	822	905
Bilateral	3,497	8,795	10,167	10,710	12,026	12,613
Private creditors	1,891	3,695	2,832	4,071	5,020	3,565
Bondholders	19	1,800	800	800	2,200	2,000
Commercial banks and others	1,872	1,895	2,032	3,271	2,820	1,565
Private nonguaranteed debt from:	1,589	10,937	10,436	8,257	8,346	8,741
Bondholders	..	..	..	..	..	..
Commercial banks and others	1,589	10,937	10,436	8,257	8,346	8,741
Use of IMF Credit	568	613	511	496	525	513
Net financial inflows						
Net debt inflows						
Use of IMF Credit	..	-1,263	-77	..	..	..
Long-term	2,451	2,291	67	-2,400	2,780	3,074
Official creditors	1,466	2,774	1,350	914	1,806	661
Multilateral	-3	-111	-293	527	563	-124
of which: World Bank	-1	33	52	83	98	83
Bilateral	1,469	2,885	1,643	387	1,243	785
Private creditors	985	-483	-1,283	-3,313	974	2,413
Bondholders	..	0	-1,000	0	1,400	-200
Banks and other private	985	-483	-283	-3,313	-426	2,613
Short-term	198	-1,236	-1,353	-852	-897	-123
Net equity inflows						
Foreign direct investment	2,016	1,546	1,434	1,086	1,068	1,378
Portfolio equity	1	5	5	0	6	3
Debt ratios						
External debt stocks to exports (%)	41	91	115	123	106	90
External debt stocks to GNI (%)	25	52	71	82	75	68
Debt service to exports (%)	4	12	15	20	12	13
Short-term to external debt stocks (%)	50	32	30	28	25	25
Multilateral to external debt stocks (%)	0	8	7	9	10	10
Reserves to external debt stocks (%)	18	9	7	9	14	13
Gross national income (GNI)	59,975	76,402	53,995	45,532	52,669	57,399

BELIZE

(US$ million, unless otherwise indicated)

	2008	2014	2015	2016	2017	2018
Summary external debt data by debtor type						
Total External debt stocks	**1,276**	**1,286**	**1,307**	**1,322**	**1,368**	**1,380**
Use of IMF Credit	28	26	25	24	25	25
Long-term external debt	1,241	1,255	1,275	1,294	1,338	1,351
Public and publicly guaranteed sector	1,021	1,101	1,153	1,177	1,231	1,259
Public Sector	1,021	1,101	1,153	1,177	1,231	1,259
of which: General Government	990	1,098	1,147	1,167	1,215	1,225
Private sector guaranteed by Public Sector	0	..	..	..	..	..
Private sector not guaranteed	219	154	121	117	107	93
Short-term external debt	7	5	7	4	5	4
Disbursements (long-term)	**109**	**90**	**95**	**69**	**107**	**76**
Public and publicly guaranteed sector	41	87	93	67	98	70
Public Sector	41	87	93	67	98	70
of which: General Government	33	87	89	63	91	52
Private sector guaranteed by Public Sector	..	..	..	..	..	..
Private sector not guaranteed	68	3	2	2	9	6
Principal repayments (long-term)	**87**	**47**	**50**	**51**	**54**	**62**
Public and publicly guaranteed sector	52	37	40	43	44	42
Public Sector	52	37	40	43	44	42
of which: General Government	47	36	39	42	44	41
Private sector guaranteed by Public Sector	0	..	..	..	..	..
Private sector not guaranteed	35	10	11	8	10	20
Interest payments (long-term)	**60**	**44**	**45**	**47**	**47**	**48**
Public and publicly guaranteed sector	49	37	37	42	42	43
Public Sector	49	37	37	42	42	43
of which: General Government	48	37	37	42	41	43
Private sector guaranteed by Public Sector	0	..	..	..	..	..
Private sector not guaranteed	12	7	7	5	5	5
Summary external debt stock by creditor type						
Long-term External debt stocks	**1,241**	**1,255**	**1,275**	**1,294**	**1,338**	**1,351**
Public and publicly guaranteed debt from:	1,021	1,101	1,153	1,177	1,231	1,259
Official creditors	428	575	627	650	679	705
Multilateral	231	291	307	317	336	348
of which: World Bank	22	13	14	17	16	19
Bilateral	197	284	320	334	344	357
Private creditors	593	527	527	527	552	554
Bondholders	22	527	527	527	527	527
Commercial banks and others	571	0	..	..	25	27
Private nonguaranteed debt from:	219	154	121	117	107	93
Bondholders	..	..	..	..	..	..
Commercial banks and others	219	154	121	117	107	93
Use of IMF Credit	28	26	25	24	25	25
Net financial inflows						
Net debt inflows						
Use of IMF Credit	..	-1	..	..	..	..
Long-term	22	43	44	17	52	14
Official creditors	-2	50	53	24	28	26
Multilateral	-6	6	16	10	18	13
of which: World Bank	-5	0	1	3	0	2
Bilateral	4	44	37	13	10	13
Private creditors	24	-7	-9	-6	24	-12
Bondholders	-2	0	0	0	0	0
Banks and other private	26	-7	-9	-6	24	-12
Short-term	0	0	0	0	0	0
Net equity inflows						
Foreign direct investment	162	141	59	33	26	120
Portfolio equity	2	..	..	..	0	0
Debt ratios						
External debt stocks to exports (%)	146	118	126	136	131	127
External debt stocks to GNI (%)	106	83	78	78	80	77
Debt service to exports (%)	17	8	9	10	10	10
Short-term to external debt stocks (%)	1	0	1	0	0	0
Multilateral to external debt stocks (%)	18	23	23	24	25	25
Reserves to external debt stocks (%)	13	38	33	28	23	21
Gross national income (GNI)	1,203	1,555	1,667	1,696	1,707	1,797

BENIN

(US$ million, unless otherwise indicated)

	2008	2014	2015	2016	2017	2018
Summary external debt data by debtor type						
Total External debt stocks	**973.6**	**2,041.5**	**2,178.0**	**2,316.2**	**2,897.8**	**3,690.6**
Use of IMF Credit	36.9	220.3	202.3	187.0	226.4	244.6
Long-term external debt	847.3	1,760.6	1,900.4	2,067.0	2,599.7	3,390.3
Public and publicly guaranteed sector	847.3	1,760.6	1,900.4	2,067.0	2,599.7	3,390.3
Public Sector	847.3	1,760.6	1,900.4	2,067.0	2,599.7	3,390.3
of which: General Government	847.3	1,760.6	1,900.4	2,067.0	2,599.7	3,390.3
Private sector guaranteed by Public Sector	..	..	..	..	..	..
Private sector not guaranteed	..	..	..	..	..	..
Short-term external debt	89.3	60.6	75.3	62.3	71.8	55.7
Disbursements (long-term)	**142.4**	**329.2**	**282.8**	**288.8**	**422.9**	**1,050.6**
Public and publicly guaranteed sector	142.4	329.2	282.8	288.8	422.9	1,050.6
Public Sector	142.4	329.2	282.8	288.8	422.9	1,050.6
of which: General Government	142.4	329.2	282.8	288.8	422.9	1,050.6
Private sector guaranteed by Public Sector	..	..	..	..	..	..
Private sector not guaranteed	..	..	..	..	..	..
Principal repayments (long-term)	**16.0**	**46.6**	**43.7**	**55.0**	**55.5**	**152.7**
Public and publicly guaranteed sector	16.0	46.6	43.7	55.0	55.5	152.7
Public Sector	16.0	46.6	43.7	55.0	55.5	152.7
of which: General Government	16.0	46.6	43.7	55.0	55.5	152.7
Private sector guaranteed by Public Sector	..	..	..	..	..	..
Private sector not guaranteed	..	..	..	..	..	..
Interest payments (long-term)	**41.1**	**24.6**	**23.9**	**28.1**	**32.7**	**39.9**
Public and publicly guaranteed sector	41.1	24.6	23.9	28.1	32.7	39.9
Public Sector	41.1	24.6	23.9	28.1	32.7	39.9
of which: General Government	41.1	24.6	23.9	28.1	32.7	39.9
Private sector guaranteed by Public Sector	..	..	..	..	..	..
Private sector not guaranteed	..	..	..	..	..	..
Summary external debt stock by creditor type						
Long-term External debt stocks	**847.3**	**1,760.6**	**1,900.4**	**2,067.0**	**2,599.7**	**3,390.3**
Public and publicly guaranteed debt from:	847.3	1,760.6	1,900.4	2,067.0	2,599.7	3,390.3
Official creditors	847.3	1,760.6	1,900.4	2,018.0	2,462.2	2,478.8
Multilateral	691.0	1,452.6	1,534.3	1,655.3	2,007.5	1,994.4
of which: World Bank	255.4	621.7	680.5	764.5	914.2	983.9
Bilateral	156.3	308.0	366.1	362.7	454.6	484.4
Private creditors	..	0.0	0.0	48.9	137.5	911.5
Bondholders	..	..	..	..	..	..
Commercial banks and others	..	0.0	0.0	48.9	137.5	911.5
Private nonguaranteed debt from:	..	..	..	..	..	..
Bondholders	..	..	..	..	..	..
Commercial banks and others	..	..	..	..	..	..
Use of IMF Credit	36.9	220.3	202.3	187.0	226.4	244.6
Net financial inflows						
Net debt inflows						
Use of IMF Credit	18.9	8.6	-8.4	-9.7	27.6	23.9
Long-term	126.4	282.6	239.1	233.7	367.4	897.8
Official creditors	126.4	282.6	239.1	182.4	290.3	93.0
Multilateral	124.1	188.5	164.9	167.8	219.6	44.5
of which: World Bank	84.1	102.4	87.0	107.9	102.5	93.4
Bilateral	2.3	94.0	74.2	14.5	70.7	48.4
Private creditors	..	..	0.0	51.3	77.1	804.9
Bondholders	..	..	..	..	..	..
Banks and other private	..	..	0.0	51.3	77.1	804.9
Short-term	-27.1	-99.4	-9.1	-7.4	8.7	-14.9
Net equity inflows						
Foreign direct investment	-48.7	176.3	96.6	31.1	44.2	207.5
Portfolio equity	-1.8	5.8	77.0	9.4	17.5	..
Debt ratios						
External debt stocks to exports (%)	58.1	63.8	102.2	103.5	108.6	133.8
External debt stocks to GNI (%)	13.7	21.2	26.5	27.1	31.6	35.9
Debt service to exports (%)	3.6	2.5	3.6	4.2	4.0	7.8
Short-term to external debt stocks (%)	9.2	3.0	3.5	2.7	2.5	1.5
Multilateral to external debt stocks (%)	71.0	71.2	70.4	71.5	69.3	54.0
Reserves to external debt stocks (%)	129.8	35.6	33.6	..	..	..
Gross national income (GNI)	7,121.5	9,646.3	8,225.6	8,535.4	9,180.4	10,277.0

BHUTAN

(US$ million, unless otherwise indicated)

	2008	2014	2015	2016	2017	2018
Summary external debt data by debtor type						
Total External debt stocks	**693.1**	**1,833.5**	**2,011.1**	**2,289.7**	**2,607.9**	**2,549.2**
Use of IMF Credit	9.2	8.7	8.3	8.1	8.5	8.3
Long-term external debt	675.9	1,821.4	2,002.8	2,281.5	2,596.4	2,536.5
Public and publicly guaranteed sector	675.9	1,819.6	1,945.1	2,221.2	2,540.8	2,481.6
Public Sector	675.9	1,819.6	1,945.1	2,221.2	2,540.8	2,481.6
of which: General Government	675.9	1,661.7	1,839.5	2,118.2	2,431.3	2,381.3
Private sector guaranteed by Public Sector	..	..	..	..	..	..
Private sector not guaranteed	..	1.9	57.7	60.3	55.6	54.9
Short-term external debt	8.0	3.4	0.0	0.1	3.0	4.3
Disbursements (long-term)	**31.7**	**424.3**	**361.4**	**402.0**	**219.8**	**165.5**
Public and publicly guaranteed sector	31.7	424.3	304.0	365.0	219.8	165.5
Public Sector	31.7	424.3	304.0	365.0	219.8	165.5
of which: General Government	31.7	424.3	304.0	365.0	219.8	165.5
Private sector guaranteed by Public Sector	..	..	..	..	..	..
Private sector not guaranteed	..	..	57.3	36.9	..	..
Principal repayments (long-term)	**43.5**	**42.3**	**91.7**	**75.4**	**46.3**	**51.6**
Public and publicly guaranteed sector	43.5	39.9	90.3	41.6	41.6	50.8
Public Sector	43.5	39.9	90.3	41.6	41.6	50.8
of which: General Government	43.5	39.9	43.5	41.6	41.6	50.8
Private sector guaranteed by Public Sector	..	..	..	..	..	..
Private sector not guaranteed	..	2.4	1.4	33.8	4.7	0.8
Interest payments (long-term)	**38.0**	**40.6**	**37.2**	**35.2**	**36.1**	**35.8**
Public and publicly guaranteed sector	38.0	40.4	37.1	34.3	33.9	34.0
Public Sector	38.0	40.4	37.1	34.3	33.9	34.0
of which: General Government	38.0	32.2	31.2	29.1	28.6	28.9
Private sector guaranteed by Public Sector	..	..	..	..	..	..
Private sector not guaranteed	..	0.2	0.1	1.0	2.2	1.7
Summary external debt stock by creditor type						
Long-term External debt stocks	**675.9**	**1,821.4**	**2,002.8**	**2,281.5**	**2,596.4**	**2,536.5**
Public and publicly guaranteed debt from:	675.9	1,819.6	1,945.1	2,221.2	2,540.8	2,481.6
Official creditors	675.9	1,769.5	1,897.6	2,179.4	2,490.7	2,434.9
Multilateral	236.9	470.9	468.9	460.2	532.5	563.4
of which: World Bank	94.3	170.3	183.4	177.6	219.0	243.7
Bilateral	439.0	1,298.6	1,428.7	1,719.2	1,958.3	1,871.5
Private creditors	..	50.1	47.5	41.8	50.1	46.7
Bondholders	..	..	..	..	..	..
Commercial banks and others	..	50.1	47.5	41.8	50.1	46.7
Private nonguaranteed debt from:	..	1.9	57.7	60.3	55.6	54.9
Bondholders	..	..	..	..	..	..
Commercial banks and others	..	1.9	57.7	60.3	55.6	54.9
Use of IMF Credit	9.2	8.7	8.3	8.1	8.5	8.3
Net financial inflows						
Net debt inflows						
Use of IMF Credit	..	0.0	..	..	..	..
Long-term	-11.8	382.0	269.7	326.6	173.5	113.9
Official creditors	-11.8	377.2	211.1	327.8	175.6	115.6
Multilateral	11.0	49.3	14.9	1.3	48.1	41.4
of which: World Bank	7.5	4.6	20.7	-0.4	29.7	30.5
Bilateral	-22.8	327.9	196.2	326.4	127.4	74.2
Private creditors	..	4.8	58.5	-1.2	-2.1	-1.7
Bondholders	..	..	..	..	..	..
Banks and other private	..	4.8	58.5	-1.2	-2.1	-1.7
Short-term	-10.0	-71.6	-3.4	0.1	2.9	1.3
Net equity inflows						
Foreign direct investment	2.4	22.4	5.7	11.5	-0.7	3.3
Portfolio equity	..	0.0	0.0	0.0	0.0	0.0
Debt ratios						
External debt stocks to exports (%)	100.7	270.2	268.8	343.4	349.4	313.1
External debt stocks to GNI (%)	56.6	99.5	104.9	112.6	112.6	109.2
Debt service to exports (%)	11.9	12.2	17.2	16.6	11.0	10.7
Short-term to external debt stocks (%)	1.2	0.2	0.0	0.0	0.1	0.2
Multilateral to external debt stocks (%)	34.2	25.7	23.3	20.1	20.4	22.1
Reserves to external debt stocks (%)	110.3	67.9	54.9	49.2	46.3	38.7
Gross national income (GNI)	1,224.3	1,841.9	1,917.0	2,034.2	2,315.2	2,333.5

BOLIVIA, PLURINATIONAL STATE OF

(US$ million, unless otherwise indicated)

	2008	2014	2015	2016	2017	2018
Summary external debt data by debtor type						
Total External debt stocks	**5,701**	**8,884**	**9,895**	**10,994**	**12,990**	**13,280**
Use of IMF Credit	41	238	227	221	234	228
Long-term external debt	5,390	8,357	9,242	10,299	12,486	12,349
Public and publicly guaranteed sector	2,421	5,745	6,336	7,010	9,151	9,904
Public Sector	2,421	5,744	6,335	7,010	9,151	9,904
of which: General Government	2,262	5,583	6,304	6,984	9,126	9,883
Private sector guaranteed by Public Sector	..	1	0	0	..	..
Private sector not guaranteed	2,969	2,612	2,906	3,289	3,336	2,445
Short-term external debt	270	289	426	475	270	703
Disbursements (long-term)	**1,302**	**1,587**	**1,408**	**1,432**	**2,661**	**1,372**
Public and publicly guaranteed sector	629	745	1,016	1,002	2,390	1,197
Public Sector	629	745	1,016	1,002	2,390	1,197
of which: General Government	589	745	1,016	1,002	2,390	1,197
Private sector guaranteed by Public Sector	..	0	0	..	..	..
Private sector not guaranteed	673	842	392	430	271	176
Principal repayments (long-term)	**768**	**817**	**811**	**550**	**688**	**640**
Public and publicly guaranteed sector	376	231	374	280	331	360
Public Sector	376	231	373	280	331	360
of which: General Government	372	219	246	276	328	356
Private sector guaranteed by Public Sector	..	0	0	0	..	..
Private sector not guaranteed	392	586	438	270	357	280
Interest payments (long-term)	**176**	**157**	**170**	**211**	**283**	**346**
Public and publicly guaranteed sector	99	140	153	185	250	316
Public Sector	99	140	153	185	250	316
of which: General Government	98	136	150	184	250	316
Private sector guaranteed by Public Sector	..	0	0	0	..	..
Private sector not guaranteed	77	18	17	26	33	30
Summary external debt stock by creditor type						
Long-term External debt stocks	**5,390**	**8,357**	**9,242**	**10,299**	**12,486**	**12,349**
Public and publicly guaranteed debt from:	2,421	5,745	6,336	7,010	9,151	9,904
Official creditors	2,324	4,729	5,323	5,999	7,141	7,896
Multilateral	1,813	3,889	4,648	5,282	6,157	6,712
of which: World Bank	282	499	735	770	830	847
Bilateral	512	840	674	717	984	1,184
Private creditors	97	1,015	1,013	1,011	2,010	2,008
Bondholders	10	1,000	1,000	1,000	2,000	2,000
Commercial banks and others	87	15	13	11	10	8
Private nonguaranteed debt from:	2,969	2,612	2,906	3,289	3,336	2,445
Bondholders	..	..	..	..	..	..
Commercial banks and others	2,969	2,612	2,906	3,289	3,336	2,445
Use of IMF Credit	41	238	227	221	234	228
Net financial inflows						
Net debt inflows						
Use of IMF Credit	..	0	..	..	..	..
Long-term	534	770	596	882	1,973	732
Official creditors	191	516	644	724	1,060	838
Multilateral	106	477	786	661	827	614
of which: World Bank	24	31	259	57	19	37
Bilateral	86	39	-142	63	233	225
Private creditors	343	254	-48	159	913	-106
Bondholders	..	0	0	0	1,000	0
Banks and other private	343	254	-48	159	-87	-106
Short-term	47	39	137	49	-205	433
Net equity inflows						
Foreign direct investment	280	626	371	193	706	227
Portfolio equity	0	21	19	21	30	22
Debt ratios						
External debt stocks to exports (%)	77	63	99	131	133	126
External debt stocks to GNI (%)	35	28	31	33	36	34
Debt service to exports (%)	13	7	10	9	10	10
Short-term to external debt stocks (%)	5	3	4	4	2	5
Multilateral to external debt stocks (%)	32	44	47	48	47	51
Reserves to external debt stocks (%)	122	152	117	77	65	54
Gross national income (GNI)	16,138	31,298	31,873	33,320	36,449	39,313

BOSNIA AND HERZEGOVINA

(US$ million, unless otherwise indicated)

	2008	2014	2015	2016	2017	2018
Summary external debt data by debtor type						
Total External debt stocks	**13,109**	**13,777**	**13,917**	**14,425**	**15,318**	**15,824**
Use of IMF Credit	32	892	800	770	592	466
Long-term external debt	11,915	12,104	12,470	13,008	14,440	15,091
Public and publicly guaranteed sector	3,008	4,734	4,390	4,401	4,841	4,966
Public Sector	3,008	4,734	4,390	4,401	4,841	4,966
of which: General Government	3,000	4,501	4,064	4,035	4,430	4,569
Private sector guaranteed by Public Sector	..	..	..	..	..	..
Private sector not guaranteed	8,907	7,370	8,080	8,606	9,599	10,125
Short-term external debt	1,162	781	647	647	286	267
Disbursements (long-term)	**1,962**	**704**	**1,239**	**1,417**	**1,447**	**1,299**
Public and publicly guaranteed sector	189	644	361	401	308	629
Public Sector	189	644	361	401	308	629
of which: General Government	189	559	235	330	293	606
Private sector guaranteed by Public Sector	..	..	..	..	..	..
Private sector not guaranteed	1,773	61	878	1,016	1,139	670
Principal repayments (long-term)	**137**	**994**	**510**	**757**	**450**	**469**
Public and publicly guaranteed sector	91	227	342	267	304	325
Public Sector	91	227	342	267	304	325
of which: General Government	91	225	332	250	286	305
Private sector guaranteed by Public Sector	..	..	..	..	..	..
Private sector not guaranteed	46	768	168	490	147	143
Interest payments (long-term)	**257**	**249**	**191**	**209**	**224**	**246**
Public and publicly guaranteed sector	80	82	56	65	63	76
Public Sector	80	82	56	65	63	76
of which: General Government	80	79	53	62	61	74
Private sector guaranteed by Public Sector	..	..	..	..	..	..
Private sector not guaranteed	176	168	135	144	160	169
Summary external debt stock by creditor type						
Long-term External debt stocks	**11,915**	**12,104**	**12,470**	**13,008**	**14,440**	**15,091**
Public and publicly guaranteed debt from:	3,008	4,734	4,390	4,401	4,841	4,966
Official creditors	2,799	4,413	4,136	4,203	4,672	4,643
Multilateral	1,984	3,495	3,319	3,397	3,769	3,741
of which: World Bank	1,520	1,564	1,551	1,514	1,572	1,610
Bilateral	815	918	817	806	903	903
Private creditors	209	321	254	198	169	322
Bondholders	..	158	121	98	89	256
Commercial banks and others	209	163	132	100	80	66
Private nonguaranteed debt from:	8,907	7,370	8,080	8,606	9,599	10,125
Bondholders	..	..	..	..	..	..
Commercial banks and others	8,907	7,370	8,080	8,606	9,599	10,125
Use of IMF Credit	32	892	800	770	592	466
Net financial inflows						
Net debt inflows						
Use of IMF Credit	-2	99	-54	-6	-218	-114
Long-term	1,825	-290	730	660	997	831
Official creditors	72	455	55	183	58	138
Multilateral	57	416	91	175	27	109
of which: World Bank	-8	27	57	0	-36	81
Bilateral	15	39	-36	8	30	29
Private creditors	1,753	-745	675	477	939	692
Bondholders	..	-25	-21	-21	-21	176
Banks and other private	1,753	-720	696	497	960	516
Short-term	-225	-239	-134	1	-362	-19
Net equity inflows						
Foreign direct investment	588	254	264	256	452	576
Portfolio equity	0	-6	2	3	5	-2
Debt ratios						
External debt stocks to exports (%)	204	198	225	220	195	181
External debt stocks to GNI (%)	66	74	85	85	85	80
Debt service to exports (%)	7	21	12	16	12	11
Short-term to external debt stocks (%)	9	6	5	4	2	2
Multilateral to external debt stocks (%)	15	25	24	24	25	24
Reserves to external debt stocks (%)	34	34	34	35	41	42
Gross national income (GNI)	19,819	18,710	16,321	16,959	18,000	19,680

BOTSWANA

(US$ million, unless otherwise indicated)

	2008	2014	2015	2016	2017	2018
Summary external debt data by debtor type						
Total External debt stocks	**448.5**	**2,545.6**	**2,225.6**	**2,109.2**	**1,717.7**	**1,748.7**
Use of IMF Credit	6.7	83.2	79.6	77.2	81.8	79.9
Long-term external debt	396.8	1,989.6	1,761.4	1,653.1	1,528.1	1,418.0
Public and publicly guaranteed sector	396.8	1,909.9	1,761.4	1,653.1	1,528.1	1,418.0
Public Sector	396.8	1,909.9	1,761.4	1,653.1	1,528.1	1,418.0
of which: General Government	379.8	1,870.0	1,730.3	1,630.9	1,514.8	1,413.6
Private sector guaranteed by Public Sector	..	..	..	..	..	..
Private sector not guaranteed	..	79.7	0.0	..	..	0.0
Short-term external debt	45.0	472.8	384.6	378.9	107.8	250.9
Disbursements (long-term)	**56.5**	**78.0**	**7.9**	**36.8**	**4.5**	**36.5**
Public and publicly guaranteed sector	56.5	78.0	7.9	36.8	4.5	36.5
Public Sector	56.5	78.0	7.9	36.8	4.5	36.5
of which: General Government	56.5	38.0	7.9	36.8	4.5	36.5
Private sector guaranteed by Public Sector	..	..	..	..	..	..
Private sector not guaranteed	..	..	..	..	..	..
Principal repayments (long-term)	**60.9**	**39.0**	**219.3**	**140.5**	**142.3**	**142.6**
Public and publicly guaranteed sector	60.9	39.0	139.6	140.5	142.3	142.6
Public Sector	60.9	39.0	139.6	140.5	142.3	142.6
of which: General Government	56.7	38.9	130.7	131.6	133.4	133.7
Private sector guaranteed by Public Sector	..	..	..	..	..	..
Private sector not guaranteed	..	..	79.7	..	..	..
Interest payments (long-term)	**7.7**	**20.1**	**20.5**	**18.5**	**29.5**	**30.8**
Public and publicly guaranteed sector	7.7	17.8	15.9	18.5	29.5	30.8
Public Sector	7.7	17.8	15.9	18.5	29.5	30.8
of which: General Government	6.9	17.8	15.7	18.2	29.3	30.6
Private sector guaranteed by Public Sector	..	..	..	..	..	..
Private sector not guaranteed	..	2.3	4.6	..	..	..
Summary external debt stock by creditor type						
Long-term External debt stocks	**396.8**	**1,989.6**	**1,761.4**	**1,653.1**	**1,528.1**	**1,418.0**
Public and publicly guaranteed debt from:	396.8	1,909.9	1,761.4	1,653.1	1,528.1	1,418.0
Official creditors	394.8	1,870.0	1,730.3	1,630.9	1,514.8	1,413.6
Multilateral	246.3	1,781.4	1,661.0	1,578.7	1,472.6	1,384.2
of which: World Bank	5.3	135.2	131.4	158.6	151.5	173.6
Bilateral	148.5	88.5	69.3	52.2	42.2	29.3
Private creditors	2.0	40.0	31.1	22.2	13.3	4.4
Bondholders	..	..	..	..	..	..
Commercial banks and others	2.0	40.0	31.1	22.2	13.3	4.4
Private nonguaranteed debt from:	..	79.7	0.0	..	..	0.0
Bondholders	..	79.7	0.0	..	..	..
Commercial banks and others	..	..	..	..	..	0.0
Use of IMF Credit	6.7	83.2	79.6	77.2	81.8	79.9
Net financial inflows						
Net debt inflows						
Use of IMF Credit	..	0.0	..	..	..	..
Long-term	-4.4	39.0	-211.3	-103.7	-137.8	-106.1
Official creditors	0.7	-0.9	-122.8	-94.8	-128.9	-97.2
Multilateral	18.0	15.8	-106.9	-79.6	-116.4	-85.4
of which: World Bank	-0.5	22.8	-1.0	27.2	-7.1	22.1
Bilateral	-17.3	-16.8	-15.8	-15.2	-12.5	-11.9
Private creditors	-5.1	40.0	-88.6	-8.9	-8.9	-8.9
Bondholders	..	..	-79.7	..	..	..
Banks and other private	-5.1	40.0	-8.9	-8.9	-8.9	-8.9
Short-term	23.0	75.5	-88.2	-5.7	-271.1	143.1
Net equity inflows						
Foreign direct investment	513.6	415.7	310.7	47.5	159.7	173.8
Portfolio equity	-36.7	-66.4	-103.6	-122.8	-46.6	-136.5
Debt ratios						
External debt stocks to exports (%)	7.6	26.1	29.9	25.0	24.0	23.0
External debt stocks to GNI (%)	4.4	16.0	15.7	14.0	10.2	9.7
Debt service to exports (%)	1.2	0.7	3.3	2.0	2.4	2.4
Short-term to external debt stocks (%)	10.0	18.6	17.3	18.0	6.3	14.3
Multilateral to external debt stocks (%)	54.9	70.0	74.6	74.8	85.7	79.2
Reserves to external debt stocks (%)	2,033.1	327.0	339.1	340.8	436.1	380.7
Gross national income (GNI)	10,196.3	15,905.2	14,205.4	15,043.5	16,826.5	17,999.6

BRAZIL

(US$ million, unless otherwise indicated)

	2008	2014	2015	2016	2017	2018
Summary external debt data by debtor type						
Total External debt stocks	**262,957**	**556,920**	**543,397**	**543,257**	**542,980**	**557,823**
Use of IMF Credit	552	4,183	4,001	3,881	4,112	4,015
Long-term external debt	225,761	494,560	487,055	482,174	486,460	486,963
Public and publicly guaranteed sector	79,918	174,931	172,887	174,683	181,161	190,143
Public Sector	78,686	171,794	170,432	172,853	179,675	189,083
of which: General Government	64,717	73,660	68,703	71,178	70,026	70,400
Private sector guaranteed by Public Sector	1,233	3,138	2,455	1,830	1,485	1,060
Private sector not guaranteed	145,842	319,629	314,168	307,492	305,299	296,820
Short-term external debt	36,644	58,177	52,341	57,202	52,408	66,844
Disbursements (long-term)	**69,560**	**115,457**	**93,786**	**106,246**	**96,709**	**105,009**
Public and publicly guaranteed sector	16,697	42,117	20,051	19,728	30,315	28,760
Public Sector	16,579	41,474	19,813	19,608	30,187	28,626
of which: General Government	12,403	13,201	3,031	5,732	7,093	4,607
Private sector guaranteed by Public Sector	119	644	238	121	128	134
Private sector not guaranteed	52,863	73,339	73,735	86,518	66,394	76,249
Principal repayments (long-term)	**40,355**	**45,025**	**71,342**	**94,709**	**75,665**	**74,379**
Public and publicly guaranteed sector	16,353	9,168	22,929	18,983	23,215	28,432
Public Sector	16,232	8,737	22,031	18,238	22,715	27,874
of which: General Government	14,319	6,849	5,140	3,809	8,450	3,645
Private sector guaranteed by Public Sector	120	431	898	745	500	558
Private sector not guaranteed	24,002	35,857	48,413	75,726	52,450	45,947
Interest payments (long-term)	**15,046**	**16,450**	**17,723**	**21,605**	**18,467**	**18,681**
Public and publicly guaranteed sector	6,057	5,726	5,895	5,537	6,696	5,679
Public Sector	5,990	5,640	5,810	5,460	6,639	5,630
of which: General Government	5,399	3,344	3,330	3,163	3,348	3,186
Private sector guaranteed by Public Sector	66	86	85	78	57	49
Private sector not guaranteed	8,989	10,724	11,828	16,068	11,771	13,002
Summary external debt stock by creditor type						
Long-term External debt stocks	**225,761**	**494,560**	**487,055**	**482,174**	**486,460**	**486,963**
Public and publicly guaranteed debt from:	79,918	174,931	172,887	174,683	181,161	190,143
Official creditors	29,329	42,412	42,083	41,064	48,327	47,811
Multilateral	24,647	31,162	31,657	32,071	32,678	33,337
of which: World Bank	10,671	15,288	15,753	16,255	16,390	16,213
Bilateral	4,682	11,250	10,426	8,993	15,650	14,474
Private creditors	50,589	132,519	130,805	133,619	132,833	142,332
Bondholders	43,237	53,854	46,628	46,843	44,874	41,979
Commercial banks and others	7,352	78,665	84,176	86,776	87,959	100,354
Private nonguaranteed debt from:	145,842	319,629	314,168	307,492	305,299	296,820
Bondholders	37,855	55,073	51,276	46,930	48,026	32,686
Commercial banks and others	107,987	264,555	262,891	260,562	257,273	264,134
Use of IMF Credit	552	4,183	4,001	3,881	4,112	4,015
Net financial inflows						
Net debt inflows						
Use of IMF Credit	..	0	..	..	..	..
Long-term	29,206	70,432	22,444	11,538	21,044	30,630
Official creditors	1,951	3,249	-236	-1,012	7,140	-406
Multilateral	1,202	2,607	507	427	633	738
of which: World Bank	914	1,597	474	516	159	-114
Bilateral	749	642	-743	-1,439	6,506	-1,144
Private creditors	27,254	67,183	22,680	12,550	13,904	31,036
Bondholders	2,587	-401	-5,442	-7,710	-642	1,287
Banks and other private	24,667	67,584	28,122	20,260	14,546	29,749
Short-term	-2,602	24,680	-5,818	4,860	-4,798	14,440
Net equity inflows						
Foreign direct investment	30,064	48,674	41,888	48,853	64,008	55,999
Portfolio equity	-7,565	11,493	9,787	11,040	5,674	-5,634
Debt ratios						
External debt stocks to exports (%)	109	205	240	236	197	186
External debt stocks to GNI (%)	16	23	31	31	27	30
Debt service to exports (%)	23	23	40	51	35	32
Short-term to external debt stocks (%)	14	10	10	11	10	12
Multilateral to external debt stocks (%)	9	6	6	6	6	6
Reserves to external debt stocks (%)	73	65	65	67	68	67
Gross national income (GNI)	1,654,242	2,407,379	1,763,308	1,758,811	2,015,527	1,840,199

BULGARIA

(US$ million, unless otherwise indicated)

	2008	2014	2015	2016	2017	2018
Summary external debt data by debtor type						
Total External debt stocks	**53,065**	**46,889**	**40,115**	**39,657**	**40,438**	**39,874**
Use of IMF Credit	941	885	847	821	870	850
Long-term external debt	33,790	34,855	30,496	30,226	30,032	29,329
Public and publicly guaranteed sector	4,830	5,715	8,571	10,818	11,321	11,138
Public Sector	4,830	5,715	8,571	10,818	11,321	11,138
of which: General Government	3,982	5,400	8,285	9,939	10,115	10,051
Private sector guaranteed by Public Sector	..	..	..	..	..	..
Private sector not guaranteed	28,960	29,139	21,925	19,408	18,711	18,192
Short-term external debt	18,334	11,149	8,773	8,609	9,536	9,695
Disbursements (long-term)	**17,394**	**5,534**	**7,135**	**6,999**	**5,276**	**4,941**
Public and publicly guaranteed sector	370	2,145	3,704	2,836	276	806
Public Sector	370	2,145	3,704	2,836	276	806
of which: General Government	266	2,145	3,664	2,177	10	782
Private sector guaranteed by Public Sector	..	..	..	..	..	..
Private sector not guaranteed	17,024	3,389	3,431	4,163	5,001	4,135
Principal repayments (long-term)	**3,960**	**4,438**	**7,173**	**5,787**	**6,833**	**4,954**
Public and publicly guaranteed sector	733	296	228	265	1,345	308
Public Sector	733	296	228	265	1,345	308
of which: General Government	672	215	172	212	1,284	211
Private sector guaranteed by Public Sector	..	..	..	..	..	..
Private sector not guaranteed	3,227	4,142	6,945	5,521	5,489	4,646
Interest payments (long-term)	**929**	**722**	**2,099**	**2,162**	**1,704**	**1,377**
Public and publicly guaranteed sector	292	124	162	239	296	260
Public Sector	292	124	162	239	296	260
of which: General Government	255	114	155	229	281	243
Private sector guaranteed by Public Sector	..	..	..	..	..	..
Private sector not guaranteed	637	598	1,936	1,923	1,408	1,118
Summary external debt stock by creditor type						
Long-term External debt stocks	**33,790**	**34,855**	**30,496**	**30,226**	**30,032**	**29,329**
Public and publicly guaranteed debt from:	4,830	5,715	8,571	10,818	11,321	11,138
Official creditors	3,019	2,744	2,477	2,817	3,357	2,847
Multilateral	2,198	2,373	2,168	2,556	3,033	2,600
of which: World Bank	1,207	969	786	920	1,129	831
Bilateral	821	371	309	261	325	247
Private creditors	1,811	2,971	6,094	8,002	7,964	8,291
Bondholders	1,775	2,966	6,089	7,997	7,960	8,286
Commercial banks and others	36	5	5	4	5	4
Private nonguaranteed debt from:	28,960	29,139	21,925	19,408	18,711	18,192
Bondholders	522	1,444	1,444	1,444	1,444	85
Commercial banks and others	28,438	27,695	20,481	17,964	17,267	18,107
Use of IMF Credit	941	885	847	821	870	850
Net financial inflows						
Net debt inflows						
Use of IMF Credit	..	0	..	..	..	..
Long-term	13,434	1,096	-38	1,212	-1,557	-13
Official creditors	-352	-117	-17	404	4	-210
Multilateral	-431	-54	37	463	-41	-134
of which: World Bank	-407	-103	-87	150	-82	-84
Bilateral	79	-63	-54	-58	45	-76
Private creditors	13,786	1,213	-20	808	-1,561	197
Bondholders	-287	1,816	3,494	2,167	-1,073	-650
Banks and other private	14,073	-602	-3,514	-1,359	-488	848
Short-term	4,298	-2,260	-2,331	-159	897	36
Net equity inflows						
Foreign direct investment	5,821	11	2,788	1,460	993	1,381
Portfolio equity	-106	-77	-9	-20	155	102
Debt ratios						
External debt stocks to exports (%)	166	123	121	112	99	91
External debt stocks to GNI (%)	102	83	82	75	69	60
Debt service to exports (%)	18	14	29	23	21	15
Short-term to external debt stocks (%)	35	24	22	22	24	24
Multilateral to external debt stocks (%)	4	5	5	6	7	7
Reserves to external debt stocks (%)	32	40	52	60	66	68
Gross national income (GNI)	52,088	56,323	49,193	53,102	58,985	66,138

BURKINA FASO

(US$ million, unless otherwise indicated)

	2008	2014	2015	2016	2017	2018
Summary external debt data by debtor type						
Total External debt stocks	**1,584**	**2,551**	**2,632**	**2,825**	**3,129**	**3,286**
Use of IMF Credit	69	283	283	286	284	269
Long-term external debt	1,507	2,268	2,349	2,539	2,845	3,017
Public and publicly guaranteed sector	1,506	2,260	2,339	2,532	2,835	3,006
Public Sector	1,506	2,260	2,339	2,532	2,835	3,006
of which: General Government	1,506	2,260	2,339	2,532	2,835	3,006
Private sector guaranteed by Public Sector	..	..	..	..	..	..
Private sector not guaranteed	1	8	10	7	10	11
Short-term external debt	9	0	0	0	0	0
Disbursements (long-term)	**293**	**221**	**274**	**264**	**184**	**340**
Public and publicly guaranteed sector	293	217	271	262	183	338
Public Sector	293	217	271	262	183	338
of which: General Government	293	217	271	262	183	338
Private sector guaranteed by Public Sector	..	..	..	..	..	..
Private sector not guaranteed	1	4	3	2	1	2
Principal repayments (long-term)	**27**	**59**	**71**	**71**	**78**	**78**
Public and publicly guaranteed sector	27	58	70	70	77	77
Public Sector	27	58	70	70	77	77
of which: General Government	27	58	70	70	77	77
Private sector guaranteed by Public Sector	..	..	..	..	..	..
Private sector not guaranteed	0	1	1	1	1	1
Interest payments (long-term)	**14**	**24**	**23**	**31**	**33**	**32**
Public and publicly guaranteed sector	14	23	22	31	32	31
Public Sector	14	23	22	31	32	31
of which: General Government	14	23	22	31	32	31
Private sector guaranteed by Public Sector	..	..	..	..	..	..
Private sector not guaranteed	0	0	0	0	0	1
Summary external debt stock by creditor type						
Long-term External debt stocks	**1,507**	**2,268**	**2,349**	**2,539**	**2,845**	**3,017**
Public and publicly guaranteed debt from:	1,506	2,260	2,339	2,532	2,835	3,006
Official creditors	1,484	2,253	2,336	2,531	2,835	3,006
Multilateral	1,198	1,987	2,039	2,195	2,506	2,664
of which: World Bank	626	949	1,038	1,171	1,334	1,458
Bilateral	286	266	298	336	329	342
Private creditors	22	7	3	1	0	..
Bondholders	..	..	..	..	..	..
Commercial banks and others	22	7	3	1	0	..
Private nonguaranteed debt from:	1	8	10	7	10	11
Bondholders	..	..	..	..	..	..
Commercial banks and others	1	8	10	7	10	11
Use of IMF Credit	69	283	283	286	284	269
Net financial inflows						
Net debt inflows						
Use of IMF Credit	18	-3	12	12	-18	-9
Long-term	266	162	203	193	106	262
Official creditors	269	162	204	194	107	261
Multilateral	228	174	163	199	129	241
of which: World Bank	159	85	130	166	78	166
Bilateral	41	-13	41	-5	-23	20
Private creditors	-2	1	-1	0	-1	1
Bondholders	..	..	..	..	..	..
Banks and other private	-2	1	-1	0	-1	1
Short-term	-147	0	0	0	0	0
Net equity inflows						
Foreign direct investment	28	241	108	165	92	480
Portfolio equity	-2	66	4	35	28	..
Debt ratios						
External debt stocks to exports (%)	148	76	90	82	80	..
External debt stocks to GNI (%)	19	21	26	27	26	23
Debt service to exports (%)	4	3	4	4	3	..
Short-term to external debt stocks (%)	1	0	0	0	0	0
Multilateral to external debt stocks (%)	76	78	77	78	80	81
Reserves to external debt stocks (%)	59	12	10	..	..	..
Gross national income (GNI)	8,348	12,018	10,082	10,496	11,921	14,030

BURUNDI

(US$ million, unless otherwise indicated)

	2008	2014	2015	2016	2017	2018
Summary external debt data by debtor type						
Total External debt stocks	**1,390.3**	**690.2**	**626.0**	**602.8**	**614.0**	**589.3**
Use of IMF Credit	138.0	238.3	217.6	193.6	188.1	166.4
Long-term external debt	1,234.3	403.6	408.1	408.9	425.6	422.7
Public and publicly guaranteed sector	1,234.3	403.6	408.1	408.9	425.6	422.7
Public Sector	1,234.3	403.6	408.1	408.9	425.6	422.7
of which: General Government	1,232.3	403.6	408.1	397.6	414.4	411.5
Private sector guaranteed by Public Sector	..	..	..	..	..	..
Private sector not guaranteed	..	..	..	..	..	..
Short-term external debt	18.0	48.3	0.3	0.3	0.3	0.3
Disbursements (long-term)	**24.8**	**39.9**	**21.0**	**19.0**	**20.1**	**10.7**
Public and publicly guaranteed sector	24.8	39.9	21.0	19.0	20.1	10.7
Public Sector	24.8	39.9	21.0	19.0	20.1	10.7
of which: General Government	24.8	39.9	21.0	7.8	20.1	10.7
Private sector guaranteed by Public Sector	..	..	..	..	..	..
Private sector not guaranteed	..	..	..	..	..	..
Principal repayments (long-term)	**11.3**	**9.6**	**5.7**	**11.5**	**15.7**	**8.4**
Public and publicly guaranteed sector	11.3	9.6	5.7	11.5	15.7	8.4
Public Sector	11.3	9.6	5.7	11.5	15.7	8.4
of which: General Government	9.7	9.6	5.7	11.5	15.7	8.4
Private sector guaranteed by Public Sector	..	..	..	..	..	..
Private sector not guaranteed	..	..	..	..	..	..
Interest payments (long-term)	**7.4**	**3.8**	**3.7**	**3.7**	**2.7**	**3.1**
Public and publicly guaranteed sector	7.4	3.8	3.7	3.7	2.7	3.1
Public Sector	7.4	3.8	3.7	3.7	2.7	3.1
of which: General Government	7.4	3.8	3.7	3.7	2.7	3.0
Private sector guaranteed by Public Sector	..	..	..	..	..	..
Private sector not guaranteed	..	..	..	..	..	..
Summary external debt stock by creditor type						
Long-term External debt stocks	**1,234.3**	**403.6**	**408.1**	**408.9**	**425.6**	**422.7**
Public and publicly guaranteed debt from:	1,234.3	403.6	408.1	408.9	425.6	422.7
Official creditors	1,234.3	399.2	403.7	404.5	421.3	418.4
Multilateral	1,145.4	313.8	307.2	310.6	318.4	314.5
of which: World Bank	818.5	160.7	150.6	143.0	148.2	141.5
Bilateral	88.9	85.4	96.5	93.9	102.9	103.9
Private creditors	0.0	4.4	4.4	4.4	4.4	4.4
Bondholders	..	..	..	..	..	..
Commercial banks and others	0.0	4.4	4.4	4.4	4.4	4.4
Private nonguaranteed debt from:	..	..	..	..	..	..
Bondholders	..	..	..	..	..	..
Commercial banks and others	..	..	..	..	..	..
Use of IMF Credit	138.0	238.3	217.6	193.6	188.1	166.4
Net financial inflows						
Net debt inflows						
Use of IMF Credit	21.7	-0.9	-10.5	-18.0	-16.6	-17.6
Long-term	13.5	30.3	15.3	7.5	4.4	2.3
Official creditors	13.5	30.3	15.3	7.5	4.4	2.3
Multilateral	14.3	15.1	2.9	9.0	-3.4	0.4
of which: World Bank	13.8	-2.6	-3.2	-3.2	-3.2	-3.3
Bilateral	-0.8	15.1	12.4	-1.5	7.7	1.9
Private creditors	..	..	..	..	0.0	0.0
Bondholders	..	..	..	..	..	..
Banks and other private	..	..	..	..	0.0	0.0
Short-term	13.0	17.0	-48.0	0.0	0.0	0.0
Net equity inflows						
Foreign direct investment	3.8	81.7	49.6	0.1	0.3	1.0
Portfolio equity	..	1.5	..	..	..	..
Debt ratios						
External debt stocks to exports (%)	848.5	316.3	323.5	289.1	245.8	..
External debt stocks to GNI (%)	86.5	25.6	20.2	20.4	19.4	19.2
Debt service to exports (%)	12.0	13.9	13.9	16.0	14.0	..
Short-term to external debt stocks (%)	1.3	7.0	0.0	0.0	0.0	0.0
Multilateral to external debt stocks (%)	82.4	45.5	49.1	51.5	51.9	53.4
Reserves to external debt stocks (%)	19.1	45.8	21.6	15.6	15.7	11.3
Gross national income (GNI)	1,607.5	2,699.0	3,102.7	2,958.3	3,167.6	3,075.6

CABO VERDE

(US$ million, unless otherwise indicated)

	2008	2014	2015	2016	2017	2018
Summary external debt data by debtor type						
Total External debt stocks	**626.1**	**1,543.5**	**1,542.5**	**1,542.6**	**1,761.7**	**1,735.4**
Use of IMF Credit	13.3	13.6	12.7	12.3	13.1	12.8
Long-term external debt	611.4	1,528.3	1,528.3	1,528.7	1,747.2	1,721.1
Public and publicly guaranteed sector	611.4	1,528.3	1,528.3	1,528.7	1,747.2	1,721.1
Public Sector	611.4	1,528.3	1,528.3	1,528.7	1,747.2	1,721.1
of which: General Government	611.4	1,528.3	1,528.3	1,528.7	1,747.2	1,721.1
Private sector guaranteed by Public Sector	..	..	..	..	..	..
Private sector not guaranteed	..	..	..	..	..	..
Short-term external debt	1.4	1.5	1.5	1.5	1.5	1.5
Disbursements (long-term)	**74.8**	**233.3**	**140.1**	**67.9**	**94.8**	**69.8**
Public and publicly guaranteed sector	74.8	233.3	140.1	67.9	94.8	69.8
Public Sector	74.8	233.3	140.1	67.9	94.8	69.8
of which: General Government	74.8	233.3	140.1	67.9	94.8	69.8
Private sector guaranteed by Public Sector	..	..	..	..	..	..
Private sector not guaranteed	..	..	..	..	..	..
Principal repayments (long-term)	**23.9**	**24.5**	**24.1**	**25.9**	**32.6**	**36.6**
Public and publicly guaranteed sector	23.9	24.5	24.1	25.9	32.6	36.6
Public Sector	23.9	24.5	24.1	25.9	32.6	36.6
of which: General Government	23.6	24.5	24.1	25.9	32.6	36.6
Private sector guaranteed by Public Sector	..	..	..	..	..	..
Private sector not guaranteed	..	..	..	..	..	..
Interest payments (long-term)	**6.6**	**18.2**	**17.9**	**18.2**	**18.1**	**19.0**
Public and publicly guaranteed sector	6.6	18.2	17.9	18.2	18.1	19.0
Public Sector	6.6	18.2	17.9	18.2	18.1	19.0
of which: General Government	6.6	18.2	17.9	18.2	18.1	19.0
Private sector guaranteed by Public Sector	..	..	..	..	..	..
Private sector not guaranteed	..	..	..	..	..	..
Summary external debt stock by creditor type						
Long-term External debt stocks	**611.4**	**1,528.3**	**1,528.3**	**1,528.7**	**1,747.2**	**1,721.1**
Public and publicly guaranteed debt from:	611.4	1,528.3	1,528.3	1,528.7	1,747.2	1,721.1
Official creditors	601.5	1,045.8	1,067.6	1,067.0	1,208.6	1,206.9
Multilateral	483.6	704.1	722.4	724.1	796.9	802.2
of which: World Bank	283.8	358.3	357.4	344.7	361.7	351.4
Bilateral	117.9	341.7	345.2	342.9	411.6	404.7
Private creditors	9.9	482.5	460.7	461.7	538.6	514.2
Bondholders	..	..	..	..	..	..
Commercial banks and others	9.9	482.5	460.7	461.7	538.6	514.2
Private nonguaranteed debt from:	..	..	..	..	..	..
Bondholders	..	..	..	..	..	..
Commercial banks and others	..	..	..	..	..	..
Use of IMF Credit	13.3	13.6	12.7	12.3	13.1	12.8
Net financial inflows						
Net debt inflows						
Use of IMF Credit	-0.8	-1.1	-0.3	..	..	..
Long-term	50.9	208.8	116.0	42.0	62.2	33.2
Official creditors	55.2	94.7	87.4	25.6	49.7	33.2
Multilateral	26.0	74.9	56.7	20.0	16.7	27.9
of which: World Bank	18.2	44.7	17.4	-2.0	-6.3	-1.0
Bilateral	29.3	19.8	30.7	5.5	33.0	5.3
Private creditors	-4.3	114.2	28.6	16.4	12.5	0.0
Bondholders	..	..	..	..	..	..
Banks and other private	-4.3	114.2	28.6	16.4	12.5	0.0
Short-term	..	..	..	..	..	..
Net equity inflows						
Foreign direct investment	210.3	173.1	99.9	125.5	120.0	101.8
Portfolio equity	0.0	0.0	0.0	0.0	0.0	0.0
Debt ratios						
External debt stocks to exports (%)	84.9	170.0	229.4	208.5	208.4	173.6
External debt stocks to GNI (%)	35.9	87.3	100.3	96.2	103.0	89.3
Debt service to exports (%)	4.3	4.8	6.3	6.0	6.0	5.6
Short-term to external debt stocks (%)	0.2	0.1	0.1	0.1	0.1	0.1
Multilateral to external debt stocks (%)	77.2	45.6	46.8	46.9	45.2	46.2
Reserves to external debt stocks (%)	57.7	33.1	32.1	37.1	35.0	34.9
Gross national income (GNI)	1,742.2	1,767.3	1,537.7	1,603.6	1,710.2	1,943.4

CAMBODIA

(US$ million, unless otherwise indicated)

	2008	2014	2015	2016	2017	2018
Summary external debt data by debtor type						
Total External debt stocks	**2,466**	**8,130**	**9,698**	**11,602**	**13,016**	**15,336**
Use of IMF Credit	24	122	116	113	120	117
Long-term external debt	2,361	6,921	8,262	9,762	11,118	12,853
Public and publicly guaranteed sector	2,361	5,065	5,451	5,647	6,389	6,731
Public Sector	2,361	5,065	5,451	5,647	6,389	6,731
of which: General Government	2,361	5,065	5,451	5,647	6,389	6,731
Private sector guaranteed by Public Sector	..	..	..	..	..	..
Private sector not guaranteed	..	1,857	2,810	4,116	4,729	6,122
Short-term external debt	81	1,087	1,320	1,727	1,778	2,366
Disbursements (long-term)	**345**	**1,312**	**1,613**	**2,331**	**1,580**	**2,422**
Public and publicly guaranteed sector	345	660	619	520	656	638
Public Sector	345	660	619	520	656	638
of which: General Government	345	660	619	520	656	638
Private sector guaranteed by Public Sector	..	..	..	..	..	..
Private sector not guaranteed	..	651	994	1,811	924	1,784
Principal repayments (long-term)	**19**	**585**	**580**	**619**	**450**	**572**
Public and publicly guaranteed sector	19	77	80	113	140	181
Public Sector	19	77	80	113	140	181
of which: General Government	19	77	80	113	140	181
Private sector guaranteed by Public Sector	..	..	..	..	..	..
Private sector not guaranteed	..	508	500	506	311	391
Interest payments (long-term)	**19**	**63**	**71**	**94**	**99**	**225**
Public and publicly guaranteed sector	19	57	57	72	72	85
Public Sector	19	57	57	72	72	85
of which: General Government	19	57	57	72	72	85
Private sector guaranteed by Public Sector	..	..	..	..	..	..
Private sector not guaranteed	..	5	14	21	27	139
Summary external debt stock by creditor type						
Long-term External debt stocks	**2,361**	**6,921**	**8,262**	**9,762**	**11,118**	**12,853**
Public and publicly guaranteed debt from:	2,361	5,065	5,451	5,647	6,389	6,731
Official creditors	2,361	5,065	5,451	5,647	6,389	6,731
Multilateral	1,420	1,690	1,681	1,735	1,936	1,954
of which: World Bank	545	577	541	518	550	544
Bilateral	941	3,375	3,770	3,912	4,453	4,777
Private creditors	..	..	..	..	..	..
Bondholders	..	..	..	..	..	..
Commercial banks and others	..	..	..	..	..	..
Private nonguaranteed debt from:	..	1,857	2,810	4,116	4,729	6,122
Bondholders	..	..	..	..	..	300
Commercial banks and others	..	1,857	2,810	4,116	4,729	5,822
Use of IMF Credit	24	122	116	113	120	117
Net financial inflows						
Net debt inflows						
Use of IMF Credit	..	0	..	..	..	..
Long-term	326	727	1,033	1,712	1,129	1,850
Official creditors	326	583	539	407	516	457
Multilateral	128	64	64	106	96	64
of which: World Bank	14	22	-11	-7	1	7
Bilateral	198	519	475	301	420	393
Private creditors	..	144	494	1,305	613	1,393
Bondholders	..	..	..	..	..	300
Banks and other private	..	144	494	1,305	613	1,093
Short-term	81	124	233	407	51	588
Net equity inflows						
Foreign direct investment	815	1,853	1,823	2,476	2,788	3,103
Portfolio equity	0	0	0	0	0	0
Debt ratios						
External debt stocks to exports (%)	48	66	71	79	80	81
External debt stocks to GNI (%)	25	51	57	62	63	67
Debt service to exports (%)	1	5	5	5	4	5
Short-term to external debt stocks (%)	3	13	14	15	14	15
Multilateral to external debt stocks (%)	58	21	17	15	15	13
Reserves to external debt stocks (%)	93	69	71	72	87	87
Gross national income (GNI)	9,926	15,826	16,945	18,788	20,800	22,915

CAMEROON

(US$ million, unless otherwise indicated)

	2008	2014	2015	2016	2017	2018
Summary external debt data by debtor type						
Total External debt stocks	**2,836**	**5,758**	**7,282**	**8,240**	**10,477**	**11,493**
Use of IMF Credit	62	406	358	318	602	714
Long-term external debt	2,733	5,175	6,625	7,659	9,347	10,336
Public and publicly guaranteed sector	2,097	4,609	5,708	6,647	8,421	9,633
Public Sector	2,097	4,609	5,708	6,647	8,421	9,633
of which: General Government	2,083	4,608	5,707	6,646	8,420	9,632
Private sector guaranteed by Public Sector	..	..	..	..	..	..
Private sector not guaranteed	636	565	918	1,012	925	703
Short-term external debt	40	177	299	262	528	443
Disbursements (long-term)	**275**	**1,255**	**1,687**	**1,605**	**1,644**	**1,783**
Public and publicly guaranteed sector	188	1,209	1,630	1,356	1,583	1,730
Public Sector	188	1,209	1,630	1,356	1,583	1,730
of which: General Government	188	1,209	1,630	1,356	1,583	1,730
Private sector guaranteed by Public Sector	..	..	..	..	..	..
Private sector not guaranteed	87	46	57	249	61	53
Principal repayments (long-term)	**341**	**375**	**316**	**614**	**413**	**623**
Public and publicly guaranteed sector	149	347	269	341	175	373
Public Sector	149	347	269	341	175	373
of which: General Government	141	347	269	341	175	373
Private sector guaranteed by Public Sector	..	..	..	..	..	..
Private sector not guaranteed	192	28	47	273	238	250
Interest payments (long-term)	**91**	**148**	**157**	**280**	**272**	**404**
Public and publicly guaranteed sector	47	136	115	168	240	237
Public Sector	47	136	115	168	240	237
of which: General Government	46	136	115	168	240	236
Private sector guaranteed by Public Sector	..	..	..	..	..	..
Private sector not guaranteed	44	12	42	112	32	168
Summary external debt stock by creditor type						
Long-term External debt stocks	**2,733**	**5,175**	**6,625**	**7,659**	**9,347**	**10,336**
Public and publicly guaranteed debt from:	2,097	4,609	5,708	6,647	8,421	9,633
Official creditors	2,095	4,436	4,723	5,695	7,346	8,212
Multilateral	612	1,609	1,688	1,894	2,555	3,303
of which: World Bank	260	743	798	897	1,306	1,432
Bilateral	1,483	2,826	3,035	3,802	4,791	4,908
Private creditors	3	174	985	951	1,075	1,422
Bondholders	..	0	750	687	687	786
Commercial banks and others	3	174	235	265	389	636
Private nonguaranteed debt from:	636	565	918	1,012	925	703
Bondholders	..	..	..	..	..	..
Commercial banks and others	636	565	918	1,012	925	703
Use of IMF Credit	62	406	358	318	602	714
Net financial inflows						
Net debt inflows						
Use of IMF Credit	8	-5	-31	-30	258	128
Long-term	-66	880	1,371	991	1,231	1,160
Official creditors	39	836	531	1,042	1,313	1,090
Multilateral	66	243	179	185	572	859
of which: World Bank	23	120	90	127	353	165
Bilateral	-27	593	352	857	741	231
Private creditors	-105	45	839	-51	-82	70
Bondholders	..	0	750	-63	..	0
Banks and other private	-105	45	89	12	-82	70
Short-term	-199	-206	123	-36	262	-95
Net equity inflows						
Foreign direct investment	56	154	65	48	219	702
Portfolio equity	-1	0	-21	0	0	..
Debt ratios						
External debt stocks to exports (%)	38	66	105	128	155	..
External debt stocks to GNI (%)	11	17	24	26	31	30
Debt service to exports (%)	6	6	7	14	11	..
Short-term to external debt stocks (%)	1	3	4	3	5	4
Multilateral to external debt stocks (%)	22	28	23	23	24	29
Reserves to external debt stocks (%)	109	55	49	27	31	30
Gross national income (GNI)	25,997	34,653	30,479	32,063	34,261	37,807

CENTRAL AFRICAN REPUBLIC

(US$ million, unless otherwise indicated)

	2008	2014	2015	2016	2017	2018
Summary external debt data by debtor type						
Total External debt stocks	**998.7**	**661.8**	**682.4**	**688.2**	**729.5**	**778.9**
Use of IMF Credit	77.4	177.3	174.9	184.6	235.4	279.1
Long-term external debt	832.1	395.8	417.2	414.8	399.7	409.5
Public and publicly guaranteed sector	832.1	395.8	417.2	414.8	399.7	409.5
Public Sector	832.1	395.8	417.2	414.8	399.7	409.5
of which: General Government	795.7	379.2	402.3	400.4	387.0	397.6
Private sector guaranteed by Public Sector	0.0	..	..	..	..	..
Private sector not guaranteed	..	..	..	..	..	..
Short-term external debt	89.2	88.7	90.3	88.7	94.4	90.3
Disbursements (long-term)	**1.9**	**94.0**	**39.1**	**11.0**	**14.6**	**38.0**
Public and publicly guaranteed sector	1.9	94.0	39.1	11.0	14.6	38.0
Public Sector	1.9	94.0	39.1	11.0	14.6	38.0
of which: General Government	1.9	94.0	39.1	11.0	14.6	38.0
Private sector guaranteed by Public Sector	0.0	..	..	..	..	..
Private sector not guaranteed	..	..	..	..	..	..
Principal repayments (long-term)	**12.5**	**3.8**	**0.9**	**4.3**	**6.1**	**3.4**
Public and publicly guaranteed sector	12.5	3.8	0.9	4.3	6.1	3.4
Public Sector	12.5	3.8	0.9	4.3	6.1	3.4
of which: General Government	11.1	3.8	0.8	4.3	2.7	3.1
Private sector guaranteed by Public Sector	..	..	..	..	..	..
Private sector not guaranteed	..	..	..	..	..	..
Interest payments (long-term)	**6.1**	**2.6**	**2.6**	**1.5**	**1.3**	**1.8**
Public and publicly guaranteed sector	6.1	2.6	2.6	1.5	1.3	1.8
Public Sector	6.1	2.6	2.6	1.5	1.3	1.8
of which: General Government	6.0	2.6	2.6	1.5	1.3	1.8
Private sector guaranteed by Public Sector	..	..	..	..	..	..
Private sector not guaranteed	..	..	..	..	..	..
Summary external debt stock by creditor type						
Long-term External debt stocks	**832.1**	**395.8**	**417.2**	**414.8**	**399.7**	**409.5**
Public and publicly guaranteed debt from:	832.1	395.8	417.2	414.8	399.7	409.5
Official creditors	797.6	369.8	371.4	369.1	353.7	371.6
Multilateral	571.3	69.3	85.5	88.4	105.8	138.3
of which: World Bank	389.9	53.1	58.6	59.9	64.2	98.5
Bilateral	226.3	300.5	285.9	280.7	247.9	233.2
Private creditors	34.5	26.0	45.8	45.7	46.0	37.9
Bondholders	..	..	..	..	..	..
Commercial banks and others	34.5	26.0	45.8	45.7	46.0	37.9
Private nonguaranteed debt from:	..	..	..	..	..	..
Bondholders	..	..	..	..	..	..
Commercial banks and others	..	..	..	..	..	..
Use of IMF Credit	77.4	177.3	174.9	184.6	235.4	279.1
Net financial inflows						
Net debt inflows						
Use of IMF Credit	15.3	7.3	5.4	15.5	38.8	50.1
Long-term	-10.6	90.2	38.2	6.7	8.5	34.6
Official creditors	-10.6	92.4	18.2	6.7	8.5	34.6
Multilateral	-7.6	33.9	18.7	4.5	13.4	35.7
of which: World Bank	-1.2	33.1	7.9	3.1	1.1	37.1
Bilateral	-2.9	58.5	-0.5	2.2	-4.9	-1.2
Private creditors	0.0	-2.2	20.0	0.0	0.0	0.0
Bondholders	..	..	..	..	..	..
Banks and other private	0.0	-2.2	20.0	0.0	0.0	0.0
Short-term	0.0	-2.5	-0.8	-2.7	0.6	-0.2
Net equity inflows						
Foreign direct investment	117.1	3.5	3.0	7.3	6.9	18.0
Portfolio equity	..	..	..	..	..	..
Debt ratios						
External debt stocks to exports (%)	..	..	..	..	..	..
External debt stocks to GNI (%)	50.9	34.6	39.8	37.3	33.6	32.7
Debt service to exports (%)	..	..	..	..	..	..
Short-term to external debt stocks (%)	8.9	13.4	13.2	12.9	12.9	11.6
Multilateral to external debt stocks (%)	57.2	10.5	12.5	12.8	14.5	17.8
Reserves to external debt stocks (%)	12.2	39.2	31.3	34.8	49.7	46.4
Gross national income (GNI)	1,962.4	1,912.0	1,716.2	1,846.5	2,172.6	2,385.6

CHAD

(US$ million, unless otherwise indicated)

	2008	2014	2015	2016	2017	2018
Summary external debt data by debtor type						
Total External debt stocks	**1,802**	**3,752**	**2,973**	**3,018**	**3,145**	**3,242**
Use of IMF Credit	55	98	137	193	254	395
Long-term external debt	1,743	3,647	2,828	2,811	2,876	2,834
Public and publicly guaranteed sector	1,743	3,647	2,828	2,811	2,876	2,834
Public Sector	1,743	3,647	2,828	2,811	2,876	2,834
of which: General Government	1,709	3,618	2,828	2,811	2,876	2,834
Private sector guaranteed by Public Sector	..	..	..	..	..	..
Private sector not guaranteed	..	..	..	..	..	..
Short-term external debt	4	8	8	15	15	14
Disbursements (long-term)	**97**	**1,472**	**43**	**38**	**49**	**26**
Public and publicly guaranteed sector	97	1,472	43	38	49	26
Public Sector	97	1,472	43	38	49	26
of which: General Government	97	1,472	43	38	49	26
Private sector guaranteed by Public Sector	..	..	..	..	..	..
Private sector not guaranteed	..	..	..	..	..	..
Principal repayments (long-term)	**105**	**539**	**31**	**30**	**43**	**43**
Public and publicly guaranteed sector	105	539	31	30	43	43
Public Sector	105	539	31	30	43	43
of which: General Government	105	538	30	30	43	43
Private sector guaranteed by Public Sector	..	..	..	..	..	..
Private sector not guaranteed	..	..	..	..	..	..
Interest payments (long-term)	**18**	**49**	**56**	**110**	**115**	**131**
Public and publicly guaranteed sector	18	49	56	110	115	131
Public Sector	18	49	56	110	115	131
of which: General Government	18	49	56	110	115	131
Private sector guaranteed by Public Sector	..	..	..	..	..	..
Private sector not guaranteed	..	..	..	..	..	..
Summary external debt stock by creditor type						
Long-term External debt stocks	**1,743**	**3,647**	**2,828**	**2,811**	**2,876**	**2,834**
Public and publicly guaranteed debt from:	1,743	3,647	2,828	2,811	2,876	2,834
Official creditors	1,710	2,096	1,278	1,260	1,326	1,283
Multilateral	1,507	1,381	575	564	605	576
of which: World Bank	905	747	187	180	189	181
Bilateral	203	715	703	696	720	707
Private creditors	33	1,551	1,550	1,550	1,550	1,550
Bondholders	..	..	..	..	..	..
Commercial banks and others	33	1,551	1,550	1,550	1,550	1,550
Private nonguaranteed debt from:	..	..	..	..	..	..
Bondholders	..	..	..	..	..	..
Commercial banks and others	..	..	..	..	..	..
Use of IMF Credit	55	98	137	193	254	395
Net financial inflows						
Net debt inflows						
Use of IMF Credit	-14	19	44	62	49	149
Long-term	-7	933	13	8	6	-16
Official creditors	-7	2	13	8	6	-16
Multilateral	-62	-23	3	3	4	-14
of which: World Bank	-83	-17	-10	-2	-1	-4
Bilateral	54	25	10	5	2	-2
Private creditors	..	931	..	..	0	0
Bondholders	..	..	..	..	..	..
Banks and other private	..	931	..	..	0	0
Short-term	-20	0	0	0	0	0
Net equity inflows						
Foreign direct investment	466	-676	560	245	335	662
Portfolio equity	..	..	..	..	..	..
Debt ratios						
External debt stocks to exports (%)	..	..	..	..	..	..
External debt stocks to GNI (%)	21	28	28	30	32	29
Debt service to exports (%)	..	..	..	..	..	..
Short-term to external debt stocks (%)	0	0	0	0	0	0
Multilateral to external debt stocks (%)	84	37	19	19	19	18
Reserves to external debt stocks (%)	75	29	12	0	0	5
Gross national income (GNI)	8,690	13,319	10,614	9,905	9,845	11,070

CHINA

(US$ million, unless otherwise indicated)

	2008	2014	2015	2016	2017	2018
Summary external debt data by debtor type						
Total External debt stocks	**380,354**	**1,770,540**	**1,325,925**	**1,415,836**	**1,709,949**	**1,962,304**
Use of IMF Credit	365	10,127	9,686	9,396	9,954	9,721
Long-term external debt	192,802	520,961	493,996	605,043	669,361	733,682
Public and publicly guaranteed sector	91,027	171,214	138,218	162,223	201,741	243,455
Public Sector	90,870	171,139	138,157	162,176	201,707	243,434
of which: General Government	48,782	81,563	91,220	96,446	99,155	97,639
Private sector guaranteed by Public Sector	158	75	61	48	34	20
Private sector not guaranteed	101,774	349,748	355,777	442,820	467,620	490,227
Short-term external debt	187,188	1,239,452	822,244	801,396	1,030,633	1,218,901
Disbursements (long-term)	**38,188**	**136,839**	**108,563**	**170,041**	**228,212**	**224,034**
Public and publicly guaranteed sector	5,449	41,161	26,473	28,666	52,239	58,739
Public Sector	5,449	41,161	26,473	28,666	52,239	58,739
of which: General Government	2,870	18,705	13,697	15,175	6,351	3,827
Private sector guaranteed by Public Sector	0	0	0	0	0	0
Private sector not guaranteed	32,739	95,678	82,090	141,374	175,973	165,295
Principal repayments (long-term)	**23,965**	**38,270**	**83,971**	**129,163**	**143,086**	**154,990**
Public and publicly guaranteed sector	6,756	12,709	32,109	14,319	13,867	15,533
Public Sector	6,741	12,696	32,096	14,306	13,854	15,519
of which: General Government	3,244	4,469	3,547	9,808	4,120	5,110
Private sector guaranteed by Public Sector	15	14	14	14	14	14
Private sector not guaranteed	17,209	25,561	51,862	114,844	129,219	139,457
Interest payments (long-term)	**4,813**	**9,433**	**9,314**	**11,102**	**16,615**	**27,299**
Public and publicly guaranteed sector	2,593	1,730	2,270	1,926	3,435	6,296
Public Sector	2,592	1,730	2,270	1,926	3,435	6,296
of which: General Government	1,667	650	555	636	1,442	2,821
Private sector guaranteed by Public Sector	1	..	1	1	1	1
Private sector not guaranteed	2,220	7,703	7,044	9,175	13,180	21,002
Summary external debt stock by creditor type						
Long-term External debt stocks	**192,802**	**520,961**	**493,996**	**605,043**	**669,361**	**733,682**
Public and publicly guaranteed debt from:	91,027	171,214	138,218	162,223	201,741	243,455
Official creditors	63,538	57,262	45,808	54,738	54,379	52,686
Multilateral	30,845	33,713	33,151	33,100	33,924	34,183
of which: World Bank	22,440	17,884	17,048	16,215	16,356	16,095
Bilateral	32,693	23,548	12,657	21,638	20,455	18,503
Private creditors	27,489	113,952	92,410	107,486	147,362	190,769
Bondholders	15,728	55,403	66,945	69,469	101,454	138,289
Commercial banks and others	11,761	58,549	25,466	38,017	45,908	52,480
Private nonguaranteed debt from:	101,774	349,748	355,777	442,820	467,620	490,227
Bondholders	5,970	89,524	84,370	101,999	152,191	179,902
Commercial banks and others	95,804	260,223	271,408	340,821	315,429	310,325
Use of IMF Credit	365	10,127	9,686	9,396	9,954	9,721
Net financial inflows						
Net debt inflows						
Use of IMF Credit	..	..	..	..	..	..
Long-term	14,223	98,569	24,592	40,878	85,126	69,044
Official creditors	1,078	-368	-3,957	-912	-786	-1,575
Multilateral	1,344	-100	-163	108	502	379
of which: World Bank	326	-741	-623	-727	-15	-205
Bilateral	-266	-268	-3,793	-1,020	-1,288	-1,955
Private creditors	13,146	98,937	28,548	41,790	85,912	70,620
Bondholders	-1,092	53,880	8,776	22,273	82,088	68,614
Banks and other private	14,238	45,057	19,773	19,517	3,824	2,006
Short-term	-16,510	162,421	-417,208	-20,848	229,237	188,268
Net equity inflows						
Foreign direct investment	144,086	210,826	211,785	164,930	140,569	154,396
Portfolio equity	8,464	51,916	14,964	23,416	36,209	60,668
Debt ratios						
External debt stocks to exports (%)	24	66	51	58	63	68
External debt stocks to GNI (%)	8	17	12	13	14	14
Debt service to exports (%)	2	3	5	7	8	8
Short-term to external debt stocks (%)	49	70	62	57	60	62
Multilateral to external debt stocks (%)	8	2	3	2	2	2
Reserves to external debt stocks (%)	512	218	252	214	185	158
Gross national income (GNI)	4,622,872	10,451,828	10,973,754	11,092,994	12,109,561	13,556,844

COLOMBIA

(US$ million, unless otherwise indicated)

	2008	2014	2015	2016	2017	2018
Summary external debt data by debtor type						
Total External debt stocks	**46,761**	**105,351**	**114,623**	**121,951**	**127,202**	**134,940**
Use of IMF Credit	176	1,070	1,023	993	1,051	1,027
Long-term external debt	40,952	92,060	101,665	109,678	113,122	118,808
Public and publicly guaranteed sector	28,928	62,364	70,359	74,473	75,624	76,044
Public Sector	28,451	62,099	70,103	74,227	75,387	75,820
of which: General Government	25,459	41,529	46,700	49,192	52,425	55,673
Private sector guaranteed by Public Sector	477	265	256	246	237	224
Private sector not guaranteed	12,024	29,696	31,306	35,205	37,498	42,764
Short-term external debt	5,633	12,221	11,935	11,280	13,029	15,105
Disbursements (long-term)	**7,095**	**19,473**	**19,254**	**18,681**	**17,325**	**23,260**
Public and publicly guaranteed sector	3,862	11,234	10,414	7,030	7,108	6,885
Public Sector	3,387	11,219	10,414	7,030	7,108	6,885
of which: General Government	2,857	5,091	6,854	4,783	5,454	5,711
Private sector guaranteed by Public Sector	476	15	0	..	0	0
Private sector not guaranteed	3,232	8,240	8,840	11,651	10,217	16,375
Principal repayments (long-term)	**4,917**	**10,320**	**9,108**	**10,471**	**16,131**	**17,848**
Public and publicly guaranteed sector	2,212	2,507	1,743	2,719	6,502	6,739
Public Sector	2,212	2,498	1,733	2,709	6,493	6,726
of which: General Government	1,746	2,305	1,374	2,035	2,752	2,128
Private sector guaranteed by Public Sector	0	10	10	10	10	13
Private sector not guaranteed	2,705	7,813	7,365	7,752	9,628	11,109
Interest payments (long-term)	**2,787**	**4,102**	**4,555**	**4,820**	**5,480**	**5,906**
Public and publicly guaranteed sector	2,099	2,709	3,103	3,117	3,528	3,596
Public Sector	2,077	2,706	3,100	3,111	3,522	3,588
of which: General Government	1,866	1,972	2,041	2,005	2,279	2,271
Private sector guaranteed by Public Sector	22	3	3	5	5	7
Private sector not guaranteed	688	1,393	1,452	1,703	1,952	2,310
Summary external debt stock by creditor type						
Long-term External debt stocks	**40,952**	**92,060**	**101,665**	**109,678**	**113,122**	**118,808**
Public and publicly guaranteed debt from:	28,928	62,364	70,359	74,473	75,624	76,044
Official creditors	13,889	22,058	23,120	25,157	25,564	27,738
Multilateral	13,240	17,201	18,090	19,759	20,320	21,803
of which: World Bank	5,439	8,348	8,610	9,516	9,520	10,233
Bilateral	649	4,857	5,029	5,398	5,244	5,935
Private creditors	15,039	40,306	47,240	49,316	50,060	48,306
Bondholders	12,280	34,704	39,730	40,822	43,932	42,208
Commercial banks and others	2,759	5,602	7,510	8,494	6,128	6,098
Private nonguaranteed debt from:	12,024	29,696	31,306	35,205	37,498	42,764
Bondholders	809	8,570	8,650	9,146	10,206	9,871
Commercial banks and others	11,215	21,126	22,656	26,058	27,292	32,892
Use of IMF Credit	176	1,070	1,023	993	1,051	1,027
Net financial inflows						
Net debt inflows						
Use of IMF Credit	..	0	..	..	..	..
Long-term	2,178	9,154	10,146	8,210	1,194	5,412
Official creditors	1,675	757	1,286	2,235	152	2,515
Multilateral	1,784	493	1,003	1,856	344	1,697
of which: World Bank	688	542	357	945	-279	908
Bilateral	-109	264	283	379	-192	818
Private creditors	503	8,396	8,860	5,975	1,042	2,897
Bondholders	14	6,807	5,409	1,606	3,955	-1,934
Banks and other private	489	1,590	3,451	4,369	-2,913	4,831
Short-term	472	1,331	-286	-655	1,749	2,077
Net equity inflows						
Foreign direct investment	10,518	13,674	9,717	9,175	12,043	9,749
Portfolio equity	-86	1,823	640	-363	472	-823
Debt ratios						
External debt stocks to exports (%)	104	155	227	260	237	225
External debt stocks to GNI (%)	20	28	40	44	42	42
Debt service to exports (%)	18	22	28	34	41	41
Short-term to external debt stocks (%)	12	12	10	9	10	11
Multilateral to external debt stocks (%)	28	16	16	16	16	16
Reserves to external debt stocks (%)	50	44	40	38	37	35
Gross national income (GNI)	233,342	369,788	289,331	279,763	306,040	319,087

COMOROS

(US$ million, unless otherwise indicated)

	2008	2014	2015	2016	2017	2018
Summary external debt data by debtor type						
Total External debt stocks	**276.2**	**141.8**	**130.6**	**160.6**	**167.0**	**191.1**
Use of IMF Credit	6.2	30.9	29.2	26.6	26.1	22.3
Long-term external debt	264.4	109.2	99.9	132.5	139.8	167.6
Public and publicly guaranteed sector	264.4	109.2	99.9	132.5	139.8	167.6
Public Sector	264.4	109.2	99.9	132.5	139.8	167.6
of which: General Government	264.4	109.2	99.9	129.7	136.8	140.6
Private sector guaranteed by Public Sector	..	..	..	..	..	..
Private sector not guaranteed	..	..	..	..	..	..
Short-term external debt	5.6	1.6	1.5	1.5	1.1	1.2
Disbursements (long-term)	**1.4**	**0.0**	**0.0**	**35.6**	**5.5**	**31.7**
Public and publicly guaranteed sector	1.4	0.0	0.0	35.6	5.5	31.7
Public Sector	1.4	0.0	0.0	35.6	5.5	31.7
of which: General Government	1.4	0.0	0.0	32.7	5.5	5.0
Private sector guaranteed by Public Sector	..	..	..	..	..	..
Private sector not guaranteed	..	..	..	..	..	..
Principal repayments (long-term)	**8.1**	**0.6**	**6.9**	**1.9**	**0.4**	**2.0**
Public and publicly guaranteed sector	8.1	0.6	6.9	1.9	0.4	2.0
Public Sector	8.1	0.6	6.9	1.9	0.4	2.0
of which: General Government	8.1	0.6	6.9	1.9	0.4	0.4
Private sector guaranteed by Public Sector	..	..	..	..	..	..
Private sector not guaranteed	..	..	..	..	..	..
Interest payments (long-term)	**4.2**	**0.2**	**0.2**	**0.2**	**0.1**	**1.0**
Public and publicly guaranteed sector	4.2	0.2	0.2	0.2	0.1	1.0
Public Sector	4.2	0.2	0.2	0.2	0.1	1.0
of which: General Government	4.2	0.2	0.2	0.2	0.1	0.7
Private sector guaranteed by Public Sector	..	..	..	..	..	..
Private sector not guaranteed	..	..	..	..	..	..
Summary external debt stock by creditor type						
Long-term External debt stocks	**264.4**	**109.2**	**99.9**	**132.5**	**139.8**	**167.6**
Public and publicly guaranteed debt from:	264.4	109.2	99.9	132.5	139.8	167.6
Official creditors	264.4	109.2	99.9	132.5	139.8	167.6
Multilateral	217.8	60.1	56.9	54.3	55.3	55.1
of which: World Bank	122.3	14.4	13.5	12.9	13.3	12.7
Bilateral	46.5	49.1	43.0	78.2	84.5	112.6
Private creditors	..	..	..	..	..	..
Bondholders	..	..	..	..	..	..
Commercial banks and others	..	..	..	..	..	..
Private nonguaranteed debt from:	..	..	..	..	..	..
Bondholders	..	..	..	..	..	..
Commercial banks and others	..	..	..	..	..	..
Use of IMF Credit	6.2	30.9	29.2	26.6	26.1	22.3
Net financial inflows						
Net debt inflows						
Use of IMF Credit	5.3	0.0	-0.4	-1.8	-2.0	-3.2
Long-term	-6.8	-0.6	-6.9	33.8	5.1	29.7
Official creditors	-6.8	-0.6	-6.9	33.8	5.1	29.7
Multilateral	-6.8	-0.6	-2.0	-1.9	-0.4	0.3
of which: World Bank	-1.2	-0.2	-0.3	-0.3	-0.3	-0.3
Bilateral	..	..	-4.9	35.6	5.4	29.4
Private creditors	..	..	..	..	..	..
Bondholders	..	..	..	..	..	..
Banks and other private	..	..	..	..	..	..
Short-term	-4.0	0.0	0.0	0.0	0.0	0.0
Net equity inflows						
Foreign direct investment	4.6	4.7	4.9	3.6	3.9	7.9
Portfolio equity	0.0	..	..	..	..	..
Debt ratios						
External debt stocks to exports (%)	346.7	117.3	129.0	145.6	125.4	..
External debt stocks to GNI (%)	30.3	12.3	13.2	15.6	15.5	16.5
Debt service to exports (%)	15.5	0.6	7.4	3.5	1.9	..
Short-term to external debt stocks (%)	2.0	1.1	1.1	0.9	0.7	0.6
Multilateral to external debt stocks (%)	78.9	42.4	43.6	33.8	33.1	28.8
Reserves to external debt stocks (%)	40.6	120.3	153.1	98.9	124.0	103.8
Gross national income (GNI)	910.2	1,149.6	992.0	1,029.6	1,074.1	1,161.0

CONGO, DEMOCRATIC REPUBLIC OF

(US$ million, unless otherwise indicated)

	2008	2014	2015	2016	2017	2018
Summary external debt data by debtor type						
Total External debt stocks	**12,306**	**5,523**	**5,374**	**5,064**	**5,126**	**4,974**
Use of IMF Credit	787	1,188	1,098	989	954	839
Long-term external debt	10,862	4,149	4,108	3,856	4,043	4,038
Public and publicly guaranteed sector	10,862	4,149	4,108	3,856	4,043	4,038
Public Sector	10,862	4,149	4,108	3,856	4,043	4,038
of which: General Government	10,338	4,144	4,102	3,851	4,038	4,033
Private sector guaranteed by Public Sector	..	..	..	..	..	..
Private sector not guaranteed	..	..	..	..	..	..
Short-term external debt	657	186	168	218	129	97
Disbursements (long-term)	**110**	**115**	**282**	**65**	**347**	**239**
Public and publicly guaranteed sector	110	115	282	65	347	239
Public Sector	110	115	282	65	347	239
of which: General Government	110	115	282	65	347	239
Private sector guaranteed by Public Sector	..	..	..	..	..	..
Private sector not guaranteed	..	..	..	..	..	..
Principal repayments (long-term)	**170**	**263**	**215**	**274**	**185**	**185**
Public and publicly guaranteed sector	170	263	215	274	185	185
Public Sector	170	263	215	274	185	185
of which: General Government	145	263	215	274	185	185
Private sector guaranteed by Public Sector	..	..	..	..	..	..
Private sector not guaranteed	..	..	..	..	..	..
Interest payments (long-term)	**275**	**146**	**134**	**132**	**119**	**98**
Public and publicly guaranteed sector	275	146	134	132	119	98
Public Sector	275	146	134	132	119	98
of which: General Government	267	146	134	132	119	98
Private sector guaranteed by Public Sector	..	..	..	..	..	..
Private sector not guaranteed	..	..	..	..	..	..
Summary external debt stock by creditor type						
Long-term External debt stocks	**10,862**	**4,149**	**4,108**	**3,856**	**4,043**	**4,038**
Public and publicly guaranteed debt from:	10,862	4,149	4,108	3,856	4,043	4,038
Official creditors	10,511	4,140	4,097	3,855	4,042	4,019
Multilateral	4,138	1,977	1,877	1,730	1,778	1,817
of which: World Bank	2,437	888	841	827	942	1,098
Bilateral	6,373	2,163	2,220	2,125	2,263	2,202
Private creditors	351	9	11	2	1	18
Bondholders	..	..	..	..	..	..
Commercial banks and others	351	9	11	2	1	18
Private nonguaranteed debt from:	..	..	..	..	..	..
Bondholders	..	..	..	..	..	..
Commercial banks and others	..	..	..	..	..	..
Use of IMF Credit	787	1,188	1,098	989	954	839
Net financial inflows						
Net debt inflows						
Use of IMF Credit	-137	0	-38	-78	-92	-94
Long-term	-60	-148	67	-208	162	54
Official creditors	-54	-140	65	-199	163	37
Multilateral	41	-156	-31	-126	-40	69
of which: World Bank	89	-19	-8	11	65	180
Bilateral	-95	16	97	-74	202	-32
Private creditors	-7	-8	2	-9	-1	17
Bondholders	..	..	..	..	..	..
Banks and other private	-7	-8	2	-9	-1	17
Short-term	12	-259	-17	15	9	-33
Net equity inflows						
Foreign direct investment	1,727	1,843	1,674	1,205	1,340	1,494
Portfolio equity	..	-14	-94	0	-10	-7
Debt ratios						
External debt stocks to exports (%)	159	43	51	42	44	31
External debt stocks to GNI (%)	67	17	15	14	14	11
Debt service to exports (%)	8	3	4	4	3	2
Short-term to external debt stocks (%)	5	3	3	4	3	2
Multilateral to external debt stocks (%)	34	36	35	34	35	37
Reserves to external debt stocks (%)	1	28	23	14	14	13
Gross national income (GNI)	18,459	32,869	35,127	36,345	36,946	45,550

CONGO, REPUBLIC OF

(US$ million, unless otherwise indicated)

	2008	2014	2015	2016	2017	2018
Summary external debt data by debtor type						
Total External debt stocks	**5,391**	**3,903**	**4,022**	**3,758**	**4,926**	**5,147**
Use of IMF Credit	53	134	123	116	120	115
Long-term external debt	5,071	3,559	3,451	3,457	4,482	4,728
Public and publicly guaranteed sector	5,071	3,559	3,451	3,457	4,482	4,728
Public Sector	5,071	3,559	3,451	3,457	4,482	4,728
of which: General Government	5,056	3,559	3,451	3,457	4,482	4,728
Private sector guaranteed by Public Sector	..	..	..	..	..	..
Private sector not guaranteed	..	..	..	..	..	..
Short-term external debt	267	210	448	186	325	305
Disbursements (long-term)	**19**	**845**	**122**	**150**	**1,153**	**505**
Public and publicly guaranteed sector	19	845	122	150	1,153	505
Public Sector	19	845	122	150	1,153	505
of which: General Government	19	845	122	150	1,153	505
Private sector guaranteed by Public Sector	..	..	..	..	..	..
Private sector not guaranteed	..	..	..	..	..	..
Principal repayments (long-term)	**107**	**263**	**185**	**114**	**191**	**210**
Public and publicly guaranteed sector	107	263	185	114	191	210
Public Sector	107	263	185	114	191	210
of which: General Government	107	263	185	114	191	210
Private sector guaranteed by Public Sector	..	..	..	..	..	..
Private sector not guaranteed	..	..	..	..	..	..
Interest payments (long-term)	**57**	**34**	**30**	**29**	**28**	**75**
Public and publicly guaranteed sector	57	34	30	29	28	75
Public Sector	57	34	30	29	28	75
of which: General Government	57	34	30	29	28	75
Private sector guaranteed by Public Sector	..	..	..	..	..	..
Private sector not guaranteed	..	..	..	..	..	..
Summary external debt stock by creditor type						
Long-term External debt stocks	**5,071**	**3,559**	**3,451**	**3,457**	**4,482**	**4,728**
Public and publicly guaranteed debt from:	5,071	3,559	3,451	3,457	4,482	4,728
Official creditors	3,964	2,435	2,364	2,395	3,438	3,715
Multilateral	443	179	189	234	665	662
of which: World Bank	299	104	110	122	153	192
Bilateral	3,521	2,256	2,175	2,160	2,773	3,053
Private creditors	1,107	1,124	1,087	1,062	1,044	1,013
Bondholders	454	418	399	377	350	322
Commercial banks and others	653	707	688	685	694	690
Private nonguaranteed debt from:	..	..	..	..	..	..
Bondholders	..	..	..	..	..	..
Commercial banks and others	..	..	..	..	..	..
Use of IMF Credit	53	134	123	116	120	115
Net financial inflows						
Net debt inflows						
Use of IMF Credit	2	-5	-5	-4	-2	-2
Long-term	-88	583	-63	36	962	294
Official creditors	-66	489	-34	60	989	322
Multilateral	-7	4	18	61	412	7
of which: World Bank	1	10	10	16	23	43
Bilateral	-59	485	-52	-1	577	315
Private creditors	-22	94	-29	-23	-28	-28
Bondholders	-24	-18	-18	-23	-27	-27
Banks and other private	2	112	-11	-1	0	0
Short-term	-61	-18	240	-266	135	-63
Net equity inflows						
Foreign direct investment	992	-732	-261	-232	4,406	4,313
Portfolio equity	0	1	..	..	..	..
Debt ratios						
External debt stocks to exports (%)	65	41	78	82	..	..
External debt stocks to GNI (%)	61	33	48	45	63	51
Debt service to exports (%)	2	3	4	3	..	..
Short-term to external debt stocks (%)	5	5	11	5	7	6
Multilateral to external debt stocks (%)	8	5	5	6	13	13
Reserves to external debt stocks (%)	72	126	55	19	8	8
Gross national income (GNI)	8,768	11,739	8,466	8,378	7,859	10,068

COSTA RICA

(US$ million, unless otherwise indicated)

	2008	2014	2015	2016	2017	2018
Summary external debt data by debtor type						
Total External debt stocks	**8,839**	**19,722**	**23,589**	**25,563**	**25,616**	**27,819**
Use of IMF Credit	37	227	217	210	223	218
Long-term external debt	4,814	17,149	20,768	22,797	22,855	24,232
Public and publicly guaranteed sector	3,224	8,819	10,147	11,054	11,037	11,340
Public Sector	3,224	8,819	10,147	11,054	11,037	11,340
of which: General Government	2,479	4,752	5,845	6,142	6,264	6,581
Private sector guaranteed by Public Sector	0	..	..	..	..	..
Private sector not guaranteed	1,590	8,329	10,621	11,744	11,817	12,891
Short-term external debt	3,989	2,347	2,604	2,555	2,538	3,370
Disbursements (long-term)	**795**	**4,988**	**4,810**	**3,991**	**1,985**	**4,480**
Public and publicly guaranteed sector	394	2,022	1,649	1,351	599	1,763
Public Sector	394	2,022	1,649	1,351	599	1,763
of which: General Government	110	1,206	1,229	434	248	449
Private sector guaranteed by Public Sector	..	..	..	..	..	..
Private sector not guaranteed	402	2,966	3,161	2,640	1,386	2,716
Principal repayments (long-term)	**1,116**	**2,409**	**1,687**	**1,721**	**1,797**	**2,484**
Public and publicly guaranteed sector	847	756	318	444	485	1,407
Public Sector	847	756	318	444	485	1,407
of which: General Government	564	361	135	134	135	127
Private sector guaranteed by Public Sector	..	..	..	..	..	..
Private sector not guaranteed	270	1,653	1,369	1,277	1,312	1,077
Interest payments (long-term)	**345**	**997**	**1,028**	**1,055**	**1,109**	**1,265**
Public and publicly guaranteed sector	248	387	823	601	638	691
Public Sector	248	387	823	601	638	691
of which: General Government	202	209	470	356	364	368
Private sector guaranteed by Public Sector	..	..	..	..	..	..
Private sector not guaranteed	97	610	205	454	471	574
Summary external debt stock by creditor type						
Long-term External debt stocks	**4,814**	**17,149**	**20,768**	**22,797**	**22,855**	**24,232**
Public and publicly guaranteed debt from:	3,224	8,819	10,147	11,054	11,037	11,340
Official creditors	1,412	2,339	2,738	3,226	3,288	4,591
Multilateral	1,089	2,060	2,417	2,801	2,835	4,128
of which: World Bank	41	600	602	736	788	903
Bilateral	323	280	321	426	453	464
Private creditors	1,812	6,480	7,409	7,827	7,749	6,749
Bondholders	1,610	4,750	5,750	6,251	6,250	5,750
Commercial banks and others	202	1,730	1,659	1,576	1,499	999
Private nonguaranteed debt from:	1,590	8,329	10,621	11,744	11,817	12,891
Bondholders	..	1,350	1,350	1,850	2,150	2,150
Commercial banks and others	1,590	6,979	9,271	9,894	9,667	10,741
Use of IMF Credit	37	227	217	210	223	218
Net financial inflows						
Net debt inflows						
Use of IMF Credit	..	0	..	..	..	..
Long-term	-321	2,579	3,123	2,270	188	1,996
Official creditors	-91	362	402	489	192	1,356
Multilateral	-111	378	358	384	179	1,344
of which: World Bank	-4	2	2	135	52	115
Bilateral	20	-16	45	105	13	12
Private creditors	-230	2,217	2,720	1,781	-5	639
Bondholders	-240	1,040	1,000	1,001	299	-500
Banks and other private	11	1,177	1,720	780	-304	1,139
Short-term	755	-64	257	-49	-16	831
Net equity inflows						
Foreign direct investment	2,243	2,330	2,291	1,468	2,410	1,970
Portfolio equity	8	8	1	42	43	44
Debt ratios						
External debt stocks to exports (%)	70	117	135	134	129	132
External debt stocks to GNI (%)	29	41	45	47	46	49
Debt service to exports (%)	13	20	16	15	15	18
Short-term to external debt stocks (%)	45	12	11	10	10	12
Multilateral to external debt stocks (%)	12	10	10	11	11	15
Reserves to external debt stocks (%)	43	37	33	30	28	27
Gross national income (GNI)	30,019	48,431	52,361	54,676	55,212	56,794

CÔTE D'IVOIRE

(US$ million, unless otherwise indicated)

	2008	2014	2015	2016	2017	2018
Summary external debt data by debtor type						
Total External debt stocks	**12,968**	**9,805**	**11,386**	**11,448**	**13,444**	**15,660**
Use of IMF Credit	247	1,492	1,508	1,495	1,738	1,814
Long-term external debt	11,377	8,313	9,878	9,684	11,678	13,708
Public and publicly guaranteed sector	10,640	6,620	8,508	8,360	10,440	12,696
Public Sector	10,640	6,620	8,508	8,360	10,440	12,696
of which: General Government	10,638	6,620	8,508	8,360	10,440	12,679
Private sector guaranteed by Public Sector	..	..	..	..	..	..
Private sector not guaranteed	738	1,693	1,370	1,324	1,238	1,011
Short-term external debt	1,344	0	0	269	28	138
Disbursements (long-term)	**310**	**1,293**	**2,659**	**1,236**	**3,229**	**3,328**
Public and publicly guaranteed sector	35	1,271	2,659	896	3,089	3,208
Public Sector	35	1,271	2,659	896	3,089	3,208
of which: General Government	35	1,271	2,659	896	3,089	3,191
Private sector guaranteed by Public Sector	..	..	..	..	..	..
Private sector not guaranteed	275	23	1	341	141	120
Principal repayments (long-term)	**782**	**645**	**460**	**1,097**	**1,725**	**1,040**
Public and publicly guaranteed sector	586	272	136	727	1,413	706
Public Sector	586	272	136	727	1,413	706
of which: General Government	586	272	136	727	1,413	706
Private sector guaranteed by Public Sector	..	..	..	..	..	..
Private sector not guaranteed	196	374	324	370	312	334
Interest payments (long-term)	**216**	**352**	**289**	**402**	**398**	**452**
Public and publicly guaranteed sector	183	323	264	315	329	405
Public Sector	183	323	264	315	329	405
of which: General Government	183	323	264	315	329	404
Private sector guaranteed by Public Sector	..	..	..	..	..	..
Private sector not guaranteed	33	29	26	87	70	47
Summary external debt stock by creditor type						
Long-term External debt stocks	**11,377**	**8,313**	**9,878**	**9,684**	**11,678**	**13,708**
Public and publicly guaranteed debt from:	10,640	6,620	8,508	8,360	10,440	12,696
Official creditors	8,141	3,475	4,372	4,096	5,008	5,224
Multilateral	2,897	750	891	1,019	1,588	1,950
of which: World Bank	1,914	240	394	522	781	982
Bilateral	5,244	2,726	3,481	3,077	3,420	3,274
Private creditors	2,499	3,144	4,136	4,263	5,432	7,472
Bondholders	2,346	3,085	4,085	4,221	5,398	7,230
Commercial banks and others	152	60	51	43	34	242
Private nonguaranteed debt from:	738	1,693	1,370	1,324	1,238	1,011
Bondholders	..	..	..	..	..	..
Commercial banks and others	738	1,693	1,370	1,324	1,238	1,011
Use of IMF Credit	247	1,492	1,508	1,495	1,738	1,814
Net financial inflows						
Net debt inflows						
Use of IMF Credit	20	166	82	33	150	119
Long-term	-472	648	2,200	139	1,505	2,288
Official creditors	-551	296	1,531	40	551	359
Multilateral	-561	139	189	156	455	425
of which: World Bank	-481	82	165	140	205	231
Bilateral	10	157	1,342	-115	96	-66
Private creditors	79	352	668	99	954	1,929
Bondholders	..	753	1,000	136	1,133	1,928
Banks and other private	79	-401	-332	-38	-179	1
Short-term	-381	0	0	269	-241	110
Net equity inflows						
Foreign direct investment	431	271	378	531	643	913
Portfolio equity	2	33	0	8	24	..
Debt ratios						
External debt stocks to exports (%)	111	70	89	95	102	..
External debt stocks to GNI (%)	56	28	35	33	37	38
Debt service to exports (%)	9	7	6	13	17	..
Short-term to external debt stocks (%)	10	0	0	2	0	1
Multilateral to external debt stocks (%)	22	8	8	9	12	12
Reserves to external debt stocks (%)	17	46	41	..	..	..
Gross national income (GNI)	23,327	34,408	32,124	35,189	36,521	41,298

DJIBOUTI

(US$ million, unless otherwise indicated)

	2008	2014	2015	2016	2017	2018
Summary external debt data by debtor type						
Total External debt stocks	**846.5**	**2,171.0**	**2,603.6**	**2,991.4**	**3,355.8**	**3,264.1**
Use of IMF Credit	19.2	52.9	49.1	45.8	44.0	36.7
Long-term external debt	680.5	2,041.1	2,550.6	2,892.0	2,978.9	2,983.6
Public and publicly guaranteed sector	680.5	810.0	1,171.2	1,599.6	1,942.1	2,040.9
Public Sector	680.5	810.0	1,171.2	1,599.6	1,942.1	2,040.9
of which: General Government	556.9	523.3	520.9	733.3	934.5	982.0
Private sector guaranteed by Public Sector	..	..	..	..	..	..
Private sector not guaranteed	..	1,231.1	1,379.3	1,292.4	1,036.8	942.8
Short-term external debt	146.7	77.0	4.0	53.7	333.0	243.7
Disbursements (long-term)	**45.9**	**436.9**	**701.2**	**515.0**	**359.4**	**261.9**
Public and publicly guaranteed sector	45.9	211.4	415.0	472.7	337.4	139.9
Public Sector	45.9	211.4	415.0	472.7	337.4	139.9
of which: General Government	45.0	31.9	28.5	244.3	196.0	74.8
Private sector guaranteed by Public Sector	..	..	..	..	..	..
Private sector not guaranteed	..	225.5	286.2	42.3	22.0	122.0
Principal repayments (long-term)	**17.6**	**149.9**	**165.5**	**160.2**	**303.0**	**244.0**
Public and publicly guaranteed sector	17.6	26.8	27.5	31.0	25.4	28.0
Public Sector	17.6	26.8	27.5	31.0	25.4	28.0
of which: General Government	7.3	20.0	19.2	23.4	18.9	18.4
Private sector guaranteed by Public Sector	..	..	..	..	..	..
Private sector not guaranteed	..	123.1	137.9	129.2	277.6	216.0
Interest payments (long-term)	**7.8**	**9.1**	**15.1**	**25.2**	**35.7**	**407.3**
Public and publicly guaranteed sector	7.8	9.1	15.1	25.2	35.7	407.3
Public Sector	7.8	9.1	15.1	25.2	35.7	407.3
of which: General Government	4.8	7.2	7.3	6.6	12.5	14.3
Private sector guaranteed by Public Sector	..	..	..	..	..	..
Private sector not guaranteed	..	..	..	..	..	..
Summary external debt stock by creditor type						
Long-term External debt stocks	**680.5**	**2,041.1**	**2,550.6**	**2,892.0**	**2,978.9**	**2,983.6**
Public and publicly guaranteed debt from:	680.5	810.0	1,171.2	1,599.6	1,942.1	2,040.9
Official creditors	653.2	802.1	1,166.3	1,595.4	1,938.1	2,037.0
Multilateral	363.0	429.4	454.3	490.3	532.8	568.6
of which: World Bank	151.6	136.6	129.9	127.9	143.6	152.2
Bilateral	290.2	372.7	712.0	1,105.1	1,405.3	1,468.4
Private creditors	27.4	7.9	4.9	4.2	4.0	3.9
Bondholders	..	..	..	..	..	..
Commercial banks and others	27.4	7.9	4.9	4.2	4.0	3.9
Private nonguaranteed debt from:	..	1,231.1	1,379.3	1,292.4	1,036.8	942.8
Bondholders	..	..	..	..	..	..
Commercial banks and others	..	1,231.1	1,379.3	1,292.4	1,036.8	942.8
Use of IMF Credit	19.2	52.9	49.1	45.8	44.0	36.7
Net financial inflows						
Net debt inflows						
Use of IMF Credit	1.8	-1.4	-1.5	-1.9	-4.4	-6.3
Long-term	28.3	287.0	535.7	354.8	56.4	17.8
Official creditors	32.2	186.5	390.1	442.4	312.2	112.0
Multilateral	15.2	17.9	40.9	42.9	24.7	42.2
of which: World Bank	5.6	-2.4	-0.7	2.0	7.8	12.1
Bilateral	16.9	168.7	349.2	399.5	287.5	69.8
Private creditors	-3.9	100.4	145.6	-87.6	-255.8	-94.1
Bondholders	..	..	..	..	..	..
Banks and other private	-3.9	100.4	145.6	-87.6	-255.8	-94.1
Short-term	11.0	-22.6	-74.0	49.1	275.3	-105.9
Net equity inflows						
Foreign direct investment	227.7	153.0	124.0	160.0	165.0	265.0
Portfolio equity	..	..	..	..	..	..
Debt ratios						
External debt stocks to exports (%)	205.8	393.0	412.0	502.9	552.3	..
External debt stocks to GNI (%)	..	137.7	147.4	157.9	171.7	157.6
Debt service to exports (%)	8.2	29.2	28.8	31.6	57.8	..
Short-term to external debt stocks (%)	17.3	3.5	0.2	1.8	9.9	7.5
Multilateral to external debt stocks (%)	42.9	19.8	17.5	16.4	15.9	17.4
Reserves to external debt stocks (%)	20.7	18.1	14.0	13.6	16.6	13.9
Gross national income (GNI)	..	1,577.0	1,766.7	1,894.3	1,954.7	2,071.0

DOMINICA

(US$ million, unless otherwise indicated)

	2008	2014	2015	2016	2017	2018
Summary external debt data by debtor type						
Total External debt stocks	**260.5**	**308.2**	**314.2**	**297.1**	**295.6**	**279.2**
Use of IMF Credit	15.9	20.9	26.5	24.2	24.4	22.4
Long-term external debt	221.9	281.8	282.1	264.1	260.3	243.7
Public and publicly guaranteed sector	221.9	281.8	282.1	264.1	260.3	243.7
Public Sector	221.9	281.8	282.1	264.1	260.3	243.7
of which: General Government	194.4	262.8	256.7	239.6	238.8	224.6
Private sector guaranteed by Public Sector	..	..	..	..	..	..
Private sector not guaranteed	..	..	..	..	..	..
Short-term external debt	22.6	5.5	5.5	8.8	10.8	13.1
Disbursements (long-term)	**8.0**	**20.4**	**20.9**	**4.0**	**9.7**	**5.0**
Public and publicly guaranteed sector	8.0	20.4	20.9	4.0	9.7	5.0
Public Sector	8.0	20.4	20.9	4.0	9.7	5.0
of which: General Government	6.8	19.1	12.2	1.7	8.6	4.3
Private sector guaranteed by Public Sector	..	..	..	..	..	..
Private sector not guaranteed	..	..	..	..	..	..
Principal repayments (long-term)	**12.9**	**11.5**	**14.3**	**18.1**	**19.5**	**18.5**
Public and publicly guaranteed sector	12.9	11.5	14.3	18.1	19.5	18.5
Public Sector	12.9	11.5	14.3	18.1	19.5	18.5
of which: General Government	9.6	9.6	12.0	14.8	15.4	15.3
Private sector guaranteed by Public Sector	..	..	..	..	..	..
Private sector not guaranteed	..	..	..	..	..	..
Interest payments (long-term)	**5.4**	**7.2**	**6.8**	**7.1**	**7.8**	**8.3**
Public and publicly guaranteed sector	5.4	7.2	6.8	7.1	7.8	8.3
Public Sector	5.4	7.2	6.8	7.1	7.8	8.3
of which: General Government	4.6	6.6	6.1	6.3	7.1	7.7
Private sector guaranteed by Public Sector	..	..	..	..	..	..
Private sector not guaranteed	..	..	..	..	..	..
Summary external debt stock by creditor type						
Long-term External debt stocks	**221.9**	**281.8**	**282.1**	**264.1**	**260.3**	**243.7**
Public and publicly guaranteed debt from:	221.9	281.8	282.1	264.1	260.3	243.7
Official creditors	156.4	232.5	234.8	218.7	216.9	201.7
Multilateral	117.1	128.6	132.6	127.1	128.7	123.9
of which: World Bank	28.3	26.4	25.5	24.0	32.8	34.0
Bilateral	39.3	103.9	102.2	91.6	88.2	77.8
Private creditors	65.5	49.3	47.3	45.4	43.4	42.0
Bondholders	60.9	25.7	25.7	25.6	25.5	25.5
Commercial banks and others	4.6	23.6	21.7	19.8	17.9	16.5
Private nonguaranteed debt from:	..	..	..	..	..	..
Bondholders	..	..	..	..	..	..
Commercial banks and others	..	..	..	..	..	..
Use of IMF Credit	15.9	20.9	26.5	24.2	24.4	22.4
Net financial inflows						
Net debt inflows						
Use of IMF Credit	3.2	-1.6	6.5	-1.6	-1.2	-1.5
Long-term	-4.9	8.9	6.6	-14.0	-9.8	-13.5
Official creditors	-6.8	11.2	8.6	-12.1	-7.8	-12.0
Multilateral	-3.2	-0.8	5.2	-4.6	0.0	-4.0
of which: World Bank	0.5	0.0	0.3	-0.8	7.3	2.1
Bilateral	-3.6	11.9	3.4	-7.5	-7.8	-8.0
Private creditors	1.9	-2.3	-2.0	-2.0	-2.0	-1.4
Bondholders	0.1	-0.4	-0.1	-0.1	-0.1	..
Banks and other private	1.7	-1.9	-1.9	-1.9	-1.9	-1.4
Short-term	0.1	-0.1	0.1	0.0	2.0	2.0
Net equity inflows						
Foreign direct investment	45.1	12.8	18.0	41.5	-1.8	13.7
Portfolio equity	..	0.0	0.0	0.0	0.1	..
Debt ratios						
External debt stocks to exports (%)	157.7	111.0	117.0	110.5	121.2	161.8
External debt stocks to GNI (%)	59.3	60.8	60.5	53.0	60.9	55.3
Debt service to exports (%)	12.3	7.3	8.7	10.0	11.7	16.5
Short-term to external debt stocks (%)	8.7	1.8	1.8	3.0	3.7	4.7
Multilateral to external debt stocks (%)	45.0	41.7	42.2	42.8	43.6	44.4
Reserves to external debt stocks (%)	21.2	32.9	40.2	74.7	71.8	68.5
Gross national income (GNI)	439.5	506.9	519.1	560.3	485.1	505.0

DOMINICAN REPUBLIC

(US$ million, unless otherwise indicated)

	2008	2014	2015	2016	2017	2018
Summary external debt data by debtor type						
Total External debt stocks	**10,609**	**26,269**	**26,727**	**28,291**	**31,168**	**33,905**
Use of IMF Credit	541	803	403	281	297	290
Long-term external debt	8,129	22,980	23,145	24,958	28,869	31,496
Public and publicly guaranteed sector	7,285	15,701	15,815	17,186	20,226	23,485
Public Sector	7,281	15,699	15,813	17,185	20,225	23,484
of which: General Government	6,285	15,381	15,579	17,044	20,136	23,436
Private sector guaranteed by Public Sector	5	2	1	1	1	1
Private sector not guaranteed	843	7,280	7,330	7,772	8,643	8,011
Short-term external debt	1,940	2,486	3,179	3,053	2,001	2,118
Disbursements (long-term)	**1,310**	**3,831**	**6,096**	**3,724**	**5,055**	**5,073**
Public and publicly guaranteed sector	1,310	2,829	5,020	2,259	3,780	4,104
Public Sector	1,310	2,829	5,020	2,259	3,780	4,104
of which: General Government	1,004	2,828	5,020	2,259	3,780	4,104
Private sector guaranteed by Public Sector	0	0	0	..	0	0
Private sector not guaranteed	..	1,003	1,076	1,465	1,275	969
Principal repayments (long-term)	**823**	**1,907**	**3,782**	**2,075**	**1,961**	**1,478**
Public and publicly guaranteed sector	823	1,226	2,757	861	808	808
Public Sector	822	1,226	2,756	861	807	808
of which: General Government	692	1,134	2,688	770	748	769
Private sector guaranteed by Public Sector	1	0	0	0	0	0
Private sector not guaranteed	1	681	1,026	1,214	1,154	670
Interest payments (long-term)	**448**	**821**	**1,022**	**1,205**	**1,012**	**1,559**
Public and publicly guaranteed sector	339	573	775	922	716	1,087
Public Sector	339	573	775	922	716	1,087
of which: General Government	289	561	767	917	713	1,085
Private sector guaranteed by Public Sector	0	0	0	0	0	0
Private sector not guaranteed	108	248	247	282	296	472
Summary external debt stock by creditor type						
Long-term External debt stocks	**8,129**	**22,980**	**23,145**	**24,958**	**28,869**	**31,496**
Public and publicly guaranteed debt from:	7,285	15,701	15,815	17,186	20,226	23,485
Official creditors	4,458	9,032	5,675	5,813	5,705	5,982
Multilateral	1,890	3,596	4,150	4,439	4,454	4,704
of which: World Bank	458	888	932	933	923	923
Bilateral	2,568	5,436	1,525	1,375	1,251	1,278
Private creditors	2,828	6,669	10,140	11,372	14,521	17,503
Bondholders	615	4,812	8,312	9,812	13,212	16,308
Commercial banks and others	2,213	1,857	1,828	1,560	1,309	1,196
Private nonguaranteed debt from:	843	7,280	7,330	7,772	8,643	8,011
Bondholders	843	1,375	1,575	1,945	1,945	1,945
Commercial banks and others	1	5,904	5,755	5,827	6,698	6,066
Use of IMF Credit	541	803	403	281	297	290
Net financial inflows						
Net debt inflows						
Use of IMF Credit	-43	-457	-368	-114	..	..
Long-term	487	1,924	2,313	1,650	3,094	3,595
Official creditors	712	-48	-1,256	155	-124	283
Multilateral	-3	-297	561	291	10	253
of which: World Bank	-24	-13	44	1	-10	0
Bilateral	715	249	-1,817	-136	-134	30
Private creditors	-225	1,972	3,569	1,495	3,218	3,313
Bondholders	-125	1,988	3,700	1,870	3,400	3,108
Banks and other private	-100	-17	-131	-375	-182	205
Short-term	-534	733	693	-127	-1,051	117
Net equity inflows						
Foreign direct investment	2,593	2,375	2,187	2,340	3,733	2,677
Portfolio equity	0	0	0	0	0	0
Debt ratios						
External debt stocks to exports (%)	106	150	152	152	160	164
External debt stocks to GNI (%)	23	42	41	41	43	44
Debt service to exports (%)	15	18	30	19	16	15
Short-term to external debt stocks (%)	18	9	12	11	6	6
Multilateral to external debt stocks (%)	18	14	16	16	14	14
Reserves to external debt stocks (%)	25	18	20	22	22	23
Gross national income (GNI)	46,506	62,818	65,866	69,090	72,138	77,454

ECUADOR

(US$ million, unless otherwise indicated)

	2008	2014	2015	2016	2017	2018
Summary external debt data by debtor type						
Total External debt stocks	**19,024**	**24,994**	**28,389**	**35,374**	**41,106**	**45,019**
Use of IMF Credit	51	418	400	739	783	765
Long-term external debt	17,319	23,731	27,095	33,966	39,450	43,502
Public and publicly guaranteed sector	13,330	17,587	20,155	25,572	31,617	35,567
Public Sector	13,313	17,557	20,128	25,547	31,595	35,547
of which: General Government	12,782	15,982	18,808	23,770	29,196	33,706
Private sector guaranteed by Public Sector	17	30	27	25	23	20
Private sector not guaranteed	3,990	6,144	6,940	8,394	7,833	7,935
Short-term external debt	1,654	845	895	668	873	751
Disbursements (long-term)	**1,369**	**8,928**	**7,370**	**9,990**	**10,203**	**10,800**
Public and publicly guaranteed sector	353	6,456	4,762	7,325	8,870	7,217
Public Sector	340	6,455	4,762	7,325	8,870	7,217
of which: General Government	332	5,433	4,742	6,480	7,824	7,005
Private sector guaranteed by Public Sector	13	1	0	..	0	0
Private sector not guaranteed	1,016	2,472	2,609	2,666	1,334	3,584
Principal repayments (long-term)	**1,485**	**3,054**	**3,807**	**3,861**	**4,547**	**6,437**
Public and publicly guaranteed sector	963	1,282	2,116	1,859	2,894	3,196
Public Sector	963	1,279	2,114	1,857	2,891	3,194
of which: General Government	907	1,229	1,841	1,469	2,463	2,425
Private sector guaranteed by Public Sector	0	2	2	2	2	2
Private sector not guaranteed	521	1,772	1,691	2,002	1,653	3,241
Interest payments (long-term)	**972**	**956**	**1,278**	**1,507**	**2,032**	**2,663**
Public and publicly guaranteed sector	781	750	1,057	1,200	1,753	2,237
Public Sector	781	749	1,056	1,199	1,752	2,236
of which: General Government	764	716	984	1,094	1,633	2,099
Private sector guaranteed by Public Sector	0	1	1	1	1	1
Private sector not guaranteed	191	206	221	306	279	425
Summary external debt stock by creditor type						
Long-term External debt stocks	**17,319**	**23,731**	**27,095**	**33,966**	**39,450**	**43,502**
Public and publicly guaranteed debt from:	13,330	17,587	20,155	25,572	31,617	35,567
Official creditors	5,913	12,212	14,137	17,155	16,901	16,951
Multilateral	4,335	5,952	7,542	8,168	8,663	9,437
of which: World Bank	624	183	257	246	399	617
Bilateral	1,578	6,260	6,596	8,987	8,238	7,514
Private creditors	7,417	5,375	6,018	8,417	14,717	18,616
Bondholders	7,189	3,021	2,352	5,068	12,020	14,705
Commercial banks and others	228	2,354	3,666	3,349	2,697	3,912
Private nonguaranteed debt from:	3,990	6,144	6,940	8,394	7,833	7,935
Bondholders	..	..	..	..	..	..
Commercial banks and others	3,990	6,144	6,940	8,394	7,833	7,935
Use of IMF Credit	51	418	400	739	783	765
Net financial inflows						
Net debt inflows						
Use of IMF Credit	..	0	..	364	0	0
Long-term	-115	5,874	3,563	6,129	5,657	4,363
Official creditors	-560	937	1,991	3,062	-308	115
Multilateral	-396	396	1,603	628	509	799
of which: World Bank	-72	-53	73	-11	153	218
Bilateral	-164	541	388	2,434	-818	-684
Private creditors	445	4,937	1,572	3,067	5,965	4,248
Bondholders	-11	1,982	-670	2,717	6,951	2,685
Banks and other private	456	2,955	2,242	350	-986	1,563
Short-term	-271	-20	34	-241	188	-137
Net equity inflows						
Foreign direct investment	527	1,162	1,272	879	682	702
Portfolio equity	1	1	2	6	4	6
Debt ratios						
External debt stocks to exports (%)	90	86	132	179	187	181
External debt stocks to GNI (%)	32	25	29	36	40	43
Debt service to exports (%)	12	14	24	27	30	37
Short-term to external debt stocks (%)	9	3	3	2	2	2
Multilateral to external debt stocks (%)	23	24	27	23	21	21
Reserves to external debt stocks (%)	20	14	7	11	4	4
Gross national income (GNI)	60,334	100,175	97,560	98,095	101,942	105,604

EGYPT, ARAB REPUBLIC OF

(US$ million, unless otherwise indicated)

	2008	2014	2015	2016	2017	2018
Summary external debt data by debtor type						
Total External debt stocks	**33,912**	**41,743**	**49,847**	**69,173**	**84,429**	**98,705**
Use of IMF Credit	209	1,302	1,245	3,856	7,401	9,220
Long-term external debt	30,860	37,120	44,178	53,372	65,899	79,144
Public and publicly guaranteed sector	30,780	37,099	44,156	53,215	65,493	78,698
Public Sector	30,214	36,966	44,046	53,138	65,435	78,671
of which: General Government	26,702	25,329	30,073	32,200	42,248	51,164
Private sector guaranteed by Public Sector	566	133	110	77	58	26
Private sector not guaranteed	80	21	23	157	406	446
Short-term external debt	2,842	3,321	4,424	11,945	11,128	10,341
Disbursements (long-term)	**1,133**	**1,684**	**10,962**	**14,683**	**15,534**	**19,089**
Public and publicly guaranteed sector	1,063	1,659	10,933	14,523	15,236	18,963
Public Sector	1,046	1,659	10,933	14,523	15,236	18,963
of which: General Government	893	1,461	7,849	6,280	11,891	11,261
Private sector guaranteed by Public Sector	17	..	0	..	..	..
Private sector not guaranteed	70	25	29	160	298	126
Principal repayments (long-term)	**2,346**	**5,134**	**2,887**	**5,105**	**4,612**	**5,108**
Public and publicly guaranteed sector	2,335	5,118	2,859	5,102	4,564	5,021
Public Sector	2,259	5,086	2,849	5,071	4,537	4,991
of which: General Government	1,459	4,683	2,286	3,987	2,704	1,994
Private sector guaranteed by Public Sector	76	32	10	31	27	30
Private sector not guaranteed	11	16	28	3	48	87
Interest payments (long-term)	**832**	**732**	**715**	**1,027**	**1,579**	**2,205**
Public and publicly guaranteed sector	829	731	714	1,026	1,565	2,188
Public Sector	796	730	713	1,024	1,563	2,187
of which: General Government	670	644	604	785	1,104	1,614
Private sector guaranteed by Public Sector	33	1	1	1	1	1
Private sector not guaranteed	3	0	0	2	14	16
Summary external debt stock by creditor type						
Long-term External debt stocks	**30,860**	**37,120**	**44,178**	**53,372**	**65,899**	**79,144**
Public and publicly guaranteed debt from:	30,780	37,099	44,156	53,215	65,493	78,698
Official creditors	28,136	33,470	38,132	47,757	52,659	55,357
Multilateral	7,732	10,884	11,716	15,854	18,809	19,843
of which: World Bank	2,700	4,909	5,597	7,114	8,435	9,930
Bilateral	20,404	22,585	26,416	31,902	33,849	35,514
Private creditors	2,643	3,629	6,023	5,458	12,834	23,341
Bondholders	2,184	3,350	4,850	3,600	10,000	15,800
Commercial banks and others	459	279	1,173	1,858	2,834	7,540
Private nonguaranteed debt from:	80	21	23	157	406	446
Bondholders	..	..	..	..	..	..
Commercial banks and others	80	21	23	157	406	446
Use of IMF Credit	209	1,302	1,245	3,856	7,401	9,220
Net financial inflows						
Net debt inflows						
Use of IMF Credit	..	0	..	2,738	3,229	2,029
Long-term	-1,212	-3,450	8,075	9,578	10,922	13,981
Official creditors	-896	-905	5,651	9,962	3,418	3,296
Multilateral	89	441	1,185	4,312	2,486	1,217
of which: World Bank	26	347	723	1,545	1,289	1,507
Bilateral	-985	-1,345	4,466	5,650	932	2,079
Private creditors	-317	-2,545	2,424	-384	7,504	10,685
Bondholders	..	-2,500	1,500	-1,250	6,400	5,868
Banks and other private	-317	-45	924	866	1,104	4,817
Short-term	607	505	1,103	7,521	-817	-787
Net equity inflows						
Foreign direct investment	9,495	4,612	6,925	8,107	7,409	6,798
Portfolio equity	-674	485	14	610	224	220
Debt ratios						
External debt stocks to exports (%)	59	88	132	203	194	188
External debt stocks to GNI (%)	21	14	15	21	37	40
Debt service to exports (%)	6	13	10	20	15	15
Short-term to external debt stocks (%)	8	8	9	17	13	10
Multilateral to external debt stocks (%)	23	26	24	23	22	20
Reserves to external debt stocks (%)	95	29	27	30	39	39
Gross national income (GNI)	164,178	298,267	326,997	328,456	230,801	244,616

EL SALVADOR

(US$ million, unless otherwise indicated)

	2008	2014	2015	2016	2017	2018
Summary external debt data by debtor type						
Total External debt stocks	**10,688**	**15,170**	**15,571**	**16,566**	**17,180**	**17,486**
Use of IMF Credit	38	237	227	220	233	228
Long-term external debt	9,108	12,915	13,327	13,813	14,903	15,188
Public and publicly guaranteed sector	5,791	8,692	8,605	8,710	9,489	9,605
Public Sector	5,788	8,691	8,604	8,710	9,489	9,605
of which: General Government	5,203	8,064	7,969	7,965	8,655	8,851
Private sector guaranteed by Public Sector	3	1	1	0	0	0
Private sector not guaranteed	3,316	4,223	4,722	5,103	5,414	5,583
Short-term external debt	1,542	2,018	2,018	2,533	2,043	2,070
Disbursements (long-term)	**1,070**	**1,777**	**1,259**	**1,028**	**3,513**	**2,913**
Public and publicly guaranteed sector	694	1,144	394	409	978	556
Public Sector	694	1,144	394	409	978	556
of which: General Government	360	935	220	130	748	496
Private sector guaranteed by Public Sector	..	..	..	..	..	..
Private sector not guaranteed	376	633	865	619	2,535	2,357
Principal repayments (long-term)	**490**	**689**	**635**	**693**	**2,994**	**2,623**
Public and publicly guaranteed sector	351	419	406	455	433	435
Public Sector	351	419	405	455	433	434
of which: General Government	255	248	241	284	292	294
Private sector guaranteed by Public Sector	0	0	0	0	0	0
Private sector not guaranteed	139	269	229	238	2,561	2,188
Interest payments (long-term)	**485**	**584**	**643**	**660**	**768**	**859**
Public and publicly guaranteed sector	369	456	494	514	547	559
Public Sector	369	456	494	514	547	559
of which: General Government	351	432	469	483	511	515
Private sector guaranteed by Public Sector	0	0	0	0	0	0
Private sector not guaranteed	116	129	149	145	221	300
Summary external debt stock by creditor type						
Long-term External debt stocks	**9,108**	**12,915**	**13,327**	**13,813**	**14,903**	**15,188**
Public and publicly guaranteed debt from:	5,791	8,692	8,605	8,710	9,489	9,605
Official creditors	3,524	4,314	4,277	4,215	4,185	4,251
Multilateral	2,796	3,861	3,839	3,783	3,757	3,860
of which: World Bank	409	949	921	912	906	876
Bilateral	728	452	437	433	428	391
Private creditors	2,267	4,379	4,328	4,495	5,304	5,354
Bondholders	2,174	4,334	4,283	4,438	5,238	5,238
Commercial banks and others	93	44	45	57	66	116
Private nonguaranteed debt from:	3,316	4,223	4,722	5,103	5,414	5,583
Bondholders	..	38	38	38	38	38
Commercial banks and others	3,316	4,185	4,684	5,065	5,376	5,545
Use of IMF Credit	38	237	227	220	233	228
Net financial inflows						
Net debt inflows						
Use of IMF Credit	..	0	..	..	..	..
Long-term	580	1,089	624	335	519	291
Official creditors	282	-82	-15	-58	-52	71
Multilateral	272	-57	-14	-51	-27	104
of which: World Bank	-2	-20	-27	-9	0	-31
Bilateral	10	-25	-1	-7	-25	-33
Private creditors	298	1,171	639	393	571	220
Bondholders	0	780	0	0	589	0
Banks and other private	298	391	639	393	-18	220
Short-term	250	165	0	515	-490	27
Net equity inflows						
Foreign direct investment	538	371	320	415	844	141
Portfolio equity	0	0	0	0	0	0
Debt ratios						
External debt stocks to exports (%)	214	225	221	237	233	225
External debt stocks to GNI (%)	61	70	70	72	73	71
Debt service to exports (%)	20	19	19	20	52	46
Short-term to external debt stocks (%)	14	13	13	15	12	12
Multilateral to external debt stocks (%)	26	25	25	23	22	22
Reserves to external debt stocks (%)	23	16	18	19	20	20
Gross national income (GNI)	17,598	21,558	22,346	22,925	23,540	24,585

ERITREA

(US$ million, unless otherwise indicated)

	2008	2014	2015	2016	2017	2018
Summary external debt data by debtor type						
Total External debt stocks	**997.8**	**907.7**	**873.0**	**796.0**	**818.5**	**791.2**
Use of IMF Credit	23.3	22.0	21.0	20.4	21.6	21.1
Long-term external debt	957.0	829.1	781.5	748.4	769.2	735.3
Public and publicly guaranteed sector	957.0	829.1	781.5	748.4	769.2	735.3
Public Sector	957.0	829.1	781.5	748.4	769.2	735.3
of which: General Government	957.0	829.1	781.5	748.4	769.2	735.3
Private sector guaranteed by Public Sector	..	..	..	..	..	..
Private sector not guaranteed	..	..	..	..	..	..
Short-term external debt	17.5	56.6	70.5	27.2	27.7	34.8
Disbursements (long-term)	**104.9**	**20.2**	**14.7**	**9.5**	**6.9**	**4.2**
Public and publicly guaranteed sector	104.9	20.2	14.7	9.5	6.9	4.2
Public Sector	104.9	20.2	14.7	9.5	6.9	4.2
of which: General Government	104.9	20.2	14.7	9.5	6.9	4.2
Private sector guaranteed by Public Sector	..	..	..	..	..	..
Private sector not guaranteed	..	..	..	..	..	..
Principal repayments (long-term)	**6.5**	**41.2**	**29.9**	**24.3**	**24.7**	**22.8**
Public and publicly guaranteed sector	6.5	41.2	29.9	24.3	24.7	22.8
Public Sector	6.5	41.2	29.9	24.3	24.7	22.8
of which: General Government	6.5	41.2	29.9	24.3	24.7	22.8
Private sector guaranteed by Public Sector	..	..	..	..	..	..
Private sector not guaranteed	..	..	..	..	..	..
Interest payments (long-term)	**9.1**	**4.9**	**4.1**	**3.8**	**3.5**	**3.2**
Public and publicly guaranteed sector	9.1	4.9	4.1	3.8	3.5	3.2
Public Sector	9.1	4.9	4.1	3.8	3.5	3.2
of which: General Government	9.1	4.9	4.1	3.8	3.5	3.2
Private sector guaranteed by Public Sector	..	..	..	..	..	..
Private sector not guaranteed	..	..	..	..	..	..
Summary external debt stock by creditor type						
Long-term External debt stocks	**957.0**	**829.1**	**781.5**	**748.4**	**769.2**	**735.3**
Public and publicly guaranteed debt from:	957.0	829.1	781.5	748.4	769.2	735.3
Official creditors	917.4	794.6	750.6	718.5	735.1	702.8
Multilateral	643.6	597.1	572.5	557.5	587.3	571.6
of which: World Bank	472.6	452.6	432.9	420.0	444.9	434.5
Bilateral	273.8	197.5	178.1	160.9	147.8	131.2
Private creditors	39.5	34.5	30.9	29.9	34.1	32.5
Bondholders	..	..	..	..	..	..
Commercial banks and others	39.5	34.5	30.9	29.9	34.1	32.5
Private nonguaranteed debt from:	..	..	..	..	..	..
Bondholders	..	..	..	..	..	..
Commercial banks and others	..	..	..	..	..	..
Use of IMF Credit	23.3	22.0	21.0	20.4	21.6	21.1
Net financial inflows						
Net debt inflows						
Use of IMF Credit	..	0.0	..	..	..	..
Long-term	98.3	-21.0	-15.3	-14.8	-17.8	-18.5
Official creditors	97.5	-21.0	-15.3	-14.8	-17.8	-18.5
Multilateral	26.5	-5.5	-0.4	-1.0	-1.6	-3.8
of which: World Bank	19.5	0.0	0.0	0.0	0.0	0.0
Bilateral	71.0	-15.4	-14.8	-13.8	-16.2	-14.7
Private creditors	0.8	0.0	..	0.0	..	..
Bondholders	..	..	..	..	..	..
Banks and other private	0.8	0.0	..	0.0	..	..
Short-term	0.0	28.0	11.7	-45.7	-4.0	4.4
Net equity inflows						
Foreign direct investment	39.0	46.5	49.3	52.3	55.5	61.0
Portfolio equity	..	..	..	..	..	..
Debt ratios						
External debt stocks to exports (%)	..	..	..	..	..	..
External debt stocks to GNI (%)	72.9	..	..	..	..	..
Debt service to exports (%)	..	..	..	..	..	..
Short-term to external debt stocks (%)	1.8	6.2	8.1	3.4	3.4	4.4
Multilateral to external debt stocks (%)	64.5	65.8	65.6	70.0	71.8	72.2
Reserves to external debt stocks (%)	5.8	..	..	..	..	..
Gross national income (GNI)	1,368.4	..	..	..	..	..

ESWATINI

(US$ million, unless otherwise indicated)

	2008	2014	2015	2016	2017	2018
Summary external debt data by debtor type						
Total External debt stocks	**475.1**	**396.7**	**367.5**	**487.1**	**652.2**	**509.2**
Use of IMF Credit	9.9	70.0	66.9	64.9	68.8	67.2
Long-term external debt	417.3	293.0	286.0	359.2	397.6	418.2
Public and publicly guaranteed sector	417.3	293.0	286.0	359.2	397.6	418.2
Public Sector	417.3	293.0	286.0	359.2	397.6	418.2
of which: General Government	404.3	288.2	281.2	348.5	386.8	407.4
Private sector guaranteed by Public Sector	..	..	..	..	..	..
Private sector not guaranteed	..	..	..	..	..	..
Short-term external debt	47.9	33.7	14.6	63.0	185.8	23.9
Disbursements (long-term)	**43.6**	**24.8**	**38.9**	**99.6**	**55.6**	**63.3**
Public and publicly guaranteed sector	43.6	24.8	38.9	99.6	55.6	63.3
Public Sector	43.6	24.8	38.9	99.6	55.6	63.3
of which: General Government	43.6	24.8	38.9	93.6	55.6	63.3
Private sector guaranteed by Public Sector	..	..	..	..	..	..
Private sector not guaranteed	..	..	..	..	..	..
Principal repayments (long-term)	**35.2**	**23.4**	**24.4**	**31.2**	**31.1**	**32.6**
Public and publicly guaranteed sector	35.2	23.4	24.4	31.2	31.1	32.6
Public Sector	35.2	23.4	24.4	31.2	31.1	32.6
of which: General Government	30.6	22.4	24.4	31.2	31.1	32.6
Private sector guaranteed by Public Sector	..	..	..	..	..	..
Private sector not guaranteed	..	..	..	..	..	..
Interest payments (long-term)	**23.3**	**12.2**	**9.7**	**8.8**	**11.2**	**13.2**
Public and publicly guaranteed sector	23.3	12.2	9.7	8.8	11.2	13.2
Public Sector	23.3	12.2	9.7	8.8	11.2	13.2
of which: General Government	21.9	12.2	9.7	8.8	11.2	13.2
Private sector guaranteed by Public Sector	..	..	..	..	..	..
Private sector not guaranteed	..	..	..	..	..	..
Summary external debt stock by creditor type						
Long-term External debt stocks	**417.3**	**293.0**	**286.0**	**359.2**	**397.6**	**418.2**
Public and publicly guaranteed debt from:	417.3	293.0	286.0	359.2	397.6	418.2
Official creditors	385.7	273.6	272.2	344.5	381.9	405.8
Multilateral	254.5	172.9	156.2	177.4	208.3	219.4
of which: World Bank	16.9	14.0	21.8	27.6	38.8	39.8
Bilateral	131.2	100.7	116.0	167.1	173.6	186.4
Private creditors	31.6	19.4	13.7	14.7	15.7	12.4
Bondholders	..	..	..	..	..	..
Commercial banks and others	31.6	19.4	13.7	14.7	15.7	12.4
Private nonguaranteed debt from:	..	..	..	..	..	..
Bondholders	..	..	..	..	..	..
Commercial banks and others	..	..	..	..	..	..
Use of IMF Credit	9.9	70.0	66.9	64.9	68.8	67.2
Net financial inflows						
Net debt inflows						
Use of IMF Credit	..	0.0	..	..	..	..
Long-term	8.4	1.4	14.5	68.3	24.6	30.7
Official creditors	9.8	2.5	15.4	69.1	25.1	31.9
Multilateral	-18.2	-7.6	-3.3	19.4	22.8	18.1
of which: World Bank	-6.2	6.3	7.7	5.8	11.2	1.0
Bilateral	28.0	10.1	18.7	49.7	2.3	13.8
Private creditors	-1.4	-1.1	-0.9	-0.8	-0.6	-1.2
Bondholders	..	..	..	..	..	..
Banks and other private	-1.4	-1.1	-0.9	-0.8	-0.6	-1.2
Short-term	11.0	-8.5	-17.6	46.7	128.3	-168.5
Net equity inflows						
Foreign direct investment	90.6	55.1	34.2	2.3	43.3	25.4
Portfolio equity	43.9	..	..	..	..	..
Debt ratios						
External debt stocks to exports (%)	23.3	18.5	18.4	26.7	31.1	24.8
External debt stocks to GNI (%)	14.4	9.0	9.1	12.8	15.0	10.9
Debt service to exports (%)	3.0	1.7	1.7	2.2	2.2	2.3
Short-term to external debt stocks (%)	10.1	8.5	4.0	12.9	28.5	4.7
Multilateral to external debt stocks (%)	53.6	43.6	42.5	36.4	31.9	43.1
Reserves to external debt stocks (%)	158.3	174.1	149.1	115.8	86.3	86.5
Gross national income (GNI)	3,288.9	4,387.8	4,060.0	3,807.2	4,352.4	4,686.3

ETHIOPIA

(US$ million, unless otherwise indicated)

	2008	2014	2015	2016	2017	2018
Summary external debt data by debtor type						
Total External debt stocks	**2,846**	**16,945**	**21,021**	**23,796**	**26,657**	**28,027**
Use of IMF Credit	17	452	397	335	301	242
Long-term external debt	2,771	16,202	20,074	22,533	25,721	27,036
Public and publicly guaranteed sector	2,771	16,202	20,074	22,533	25,721	27,036
Public Sector	2,771	16,202	20,074	22,533	25,721	27,036
of which: General Government	2,531	9,659	10,635	12,239	14,352	15,474
Private sector guaranteed by Public Sector	..	..	..	..	..	..
Private sector not guaranteed	..	..	..	..	..	..
Short-term external debt	58	292	550	927	634	749
Disbursements (long-term)	**379**	**4,733**	**4,903**	**3,497**	**3,518**	**3,622**
Public and publicly guaranteed sector	379	4,733	4,903	3,497	3,518	3,622
Public Sector	379	4,733	4,903	3,497	3,518	3,622
of which: General Government	379	2,582	1,375	1,969	1,758	2,075
Private sector guaranteed by Public Sector	..	..	..	..	..	..
Private sector not guaranteed	..	..	..	..	..	..
Principal repayments (long-term)	**68**	**563**	**693**	**762**	**894**	**1,494**
Public and publicly guaranteed sector	68	563	693	762	894	1,494
Public Sector	68	563	693	762	894	1,494
of which: General Government	35	89	95	104	145	171
Private sector guaranteed by Public Sector	..	..	..	..	..	..
Private sector not guaranteed	..	..	..	..	..	..
Interest payments (long-term)	**35**	**188**	**302**	**397**	**429**	**436**
Public and publicly guaranteed sector	35	188	302	397	429	436
Public Sector	35	188	302	397	429	436
of which: General Government	23	81	158	168	166	205
Private sector guaranteed by Public Sector	..	..	..	..	..	..
Private sector not guaranteed	..	..	..	..	..	..
Summary external debt stock by creditor type						
Long-term External debt stocks	**2,771**	**16,202**	**20,074**	**22,533**	**25,721**	**27,036**
Public and publicly guaranteed debt from:	2,771	16,202	20,074	22,533	25,721	27,036
Official creditors	2,532	11,518	13,725	16,293	19,012	20,096
Multilateral	1,603	5,981	6,775	8,155	10,106	11,063
of which: World Bank	859	4,259	4,753	5,746	7,040	8,338
Bilateral	930	5,537	6,950	8,137	8,906	9,034
Private creditors	239	4,684	6,349	6,241	6,710	6,939
Bondholders	..	1,000	1,000	1,000	1,000	1,000
Commercial banks and others	239	3,684	5,349	5,241	5,710	5,939
Private nonguaranteed debt from:	..	..	..	..	..	..
Bondholders	..	..	..	..	..	..
Commercial banks and others	..	..	..	..	..	..
Use of IMF Credit	17	452	397	335	301	242
Net financial inflows						
Net debt inflows						
Use of IMF Credit	..	-5	-36	-52	-52	-53
Long-term	311	4,170	4,211	2,735	2,623	2,128
Official creditors	344	2,834	2,527	2,839	2,193	1,876
Multilateral	254	1,008	1,058	1,613	1,503	1,703
of which: World Bank	157	854	685	1,177	933	1,494
Bilateral	90	1,826	1,469	1,225	690	173
Private creditors	-33	1,336	1,684	-104	431	252
Bondholders	..	1,000	..	..	..	0
Banks and other private	-33	336	1,684	-104	431	252
Short-term	-8	88	258	378	-293	115
Net equity inflows						
Foreign direct investment	109	1,855	2,627	3,989	4,017	3,310
Portfolio equity	0	..	..	..	..	..
Debt ratios						
External debt stocks to exports (%)	81	265	349	402	399	..
External debt stocks to GNI (%)	11	31	33	32	33	33
Debt service to exports (%)	3	12	17	21	21	..
Short-term to external debt stocks (%)	2	2	3	4	2	3
Multilateral to external debt stocks (%)	56	35	32	34	38	39
Reserves to external debt stocks (%)	31	21	18	13	11	14
Gross national income (GNI)	27,087	55,459	64,203	74,029	81,231	83,806

FIJI

(US$ million, unless otherwise indicated)

	2008	2014	2015	2016	2017	2018
Summary external debt data by debtor type						
Total External debt stocks	**342.9**	**833.7**	**791.8**	**849.5**	**876.5**	**851.8**
Use of IMF Credit	10.7	97.2	93.0	90.2	95.6	93.3
Long-term external debt	314.8	668.6	617.3	662.0	717.3	713.9
Public and publicly guaranteed sector	314.4	668.2	616.9	661.6	716.9	713.6
Public Sector	314.4	668.2	616.9	661.6	716.9	713.6
of which: General Government	287.2	628.0	580.9	628.7	683.0	681.3
Private sector guaranteed by Public Sector	..	..	..	..	..	..
Private sector not guaranteed	0.4	0.4	0.4	0.4	0.4	0.4
Short-term external debt	17.4	67.9	81.5	97.3	63.6	44.6
Disbursements (long-term)	**21.9**	**71.9**	**227.9**	**96.6**	**59.5**	**36.9**
Public and publicly guaranteed sector	21.8	71.9	227.9	96.5	59.4	36.8
Public Sector	21.8	71.9	227.9	96.5	59.4	36.8
of which: General Government	13.2	70.5	226.0	95.4	58.5	36.0
Private sector guaranteed by Public Sector	..	..	..	..	..	..
Private sector not guaranteed	0.2	0.0	0.0	0.1	0.1	0.0
Principal repayments (long-term)	**7.8**	**21.1**	**265.6**	**35.8**	**20.8**	**28.3**
Public and publicly guaranteed sector	7.7	21.0	265.6	35.8	20.7	28.3
Public Sector	7.7	21.0	265.6	35.8	20.7	28.3
of which: General Government	7.7	21.0	259.5	31.6	20.7	25.8
Private sector guaranteed by Public Sector	..	..	..	..	..	..
Private sector not guaranteed	0.0	0.1	0.0	0.0	0.1	0.1
Interest payments (long-term)	**16.2**	**28.7**	**35.7**	**21.3**	**22.6**	**24.7**
Public and publicly guaranteed sector	16.2	28.7	35.7	21.3	22.6	24.7
Public Sector	16.2	28.7	35.7	21.3	22.6	24.7
of which: General Government	14.9	28.7	35.7	21.0	22.6	24.7
Private sector guaranteed by Public Sector	..	..	..	..	..	..
Private sector not guaranteed	0.0	0.0	0.0	0.0	0.0	0.0
Summary external debt stock by creditor type						
Long-term External debt stocks	**314.8**	**668.6**	**617.3**	**662.0**	**717.3**	**713.9**
Public and publicly guaranteed debt from:	314.4	668.2	616.9	661.6	716.9	713.6
Official creditors	164.4	418.2	410.1	461.6	516.9	513.6
Multilateral	108.6	137.8	130.1	172.8	224.3	253.4
of which: World Bank	1.5	..	..	50.2	53.6	73.1
Bilateral	55.8	280.4	280.0	288.8	292.6	260.1
Private creditors	150.0	250.0	206.9	200.0	200.0	200.0
Bondholders	150.0	250.0	206.9	200.0	200.0	200.0
Commercial banks and others	..	..	..	..	..	..
Private nonguaranteed debt from:	0.4	0.4	0.4	0.4	0.4	0.4
Bondholders	..	..	..	..	..	..
Commercial banks and others	0.4	0.4	0.4	0.4	0.4	0.4
Use of IMF Credit	10.7	97.2	93.0	90.2	95.6	93.3
Net financial inflows						
Net debt inflows						
Use of IMF Credit	..	0.0	..	..	..	..
Long-term	14.2	50.8	-37.7	60.8	38.7	8.5
Official creditors	14.1	50.9	5.4	67.6	38.7	8.5
Multilateral	3.7	-0.6	-7.7	42.5	51.4	29.1
of which: World Bank	-1.3	..	..	50.2	3.4	19.5
Bilateral	10.4	51.5	13.1	25.1	-12.7	-20.6
Private creditors	0.1	-0.1	-43.2	-6.8	0.0	0.0
Bondholders	..	..	-43.2	-6.9	0.0	0.0
Banks and other private	0.1	-0.1	0.0	0.0	0.0	0.0
Short-term	-4.0	31.6	13.6	15.8	-33.6	-19.1
Net equity inflows						
Foreign direct investment	350.5	409.8	208.9	379.2	418.3	307.1
Portfolio equity	1.4	..	..	..	..	..
Debt ratios						
External debt stocks to exports (%)	16.4	32.0	33.7	35.6	34.5	31.3
External debt stocks to GNI (%)	10.0	18.0	17.7	18.0	17.7	16.7
Debt service to exports (%)	1.2	1.9	12.9	2.5	1.8	2.0
Short-term to external debt stocks (%)	5.1	8.1	10.3	11.5	7.3	5.2
Multilateral to external debt stocks (%)	31.7	16.5	16.4	20.3	25.6	29.8
Reserves to external debt stocks (%)	93.8	109.8	115.9	106.8	127.2	111.1
Gross national income (GNI)	3,436.1	4,631.6	4,477.2	4,717.5	4,944.0	5,103.8

GABON

(US$ million, unless otherwise indicated)

	2008	2014	2015	2016	2017	2018
Summary external debt data by debtor type						
Total External debt stocks	**2,363**	**4,542**	**5,059**	**5,286**	**6,459**	**6,767**
Use of IMF Credit	22	213	203	197	412	601
Long-term external debt	2,227	4,256	4,646	4,848	5,839	5,978
Public and publicly guaranteed sector	2,227	4,256	4,646	4,848	5,839	5,978
Public Sector	2,227	4,256	4,646	4,848	5,839	5,978
of which: General Government	2,225	4,251	4,638	4,834	5,789	5,922
Private sector guaranteed by Public Sector	..	..	..	..	..	..
Private sector not guaranteed	..	..	..	..	..	..
Short-term external debt	115	73	210	240	207	187
Disbursements (long-term)	**181**	**568**	**834**	**431**	**1,175**	**720**
Public and publicly guaranteed sector	181	568	834	431	1,175	720
Public Sector	181	568	834	431	1,175	720
of which: General Government	181	568	831	423	1,155	693
Private sector guaranteed by Public Sector	..	..	..	..	..	..
Private sector not guaranteed	..	..	..	..	..	..
Principal repayments (long-term)	**2,250**	**263**	**227**	**160**	**439**	**435**
Public and publicly guaranteed sector	2,250	263	227	160	439	435
Public Sector	2,250	263	227	160	439	435
of which: General Government	2,249	261	227	159	438	434
Private sector guaranteed by Public Sector	..	..	..	..	..	..
Private sector not guaranteed	..	..	..	..	..	..
Interest payments (long-term)	**360**	**159**	**192**	**193**	**201**	**217**
Public and publicly guaranteed sector	360	159	192	193	201	217
Public Sector	360	159	192	193	201	217
of which: General Government	360	158	192	193	201	216
Private sector guaranteed by Public Sector	..	..	..	..	..	..
Private sector not guaranteed	..	..	..	..	..	..
Summary external debt stock by creditor type						
Long-term External debt stocks	**2,227**	**4,256**	**4,646**	**4,848**	**5,839**	**5,978**
Public and publicly guaranteed debt from:	2,227	4,256	4,646	4,848	5,839	5,978
Official creditors	1,126	1,615	1,639	1,820	2,863	3,255
Multilateral	410	589	568	562	1,449	1,696
of which: World Bank	20	32	46	67	336	369
Bilateral	716	1,026	1,071	1,259	1,414	1,560
Private creditors	1,100	2,642	3,007	3,028	2,976	2,722
Bondholders	946	1,718	2,218	2,218	2,200	2,186
Commercial banks and others	154	923	789	810	776	536
Private nonguaranteed debt from:	..	..	..	..	..	..
Bondholders	..	..	..	..	..	..
Commercial banks and others	..	..	..	..	..	..
Use of IMF Credit	22	213	203	197	412	601
Net financial inflows						
Net debt inflows						
Use of IMF Credit	-25	0	..	..	198	202
Long-term	-2,069	304	607	271	736	285
Official creditors	-2,069	172	149	224	887	510
Multilateral	-12	43	23	8	786	331
of which: World Bank	9	-1	17	21	249	64
Bilateral	-2,057	130	126	216	101	179
Private creditors	0	132	458	48	-151	-225
Bondholders	..	..	500	..	-18	-14
Banks and other private	0	132	-42	48	-133	-211
Short-term	-105	-200	135	21	-37	-11
Net equity inflows						
Foreign direct investment	696	242	-125	1,241	1,498	846
Portfolio equity	0	-1	4	..	..	..
Debt ratios						
External debt stocks to exports (%)	25	53	92	..	..	..
External debt stocks to GNI (%)	18	26	38	41	46	43
Debt service to exports (%)	28	5	8	..	..	..
Short-term to external debt stocks (%)	5	2	4	5	3	3
Multilateral to external debt stocks (%)	17	13	11	11	22	25
Reserves to external debt stocks (%)	81	55	37	15	15	20
Gross national income (GNI)	13,353	17,233	13,183	12,926	13,951	15,747

GAMBIA, THE

(US$ million, unless otherwise indicated)

	2008	2014	2015	2016	2017	2018
Summary external debt data by debtor type						
Total External debt stocks	**401.9**	**528.0**	**532.9**	**516.0**	**653.6**	**681.4**
Use of IMF Credit	20.2	86.8	88.4	80.0	93.9	84.1
Long-term external debt	365.7	428.0	432.8	418.0	545.7	579.4
Public and publicly guaranteed sector	365.7	428.0	432.8	418.0	545.7	579.4
Public Sector	365.7	428.0	432.8	418.0	545.7	579.4
of which: General Government	350.4	411.2	420.4	408.8	539.1	576.1
Private sector guaranteed by Public Sector	..	..	..	..	..	..
Private sector not guaranteed	..	..	..	..	..	..
Short-term external debt	15.9	13.3	11.6	17.9	14.0	17.9
Disbursements (long-term)	**37.4**	**41.2**	**44.7**	**17.0**	**143.5**	**71.0**
Public and publicly guaranteed sector	37.4	41.2	44.7	17.0	143.5	71.0
Public Sector	37.4	41.2	44.7	17.0	143.5	71.0
of which: General Government	32.0	38.6	44.7	17.0	143.5	71.0
Private sector guaranteed by Public Sector	..	..	..	..	..	..
Private sector not guaranteed	..	..	..	..	..	..
Principal repayments (long-term)	**10.3**	**39.1**	**27.8**	**25.9**	**30.5**	**30.4**
Public and publicly guaranteed sector	10.3	39.1	27.8	25.9	30.5	30.4
Public Sector	10.3	39.1	27.8	25.9	30.5	30.4
of which: General Government	9.1	35.6	24.4	22.8	27.4	27.2
Private sector guaranteed by Public Sector	..	..	..	..	..	..
Private sector not guaranteed	..	..	..	..	..	..
Interest payments (long-term)	**5.8**	**5.3**	**5.1**	**5.6**	**6.1**	**6.6**
Public and publicly guaranteed sector	5.8	5.3	5.1	5.6	6.1	6.6
Public Sector	5.8	5.3	5.1	5.6	6.1	6.6
of which: General Government	5.2	5.0	4.7	5.4	6.0	6.4
Private sector guaranteed by Public Sector	..	..	..	..	..	..
Private sector not guaranteed	..	..	..	..	..	..
Summary external debt stock by creditor type						
Long-term External debt stocks	**365.7**	**428.0**	**432.8**	**418.0**	**545.7**	**579.4**
Public and publicly guaranteed debt from:	365.7	428.0	432.8	418.0	545.7	579.4
Official creditors	363.2	419.1	426.6	413.7	542.7	578.5
Multilateral	245.5	310.4	306.8	293.4	392.4	422.3
of which: World Bank	61.9	57.7	55.0	57.2	105.1	115.8
Bilateral	117.7	108.7	119.9	120.3	150.3	156.1
Private creditors	2.5	8.9	6.2	4.3	2.9	0.9
Bondholders	..	..	..	..	..	..
Commercial banks and others	2.5	8.9	6.2	4.3	2.9	0.9
Private nonguaranteed debt from:	..	..	..	..	..	..
Bondholders	..	..	..	..	..	..
Commercial banks and others	..	..	..	..	..	..
Use of IMF Credit	20.2	86.8	88.4	80.0	93.9	84.1
Net financial inflows						
Net debt inflows						
Use of IMF Credit	6.3	-3.2	5.5	-5.9	8.9	-7.8
Long-term	27.2	2.2	16.9	-8.9	113.0	40.6
Official creditors	25.7	3.0	18.7	-7.1	114.8	42.5
Multilateral	25.1	12.4	6.1	-7.9	85.8	36.3
of which: World Bank	2.3	-0.5	-0.2	4.0	43.9	13.3
Bilateral	0.5	-9.4	12.7	0.8	29.0	6.2
Private creditors	1.5	-0.9	-1.8	-1.8	-1.8	-1.9
Bondholders	..	..	..	..	..	..
Banks and other private	1.5	-0.9	-1.8	-1.8	-1.8	-1.9
Short-term	-7.0	-0.9	-1.0	7.9	-3.9	3.7
Net equity inflows						
Foreign direct investment	70.8	33.7	7.9	7.9	12.3	29.1
Portfolio equity	..	..	..	..	..	..
Debt ratios						
External debt stocks to exports (%)	127.1	194.7	200.3	210.2	248.9	..
External debt stocks to GNI (%)	42.7	42.9	39.1	36.5	44.7	42.7
Debt service to exports (%)	5.4	17.6	14.4	15.3	16.8	..
Short-term to external debt stocks (%)	4.0	2.5	2.2	3.5	2.1	2.6
Multilateral to external debt stocks (%)	61.1	58.8	57.6	56.9	60.0	62.0
Reserves to external debt stocks (%)	29.0	30.2	20.8	17.0	26.0	28.1
Gross national income (GNI)	940.2	1,230.1	1,361.1	1,414.8	1,461.2	1,595.4

GEORGIA

(US$ million, unless otherwise indicated)

	2008	2014	2015	2016	2017	2018
Summary external debt data by debtor type						
Total External debt stocks	**7,722**	**13,657**	**14,375**	**15,820**	**15,924**	**17,118**
Use of IMF Credit	682	420	330	307	397	416
Long-term external debt	6,003	11,086	12,001	13,159	13,084	14,033
Public and publicly guaranteed sector	2,974	5,076	5,221	5,724	6,115	6,280
Public Sector	2,974	5,076	5,221	5,724	6,115	6,280
of which: General Government	2,281	4,039	4,233	4,443	5,032	5,257
Private sector guaranteed by Public Sector	0	..	..	..	..	..
Private sector not guaranteed	3,029	6,010	6,781	7,435	6,969	7,754
Short-term external debt	1,037	2,151	2,043	2,354	2,443	2,669
Disbursements (long-term)	**893**	**1,467**	**2,545**	**2,780**	**2,003**	**2,467**
Public and publicly guaranteed sector	725	627	733	839	536	567
Public Sector	725	627	733	839	536	567
of which: General Government	725	461	464	424	524	555
Private sector guaranteed by Public Sector	..	..	..	..	..	..
Private sector not guaranteed	168	841	1,812	1,941	1,467	1,900
Principal repayments (long-term)	**423**	**1,207**	**1,387**	**1,634**	**1,974**	**1,681**
Public and publicly guaranteed sector	110	191	435	256	434	300
Public Sector	110	191	435	256	434	300
of which: General Government	40	98	118	132	165	227
Private sector guaranteed by Public Sector	..	..	..	..	..	..
Private sector not guaranteed	314	1,016	952	1,379	1,540	1,381
Interest payments (long-term)	**225**	**387**	**623**	**867**	**487**	**571**
Public and publicly guaranteed sector	54	127	127	114	136	128
Public Sector	54	127	127	114	136	128
of which: General Government	46	80	79	87	99	111
Private sector guaranteed by Public Sector	..	..	..	..	..	..
Private sector not guaranteed	171	260	495	752	351	442
Summary external debt stock by creditor type						
Long-term External debt stocks	**6,003**	**11,086**	**12,001**	**13,159**	**13,084**	**14,033**
Public and publicly guaranteed debt from:	2,974	5,076	5,221	5,724	6,115	6,280
Official creditors	1,780	3,526	3,712	3,892	4,432	4,663
Multilateral	1,190	2,746	2,962	3,154	3,664	3,794
of which: World Bank	989	1,774	1,849	1,830	2,026	1,960
Bilateral	590	780	750	738	768	870
Private creditors	1,194	1,550	1,509	1,831	1,683	1,616
Bondholders	500	1,000	750	1,000	750	750
Commercial banks and others	694	550	759	831	933	866
Private nonguaranteed debt from:	3,029	6,010	6,781	7,435	6,969	7,754
Bondholders	..	750	900	1,054	1,152	1,660
Commercial banks and others	3,029	5,260	5,881	6,381	5,817	6,094
Use of IMF Credit	682	420	330	307	397	416
Net financial inflows						
Net debt inflows						
Use of IMF Credit	221	-132	-73	-14	70	28
Long-term	470	261	1,158	1,146	28	787
Official creditors	185	363	337	259	320	330
Multilateral	183	347	330	265	337	211
of which: World Bank	110	109	133	19	125	-31
Bilateral	2	16	7	-6	-17	118
Private creditors	285	-103	821	887	-291	457
Bondholders	500	0	-100	404	-454	236
Banks and other private	-215	-103	921	483	163	221
Short-term	373	58	248	230	181	89
Net equity inflows						
Foreign direct investment	1,177	1,572	1,704	2,132	1,845	1,259
Portfolio equity	115	210	5	-4	-2	4
Debt ratios						
External debt stocks to exports (%)	182	169	207	223	183	168
External debt stocks to GNI (%)	61	83	106	116	112	111
Debt service to exports (%)	17	23	30	36	29	24
Short-term to external debt stocks (%)	13	16	14	15	15	16
Multilateral to external debt stocks (%)	15	20	21	20	23	22
Reserves to external debt stocks (%)	19	20	18	17	19	19
Gross national income (GNI)	12,623	16,358	13,610	13,665	14,263	15,473

GHANA

(US$ million, unless otherwise indicated)

	2008	2014	2015	2016	2017	2018
Summary external debt data by debtor type						
Total External debt stocks	**4,712**	**17,839**	**20,105**	**21,166**	**22,354**	**23,315**
Use of IMF Credit	259	1,120	1,242	1,366	1,465	1,508
Long-term external debt	3,326	13,637	15,559	17,012	17,566	18,174
Public and publicly guaranteed sector	3,326	13,384	15,306	16,759	17,313	17,920
Public Sector	3,326	13,384	15,306	16,759	17,313	17,920
of which: General Government	3,179	12,450	14,282	15,739	16,214	16,836
Private sector guaranteed by Public Sector	..	..	..	..	..	..
Private sector not guaranteed	0	253	253	253	253	253
Short-term external debt	1,127	3,082	3,304	2,789	3,323	3,634
Disbursements (long-term)	**756**	**3,306**	**2,852**	**2,510**	**1,148**	**2,585**
Public and publicly guaranteed sector	756	3,053	2,852	2,510	1,148	2,585
Public Sector	756	3,053	2,852	2,510	1,148	2,585
of which: General Government	756	2,835	2,705	2,473	1,122	2,565
Private sector guaranteed by Public Sector	..	..	..	..	..	..
Private sector not guaranteed	..	253	..	..	..	..
Principal repayments (long-term)	**137**	**450**	**558**	**848**	**1,063**	**1,774**
Public and publicly guaranteed sector	137	450	558	848	1,063	1,774
Public Sector	137	450	558	848	1,063	1,774
of which: General Government	114	432	544	835	1,053	1,767
Private sector guaranteed by Public Sector	..	..	..	..	..	..
Private sector not guaranteed	..	..	..	..	..	..
Interest payments (long-term)	**66**	**255**	**336**	**554**	**745**	**676**
Public and publicly guaranteed sector	66	255	330	548	739	669
Public Sector	66	255	330	548	739	669
of which: General Government	56	248	322	539	730	661
Private sector guaranteed by Public Sector	..	..	..	..	..	..
Private sector not guaranteed	..	..	6	6	6	6
Summary external debt stock by creditor type						
Long-term External debt stocks	**3,326**	**13,637**	**15,559**	**17,012**	**17,566**	**18,174**
Public and publicly guaranteed debt from:	3,326	13,384	15,306	16,759	17,313	17,920
Official creditors	2,591	8,147	8,775	8,781	9,305	8,974
Multilateral	1,899	4,157	4,579	4,728	5,386	5,362
of which: World Bank	1,330	2,946	3,285	3,415	3,945	3,926
Bilateral	691	3,990	4,195	4,052	3,919	3,612
Private creditors	735	5,237	6,531	7,978	8,008	8,946
Bondholders	..	2,000	3,000	3,750	3,750	5,048
Commercial banks and others	735	3,237	3,531	4,228	4,258	3,898
Private nonguaranteed debt from:	0	253	253	253	253	253
Bondholders	0	253	253	253	253	253
Commercial banks and others	..	..	..	..	..	..
Use of IMF Credit	259	1,120	1,242	1,366	1,465	1,508
Net financial inflows						
Net debt inflows						
Use of IMF Credit	0	-32	172	166	18	78
Long-term	619	2,856	2,294	1,662	84	810
Official creditors	537	1,007	883	180	168	-170
Multilateral	387	336	596	282	402	91
of which: World Bank	256	296	474	235	323	75
Bilateral	149	672	288	-102	-233	-261
Private creditors	83	1,849	1,411	1,482	-84	980
Bondholders	..	1,253	1,000	750	0	1,298
Banks and other private	83	596	411	732	-84	-318
Short-term	-73	-509	230	-503	409	290
Net equity inflows						
Foreign direct investment	1,429	3,363	3,192	3,485	3,255	2,989
Portfolio equity	..	..	..	..	..	..
Debt ratios						
External debt stocks to exports (%)	66	116	119	120	108	..
External debt stocks to GNI (%)	17	34	41	39	39	36
Debt service to exports (%)	3	5	6	9	9	..
Short-term to external debt stocks (%)	24	17	16	13	15	16
Multilateral to external debt stocks (%)	40	23	23	22	24	23
Reserves to external debt stocks (%)	38	29	27	26	30	25
Gross national income (GNI)	28,411	51,863	48,530	53,962	57,430	64,270

GRENADA

(US$ million, unless otherwise indicated)

	2008	2014	2015	2016	2017	2018
Summary external debt data by debtor type						
Total External debt stocks	**538.9**	**637.7**	**597.7**	**597.1**	**537.4**	**644.9**
Use of IMF Credit	14.4	45.7	44.8	43.9	44.5	38.6
Long-term external debt	460.3	513.0	533.9	526.4	470.9	488.6
Public and publicly guaranteed sector	460.3	513.0	533.9	526.4	470.9	488.6
Public Sector	460.3	513.0	533.9	526.4	470.9	488.6
of which: General Government	457.7	511.5	532.8	525.6	470.5	488.6
Private sector guaranteed by Public Sector	..	..	..	..	..	..
Private sector not guaranteed	..	..	..	..	..	..
Short-term external debt	64.2	79.0	19.0	26.8	22.0	117.7
Disbursements (long-term)	**34.8**	**35.3**	**50.6**	**21.3**	**13.8**	**51.9**
Public and publicly guaranteed sector	34.8	35.3	50.6	21.3	13.8	51.9
Public Sector	34.8	35.3	50.6	21.3	13.8	51.9
of which: General Government	34.3	35.3	50.6	21.3	13.8	51.9
Private sector guaranteed by Public Sector	..	..	..	..	..	..
Private sector not guaranteed	..	..	..	..	..	..
Principal repayments (long-term)	**8.9**	**12.0**	**16.4**	**24.3**	**30.5**	**31.7**
Public and publicly guaranteed sector	8.9	12.0	16.4	24.3	30.5	31.7
Public Sector	8.9	12.0	16.4	24.3	30.5	31.7
of which: General Government	8.6	11.6	16.0	24.0	30.1	31.3
Private sector guaranteed by Public Sector	..	..	..	..	..	..
Private sector not guaranteed	..	..	..	..	..	..
Interest payments (long-term)	**8.1**	**6.0**	**5.9**	**18.4**	**20.5**	**16.2**
Public and publicly guaranteed sector	8.1	6.0	5.9	18.4	20.5	16.2
Public Sector	8.1	6.0	5.9	18.4	20.5	16.2
of which: General Government	8.0	6.0	5.9	18.3	20.5	16.2
Private sector guaranteed by Public Sector	..	..	..	..	..	..
Private sector not guaranteed	..	..	..	..	..	..
Summary external debt stock by creditor type						
Long-term External debt stocks	**460.3**	**513.0**	**533.9**	**526.4**	**470.9**	**488.6**
Public and publicly guaranteed debt from:	460.3	513.0	533.9	526.4	470.9	488.6
Official creditors	257.4	316.1	346.4	350.6	353.0	379.8
Multilateral	169.0	209.7	244.3	251.0	256.0	278.6
of which: World Bank	48.1	74.7	89.8	89.5	102.0	131.1
Bilateral	88.4	106.4	102.1	99.6	97.0	101.1
Private creditors	202.8	196.9	187.4	175.7	117.8	108.8
Bondholders	193.2	193.2	184.8	175.4	117.5	108.5
Commercial banks and others	9.6	3.7	2.6	0.3	0.3	0.3
Private nonguaranteed debt from:	..	..	..	..	..	..
Bondholders	..	..	..	..	..	..
Commercial banks and others	..	..	..	..	..	..
Use of IMF Credit	14.4	45.7	44.8	43.9	44.5	38.6
Net financial inflows						
Net debt inflows						
Use of IMF Credit	5.6	3.4	1.1	0.5	-2.0	-4.9
Long-term	25.9	23.3	34.2	-3.1	-16.7	20.2
Official creditors	25.9	23.3	35.3	6.3	-7.7	29.2
Multilateral	20.6	21.8	37.8	9.2	-0.4	24.8
of which: World Bank	1.7	15.0	18.1	2.1	7.3	31.3
Bilateral	5.3	1.5	-2.5	-2.9	-7.4	4.3
Private creditors	..	..	-1.1	-9.4	-9.0	-9.0
Bondholders	..	..	..	-9.4	-9.0	-9.0
Banks and other private	..	..	-1.1	..	..	0.0
Short-term	20.0	20.9	-9.0	5.9	-5.3	95.2
Net equity inflows						
Foreign direct investment	115.7	84.4	157.8	93.4	110.1	143.4
Portfolio equity	..	0.0	0.0	0.0	0.0	..
Debt ratios						
External debt stocks to exports (%)	249.6	130.4	115.0	111.1	89.9	97.4
External debt stocks to GNI (%)	68.8	77.0	67.7	61.9	52.6	58.8
Debt service to exports (%)	9.9	4.3	5.2	8.9	9.4	8.4
Short-term to external debt stocks (%)	11.9	12.4	3.2	4.5	4.1	18.3
Multilateral to external debt stocks (%)	31.4	32.9	40.9	42.0	47.6	43.2
Reserves to external debt stocks (%)	19.5	26.7	33.1	34.8	37.1	36.3
Gross national income (GNI)	783.3	828.7	882.8	964.6	1,022.4	1,096.3

GUATEMALA

(US$ million, unless otherwise indicated)

	2008	2014	2015	2016	2017	2018
Summary external debt data by debtor type						
Total External debt stocks	**13,823**	**19,512**	**20,378**	**21,480**	**22,972**	**22,349**
Use of IMF Credit	43	291	278	270	286	279
Long-term external debt	11,629	18,270	19,256	20,289	21,643	21,155
Public and publicly guaranteed sector	4,385	7,000	7,544	8,148	8,366	8,428
Public Sector	4,385	7,000	7,544	8,148	8,366	8,428
of which: General Government	3,899	6,655	7,237	7,878	8,134	8,234
Private sector guaranteed by Public Sector	..	..	..	..	..	..
Private sector not guaranteed	7,245	11,270	11,711	12,142	13,277	12,727
Short-term external debt	2,151	951	844	920	1,042	914
Disbursements (long-term)	**958**	**3,318**	**2,423**	**3,212**	**4,554**	**2,699**
Public and publicly guaranteed sector	396	290	906	953	662	406
Public Sector	396	290	906	953	662	406
of which: General Government	366	290	906	953	662	406
Private sector guaranteed by Public Sector	..	..	..	..	..	..
Private sector not guaranteed	562	3,028	1,516	2,260	3,893	2,293
Principal repayments (long-term)	**917**	**1,240**	**1,424**	**2,116**	**3,225**	**3,182**
Public and publicly guaranteed sector	260	311	350	352	457	342
Public Sector	260	311	350	352	457	342
of which: General Government	257	274	312	314	419	305
Private sector guaranteed by Public Sector	..	..	..	..	..	..
Private sector not guaranteed	656	928	1,074	1,765	2,768	2,839
Interest payments (long-term)	**621**	**719**	**676**	**953**	**950**	**752**
Public and publicly guaranteed sector	257	280	288	354	376	267
Public Sector	257	280	288	354	376	267
of which: General Government	227	260	271	338	362	255
Private sector guaranteed by Public Sector	..	..	..	..	..	..
Private sector not guaranteed	365	439	388	600	574	485
Summary external debt stock by creditor type						
Long-term External debt stocks	**11,629**	**18,270**	**19,256**	**20,289**	**21,643**	**21,155**
Public and publicly guaranteed debt from:	4,385	7,000	7,544	8,148	8,366	8,428
Official creditors	3,427	5,247	5,783	5,684	5,406	5,470
Multilateral	3,062	4,850	5,353	5,197	4,911	4,977
of which: World Bank	806	1,497	1,765	1,679	1,555	1,718
Bilateral	366	397	430	486	496	493
Private creditors	957	1,753	1,762	2,464	2,960	2,958
Bondholders	955	1,730	1,730	2,430	2,930	2,930
Commercial banks and others	2	23	32	34	30	28
Private nonguaranteed debt from:	7,245	11,270	11,711	12,142	13,277	12,727
Bondholders	55	1,155	1,150	1,500	2,330	2,330
Commercial banks and others	7,190	10,115	10,561	10,642	10,947	10,397
Use of IMF Credit	43	291	278	270	286	279
Net financial inflows						
Net debt inflows						
Use of IMF Credit	..	0	..	..	..	..
Long-term	41	2,078	998	1,096	1,329	-483
Official creditors	136	-22	548	-101	-290	65
Multilateral	160	-141	508	-154	-289	68
of which: World Bank	66	-52	269	-86	-124	163
Bilateral	-24	119	39	53	-1	-2
Private creditors	-95	2,100	451	1,197	1,620	-548
Bondholders	5	800	-5	1,050	1,330	..
Banks and other private	-100	1,300	456	147	290	-548
Short-term	147	6	-107	76	122	-129
Net equity inflows						
Foreign direct investment	679	958	1,673	1,135	931	1,041
Portfolio equity	85	-6	-34	..	..	..
Debt ratios						
External debt stocks to exports (%)	131	136	144	154	157	151
External debt stocks to GNI (%)	36	34	33	32	31	29
Debt service to exports (%)	15	14	15	22	29	27
Short-term to external debt stocks (%)	16	5	4	4	5	4
Multilateral to external debt stocks (%)	22	25	26	24	21	22
Reserves to external debt stocks (%)	32	36	37	41	50	55
Gross national income (GNI)	38,297	57,315	62,369	67,156	74,257	77,150

GUINEA

(US$ million, unless otherwise indicated)

	2008	2014	2015	2016	2017	2018
Summary external debt data by debtor type						
Total External debt stocks	**3,412**	**1,420**	**1,389**	**1,381**	**1,491**	**1,699**
Use of IMF Credit	98	321	340	379	426	464
Long-term external debt	3,172	1,017	930	911	947	1,083
Public and publicly guaranteed sector	3,172	1,017	930	911	947	1,083
Public Sector	3,172	1,017	930	911	947	1,083
of which: General Government	2,820	898	826	816	847	989
Private sector guaranteed by Public Sector	..	..	..	..	..	..
Private sector not guaranteed	..	..	..	..	..	..
Short-term external debt	142	82	119	90	118	152
Disbursements (long-term)	**63**	**99**	**22**	**52**	**40**	**194**
Public and publicly guaranteed sector	63	99	22	52	40	194
Public Sector	63	99	22	52	40	194
of which: General Government	48	99	22	52	40	190
Private sector guaranteed by Public Sector	..	..	..	..	..	..
Private sector not guaranteed	..	..	..	..	..	..
Principal repayments (long-term)	**100**	**64**	**58**	**52**	**52**	**38**
Public and publicly guaranteed sector	100	64	58	52	52	38
Public Sector	100	64	58	52	52	38
of which: General Government	91	57	52	46	46	32
Private sector guaranteed by Public Sector	..	..	..	..	..	..
Private sector not guaranteed	..	..	..	..	..	..
Interest payments (long-term)	**33**	**12**	**10**	**10**	**10**	**11**
Public and publicly guaranteed sector	33	12	10	10	10	11
Public Sector	33	12	10	10	10	11
of which: General Government	20	8	7	7	7	8
Private sector guaranteed by Public Sector	..	..	..	..	..	..
Private sector not guaranteed	..	..	..	..	..	..
Summary external debt stock by creditor type						
Long-term External debt stocks	**3,172**	**1,017**	**930**	**911**	**947**	**1,083**
Public and publicly guaranteed debt from:	3,172	1,017	930	911	947	1,083
Official creditors	3,008	950	880	873	917	1,053
Multilateral	1,912	649	609	615	657	754
of which: World Bank	1,288	197	186	222	252	344
Bilateral	1,096	301	270	258	260	300
Private creditors	165	67	50	38	30	29
Bondholders	146	55	38	26	18	17
Commercial banks and others	18	12	12	12	12	12
Private nonguaranteed debt from:	..	..	..	..	..	..
Bondholders	..	..	..	..	..	..
Commercial banks and others	..	..	..	..	..	..
Use of IMF Credit	98	321	340	379	426	464
Net financial inflows						
Net debt inflows						
Use of IMF Credit	8	96	33	51	24	49
Long-term	-37	35	-36	0	-11	156
Official creditors	-23	48	-25	11	0	156
Multilateral	-8	60	-13	20	9	111
of which: World Bank	-3	39	-2	43	17	98
Bilateral	-14	-12	-12	-9	-9	45
Private creditors	-15	-13	-11	-11	-11	..
Bondholders	-15	-13	-11	-11	-11	..
Banks and other private	..	0	..	0	..	..
Short-term	48	-35	39	-28	28	34
Net equity inflows						
Foreign direct investment	379	32	9	3	40	483
Portfolio equity	0	0	-2	0	1	..
Debt ratios						
External debt stocks to exports (%)	235	66	73	55	32	41
External debt stocks to GNI (%)	53	17	16	16	15	16
Debt service to exports (%)	11	4	5	3	1	1
Short-term to external debt stocks (%)	4	6	9	7	8	9
Multilateral to external debt stocks (%)	56	46	44	45	44	44
Reserves to external debt stocks (%)	1	69	41	58	63	68
Gross national income (GNI)	6,445	8,490	8,535	8,450	9,864	10,372

GUINEA-BISSAU

(US$ million, unless otherwise indicated)

	2008	2014	2015	2016	2017	2018
Summary external debt data by debtor type						
Total External debt stocks	**1,099.3**	**271.4**	**314.8**	**295.2**	**343.0**	**420.7**
Use of IMF Credit	10.5	35.3	37.7	42.5	51.6	52.6
Long-term external debt	942.4	203.2	223.8	219.9	257.5	325.6
Public and publicly guaranteed sector	942.4	203.2	223.8	219.9	257.5	325.6
Public Sector	942.4	203.2	223.8	219.9	257.5	325.6
of which: General Government	931.8	203.2	223.8	219.9	257.5	325.6
Private sector guaranteed by Public Sector	..	..	..	..	..	..
Private sector not guaranteed	..	..	..	..	..	..
Short-term external debt	146.5	32.9	53.3	32.8	33.9	42.5
Disbursements (long-term)	**7.6**	**2.5**	**29.7**	**4.6**	**59.0**	**77.6**
Public and publicly guaranteed sector	7.6	2.5	29.7	4.6	59.0	77.6
Public Sector	7.6	2.5	29.7	4.6	59.0	77.6
of which: General Government	7.6	2.5	29.7	4.6	59.0	77.6
Private sector guaranteed by Public Sector	..	..	..	..	..	..
Private sector not guaranteed	..	..	..	..	..	..
Principal repayments (long-term)	**4.1**	**2.5**	**2.4**	**4.9**	**5.0**	**3.8**
Public and publicly guaranteed sector	4.1	2.5	2.4	4.9	5.0	3.8
Public Sector	4.1	2.5	2.4	4.9	5.0	3.8
of which: General Government	3.8	2.5	2.4	4.9	5.0	3.8
Private sector guaranteed by Public Sector	..	..	..	..	..	..
Private sector not guaranteed	..	..	..	..	..	..
Interest payments (long-term)	**3.4**	**0.9**	**0.8**	**0.9**	**1.0**	**2.0**
Public and publicly guaranteed sector	3.4	0.9	0.8	0.9	1.0	2.0
Public Sector	3.4	0.9	0.8	0.9	1.0	2.0
of which: General Government	3.3	0.9	0.8	0.9	1.0	2.0
Private sector guaranteed by Public Sector	..	..	..	..	..	..
Private sector not guaranteed	..	..	..	..	..	..
Summary external debt stock by creditor type						
Long-term External debt stocks	**942.4**	**203.2**	**223.8**	**219.9**	**257.5**	**325.6**
Public and publicly guaranteed debt from:	942.4	203.2	223.8	219.9	257.5	325.6
Official creditors	942.4	203.2	223.8	219.9	257.5	325.6
Multilateral	519.8	101.7	123.3	119.7	150.2	213.0
of which: World Bank	308.7	53.1	53.0	54.1	67.0	111.1
Bilateral	422.6	101.5	100.5	100.2	107.3	112.6
Private creditors	..	..	..	..	..	..
Bondholders	..	..	..	..	..	..
Commercial banks and others	..	..	..	..	..	..
Private nonguaranteed debt from:	..	..	..	..	..	..
Bondholders	..	..	..	..	..	..
Commercial banks and others	..	..	..	..	..	..
Use of IMF Credit	10.5	35.3	37.7	42.5	51.6	52.6
Net financial inflows						
Net debt inflows						
Use of IMF Credit	3.6	5.4	4.0	6.1	6.4	2.2
Long-term	3.5	0.0	27.3	-0.2	54.0	73.8
Official creditors	3.5	0.0	27.3	-0.2	54.0	73.7
Multilateral	3.5	0.1	27.4	-0.2	47.3	68.4
of which: World Bank	3.1	1.2	2.2	2.8	9.4	46.1
Bilateral	..	-0.1	-0.1	-0.1	6.8	5.4
Private creditors	..	..	..	..	..	..
Bondholders	..	..	..	..	..	..
Banks and other private	..	..	..	..	..	..
Short-term	-5.0	0.0	20.7	-20.4	1.0	8.7
Net equity inflows						
Foreign direct investment	5.1	28.9	18.6	14.2	15.7	17.3
Portfolio equity	..	-0.1	..	..	..	..
Debt ratios						
External debt stocks to exports (%)	638.8	98.4	92.0	135.5	81.5	..
External debt stocks to GNI (%)	129.2	24.9	29.3	24.4	25.4	28.9
Debt service to exports (%)	5.7	1.2	1.0	3.1	1.9	..
Short-term to external debt stocks (%)	13.3	12.1	16.9	11.1	9.9	10.1
Multilateral to external debt stocks (%)	47.3	37.5	39.2	40.5	43.8	50.6
Reserves to external debt stocks (%)	11.3	105.7	105.5	..	..	..
Gross national income (GNI)	851.1	1,090.8	1,073.4	1,207.9	1,349.6	1,456.1

GUYANA

(US$ million, unless otherwise indicated)

	2008	2014	2015	2016	2017	2018
Summary external debt data by debtor type						
Total External debt stocks	**990.5**	**2,341.9**	**1,636.9**	**1,643.9**	**1,582.9**	**1,609.1**
Use of IMF Credit	79.5	139.6	124.5	117.1	124.0	121.1
Long-term external debt	675.2	1,283.3	1,201.3	1,283.6	1,342.6	1,362.9
Public and publicly guaranteed sector	675.2	1,098.3	1,031.3	1,049.0	1,135.0	1,205.9
Public Sector	675.2	1,098.3	1,031.3	1,049.0	1,135.0	1,205.9
of which: General Government	610.5	1,061.6	995.1	1,013.2	1,099.3	1,170.6
Private sector guaranteed by Public Sector	..	..	..	..	..	..
Private sector not guaranteed	0.0	185.1	170.0	234.5	207.7	157.0
Short-term external debt	235.8	919.0	311.1	243.2	116.2	125.1
Disbursements (long-term)	**138.4**	**353.6**	**73.9**	**140.9**	**109.4**	**137.6**
Public and publicly guaranteed sector	138.4	168.6	73.9	60.9	109.4	137.6
Public Sector	138.4	168.6	73.9	60.9	109.4	137.6
of which: General Government	138.4	168.6	73.9	60.9	109.4	137.6
Private sector guaranteed by Public Sector	..	..	..	..	..	..
Private sector not guaranteed	..	185.0	..	80.0	..	..
Principal repayments (long-term)	**16.1**	**23.5**	**43.7**	**47.7**	**65.6**	**105.5**
Public and publicly guaranteed sector	16.1	23.5	28.7	32.2	38.7	54.8
Public Sector	16.1	23.5	28.7	32.2	38.7	54.8
of which: General Government	11.2	23.3	28.4	31.9	38.4	54.5
Private sector guaranteed by Public Sector	..	..	..	..	..	..
Private sector not guaranteed	..	..	15.0	15.5	26.9	50.7
Interest payments (long-term)	**10.3**	**15.9**	**16.9**	**28.2**	**31.6**	**33.5**
Public and publicly guaranteed sector	10.3	15.9	16.9	17.5	19.1	22.1
Public Sector	10.3	15.9	16.9	17.5	19.1	22.1
of which: General Government	10.2	15.8	16.8	17.4	19.0	22.0
Private sector guaranteed by Public Sector	..	..	..	..	..	..
Private sector not guaranteed	..	..	..	10.7	12.5	11.3
Summary external debt stock by creditor type						
Long-term External debt stocks	**675.2**	**1,283.3**	**1,201.3**	**1,283.6**	**1,342.6**	**1,362.9**
Public and publicly guaranteed debt from:	675.2	1,098.3	1,031.3	1,049.0	1,135.0	1,205.9
Official creditors	658.8	1,081.9	1,014.9	1,032.8	1,101.4	1,173.1
Multilateral	381.1	678.5	688.4	693.8	725.5	787.9
of which: World Bank	9.8	14.2	20.4	25.0	35.6	75.5
Bilateral	277.7	403.4	326.6	339.0	375.9	385.2
Private creditors	16.4	16.4	16.4	16.2	33.6	32.8
Bondholders	0.0	0.0	0.0	0.0	0.0	0.0
Commercial banks and others	16.4	16.3	16.3	16.2	33.5	32.8
Private nonguaranteed debt from:	0.0	185.1	170.0	234.5	207.7	157.0
Bondholders	..	..	..	..	..	..
Commercial banks and others	0.0	185.1	170.0	234.5	207.7	157.0
Use of IMF Credit	79.5	139.6	124.5	117.1	124.0	121.1
Net financial inflows						
Net debt inflows						
Use of IMF Credit	0.0	-11.3	-9.1	-3.9	..	..
Long-term	122.3	330.0	30.3	93.3	43.8	32.1
Official creditors	122.3	145.0	45.3	28.8	53.4	83.5
Multilateral	46.9	25.4	26.1	6.9	26.3	64.4
of which: World Bank	-0.1	2.2	6.9	5.4	8.7	41.1
Bilateral	75.4	119.7	19.1	21.9	27.0	19.1
Private creditors	..	185.0	-15.0	64.5	-9.6	-51.4
Bondholders	..	0.0	..	..	..	..
Banks and other private	..	185.0	-15.0	64.5	-9.6	-51.4
Short-term	50.0	-103.3	-608.2	-80.3	-121.7	5.7
Net equity inflows						
Foreign direct investment	34.4	32.5	113.4	25.6	212.2	494.8
Portfolio equity	..	..	0.0	0.0	..	..
Debt ratios						
External debt stocks to exports (%)	93.9	166.9	119.8	99.7	..	..
External debt stocks to GNI (%)	51.3	76.8	51.6	46.9	44.3	44.6
Debt service to exports (%)	2.5	4.3	5.3	5.0	..	..
Short-term to external debt stocks (%)	23.8	39.2	19.0	14.8	7.3	7.8
Multilateral to external debt stocks (%)	38.5	29.0	42.1	42.2	45.8	49.0
Reserves to external debt stocks (%)	35.9	28.5	32.5	35.3	35.7	32.2
Gross national income (GNI)	1,931.6	3,050.9	3,172.6	3,508.7	3,576.1	3,609.8

HAITI

(US$ million, unless otherwise indicated)

	2008	2014	2015	2016	2017	2018
Summary external debt data by debtor type						
Total External debt stocks	**1,964**	**1,952**	**2,096**	**2,168**	**2,170**	**2,213**
Use of IMF Credit	126	177	178	216	213	201
Long-term external debt	1,838	1,774	1,915	1,951	1,955	2,012
Public and publicly guaranteed sector	1,838	1,773	1,914	1,947	1,954	2,012
Public Sector	1,838	1,773	1,914	1,947	1,954	2,012
of which: General Government	1,728	1,734	1,877	1,913	1,923	1,987
Private sector guaranteed by Public Sector	..	..	..	..	..	..
Private sector not guaranteed	..	1	1	4	1	0
Short-term external debt	0	1	4	1	2	0
Disbursements (long-term)	**348**	**408**	**173**	**106**	**16**	**1**
Public and publicly guaranteed sector	348	408	173	102	16	1
Public Sector	348	408	173	102	16	1
of which: General Government	348	408	173	102	16	..
Private sector guaranteed by Public Sector	..	..	..	..	..	..
Private sector not guaranteed	..	..	..	4	..	..
Principal repayments (long-term)	**34**	**21**	**27**	**68**	**9**	**8**
Public and publicly guaranteed sector	34	19	27	67	6	8
Public Sector	34	19	27	67	6	8
of which: General Government	29	19	25	64	3	5
Private sector guaranteed by Public Sector	..	..	..	..	..	..
Private sector not guaranteed	..	2	0	0	4	0
Interest payments (long-term)	**23**	**5**	**8**	**19**	**5**	**4**
Public and publicly guaranteed sector	23	5	8	19	5	4
Public Sector	23	5	8	19	5	4
of which: General Government	21	5	8	18	4	3
Private sector guaranteed by Public Sector	..	..	..	..	..	..
Private sector not guaranteed	..	0	0	0	0	0
Summary external debt stock by creditor type						
Long-term External debt stocks	**1,838**	**1,774**	**1,915**	**1,951**	**1,955**	**2,012**
Public and publicly guaranteed debt from:	1,838	1,773	1,914	1,947	1,954	2,012
Official creditors	1,788	1,728	1,868	1,901	1,909	1,969
Multilateral	1,329	79	81	89	101	99
of which: World Bank	507	..	..	..	..	..
Bilateral	460	1,649	1,787	1,812	1,808	1,870
Private creditors	50	45	45	45	45	43
Bondholders	..	..	..	..	..	..
Commercial banks and others	50	45	45	45	45	43
Private nonguaranteed debt from:	..	1	1	4	1	0
Bondholders	..	..	..	..	..	..
Commercial banks and others	..	1	1	4	1	0
Use of IMF Credit	126	177	178	216	213	201
Net financial inflows						
Net debt inflows						
Use of IMF Credit	50	5	10	39	-6	-10
Long-term	313	387	146	38	7	-8
Official creditors	263	392	146	35	11	-5
Multilateral	91	6	8	10	15	-2
of which: World Bank	-16	..	..	..	..	..
Bilateral	172	386	138	25	-4	-3
Private creditors	50	-4	0	4	-4	-3
Bondholders	..	..	..	..	..	..
Banks and other private	50	-4	0	4	-4	-3
Short-term	0	0	0	0	0	0
Net equity inflows						
Foreign direct investment	30	99	106	105	375	105
Portfolio equity	0	..	..	..	..	..
Debt ratios						
External debt stocks to exports (%)	208	113	116	129	136	120
External debt stocks to GNI (%)	30	22	24	27	26	23
Debt service to exports (%)	6	2	2	5	1	1
Short-term to external debt stocks (%)	0	0	0	0	0	0
Multilateral to external debt stocks (%)	68	4	4	4	5	4
Reserves to external debt stocks (%)	36	101	91	97	108	104
Gross national income (GNI)	6,554	8,825	8,765	8,023	8,462	9,711

HONDURAS

(US$ million, unless otherwise indicated)

	2008	2014	2015	2016	2017	2018
Summary external debt data by debtor type						
Total External debt stocks	**3,489**	**7,329**	**7,585**	**7,582**	**8,809**	**9,548**
Use of IMF Credit	61	185	173	166	176	172
Long-term external debt	2,963	6,640	6,921	6,976	8,140	8,672
Public and publicly guaranteed sector	2,306	5,528	5,879	6,017	7,032	7,031
Public Sector	2,306	5,528	5,879	6,017	7,032	7,031
of which: General Government	2,131	5,387	5,704	5,780	6,700	6,915
Private sector guaranteed by Public Sector	0	..	..	..	..	..
Private sector not guaranteed	657	1,112	1,042	960	1,107	1,641
Short-term external debt	466	504	491	439	493	703
Disbursements (long-term)	**649**	**900**	**1,453**	**896**	**2,598**	**2,126**
Public and publicly guaranteed sector	431	582	561	364	1,135	320
Public Sector	431	582	561	364	1,135	320
of which: General Government	415	574	513	289	1,038	318
Private sector guaranteed by Public Sector	..	..	..	..	..	..
Private sector not guaranteed	218	318	893	531	1,463	1,806
Principal repayments (long-term)	**277**	**492**	**1,059**	**791**	**1,574**	**1,784**
Public and publicly guaranteed sector	54	111	137	178	202	227
Public Sector	54	111	137	178	202	227
of which: General Government	45	106	125	166	198	220
Private sector guaranteed by Public Sector	..	..	..	..	..	..
Private sector not guaranteed	223	381	922	613	1,372	1,557
Interest payments (long-term)	**77**	**198**	**214**	**237**	**237**	**260**
Public and publicly guaranteed sector	49	178	192	217	218	242
Public Sector	49	178	192	217	218	242
of which: General Government	43	176	188	213	205	238
Private sector guaranteed by Public Sector	..	..	..	..	..	..
Private sector not guaranteed	27	20	22	20	19	18
Summary external debt stock by creditor type						
Long-term External debt stocks	**2,963**	**6,640**	**6,921**	**6,976**	**8,140**	**8,672**
Public and publicly guaranteed debt from:	2,306	5,528	5,879	6,017	7,032	7,031
Official creditors	2,254	4,282	4,650	4,824	5,160	5,127
Multilateral	1,437	3,531	3,782	3,871	4,094	4,466
of which: World Bank	449	936	965	940	985	937
Bilateral	818	751	869	953	1,066	661
Private creditors	52	1,246	1,229	1,193	1,872	1,904
Bondholders	..	1,000	1,000	1,000	1,700	1,700
Commercial banks and others	52	246	229	193	172	204
Private nonguaranteed debt from:	657	1,112	1,042	960	1,107	1,641
Bondholders	..	..	..	..	..	..
Commercial banks and others	657	1,112	1,042	960	1,107	1,641
Use of IMF Credit	61	185	173	166	176	172
Net financial inflows						
Net debt inflows						
Use of IMF Credit	0	-6	-4	-1	..	..
Long-term	372	408	394	105	1,024	341
Official creditors	378	349	428	216	267	105
Multilateral	162	368	291	120	165	149
of which: World Bank	51	91	68	1	-4	-28
Bilateral	216	-20	137	96	102	-45
Private creditors	-7	59	-34	-111	757	237
Bondholders	..	..	..	..	700	..
Banks and other private	-7	59	-34	-111	57	237
Short-term	151	-8	-13	-54	55	210
Net equity inflows						
Foreign direct investment	1,046	1,165	974	1,181	1,051	1,105
Portfolio equity	..	20	-1	-22	..	..
Debt ratios						
External debt stocks to exports (%)	70	108	109	109	117	128
External debt stocks to GNI (%)	26	41	39	38	41	43
Debt service to exports (%)	7	10	18	15	24	28
Short-term to external debt stocks (%)	13	7	6	6	6	7
Multilateral to external debt stocks (%)	41	48	50	51	46	47
Reserves to external debt stocks (%)	71	47	49	50	53	50
Gross national income (GNI)	13,269	18,013	19,408	20,059	21,305	22,203

INDIA

(US$ million, unless otherwise indicated)

	2008	2014	2015	2016	2017	2018
Summary external debt data by debtor type						
Total External debt stocks	**227,112**	**457,507**	**478,834**	**455,510**	**511,484**	**521,391**
Use of IMF Credit	1,049	5,764	5,513	5,348	5,666	5,533
Long-term external debt	182,241	366,169	391,759	366,229	408,210	411,686
Public and publicly guaranteed sector	76,316	152,515	162,314	152,982	182,926	180,508
Public Sector	76,221	152,515	162,314	152,982	182,926	180,508
of which: General Government	59,041	109,162	116,713	111,062	141,987	134,213
Private sector guaranteed by Public Sector	95	0	..	..	..	..
Private sector not guaranteed	105,925	213,654	229,445	213,248	225,284	231,179
Short-term external debt	43,821	85,574	81,563	83,933	97,609	104,171
Disbursements (long-term)	**38,712**	**130,004**	**66,345**	**41,942**	**78,142**	**52,234**
Public and publicly guaranteed sector	18,824	46,998	23,121	11,570	39,421	19,092
Public Sector	18,824	46,998	23,121	11,570	39,421	19,092
of which: General Government	16,023	32,974	12,562	6,194	33,035	7,866
Private sector guaranteed by Public Sector	0	0	..	..	..	..
Private sector not guaranteed	19,888	83,006	43,224	30,372	38,721	33,141
Principal repayments (long-term)	**23,685**	**80,786**	**38,772**	**65,971**	**38,666**	**46,229**
Public and publicly guaranteed sector	13,447	11,649	11,774	20,472	11,982	21,016
Public Sector	13,426	11,648	11,774	20,472	11,982	21,016
of which: General Government	11,954	3,374	3,746	11,409	4,189	15,244
Private sector guaranteed by Public Sector	21	1	..	..	..	..
Private sector not guaranteed	10,238	69,137	26,998	45,499	26,684	25,213
Interest payments (long-term)	**5,718**	**10,971**	**9,814**	**9,540**	**10,348**	**13,977**
Public and publicly guaranteed sector	1,524	1,841	1,899	2,105	2,153	2,617
Public Sector	1,521	1,841	1,899	2,105	2,153	2,617
of which: General Government	964	653	623	770	954	1,217
Private sector guaranteed by Public Sector	3	0	..	..	..	..
Private sector not guaranteed	4,194	9,131	7,916	7,435	8,195	11,361
Summary external debt stock by creditor type						
Long-term External debt stocks	**182,241**	**366,169**	**391,759**	**366,229**	**408,210**	**411,686**
Public and publicly guaranteed debt from:	76,316	152,515	162,314	152,982	182,926	180,508
Official creditors	62,581	71,748	71,726	73,258	78,072	81,023
Multilateral	39,409	50,660	50,462	50,789	52,976	54,165
of which: World Bank	32,794	37,238	36,509	36,348	37,234	36,464
Bilateral	23,172	21,088	21,264	22,469	25,096	26,858
Private creditors	13,735	80,767	90,588	79,724	104,854	99,485
Bondholders	4,520	50,811	59,512	53,246	81,997	73,809
Commercial banks and others	9,215	29,956	31,076	26,478	22,857	25,676
Private nonguaranteed debt from:	105,925	213,654	229,445	213,248	225,284	231,179
Bondholders	14,732	6,214	7,783	10,040	14,645	13,962
Commercial banks and others	91,193	207,440	221,661	203,208	210,639	217,216
Use of IMF Credit	1,049	5,764	5,513	5,348	5,666	5,533
Net financial inflows						
Net debt inflows						
Use of IMF Credit	..	0	..	..	..	..
Long-term	15,027	49,217	27,573	-24,029	39,476	6,005
Official creditors	2,874	2,035	1,428	1,972	2,445	3,416
Multilateral	2,359	1,361	843	1,014	885	1,747
of which: World Bank	928	487	260	506	-369	-243
Bilateral	515	674	585	958	1,560	1,668
Private creditors	12,153	47,183	26,145	-26,001	37,031	2,589
Bondholders	1,754	27,437	10,705	-3,796	33,309	-8,417
Banks and other private	10,399	19,746	15,439	-22,205	3,721	11,006
Short-term	7,728	-7,132	-4,012	2,370	13,676	6,315
Net equity inflows						
Foreign direct investment	42,690	32,354	39,663	41,987	37,098	39,396
Portfolio equity	-15,030	12,369	1,933	2,337	5,928	-4,361
Debt ratios						
External debt stocks to exports (%)	71	92	108	102	101	93
External debt stocks to GNI (%)	19	23	23	20	19	19
Debt service to exports (%)	10	19	11	17	10	11
Short-term to external debt stocks (%)	19	19	17	18	19	20
Multilateral to external debt stocks (%)	17	11	11	11	10	10
Reserves to external debt stocks (%)	109	66	70	75	76	72
Gross national income (GNI)	1,191,737	2,015,015	2,077,985	2,264,132	2,623,875	2,698,618

INDONESIA

(US$ million, unless otherwise indicated)

	2008	2014	2015	2016	2017	2018
Summary external debt data by debtor type						
Total External debt stocks	**157,916**	**292,991**	**306,224**	**319,013**	**350,133**	**369,840**
Use of IMF Credit	368	2,869	2,744	2,662	2,820	2,754
Long-term external debt	137,060	244,162	265,049	275,665	300,582	314,078
Public and publicly guaranteed sector	87,763	142,190	159,576	177,138	195,052	217,684
Public Sector	87,763	142,190	159,576	177,138	195,052	217,684
of which: General Government	84,461	122,211	135,953	154,827	175,699	185,868
Private sector guaranteed by Public Sector	..	..	..	..	..	..
Private sector not guaranteed	49,297	101,972	105,473	98,528	105,530	96,395
Short-term external debt	20,488	45,960	38,431	40,685	46,731	53,007
Disbursements (long-term)	**22,932**	**69,966**	**66,895**	**68,848**	**78,999**	**52,617**
Public and publicly guaranteed sector	9,065	28,164	27,260	26,730	27,573	31,047
Public Sector	9,065	28,164	27,260	26,730	27,573	31,047
of which: General Government	9,065	22,955	20,159	23,964	24,729	15,809
Private sector guaranteed by Public Sector	..	..	..	..	..	..
Private sector not guaranteed	13,867	41,802	39,635	42,117	51,426	21,571
Principal repayments (long-term)	**17,001**	**52,844**	**45,160**	**59,092**	**56,200**	**12,546**
Public and publicly guaranteed sector	6,779	23,903	9,026	10,029	11,772	8,087
Public Sector	6,779	23,903	9,026	10,029	11,772	8,087
of which: General Government	6,581	23,249	5,568	5,952	5,969	5,337
Private sector guaranteed by Public Sector	..	..	..	..	..	..
Private sector not guaranteed	10,221	28,941	36,134	49,063	44,427	4,458
Interest payments (long-term)	**4,461**	**8,258**	**9,770**	**10,489**	**10,745**	**9,267**
Public and publicly guaranteed sector	2,718	4,443	5,201	5,961	6,580	7,978
Public Sector	2,718	4,443	5,201	5,961	6,580	7,978
of which: General Government	2,488	3,521	4,235	4,909	5,521	7,084
Private sector guaranteed by Public Sector	..	..	..	..	..	..
Private sector not guaranteed	1,743	3,814	4,569	4,527	4,165	1,290
Summary external debt stock by creditor type						
Long-term External debt stocks	**137,060**	**244,162**	**265,049**	**275,665**	**300,582**	**314,078**
Public and publicly guaranteed debt from:	87,763	142,190	159,576	177,138	195,052	217,684
Official creditors	63,184	50,870	51,138	51,878	52,090	53,426
Multilateral	19,962	22,707	25,202	26,720	27,499	29,118
of which: World Bank	8,974	14,053	16,044	17,224	17,941	18,507
Bilateral	43,222	28,163	25,936	25,158	24,591	24,308
Private creditors	24,579	91,320	108,438	125,260	142,962	164,258
Bondholders	18,451	82,317	96,484	114,376	135,396	153,532
Commercial banks and others	6,128	9,003	11,954	10,884	7,566	10,726
Private nonguaranteed debt from:	49,297	101,972	105,473	98,528	105,530	96,395
Bondholders	6,592	13,267	14,279	13,306	14,383	15,038
Commercial banks and others	42,705	88,705	91,195	85,222	91,147	81,357
Use of IMF Credit	368	2,869	2,744	2,662	2,820	2,754
Net financial inflows						
Net debt inflows						
Use of IMF Credit	..	0	..	..	..	..
Long-term	5,932	17,122	21,736	9,755	22,800	40,072
Official creditors	-1,127	-1,811	761	-407	-847	1,344
Multilateral	922	69	2,614	1,576	659	1,663
of which: World Bank	613	733	2,060	1,221	645	594
Bilateral	-2,049	-1,880	-1,852	-1,982	-1,506	-320
Private creditors	7,059	18,933	20,974	10,162	23,647	38,728
Bondholders	3,890	3,087	15,319	17,143	21,257	19,027
Banks and other private	3,169	15,846	5,655	-6,981	2,390	19,701
Short-term	1,833	-150	-7,529	2,254	6,046	2,828
Net equity inflows						
Foreign direct investment	9,105	21,895	18,822	4,684	18,839	21,016
Portfolio equity	322	3,259	-1,547	1,319	-2,538	-3,668
Debt ratios						
External debt stocks to exports (%)	106	146	176	186	175	170
External debt stocks to GNI (%)	32	34	37	35	36	37
Debt service to exports (%)	14	31	32	41	34	11
Short-term to external debt stocks (%)	13	16	13	13	13	14
Multilateral to external debt stocks (%)	13	8	8	8	8	8
Reserves to external debt stocks (%)	31	37	34	36	36	32
Gross national income (GNI)	492,096	860,947	832,299	902,045	982,443	1,009,863

IRAN, ISLAMIC REPUBLIC OF

(US$ million, unless otherwise indicated)

	2008	2014	2015	2016	2017	2018
Summary external debt data by debtor type						
Total External debt stocks	**16,027**	**5,797**	**6,375**	**5,971**	**6,761**	**6,324**
Use of IMF Credit	376	2,066	1,976	1,917	2,031	1,983
Long-term external debt	9,052	3,299	2,380	740	531	382
Public and publicly guaranteed sector	9,052	3,299	2,380	740	531	382
Public Sector	9,049	3,299	2,380	740	531	382
of which: General Government	900	554	462	378	280	206
Private sector guaranteed by Public Sector	3	0	..	..	..	..
Private sector not guaranteed	0	0	0	0	0	0
Short-term external debt	6,599	432	2,019	3,314	4,199	3,959
Disbursements (long-term)	**804**	**0**	**2**	**24**	**99**	**0**
Public and publicly guaranteed sector	804	0	2	24	99	0
Public Sector	804	0	2	24	99	0
of which: General Government	125	0	0	0	0	0
Private sector guaranteed by Public Sector	..	0	..	..	..	..
Private sector not guaranteed	..	..	..	..	..	..
Principal repayments (long-term)	**2,167**	**471**	**703**	**1,931**	**329**	**138**
Public and publicly guaranteed sector	2,167	471	703	1,931	329	138
Public Sector	2,164	470	703	1,931	329	138
of which: General Government	80	129	91	99	99	74
Private sector guaranteed by Public Sector	3	1	..	..	..	..
Private sector not guaranteed	..	..	..	..	..	..
Interest payments (long-term)	**509**	**34**	**40**	**87**	**21**	**18**
Public and publicly guaranteed sector	509	34	40	87	21	18
Public Sector	509	34	40	87	21	18
of which: General Government	27	16	5	6	7	6
Private sector guaranteed by Public Sector	0	0	..	..	..	..
Private sector not guaranteed	..	..	..	..	..	..
Summary external debt stock by creditor type						
Long-term External debt stocks	**9,052**	**3,299**	**2,380**	**740**	**531**	**382**
Public and publicly guaranteed debt from:	9,052	3,299	2,380	740	531	382
Official creditors	2,500	965	653	498	462	358
Multilateral	761	536	454	372	284	217
of which: World Bank	761	520	438	355	271	206
Bilateral	1,739	428	199	126	177	141
Private creditors	6,551	2,334	1,727	241	70	24
Bondholders	..	..	..	..	..	..
Commercial banks and others	6,551	2,334	1,727	241	70	24
Private nonguaranteed debt from:	0	0	0	0	0	0
Bondholders	..	..	..	..	..	..
Commercial banks and others	0	0	0	0	0	0
Use of IMF Credit	376	2,066	1,976	1,917	2,031	1,983
Net financial inflows						
Net debt inflows						
Use of IMF Credit	..	..	..	..	..	..
Long-term	-1,363	-471	-702	-1,907	-229	-138
Official creditors	-43	-237	-299	-172	-46	-93
Multilateral	77	-96	-81	-83	-90	-67
of which: World Bank	77	-92	-82	-83	-84	-65
Bilateral	-120	-142	-218	-88	44	-26
Private creditors	-1,320	-234	-403	-1,735	-184	-45
Bondholders	..	..	..	..	..	..
Banks and other private	-1,320	-234	-403	-1,735	-184	-45
Short-term	-3,292	-345	1,588	1,292	886	-241
Net equity inflows						
Foreign direct investment	1,980	2,105	2,050	3,372	5,019	3,480
Portfolio equity	..	..	..	..	..	..
Debt ratios						
External debt stocks to exports (%)	15	5	6	8	7	5
External debt stocks to GNI (%)	4	1	2	1	1	..
Debt service to exports (%)	3	0	1	3	0	1
Short-term to external debt stocks (%)	41	7	32	56	62	63
Multilateral to external debt stocks (%)	5	9	7	6	4	3
Reserves to external debt stocks (%)	..	..	..	..	..	..
Gross national income (GNI)	407,406	435,771	386,850	420,281	454,858	..

JAMAICA

(US$ million, unless otherwise indicated)

	2008	2014	2015	2016	2017	2018
Summary external debt data by debtor type						
Total External debt stocks	**10,438**	**14,082**	**14,113**	**14,097**	**14,722**	**16,307**
Use of IMF Credit	63	1,046	1,025	1,103	1,152	1,074
Long-term external debt	9,116	11,567	11,597	11,363	11,874	13,240
Public and publicly guaranteed sector	6,952	7,996	9,648	9,507	9,941	9,772
Public Sector	6,950	7,996	9,648	9,507	9,941	9,772
of which: General Government	5,676	6,664	8,497	8,398	9,190	9,116
Private sector guaranteed by Public Sector	1	..	..	..	..	..
Private sector not guaranteed	2,164	3,571	1,949	1,856	1,932	3,468
Short-term external debt	1,259	1,469	1,492	1,632	1,696	1,993
Disbursements (long-term)	**707**	**1,918**	**3,322**	**1,097**	**1,184**	**1,389**
Public and publicly guaranteed sector	707	1,166	2,394	1,054	1,079	294
Public Sector	707	1,166	2,394	1,054	1,079	294
of which: General Government	670	1,110	2,373	1,018	1,073	285
Private sector guaranteed by Public Sector	..	..	..	..	..	..
Private sector not guaranteed	..	752	928	44	105	1,096
Principal repayments (long-term)	**474**	**517**	**3,246**	**1,206**	**700**	**460**
Public and publicly guaranteed sector	466	515	707	1,170	671	455
Public Sector	466	515	707	1,170	671	455
of which: General Government	363	438	508	1,093	595	352
Private sector guaranteed by Public Sector	..	..	..	..	..	..
Private sector not guaranteed	9	1	2,539	37	28	4
Interest payments (long-term)	**676**	**613**	**666**	**667**	**652**	**688**
Public and publicly guaranteed sector	483	407	427	575	558	591
Public Sector	483	407	427	575	558	591
of which: General Government	429	336	357	514	503	541
Private sector guaranteed by Public Sector	..	..	..	..	..	..
Private sector not guaranteed	193	206	239	92	94	96
Summary external debt stock by creditor type						
Long-term External debt stocks	**9,116**	**11,567**	**11,597**	**11,363**	**11,874**	**13,240**
Public and publicly guaranteed debt from:	6,952	7,996	9,648	9,507	9,941	9,772
Official creditors	2,311	3,441	3,601	3,643	3,609	3,645
Multilateral	1,342	2,695	2,878	2,967	2,922	2,940
of which: World Bank	327	754	826	809	862	865
Bilateral	969	747	723	677	687	705
Private creditors	4,641	4,555	6,047	5,863	6,332	6,126
Bondholders	4,218	4,181	5,736	5,632	6,163	6,064
Commercial banks and others	423	373	311	232	169	62
Private nonguaranteed debt from:	2,164	3,571	1,949	1,856	1,932	3,468
Bondholders	2,130	2,750	1,175	1,175	1,175	1,175
Commercial banks and others	34	821	774	681	757	2,293
Use of IMF Credit	63	1,046	1,025	1,103	1,152	1,074
Net financial inflows						
Net debt inflows						
Use of IMF Credit	..	-126	25	113	-16	-53
Long-term	233	1,402	76	-109	484	929
Official creditors	13	117	178	51	-50	42
Multilateral	69	116	189	90	-49	18
of which: World Bank	-34	-25	72	-16	53	3
Bilateral	-56	1	-11	-39	-1	24
Private creditors	220	1,284	-102	-160	534	887
Bondholders	212	555	-20	-90	532	-99
Banks and other private	8	729	-82	-70	3	987
Short-term	-259	23	45	110	62	296
Net equity inflows						
Foreign direct investment	1,322	582	925	928	888	775
Portfolio equity	0	138	72	33	251	181
Debt ratios						
External debt stocks to exports (%)	173	300	305	299	284	268
External debt stocks to GNI (%)	80	104	104	105	103	108
Debt service to exports (%)	20	33	88	41	27	20
Short-term to external debt stocks (%)	12	10	11	12	12	12
Multilateral to external debt stocks (%)	13	19	20	21	20	18
Reserves to external debt stocks (%)	17	18	21	23	26	22
Gross national income (GNI)	13,118	13,487	13,631	13,395	14,280	15,097

JORDAN

(US$ million, unless otherwise indicated)

	2008	2014	2015	2016	2017	2018
Summary external debt data by debtor type						
Total External debt stocks	**13,969**	**24,283**	**25,739**	**27,239**	**30,151**	**32,045**
Use of IMF Credit	54	1,593	2,070	1,820	1,500	981
Long-term external debt	5,319	11,802	13,362	14,950	17,718	19,553
Public and publicly guaranteed sector	5,126	9,689	10,995	12,635	15,258	16,482
Public Sector	4,978	9,594	10,910	12,559	15,189	16,448
of which: General Government	4,847	8,934	10,297	11,968	14,579	15,853
Private sector guaranteed by Public Sector	148	96	85	76	69	34
Private sector not guaranteed	193	2,113	2,367	2,314	2,460	3,071
Short-term external debt	8,596	10,888	10,307	10,470	10,933	11,511
Disbursements (long-term)	**330**	**2,278**	**3,261**	**3,499**	**3,226**	**2,782**
Public and publicly guaranteed sector	230	1,980	2,969	3,239	2,979	2,013
Public Sector	229	1,980	2,969	3,239	2,979	2,013
of which: General Government	188	1,890	2,958	3,230	2,934	1,884
Private sector guaranteed by Public Sector	1	0	0	0	0	0
Private sector not guaranteed	100	297	292	259	247	769
Principal repayments (long-term)	**2,430**	**911**	**1,601**	**1,652**	**670**	**760**
Public and publicly guaranteed sector	2,412	875	1,537	1,577	572	602
Public Sector	2,410	866	1,529	1,569	564	595
of which: General Government	2,394	848	1,495	1,543	526	553
Private sector guaranteed by Public Sector	1	8	8	8	8	8
Private sector not guaranteed	19	37	64	75	98	158
Interest payments (long-term)	**207**	**277**	**312**	**326**	**443**	**604**
Public and publicly guaranteed sector	200	255	283	284	388	505
Public Sector	193	250	279	281	385	502
of which: General Government	187	231	258	260	365	481
Private sector guaranteed by Public Sector	7	4	4	4	3	3
Private sector not guaranteed	7	23	29	42	55	99
Summary external debt stock by creditor type						
Long-term External debt stocks	**5,319**	**11,802**	**13,362**	**14,950**	**17,718**	**19,553**
Public and publicly guaranteed debt from:	5,126	9,689	10,995	12,635	15,258	16,482
Official creditors	4,815	5,352	5,428	6,045	6,671	7,224
Multilateral	1,956	2,919	2,881	3,290	3,443	3,790
of which: World Bank	872	1,394	1,550	1,857	1,876	2,252
Bilateral	2,859	2,433	2,547	2,755	3,229	3,435
Private creditors	311	4,337	5,567	6,590	8,586	9,258
Bondholders	145	4,223	5,458	6,444	8,429	9,115
Commercial banks and others	166	114	109	147	157	143
Private nonguaranteed debt from:	193	2,113	2,367	2,314	2,460	3,071
Bondholders	..	..	..	..	..	..
Commercial banks and others	193	2,113	2,367	2,314	2,460	3,071
Use of IMF Credit	54	1,593	2,070	1,820	1,500	981
Net financial inflows						
Net debt inflows						
Use of IMF Credit	-59	389	552	-195	-416	-493
Long-term	-2,100	1,366	1,660	1,846	2,556	2,022
Official creditors	-2,116	126	201	636	422	736
Multilateral	-27	123	6	428	95	371
of which: World Bank	-47	251	155	308	19	376
Bilateral	-2,089	3	196	209	327	365
Private creditors	16	1,240	1,459	1,210	2,134	1,286
Bondholders	..	986	1,236	986	1,986	686
Banks and other private	16	255	224	225	149	600
Short-term	1,152	14	-581	163	463	578
Net equity inflows						
Foreign direct investment	2,826	2,178	1,600	1,553	2,030	950
Portfolio equity	521	-31	15	334	-476	41
Debt ratios						
External debt stocks to exports (%)	102	148	173	190	199	199
External debt stocks to GNI (%)	62	68	69	70	74	76
Debt service to exports (%)	21	8	14	17	12	14
Short-term to external debt stocks (%)	62	45	40	38	36	36
Multilateral to external debt stocks (%)	14	12	11	12	11	12
Reserves to external debt stocks (%)	61	63	59	51	..	..
Gross national income (GNI)	22,631	35,687	37,536	38,946	40,560	42,091

KAZAKHSTAN

(US$ million, unless otherwise indicated)

	2008	2014	2015	2016	2017	2018
Summary external debt data by debtor type						
Total External debt stocks	**106,739**	**157,698**	**153,398**	**163,717**	**158,917**	**156,921**
Use of IMF Credit	529	498	476	462	489	478
Long-term external debt	96,723	147,419	146,443	156,294	150,781	148,077
Public and publicly guaranteed sector	1,915	15,124	20,114	21,425	21,295	24,181
Public Sector	1,915	15,124	20,114	21,425	21,295	24,181
of which: General Government	1,607	7,997	13,001	14,071	13,806	14,652
Private sector guaranteed by Public Sector	..	..	..	..	..	..
Private sector not guaranteed	94,808	132,295	126,329	134,869	129,486	123,896
Short-term external debt	9,487	9,781	6,478	6,961	7,647	8,365
Disbursements (long-term)	**40,803**	**39,152**	**34,595**	**30,505**	**31,525**	**33,912**
Public and publicly guaranteed sector	145	3,376	5,375	1,712	892	3,504
Public Sector	145	3,376	5,375	1,712	892	3,504
of which: General Government	117	3,364	5,375	1,454	243	1,447
Private sector guaranteed by Public Sector	..	..	..	..	..	..
Private sector not guaranteed	40,658	35,776	29,220	28,793	30,632	30,408
Principal repayments (long-term)	**29,012**	**27,854**	**31,267**	**17,415**	**24,529**	**29,807**
Public and publicly guaranteed sector	131	459	326	418	1,042	581
Public Sector	131	459	326	418	1,042	581
of which: General Government	89	448	313	401	528	565
Private sector guaranteed by Public Sector	..	..	..	..	..	..
Private sector not guaranteed	28,882	27,396	30,941	16,997	23,487	29,226
Interest payments (long-term)	**4,106**	**2,981**	**3,468**	**2,668**	**3,185**	**3,518**
Public and publicly guaranteed sector	67	406	526	801	859	902
Public Sector	67	406	526	801	859	902
of which: General Government	54	56	166	434	489	525
Private sector guaranteed by Public Sector	..	..	..	..	..	..
Private sector not guaranteed	4,039	2,576	2,942	1,866	2,325	2,617
Summary external debt stock by creditor type						
Long-term External debt stocks	**96,723**	**147,419**	**146,443**	**156,294**	**150,781**	**148,077**
Public and publicly guaranteed debt from:	1,915	15,124	20,114	21,425	21,295	24,181
Official creditors	1,912	5,689	6,679	7,990	8,361	8,372
Multilateral	748	5,058	6,094	7,175	6,925	6,638
of which: World Bank	463	3,429	3,261	4,313	4,185	3,977
Bilateral	1,164	631	585	815	1,435	1,734
Private creditors	3	9,435	13,435	13,435	12,935	15,810
Bondholders	..	9,435	13,435	13,435	12,935	15,810
Commercial banks and others	3	..	..	..	..	..
Private nonguaranteed debt from:	94,808	132,295	126,329	134,869	129,486	123,896
Bondholders	24,125	13,682	6,683	6,273	9,272	7,908
Commercial banks and others	70,682	118,613	119,647	128,596	120,213	115,988
Use of IMF Credit	529	498	476	462	489	478
Net financial inflows						
Net debt inflows						
Use of IMF Credit	..	0	..	..	..	..
Long-term	11,791	11,297	3,328	13,090	6,995	4,105
Official creditors	26	417	1,049	1,294	350	9
Multilateral	37	465	1,093	1,082	-250	-281
of which: World Bank	36	332	-168	1,053	-128	-208
Bilateral	-11	-48	-44	212	600	290
Private creditors	11,765	10,880	2,280	11,796	6,645	4,096
Bondholders	-310	6,101	-2,998	-482	1,499	2,797
Banks and other private	12,075	4,780	5,277	12,278	5,146	1,299
Short-term	-2,043	217	-3,235	310	669	692
Net equity inflows						
Foreign direct investment	6,949	4,750	1,979	9,042	5,748	2,758
Portfolio equity	-1,280	-135	6	-27	22	-1,520
Debt ratios						
External debt stocks to exports (%)	133	179	288	374	282	226
External debt stocks to GNI (%)	94	79	88	132	110	106
Debt service to exports (%)	42	35	66	46	50	48
Short-term to external debt stocks (%)	9	6	4	4	5	5
Multilateral to external debt stocks (%)	1	3	4	4	4	4
Reserves to external debt stocks (%)	17	14	13	12	11	11
Gross national income (GNI)	114,115	198,777	173,350	124,343	144,738	148,451

KENYA

(US$ million, unless otherwise indicated)

	2008	2014	2015	2016	2017	2018
Summary external debt data by debtor type						
Total External debt stocks	**7,669**	**16,900**	**19,767**	**21,694**	**26,830**	**31,511**
Use of IMF Credit	309	1,328	1,205	1,103	1,047	879
Long-term external debt	6,410	13,575	15,864	18,456	23,126	28,086
Public and publicly guaranteed sector	6,410	13,289	15,129	17,783	22,277	26,876
Public Sector	6,410	13,289	15,129	17,783	22,277	26,876
of which: General Government	5,992	12,910	14,734	17,286	21,717	26,117
Private sector guaranteed by Public Sector	..	..	..	..	..	..
Private sector not guaranteed	..	286	735	673	849	1,210
Short-term external debt	950	1,997	2,698	2,134	2,657	2,546
Disbursements (long-term)	**350**	**5,301**	**3,149**	**3,398**	**4,462**	**6,788**
Public and publicly guaranteed sector	350	5,120	2,609	3,263	4,427	6,253
Public Sector	350	5,120	2,609	3,263	4,427	6,253
of which: General Government	336	5,100	2,574	3,148	4,340	6,022
Private sector guaranteed by Public Sector	..	..	..	..	..	..
Private sector not guaranteed	..	181	540	135	34	535
Principal repayments (long-term)	**289**	**971**	**435**	**532**	**711**	**1,534**
Public and publicly guaranteed sector	289	961	344	336	570	1,366
Public Sector	289	961	344	336	570	1,366
of which: General Government	254	939	325	314	523	1,328
Private sector guaranteed by Public Sector	..	..	..	..	..	..
Private sector not guaranteed	..	10	91	196	141	168
Interest payments (long-term)	**91**	**294**	**364**	**492**	**695**	**1,018**
Public and publicly guaranteed sector	91	288	350	450	644	964
Public Sector	91	288	350	450	644	964
of which: General Government	85	282	346	448	640	960
Private sector guaranteed by Public Sector	..	..	..	..	..	..
Private sector not guaranteed	..	6	14	42	51	55
Summary external debt stock by creditor type						
Long-term External debt stocks	**6,410**	**13,575**	**15,864**	**18,456**	**23,126**	**28,086**
Public and publicly guaranteed debt from:	6,410	13,289	15,129	17,783	22,277	26,876
Official creditors	6,092	10,268	11,371	13,883	17,374	20,206
Multilateral	3,727	6,011	6,370	6,981	8,778	10,115
of which: World Bank	3,050	4,199	4,382	4,568	5,303	5,802
Bilateral	2,365	4,257	5,000	6,902	8,595	10,091
Private creditors	318	3,021	3,759	3,900	4,904	6,670
Bondholders	..	2,750	2,750	2,750	2,750	4,750
Commercial banks and others	318	271	1,009	1,150	2,154	1,920
Private nonguaranteed debt from:	..	286	735	673	849	1,210
Bondholders	..	..	..	..	..	..
Commercial banks and others	..	286	735	673	849	1,210
Use of IMF Credit	309	1,328	1,205	1,103	1,047	879
Net financial inflows						
Net debt inflows						
Use of IMF Credit	-11	-59	-66	-68	-119	-146
Long-term	61	4,330	2,714	2,866	3,751	5,254
Official creditors	70	2,029	1,507	2,775	2,896	3,093
Multilateral	150	777	615	813	1,421	1,510
of which: World Bank	104	470	365	334	455	631
Bilateral	-81	1,252	893	1,962	1,476	1,583
Private creditors	-9	2,301	1,207	91	854	2,161
Bondholders	..	2,750	..	..	..	2,000
Banks and other private	-9	-449	1,207	91	854	161
Short-term	-26	-391	696	-593	457	-132
Net equity inflows						
Foreign direct investment	23	237	90	146	198	1,626
Portfolio equity	5	954	11	23	-112	-293
Debt ratios						
External debt stocks to exports (%)	91	144	178	210	248	256
External debt stocks to GNI (%)	21	28	31	32	34	36
Debt service to exports (%)	5	12	8	11	15	23
Short-term to external debt stocks (%)	12	12	14	10	10	8
Multilateral to external debt stocks (%)	49	36	32	32	33	32
Reserves to external debt stocks (%)	38	47	38	35	27	26
Gross national income (GNI)	35,863	60,580	63,324	68,803	78,082	87,180

KOSOVO

(US$ million, unless otherwise indicated)

	2008	2014	2015	2016	2017	2018
Summary external debt data by debtor type						
Total External debt stocks	**709.9**	**2,242.3**	**2,158.3**	**2,124.8**	**2,504.2**	**2,297.2**
Use of IMF Credit	85.3	203.7	215.8	194.6	271.7	260.4
Long-term external debt	430.4	1,258.4	1,263.3	1,309.2	1,396.6	1,240.7
Public and publicly guaranteed sector	..	273.0	265.1	274.2	313.4	299.6
Public Sector	..	273.0	265.1	274.2	313.4	297.3
of which: General Government	..	261.5	248.0	239.8	263.2	249.8
Private sector guaranteed by Public Sector	..	0.0	0.0	0.0	0.0	2.3
Private sector not guaranteed	430.4	985.4	998.2	1,035.0	1,083.2	941.1
Short-term external debt	194.2	780.2	679.1	621.0	836.0	796.0
Disbursements (long-term)	**160.6**	**76.0**	**111.3**	**193.1**	**196.1**	**220.2**
Public and publicly guaranteed sector	..	22.2	33.3	36.5	24.7	20.3
Public Sector	..	22.2	33.3	36.5	24.7	18.0
of which: General Government	..	12.3	24.9	14.0	9.5	12.8
Private sector guaranteed by Public Sector	..	..	..	..	..	2.4
Private sector not guaranteed	160.6	53.8	78.0	156.6	171.4	199.9
Principal repayments (long-term)	**36.8**	**93.3**	**79.0**	**107.5**	**97.5**	**208.6**
Public and publicly guaranteed sector	..	15.2	13.9	18.7	19.8	21.6
Public Sector	..	15.2	13.9	18.7	19.8	21.6
of which: General Government	..	15.2	12.4	14.9	15.1	16.1
Private sector guaranteed by Public Sector	..	..	..	..	..	..
Private sector not guaranteed	36.8	78.1	65.2	88.8	77.6	187.0
Interest payments (long-term)	**15.3**	**43.5**	**62.1**	**55.8**	**49.8**	**55.3**
Public and publicly guaranteed sector	..	11.9	10.0	10.6	10.6	10.8
Public Sector	..	11.9	10.0	10.6	10.6	10.8
of which: General Government	..	11.6	9.3	9.6	9.2	9.2
Private sector guaranteed by Public Sector	..	..	..	..	..	..
Private sector not guaranteed	15.3	31.7	52.2	45.2	39.2	44.5
Summary external debt stock by creditor type						
Long-term External debt stocks	**430.4**	**1,258.4**	**1,263.3**	**1,309.2**	**1,396.6**	**1,240.7**
Public and publicly guaranteed debt from:	..	273.0	265.1	274.2	313.4	299.6
Official creditors	..	270.6	245.7	251.5	289.3	279.0
Multilateral	..	259.1	228.5	217.1	239.2	235.3
of which: World Bank	..	259.1	228.5	217.1	239.1	225.0
Bilateral	..	11.5	17.1	34.4	50.1	43.7
Private creditors	..	2.4	19.4	22.7	24.0	20.7
Bondholders	..	..	..	..	..	..
Commercial banks and others	..	2.4	19.4	22.7	24.0	20.7
Private nonguaranteed debt from:	430.4	985.4	998.2	1,035.0	1,083.2	941.1
Bondholders	..	..	..	..	..	..
Commercial banks and others	430.4	985.4	998.2	1,035.0	1,083.2	941.1
Use of IMF Credit	85.3	203.7	215.8	194.6	271.7	260.4
Net financial inflows						
Net debt inflows						
Use of IMF Credit	..	-14.3	21.1	-15.3	63.8	-5.0
Long-term	123.8	-17.3	32.3	85.6	98.6	11.7
Official creditors	..	4.3	1.9	13.7	6.5	1.1
Multilateral	..	-5.6	-5.1	-5.0	-3.9	5.4
of which: World Bank	..	-5.6	-5.1	-5.0	-4.0	-5.0
Bilateral	..	9.9	7.0	18.7	10.3	-4.3
Private creditors	123.8	-21.6	30.4	71.9	92.1	10.5
Bondholders	..	..	..	..	..	..
Banks and other private	123.8	-21.6	30.4	71.9	92.1	10.5
Short-term	53.6	105.2	-101.0	-58.1	215.0	-40.0
Net equity inflows						
Foreign direct investment	407.9	154.0	253.3	202.2	299.7	245.7
Portfolio equity	0.0	0.0	0.0	0.0	0.0	0.0
Debt ratios						
External debt stocks to exports (%)	62.1	114.9	130.0	116.0	112.7	95.9
External debt stocks to GNI (%)	12.0	29.7	33.0	31.2	33.7	28.5
Debt service to exports (%)	4.6	7.8	9.7	12.0	8.8	11.4
Short-term to external debt stocks (%)	27.4	34.8	31.5	29.2	33.4	34.7
Multilateral to external debt stocks (%)	0.0	11.6	10.6	10.2	9.6	10.2
Reserves to external debt stocks (%)	131.4	34.9	35.7	30.0	32.7	38.4
Gross national income (GNI)	5,927.6	7,537.9	6,543.3	6,804.2	7,421.1	8,047.8

KYRGYZ REPUBLIC

(US$ million, unless otherwise indicated)

	2008	2014	2015	2016	2017	2018
Summary external debt data by debtor type						
Total External debt stocks	**3,628**	**7,296**	**7,564**	**7,950**	**8,168**	**8,120**
Use of IMF Credit	295	308	306	302	321	285
Long-term external debt	2,942	6,675	6,906	7,286	7,491	7,375
Public and publicly guaranteed sector	1,963	3,261	3,445	3,627	3,918	3,685
Public Sector	1,963	3,261	3,445	3,627	3,918	3,685
of which: General Government	1,960	3,261	3,445	3,627	3,918	3,685
Private sector guaranteed by Public Sector	..	..	..	..	..	..
Private sector not guaranteed	980	3,414	3,461	3,659	3,573	3,689
Short-term external debt	391	313	352	362	356	460
Disbursements (long-term)	**880**	**951**	**615**	**800**	**791**	**654**
Public and publicly guaranteed sector	53	502	321	349	292	150
Public Sector	53	502	321	349	292	150
of which: General Government	53	502	321	349	292	150
Private sector guaranteed by Public Sector	..	..	..	..	..	..
Private sector not guaranteed	827	449	294	451	499	504
Principal repayments (long-term)	**261**	**310**	**320**	**341**	**668**	**692**
Public and publicly guaranteed sector	35	58	73	87	83	102
Public Sector	35	58	73	87	83	102
of which: General Government	33	58	73	87	83	102
Private sector guaranteed by Public Sector	..	..	..	..	..	..
Private sector not guaranteed	225	252	247	253	585	590
Interest payments (long-term)	**42**	**69**	**71**	**75**	**83**	**87**
Public and publicly guaranteed sector	17	42	44	47	51	54
Public Sector	17	42	44	47	51	54
of which: General Government	17	42	44	47	51	54
Private sector guaranteed by Public Sector	..	..	..	..	..	..
Private sector not guaranteed	24	28	27	28	32	33
Summary external debt stock by creditor type						
Long-term External debt stocks	**2,942**	**6,675**	**6,906**	**7,286**	**7,491**	**7,375**
Public and publicly guaranteed debt from:	1,963	3,261	3,445	3,627	3,918	3,685
Official creditors	1,963	3,261	3,445	3,627	3,918	3,685
Multilateral	1,290	1,383	1,370	1,372	1,477	1,474
of which: World Bank	655	672	652	631	667	660
Bilateral	672	1,878	2,075	2,256	2,440	2,211
Private creditors	..	..	..	..	..	..
Bondholders	..	..	..	..	..	..
Commercial banks and others	..	..	..	..	..	..
Private nonguaranteed debt from:	980	3,414	3,461	3,659	3,573	3,689
Bondholders	..	..	..	..	..	..
Commercial banks and others	980	3,414	3,461	3,659	3,573	3,689
Use of IMF Credit	295	308	306	302	321	285
Net financial inflows						
Net debt inflows						
Use of IMF Credit	19	-6	11	6	1	-29
Long-term	619	640	295	459	123	-38
Official creditors	18	444	248	262	209	49
Multilateral	23	47	47	37	22	32
of which: World Bank	9	17	9	-2	-1	8
Bilateral	-5	398	201	225	187	16
Private creditors	601	196	47	198	-86	-86
Bondholders	..	..	..	..	..	..
Banks and other private	601	196	47	198	-86	-86
Short-term	73	5	40	10	-6	104
Net equity inflows						
Foreign direct investment	178	355	890	446	-17	64
Portfolio equity	6	0	0	-1	0	0
Debt ratios						
External debt stocks to exports (%)	133	220	308	327	314	307
External debt stocks to GNI (%)	74	102	118	123	111	103
Debt service to exports (%)	12	12	17	18	30	31
Short-term to external debt stocks (%)	11	4	5	5	4	6
Multilateral to external debt stocks (%)	36	19	18	17	18	18
Reserves to external debt stocks (%)	32	25	22	23	23	21
Gross national income (GNI)	4,933	7,161	6,420	6,458	7,331	7,885

LAO PEOPLE'S DEMOCRATIC REPUBLIC

(US$ million, unless otherwise indicated)

	2008	2014	2015	2016	2017	2018
Summary external debt data by debtor type						
Total External debt stocks	**5,653**	**9,640**	**11,642**	**13,535**	**14,651**	**15,588**
Use of IMF Credit	35	73	70	68	72	70
Long-term external debt	5,469	8,743	10,873	12,745	13,834	15,113
Public and publicly guaranteed sector	3,202	5,601	6,689	7,313	8,374	9,161
Public Sector	3,202	5,601	6,689	7,313	8,374	9,161
of which: General Government	2,981	5,395	6,489	7,117	8,252	9,051
Private sector guaranteed by Public Sector	..	..	..	..	..	..
Private sector not guaranteed	2,267	3,142	4,183	5,433	5,461	5,952
Short-term external debt	149	823	699	722	745	404
Disbursements (long-term)	**813**	**1,819**	**2,517**	**2,308**	**1,332**	**1,949**
Public and publicly guaranteed sector	231	765	1,384	968	1,156	1,338
Public Sector	231	765	1,384	968	1,156	1,338
of which: General Government	227	765	1,384	968	1,156	1,277
Private sector guaranteed by Public Sector	..	..	..	..	..	..
Private sector not guaranteed	581	1,054	1,133	1,340	176	611
Principal repayments (long-term)	**149**	**227**	**238**	**326**	**491**	**581**
Public and publicly guaranteed sector	49	129	145	236	343	461
Public Sector	49	129	145	236	343	461
of which: General Government	45	124	140	231	269	389
Private sector guaranteed by Public Sector	..	..	..	..	..	..
Private sector not guaranteed	100	98	92	91	148	120
Interest payments (long-term)	**62**	**157**	**176**	**223**	**283**	**341**
Public and publicly guaranteed sector	25	94	104	138	178	223
Public Sector	25	94	104	138	178	223
of which: General Government	24	93	103	138	176	222
Private sector guaranteed by Public Sector	..	..	..	..	..	..
Private sector not guaranteed	37	63	72	85	105	118
Summary external debt stock by creditor type						
Long-term External debt stocks	**5,469**	**8,743**	**10,873**	**12,745**	**13,834**	**15,113**
Public and publicly guaranteed debt from:	3,202	5,601	6,689	7,313	8,374	9,161
Official creditors	3,202	5,282	5,759	6,105	6,705	7,326
Multilateral	1,998	1,659	1,546	1,478	1,600	1,577
of which: World Bank	685	556	511	493	582	588
Bilateral	1,204	3,622	4,214	4,627	5,106	5,749
Private creditors	..	320	930	1,208	1,669	1,835
Bondholders	..	300	838	1,082	1,484	1,596
Commercial banks and others	..	19	92	126	184	239
Private nonguaranteed debt from:	2,267	3,142	4,183	5,433	5,461	5,952
Bondholders	..	246	246	558	510	924
Commercial banks and others	2,267	2,896	3,937	4,874	4,951	5,028
Use of IMF Credit	35	73	70	68	72	70
Net financial inflows						
Net debt inflows						
Use of IMF Credit	-4	0	..	..	..	..
Long-term	664	1,592	2,280	1,982	841	1,368
Official creditors	182	466	624	447	413	707
Multilateral	41	-44	-44	-25	36	13
of which: World Bank	4	-21	-21	-4	60	19
Bilateral	141	510	668	472	376	694
Private creditors	482	1,126	1,655	1,534	429	661
Bondholders	..	403	538	560	309	521
Banks and other private	482	723	1,117	974	119	140
Short-term	-19	21	-125	23	23	-341
Net equity inflows						
Foreign direct investment	228	868	1,078	935	1,693	1,320
Portfolio equity	0	4	0	-5	-34	2
Debt ratios						
External debt stocks to exports (%)	371	232	252	260	254	245
External debt stocks to GNI (%)	109	76	85	89	92	90
Debt service to exports (%)	14	9	9	11	14	15
Short-term to external debt stocks (%)	3	9	6	5	5	3
Multilateral to external debt stocks (%)	35	17	13	11	11	10
Reserves to external debt stocks (%)	11	9	9	6	8	6
Gross national income (GNI)	5,188	12,683	13,750	15,126	15,964	17,285

LEBANON

(US$ million, unless otherwise indicated)

	2008	2014	2015	2016	2017	2018
Summary external debt data by debtor type						
Total External debt stocks	**44,018**	**64,337**	**67,707**	**70,577**	**73,993**	**79,345**
Use of IMF Credit	124	280	268	260	275	269
Long-term external debt	40,817	56,052	59,060	62,463	64,954	73,529
Public and publicly guaranteed sector	20,739	25,232	26,724	27,703	29,985	33,070
Public Sector	20,739	25,232	26,724	27,703	29,985	33,070
of which: General Government	20,739	25,232	26,724	27,703	29,985	33,070
Private sector guaranteed by Public Sector	..	..	..	..	..	..
Private sector not guaranteed	20,078	30,820	32,336	34,760	34,969	40,459
Short-term external debt	3,077	8,006	8,379	7,854	8,764	5,547
Disbursements (long-term)	**2,759**	**11,534**	**13,611**	**14,458**	**14,993**	**20,567**
Public and publicly guaranteed sector	2,759	2,016	3,962	3,651	5,152	5,717
Public Sector	2,759	2,016	3,962	3,651	5,152	5,717
of which: General Government	2,759	2,016	3,962	3,651	5,152	5,717
Private sector guaranteed by Public Sector	..	..	..	..	..	..
Private sector not guaranteed	..	9,517	9,648	10,807	9,841	14,851
Principal repayments (long-term)	**2,917**	**9,905**	**10,420**	**11,169**	**12,685**	**11,951**
Public and publicly guaranteed sector	2,857	2,285	2,288	2,627	3,031	2,590
Public Sector	2,857	2,285	2,288	2,627	3,031	2,590
of which: General Government	2,856	2,285	2,288	2,627	3,031	2,590
Private sector guaranteed by Public Sector	..	..	..	..	..	..
Private sector not guaranteed	60	7,620	8,132	8,542	9,653	9,361
Interest payments (long-term)	**1,443**	**3,400**	**3,472**	**3,658**	**3,843**	**4,265**
Public and publicly guaranteed sector	1,403	1,665	1,623	1,718	1,760	2,150
Public Sector	1,403	1,665	1,623	1,718	1,760	2,150
of which: General Government	1,403	1,665	1,623	1,718	1,760	2,150
Private sector guaranteed by Public Sector	..	..	..	..	..	..
Private sector not guaranteed	40	1,735	1,849	1,940	2,082	2,114
Summary external debt stock by creditor type						
Long-term External debt stocks	**40,817**	**56,052**	**59,060**	**62,463**	**64,954**	**73,529**
Public and publicly guaranteed debt from:	20,739	25,232	26,724	27,703	29,985	33,070
Official creditors	2,575	2,068	1,829	1,759	2,023	1,941
Multilateral	1,429	1,057	985	1,034	1,331	1,367
of which: World Bank	368	176	189	254	441	510
Bilateral	1,145	1,011	844	726	692	574
Private creditors	18,165	23,164	24,895	25,944	27,961	31,128
Bondholders	17,490	22,838	24,628	25,727	27,768	30,964
Commercial banks and others	675	326	266	217	193	164
Private nonguaranteed debt from:	20,078	30,820	32,336	34,760	34,969	40,459
Bondholders	470	700	700	500	300	600
Commercial banks and others	19,608	30,120	31,636	34,260	34,669	39,859
Use of IMF Credit	124	280	268	260	275	269
Net financial inflows						
Net debt inflows						
Use of IMF Credit	40	0	..	..	..	..
Long-term	-158	1,629	3,190	3,289	2,308	8,617
Official creditors	85	150	-124	-43	177	-52
Multilateral	-31	-115	-31	63	264	53
of which: World Bank	-76	-33	13	67	186	70
Bilateral	115	265	-93	-106	-86	-105
Private creditors	-242	1,478	3,314	3,332	2,131	8,669
Bondholders	-233	-369	1,846	1,114	1,776	3,504
Banks and other private	-9	1,848	1,468	2,218	355	5,164
Short-term	-1,206	846	373	-525	909	-3,217
Net equity inflows						
Foreign direct investment	4,333	2,859	2,158	2,568	2,558	2,880
Portfolio equity	466	220	-1,002	-135	-290	..
Debt ratios						
External debt stocks to exports (%)	177	302	310	331	343	349
External debt stocks to GNI (%)	148	135	137	140	139	145
Debt service to exports (%)	18	63	64	70	78	72
Short-term to external debt stocks (%)	7	12	12	11	12	7
Multilateral to external debt stocks (%)	3	2	1	1	2	2
Reserves to external debt stocks (%)	46	61	57	61	59	51
Gross national income (GNI)	29,660	47,719	49,465	50,421	53,354	54,679

LESOTHO

(US$ million, unless otherwise indicated)

	2008	2014	2015	2016	2017	2018
Summary external debt data by debtor type						
Total External debt stocks	**700.0**	**890.5**	**888.4**	**883.2**	**935.6**	**914.8**
Use of IMF Credit	35.4	121.0	114.6	108.3	108.1	93.8
Long-term external debt	662.6	769.3	773.8	774.8	827.5	820.5
Public and publicly guaranteed sector	662.6	769.3	773.8	774.8	827.5	820.5
Public Sector	662.6	769.3	773.8	774.8	827.5	820.5
of which: General Government	652.0	764.4	773.4	774.1	826.4	818.2
Private sector guaranteed by Public Sector	..	..	..	..	..	..
Private sector not guaranteed	..	..	..	..	..	..
Short-term external debt	2.0	0.2	0.1	0.1	0.1	0.5
Disbursements (long-term)	**49.5**	**74.0**	**70.6**	**59.6**	**38.9**	**43.7**
Public and publicly guaranteed sector	49.5	74.0	70.6	59.6	38.9	43.7
Public Sector	49.5	74.0	70.6	59.6	38.9	43.7
of which: General Government	49.5	73.8	70.4	59.3	38.5	42.5
Private sector guaranteed by Public Sector	..	..	..	..	..	..
Private sector not guaranteed	..	..	..	..	..	..
Principal repayments (long-term)	**24.5**	**28.5**	**31.3**	**40.2**	**33.2**	**31.6**
Public and publicly guaranteed sector	24.5	28.5	31.3	40.2	33.2	31.6
Public Sector	24.5	28.5	31.3	40.2	33.2	31.6
of which: General Government	20.1	28.4	27.0	40.1	33.2	31.6
Private sector guaranteed by Public Sector	..	..	..	..	..	..
Private sector not guaranteed	..	..	..	..	..	..
Interest payments (long-term)	**7.8**	**12.4**	**20.3**	**14.2**	**16.1**	**16.9**
Public and publicly guaranteed sector	7.8	12.4	20.3	14.2	16.1	16.9
Public Sector	7.8	12.4	20.3	14.2	16.1	16.9
of which: General Government	6.4	11.6	19.7	14.2	16.1	16.9
Private sector guaranteed by Public Sector	..	..	..	..	..	..
Private sector not guaranteed	..	..	..	..	..	..
Summary external debt stock by creditor type						
Long-term External debt stocks	**662.6**	**769.3**	**773.8**	**774.8**	**827.5**	**820.5**
Public and publicly guaranteed debt from:	662.6	769.3	773.8	774.8	827.5	820.5
Official creditors	650.1	760.7	770.3	771.6	824.1	817.3
Multilateral	603.4	652.0	655.8	648.5	703.5	708.1
of which: World Bank	306.0	293.2	283.7	284.1	321.4	338.3
Bilateral	46.7	108.7	114.5	123.1	120.6	109.2
Private creditors	12.5	8.6	3.5	3.2	3.5	3.1
Bondholders	..	..	..	..	..	..
Commercial banks and others	12.5	8.6	3.5	3.2	3.5	3.1
Private nonguaranteed debt from:	..	..	..	..	..	..
Bondholders	..	..	..	..	..	..
Commercial banks and others	..	..	..	..	..	..
Use of IMF Credit	35.4	121.0	114.6	108.3	108.1	93.8
Net financial inflows						
Net debt inflows						
Use of IMF Credit	-5.0	-1.6	-1.1	-3.0	-6.5	-11.9
Long-term	25.0	45.5	39.3	19.4	5.7	12.1
Official creditors	28.2	45.8	43.7	19.6	5.8	12.3
Multilateral	15.4	25.1	33.9	7.5	12.3	21.1
of which: World Bank	9.9	1.9	2.4	8.7	20.9	24.6
Bilateral	12.8	20.6	9.8	12.1	-6.4	-8.8
Private creditors	-3.2	-0.3	-4.4	-0.2	-0.2	-0.2
Bondholders	..	..	..	..	..	..
Banks and other private	-3.2	-0.3	-4.4	-0.2	-0.2	-0.2
Short-term	0.0	0.0	0.0	0.0	0.0	0.0
Net equity inflows						
Foreign direct investment	62.4	2.2	-40.4	-35.0	-34.0	-38.5
Portfolio equity	0.0	0.3	0.3	0.2	0.2	0.3
Debt ratios						
External debt stocks to exports (%)	41.6	64.6	62.2	64.7	61.3	53.8
External debt stocks to GNI (%)	29.4	30.8	31.8	33.7	32.3	29.2
Debt service to exports (%)	2.2	3.1	3.7	4.2	3.7	3.6
Short-term to external debt stocks (%)	0.3	0.0	0.0	0.0	0.0	0.1
Multilateral to external debt stocks (%)	86.2	73.2	73.8	73.4	75.2	77.4
Reserves to external debt stocks (%)	138.8	120.3	112.3	104.8	70.3	79.6
Gross national income (GNI)	2,384.2	2,893.2	2,789.7	2,623.2	2,896.3	3,130.2

LIBERIA

(US$ million, unless otherwise indicated)

	2008	2014	2015	2016	2017	2018
Summary external debt data by debtor type						
Total External debt stocks	**3,160.8**	**686.5**	**845.6**	**970.2**	**1,146.8**	**1,255.9**
Use of IMF Credit	890.3	327.2	332.1	359.4	401.8	389.5
Long-term external debt	865.0	359.2	513.4	610.8	745.0	866.4
Public and publicly guaranteed sector	865.0	301.2	442.4	545.9	686.2	815.3
Public Sector	865.0	301.2	442.4	545.9	686.2	815.3
of which: General Government	837.2	301.2	442.4	545.9	686.2	815.3
Private sector guaranteed by Public Sector	..	..	..	..	..	..
Private sector not guaranteed	..	58.0	71.0	64.9	58.8	51.2
Short-term external debt	1,405.5	0.0	0.0	0.0	0.0	0.0
Disbursements (long-term)	**0.0**	**143.9**	**168.6**	**115.0**	**116.4**	**156.8**
Public and publicly guaranteed sector	0.0	85.9	152.6	115.0	116.4	156.8
Public Sector	0.0	85.9	152.6	115.0	116.4	156.8
of which: General Government	0.0	85.9	152.6	115.0	116.4	156.8
Private sector guaranteed by Public Sector	..	..	..	..	..	..
Private sector not guaranteed	..	58.0	16.0	..	..	..
Principal repayments (long-term)	**37.5**	**5.6**	**5.4**	**7.7**	**6.8**	**21.9**
Public and publicly guaranteed sector	37.5	5.6	2.4	1.6	0.6	14.2
Public Sector	37.5	5.6	2.4	1.6	0.6	14.2
of which: General Government	37.4	5.6	2.4	1.6	0.6	14.2
Private sector guaranteed by Public Sector	..	..	..	..	..	..
Private sector not guaranteed	..	..	3.0	6.1	6.1	7.6
Interest payments (long-term)	**69.0**	**8.6**	**3.9**	**4.3**	**5.8**	**8.6**
Public and publicly guaranteed sector	69.0	8.6	2.7	3.1	4.9	7.6
Public Sector	69.0	8.6	2.7	3.1	4.9	7.6
of which: General Government	64.5	7.4	2.7	3.1	4.9	7.6
Private sector guaranteed by Public Sector	..	..	..	..	..	..
Private sector not guaranteed	..	..	1.1	1.2	0.9	1.0
Summary external debt stock by creditor type						
Long-term External debt stocks	**865.0**	**359.2**	**513.4**	**610.8**	**745.0**	**866.4**
Public and publicly guaranteed debt from:	865.0	301.2	442.4	545.9	686.2	815.3
Official creditors	669.8	301.2	442.4	545.9	686.2	815.3
Multilateral	157.9	187.6	328.0	413.2	532.8	621.2
of which: World Bank	72.0	102.3	164.3	231.3	306.4	367.6
Bilateral	511.9	113.6	114.4	132.7	153.3	194.1
Private creditors	195.2	..	..	..	..	0.0
Bondholders	..	..	..	..	..	..
Commercial banks and others	195.2	..	..	..	..	0.0
Private nonguaranteed debt from:	..	58.0	71.0	64.9	58.8	51.2
Bondholders	..	..	..	..	..	..
Commercial banks and others	..	58.0	71.0	64.9	58.8	51.2
Use of IMF Credit	890.3	327.2	332.1	359.4	401.8	389.5
Net financial inflows						
Net debt inflows						
Use of IMF Credit	528.5	57.1	19.4	38.5	20.5	-3.0
Long-term	-37.5	138.3	163.2	107.3	109.6	134.9
Official creditors	-37.5	80.3	150.2	113.4	115.7	142.6
Multilateral	-37.5	81.7	150.1	95.0	95.8	99.7
of which: World Bank	-4.3	48.9	67.2	74.3	59.6	69.3
Bilateral	0.0	-1.4	0.1	18.4	20.0	42.9
Private creditors	..	58.0	13.0	-6.1	-6.1	-7.6
Bondholders	..	..	..	..	..	..
Banks and other private	..	58.0	13.0	-6.1	-6.1	-7.6
Short-term	0.0	0.0	0.0	0.0	0.0	0.0
Net equity inflows						
Foreign direct investment	11.3	409.1	53.1	141.7	188.4	122.2
Portfolio equity	0.0	6.1	0.0	0.0	0.0	..
Debt ratios						
External debt stocks to exports (%)	404.7	94.2	162.2	244.4	255.0	..
External debt stocks to GNI (%)	201.8	24.4	29.2	32.4	38.4	44.7
Debt service to exports (%)	119.7	2.4	8.7	3.1	2.8	..
Short-term to external debt stocks (%)	44.5	0.0	0.0	0.0	0.0	0.0
Multilateral to external debt stocks (%)	5.0	27.3	38.8	42.6	46.5	49.5
Reserves to external debt stocks (%)	5.1	72.7	61.8	54.6	41.4	..
Gross national income (GNI)	1,566.4	2,811.0	2,897.0	2,996.8	2,982.6	2,812.0

MADAGASCAR

(US$ million, unless otherwise indicated)

	2008	2014	2015	2016	2017	2018
Summary external debt data by debtor type						
Total External debt stocks	**2,533**	**2,962**	**3,007**	**2,976**	**3,382**	**3,716**
Use of IMF Credit	129	267	281	301	440	465
Long-term external debt	1,791	2,410	2,522	2,470	2,765	2,980
Public and publicly guaranteed sector	1,770	2,404	2,509	2,465	2,735	2,888
Public Sector	1,767	2,404	2,509	2,465	2,735	2,888
of which: General Government	1,754	2,378	2,422	2,387	2,670	2,824
Private sector guaranteed by Public Sector	3	..	..	..	..	..
Private sector not guaranteed	21	5	13	5	30	92
Short-term external debt	613	286	204	204	177	271
Disbursements (long-term)	**345**	**243**	**323**	**133**	**271**	**349**
Public and publicly guaranteed sector	342	243	323	133	245	283
Public Sector	342	243	323	133	245	283
of which: General Government	331	243	251	133	245	283
Private sector guaranteed by Public Sector	0	..	..	..	..	..
Private sector not guaranteed	3	..	..	..	26	66
Principal repayments (long-term)	**15**	**58**	**96**	**84**	**93**	**72**
Public and publicly guaranteed sector	15	56	95	76	92	72
Public Sector	14	56	95	76	92	72
of which: General Government	7	56	85	68	77	72
Private sector guaranteed by Public Sector	1	..	..	..	..	..
Private sector not guaranteed	1	1	1	8	1	..
Interest payments (long-term)	**11**	**19**	**26**	**20**	**23**	**30**
Public and publicly guaranteed sector	11	19	25	20	23	29
Public Sector	11	19	25	20	23	29
of which: General Government	10	19	25	20	22	29
Private sector guaranteed by Public Sector	0	..	..	..	..	..
Private sector not guaranteed	0	0	0	0	0	1
Summary external debt stock by creditor type						
Long-term External debt stocks	**1,791**	**2,410**	**2,522**	**2,470**	**2,765**	**2,980**
Public and publicly guaranteed debt from:	1,770	2,404	2,509	2,465	2,735	2,888
Official creditors	1,763	2,379	2,423	2,388	2,609	2,725
Multilateral	1,418	1,913	1,973	2,015	2,254	2,335
of which: World Bank	1,066	1,366	1,412	1,433	1,595	1,648
Bilateral	345	466	451	373	356	390
Private creditors	7	25	86	77	126	163
Bondholders	..	..	..	..	..	..
Commercial banks and others	7	25	86	77	126	163
Private nonguaranteed debt from:	21	5	13	5	30	92
Bondholders	..	..	..	..	..	..
Commercial banks and others	21	5	13	5	30	92
Use of IMF Credit	129	267	281	301	440	465
Net financial inflows						
Net debt inflows						
Use of IMF Credit	59	27	26	29	118	36
Long-term	330	185	227	49	178	277
Official creditors	327	187	166	65	110	171
Multilateral	293	161	133	94	133	131
of which: World Bank	210	118	106	65	77	93
Bilateral	34	26	33	-30	-23	40
Private creditors	3	-1	61	-15	68	106
Bondholders	..	..	..	..	..	..
Banks and other private	3	-1	61	-15	68	106
Short-term	-186	-50	-74	26	-26	94
Net equity inflows						
Foreign direct investment	78	38	20	31	30	36
Portfolio equity	0	0	0	0	0	..
Debt ratios						
External debt stocks to exports (%)	95	84	96	88	82	84
External debt stocks to GNI (%)	27	29	32	31	30	32
Debt service to exports (%)	1	3	4	4	3	3
Short-term to external debt stocks (%)	24	10	7	7	5	7
Multilateral to external debt stocks (%)	56	65	66	68	67	63
Reserves to external debt stocks (%)	39	26	28	40	47	47
Gross national income (GNI)	9,363	10,374	9,368	9,551	11,112	11,702

MALAWI

(US$ million, unless otherwise indicated)

	2008	2014	2015	2016	2017	2018
Summary external debt data by debtor type						
Total External debt stocks	**994.6**	**1,666.4**	**1,721.1**	**1,849.7**	**2,183.6**	**2,266.0**
Use of IMF Credit	141.6	272.5	254.7	295.9	318.9	314.1
Long-term external debt	769.0	1,372.4	1,453.8	1,509.8	1,811.1	1,928.9
Public and publicly guaranteed sector	769.0	1,372.4	1,453.8	1,509.8	1,811.1	1,928.9
Public Sector	769.0	1,372.4	1,453.8	1,509.8	1,811.1	1,928.9
of which: General Government	769.0	1,353.0	1,438.1	1,495.7	1,796.0	1,914.5
Private sector guaranteed by Public Sector	..	..	..	..	..	..
Private sector not guaranteed	..	..	..	..	..	..
Short-term external debt	84.0	21.5	12.7	44.0	53.7	23.0
Disbursements (long-term)	**65.6**	**213.0**	**175.3**	**137.6**	**256.2**	**185.6**
Public and publicly guaranteed sector	65.6	213.0	175.3	137.6	256.2	185.6
Public Sector	65.6	213.0	175.3	137.6	256.2	185.6
of which: General Government	65.6	211.5	175.3	137.6	256.2	185.6
Private sector guaranteed by Public Sector	..	..	..	..	..	..
Private sector not guaranteed	..	..	..	..	..	..
Principal repayments (long-term)	**16.7**	**26.1**	**30.3**	**32.8**	**32.7**	**27.0**
Public and publicly guaranteed sector	16.7	26.1	30.3	32.8	32.7	27.0
Public Sector	16.7	26.1	30.3	32.8	32.7	27.0
of which: General Government	16.7	23.2	28.4	31.7	31.8	27.0
Private sector guaranteed by Public Sector	..	..	..	..	..	..
Private sector not guaranteed	..	..	..	..	..	..
Interest payments (long-term)	**14.9**	**15.8**	**15.6**	**17.0**	**15.7**	**16.0**
Public and publicly guaranteed sector	14.9	15.8	15.6	17.0	15.7	16.0
Public Sector	14.9	15.8	15.6	17.0	15.7	16.0
of which: General Government	14.9	15.3	15.3	16.7	15.7	16.0
Private sector guaranteed by Public Sector	..	..	..	..	..	..
Private sector not guaranteed	..	..	..	..	..	..
Summary external debt stock by creditor type						
Long-term External debt stocks	**769.0**	**1,372.4**	**1,453.8**	**1,509.8**	**1,811.1**	**1,928.9**
Public and publicly guaranteed debt from:	769.0	1,372.4	1,453.8	1,509.8	1,811.1	1,928.9
Official creditors	763.4	1,370.3	1,453.8	1,509.8	1,811.1	1,928.9
Multilateral	486.3	933.9	1,012.9	1,090.6	1,390.6	1,495.4
of which: World Bank	187.7	501.4	588.2	642.2	862.2	916.7
Bilateral	277.1	436.4	440.9	419.1	420.4	433.5
Private creditors	5.6	2.1	0.0	..	..	..
Bondholders	..	..	..	..	..	..
Commercial banks and others	5.6	2.1	0.0	..	..	..
Private nonguaranteed debt from:	..	..	..	..	..	..
Bondholders	..	..	..	..	..	..
Commercial banks and others	..	..	..	..	..	..
Use of IMF Credit	141.6	272.5	254.7	295.9	318.9	314.1
Net financial inflows						
Net debt inflows						
Use of IMF Credit	97.0	-5.5	-6.1	50.5	5.3	2.7
Long-term	48.9	186.9	145.0	104.8	223.5	158.6
Official creditors	49.0	190.0	147.0	104.8	223.5	158.6
Multilateral	55.3	155.5	126.4	110.6	237.3	137.8
of which: World Bank	11.9	114.6	111.6	75.8	180.3	78.4
Bilateral	-6.3	34.5	20.6	-5.8	-13.7	20.8
Private creditors	-0.1	-3.1	-1.9	..	..	..
Bondholders	..	..	..	..	..	..
Banks and other private	-0.1	-3.1	-1.9	..	..	..
Short-term	23.0	0.0	-8.3	31.3	5.0	-26.0
Net equity inflows						
Foreign direct investment	145.9	378.3	279.2	194.0	154.1	101.6
Portfolio equity	-1.5	0.4	0.5	0.4	0.5	..
Debt ratios						
External debt stocks to exports (%)	96.9	101.3	111.0	151.5	174.8	..
External debt stocks to GNI (%)	18.8	28.3	27.8	34.3	34.8	32.2
Debt service to exports (%)	3.1	4.1	4.5	6.2	5.7	..
Short-term to external debt stocks (%)	8.4	1.3	0.7	2.4	2.5	1.0
Multilateral to external debt stocks (%)	48.9	56.0	58.9	59.0	63.7	66.0
Reserves to external debt stocks (%)	24.4	36.0	39.4	32.9	35.3	33.5
Gross national income (GNI)	5,298.6	5,887.2	6,200.0	5,389.7	6,279.4	7,045.7

MALDIVES

(US$ million, unless otherwise indicated)

	2008	2014	2015	2016	2017	2018
Summary external debt data by debtor type						
Total External debt stocks	**1,147**	**1,098**	**1,009**	**1,196**	**1,460**	**2,332**
Use of IMF Credit	4	15	13	12	12	11
Long-term external debt	678	936	838	1,054	1,336	2,058
Public and publicly guaranteed sector	470	747	685	937	1,249	2,003
Public Sector	452	747	685	937	1,249	1,949
of which: General Government	436	705	654	760	1,078	1,320
Private sector guaranteed by Public Sector	18	0	..	0	0	54
Private sector not guaranteed	209	189	153	117	87	55
Short-term external debt	465	146	157	130	111	263
Disbursements (long-term)	**145**	**209**	**48**	**356**	**377**	**1,013**
Public and publicly guaranteed sector	100	59	48	356	377	1,013
Public Sector	100	59	48	356	377	958
of which: General Government	99	59	42	199	350	333
Private sector guaranteed by Public Sector	..	0	..	..	..	54
Private sector not guaranteed	45	150	..	..	..	..
Principal repayments (long-term)	**62**	**158**	**118**	**119**	**139**	**275**
Public and publicly guaranteed sector	38	155	81	83	102	238
Public Sector	35	152	81	83	102	238
of which: General Government	34	61	65	72	68	71
Private sector guaranteed by Public Sector	3	3	..	..	..	0
Private sector not guaranteed	24	2	36	36	36	37
Interest payments (long-term)	**19**	**11**	**15**	**16**	**17**	**57**
Public and publicly guaranteed sector	12	11	14	14	16	55
Public Sector	11	11	14	14	16	54
of which: General Government	10	11	12	12	12	31
Private sector guaranteed by Public Sector	1	0	..	..	..	1
Private sector not guaranteed	7	1	1	1	2	2
Summary external debt stock by creditor type						
Long-term External debt stocks	**678**	**936**	**838**	**1,054**	**1,336**	**2,058**
Public and publicly guaranteed debt from:	470	747	685	937	1,249	2,003
Official creditors	372	687	625	891	949	1,537
Multilateral	273	287	269	253	276	339
of which: World Bank	79	99	93	88	90	85
Bilateral	99	400	356	639	673	1,198
Private creditors	98	60	60	46	300	466
Bondholders	..	..	..	..	250	350
Commercial banks and others	98	60	60	46	50	116
Private nonguaranteed debt from:	209	189	153	117	87	55
Bondholders	..	..	..	..	..	..
Commercial banks and others	209	189	153	117	87	55
Use of IMF Credit	4	15	13	12	12	11
Net financial inflows						
Net debt inflows						
Use of IMF Credit	-2	-6	-1	-1	-1	-1
Long-term	83	51	-69	236	239	738
Official creditors	33	-93	-38	286	24	608
Multilateral	21	-4	-9	-9	8	69
of which: World Bank	3	-2	-2	-2	-2	-3
Bilateral	12	-89	-29	295	17	539
Private creditors	50	144	-32	-50	214	130
Bondholders	..	..	..	..	250	100
Banks and other private	50	144	-32	-50	-36	30
Short-term	333	60	12	-26	-18	126
Net equity inflows						
Foreign direct investment	181	333	298	457	493	552
Portfolio equity	14	-1	2	-1	-1	0
Debt ratios						
External debt stocks to exports (%)	58	33	32	38	44	63
External debt stocks to GNI (%)	58	33	27	29	33	48
Debt service to exports (%)	5	5	4	4	5	9
Short-term to external debt stocks (%)	40	13	16	11	8	11
Multilateral to external debt stocks (%)	24	26	27	21	19	15
Reserves to external debt stocks (%)	21	57	57	40	41	31
Gross national income (GNI)	1,990	3,342	3,777	4,061	4,464	4,861

MALI

(US$ million, unless otherwise indicated)

	2008	2014	2015	2016	2017	2018
Summary external debt data by debtor type						
Total External debt stocks	**2,055**	**3,458**	**3,692**	**3,789**	**4,375**	**4,896**
Use of IMF Credit	65	264	256	288	334	441
Long-term external debt	1,984	3,137	3,354	3,420	3,947	4,344
Public and publicly guaranteed sector	1,984	3,137	3,354	3,420	3,947	4,344
Public Sector	1,984	3,137	3,354	3,420	3,947	4,344
of which: General Government	1,978	3,135	3,352	3,419	3,945	4,342
Private sector guaranteed by Public Sector	..	..	..	..	..	..
Private sector not guaranteed	..	..	..	..	..	..
Short-term external debt	7	57	82	80	94	111
Disbursements (long-term)	**234**	**304**	**453**	**244**	**386**	**708**
Public and publicly guaranteed sector	234	304	453	244	386	708
Public Sector	234	304	453	244	386	708
of which: General Government	234	304	453	244	386	708
Private sector guaranteed by Public Sector	..	..	..	..	..	..
Private sector not guaranteed	..	..	..	..	..	..
Principal repayments (long-term)	**44**	**65**	**65**	**72**	**99**	**187**
Public and publicly guaranteed sector	44	65	65	72	99	187
Public Sector	44	65	65	72	99	187
of which: General Government	43	65	65	71	99	187
Private sector guaranteed by Public Sector	..	..	..	..	..	..
Private sector not guaranteed	..	..	..	..	..	..
Interest payments (long-term)	**25**	**26**	**33**	**36**	**37**	**46**
Public and publicly guaranteed sector	25	26	33	36	37	46
Public Sector	25	26	33	36	37	46
of which: General Government	24	26	33	36	37	46
Private sector guaranteed by Public Sector	..	..	..	..	..	..
Private sector not guaranteed	..	..	..	..	..	..
Summary external debt stock by creditor type						
Long-term External debt stocks	**1,984**	**3,137**	**3,354**	**3,420**	**3,947**	**4,344**
Public and publicly guaranteed debt from:	1,984	3,137	3,354	3,420	3,947	4,344
Official creditors	1,979	3,135	3,354	3,420	3,946	4,344
Multilateral	1,148	2,388	2,490	2,505	2,936	3,228
of which: World Bank	534	1,232	1,349	1,364	1,574	1,682
Bilateral	831	747	863	915	1,011	1,116
Private creditors	5	1	1	0	0	0
Bondholders	..	..	..	..	..	..
Commercial banks and others	5	1	1	0	0	0
Private nonguaranteed debt from:	..	..	..	..	..	..
Bondholders	..	..	..	..	..	..
Commercial banks and others	..	..	..	..	..	..
Use of IMF Credit	65	264	256	288	334	441
Net financial inflows						
Net debt inflows						
Use of IMF Credit	28	4	3	41	28	116
Long-term	190	239	389	173	287	521
Official creditors	191	240	389	173	287	521
Multilateral	196	160	236	87	234	383
of which: World Bank	87	105	172	57	123	149
Bilateral	-5	79	153	86	52	138
Private creditors	-1	-1	-1	0	0	0
Bondholders	..	..	..	..	..	..
Banks and other private	-1	-1	-1	0	0	0
Short-term	0	-13	23	-3	12	19
Net equity inflows						
Foreign direct investment	268	121	92	237	365	366
Portfolio equity	-3	2	4	5	2	..
Debt ratios						
External debt stocks to exports (%)	77	104	114	112	124	..
External debt stocks to GNI (%)	22	25	29	28	29	29
Debt service to exports (%)	3	3	3	4	4	..
Short-term to external debt stocks (%)	0	2	2	2	2	2
Multilateral to external debt stocks (%)	56	69	67	66	67	66
Reserves to external debt stocks (%)	52	25	17	..	..	..
Gross national income (GNI)	9,528	13,962	12,804	13,636	15,006	16,616

MAURITANIA

(US$ million, unless otherwise indicated)

	2008	2014	2015	2016	2017	2018
Summary external debt data by debtor type						
Total External debt stocks	**2,855**	**4,365**	**4,647**	**4,786**	**4,968**	**4,984**
Use of IMF Credit	31	210	196	180	200	221
Long-term external debt	1,674	3,129	3,364	3,570	3,728	3,710
Public and publicly guaranteed sector	1,674	3,129	3,364	3,570	3,728	3,710
Public Sector	1,674	3,129	3,364	3,570	3,728	3,710
of which: General Government	1,395	2,569	2,789	3,058	3,268	3,308
Private sector guaranteed by Public Sector	..	..	..	..	..	..
Private sector not guaranteed	..	..	..	..	..	..
Short-term external debt	1,150	1,026	1,087	1,036	1,040	1,053
Disbursements (long-term)	**296**	**311**	**463**	**420**	**235**	**266**
Public and publicly guaranteed sector	296	311	463	420	235	266
Public Sector	296	311	463	420	235	266
of which: General Government	234	289	383	420	235	266
Private sector guaranteed by Public Sector	..	..	..	..	..	..
Private sector not guaranteed	..	..	..	..	..	..
Principal repayments (long-term)	**38**	**155**	**125**	**150**	**189**	**233**
Public and publicly guaranteed sector	38	155	125	150	189	233
Public Sector	38	155	125	150	189	233
of which: General Government	13	73	62	89	130	177
Private sector guaranteed by Public Sector	..	..	..	..	..	..
Private sector not guaranteed	..	..	..	..	..	..
Interest payments (long-term)	**21**	**62**	**86**	**62**	**68**	**71**
Public and publicly guaranteed sector	21	62	86	62	68	71
Public Sector	21	62	86	62	68	71
of which: General Government	14	38	41	42	49	53
Private sector guaranteed by Public Sector	..	..	..	..	..	..
Private sector not guaranteed	..	..	..	..	..	..
Summary external debt stock by creditor type						
Long-term External debt stocks	**1,674**	**3,129**	**3,364**	**3,570**	**3,728**	**3,710**
Public and publicly guaranteed debt from:	1,674	3,129	3,364	3,570	3,728	3,710
Official creditors	1,660	3,129	3,364	3,570	3,728	3,710
Multilateral	926	1,777	1,880	2,069	2,192	2,159
of which: World Bank	243	379	369	366	390	382
Bilateral	734	1,352	1,485	1,501	1,536	1,551
Private creditors	14	..	..	..	..	..
Bondholders	..	..	..	..	..	..
Commercial banks and others	14	..	..	..	..	..
Private nonguaranteed debt from:	..	..	..	..	..	..
Bondholders	..	..	..	..	..	..
Commercial banks and others	..	..	..	..	..	..
Use of IMF Credit	31	210	196	180	200	221
Net financial inflows						
Net debt inflows						
Use of IMF Credit	3	-3	-4	-10	9	26
Long-term	258	156	339	269	46	33
Official creditors	265	156	339	269	46	33
Multilateral	136	196	163	225	52	-4
of which: World Bank	43	9	6	9	2	2
Bilateral	129	-40	176	45	-6	37
Private creditors	-6	..	..	..	..	..
Bondholders	..	..	..	..	..	..
Banks and other private	-6	..	..	..	..	..
Short-term	40	-22	63	-50	4	13
Net equity inflows						
Foreign direct investment	343	503	502	271	588	71
Portfolio equity	..	0	0	..	..	..
Debt ratios						
External debt stocks to exports (%)	139	195	271	277	243	..
External debt stocks to GNI (%)	71	85	100	104	101	93
Debt service to exports (%)	3	10	13	13	13	..
Short-term to external debt stocks (%)	40	24	23	22	21	21
Multilateral to external debt stocks (%)	32	41	40	43	44	43
Reserves to external debt stocks (%)	7	14	17	17	17	18
Gross national income (GNI)	4,008	5,121	4,652	4,612	4,897	5,333

MAURITIUS

(US$ million, unless otherwise indicated)

	2008	2014	2015	2016	2017	2018
Summary external debt data by debtor type						
Total External debt stocks	**6,515**	**12,769**	**10,312**	**10,454**	**10,637**	**11,207**
Use of IMF Credit	24	140	134	130	138	135
Long-term external debt	6,491	7,296	5,439	5,707	5,314	6,279
Public and publicly guaranteed sector	597	1,812	1,718	1,628	1,547	1,430
Public Sector	597	1,812	1,718	1,628	1,547	1,430
of which: General Government	396	1,460	1,371	1,320	1,273	1,151
Private sector guaranteed by Public Sector	..	..	..	..	..	..
Private sector not guaranteed	5,893	5,484	3,721	4,079	3,766	4,849
Short-term external debt	0	5,332	4,738	4,617	5,186	4,794
Disbursements (long-term)	**2,116**	**3,881**	**2,199**	**1,830**	**2,152**	**3,846**
Public and publicly guaranteed sector	88	275	75	74	71	63
Public Sector	88	275	75	74	71	63
of which: General Government	80	245	50	73	70	18
Private sector guaranteed by Public Sector	..	..	..	..	..	..
Private sector not guaranteed	2,028	3,606	2,124	1,756	2,081	3,782
Principal repayments (long-term)	**1,266**	**5,861**	**3,979**	**1,510**	**2,637**	**2,845**
Public and publicly guaranteed sector	111	109	92	111	243	146
Public Sector	111	109	92	111	243	146
of which: General Government	35	94	68	73	204	106
Private sector guaranteed by Public Sector	..	..	..	..	..	..
Private sector not guaranteed	1,156	5,752	3,887	1,398	2,394	2,699
Interest payments (long-term)	**55**	**298**	**228**	**205**	**197**	**297**
Public and publicly guaranteed sector	25	29	27	27	30	28
Public Sector	25	29	27	27	30	28
of which: General Government	12	22	19	20	21	22
Private sector guaranteed by Public Sector	..	..	..	..	..	..
Private sector not guaranteed	30	269	201	178	167	269
Summary external debt stock by creditor type						
Long-term External debt stocks	**6,491**	**7,296**	**5,439**	**5,707**	**5,314**	**6,279**
Public and publicly guaranteed debt from:	597	1,812	1,718	1,628	1,547	1,430
Official creditors	501	1,767	1,685	1,601	1,522	1,411
Multilateral	270	959	890	877	815	757
of which: World Bank	111	324	294	271	263	231
Bilateral	231	809	795	724	706	654
Private creditors	96	45	34	28	26	19
Bondholders	..	..	..	..	..	..
Commercial banks and others	96	45	34	28	26	19
Private nonguaranteed debt from:	5,893	5,484	3,721	4,079	3,766	4,849
Bondholders	..	..	..	..	..	..
Commercial banks and others	5,893	5,484	3,721	4,079	3,766	4,849
Use of IMF Credit	24	140	134	130	138	135
Net financial inflows						
Net debt inflows						
Use of IMF Credit	..	0	..	..	..	..
Long-term	849	-1,981	-1,780	320	-485	1,000
Official creditors	5	176	-10	-33	-167	-77
Multilateral	21	118	-37	8	-108	-42
of which: World Bank	20	1	-24	-8	-26	-25
Bilateral	-17	57	27	-41	-59	-34
Private creditors	845	-2,156	-1,770	353	-318	1,077
Bondholders	..	..	..	..	..	..
Banks and other private	845	-2,156	-1,770	353	-318	1,077
Short-term	..	2,429	-594	-123	568	-389
Net equity inflows						
Foreign direct investment	378	456	216	379	443	372
Portfolio equity	34	-1,191	1,417	-3,781	3,306	-2,269
Debt ratios						
External debt stocks to exports (%)	113	89	79	75	62	81
External debt stocks to GNI (%)	64	93	81	79	73	72
Debt service to exports (%)	23	43	33	13	17	23
Short-term to external debt stocks (%)	0	42	46	44	49	43
Multilateral to external debt stocks (%)	4	8	9	8	8	7
Reserves to external debt stocks (%)	27	28	38	43	51	52
Gross national income (GNI)	10,163	13,796	12,684	13,230	14,588	15,615

MEXICO

(US$ million, unless otherwise indicated)

	2008	2014	2015	2016	2017	2018
Summary external debt data by debtor type						
Total External debt stocks	**197,672**	**442,414**	**426,905**	**422,601**	**441,577**	**452,991**
Use of IMF Credit	447	4,131	3,951	3,833	4,060	3,965
Long-term external debt	173,047	346,355	352,699	364,970	385,081	387,931
Public and publicly guaranteed sector	128,375	247,441	259,350	266,767	286,638	295,042
Public Sector	128,375	247,441	259,350	266,767	286,438	294,842
of which: General Government	53,426	181,082	180,944	176,253	185,818	191,327
Private sector guaranteed by Public Sector	1	..	..	0	200	200
Private sector not guaranteed	44,672	98,914	93,349	98,203	98,443	92,888
Short-term external debt	24,178	91,928	70,255	53,798	52,435	61,095
Disbursements (long-term)	**33,704**	**67,150**	**49,797**	**60,841**	**59,293**	**37,523**
Public and publicly guaranteed sector	24,746	41,539	27,847	40,966	34,930	25,469
Public Sector	24,746	41,539	27,847	40,966	34,730	25,469
of which: General Government	5,782	28,727	9,703	12,805	13,424	8,417
Private sector guaranteed by Public Sector	..	..	..	..	200	0
Private sector not guaranteed	8,958	25,610	21,950	19,875	24,364	12,054
Principal repayments (long-term)	**24,602**	**29,394**	**31,756**	**59,129**	**38,062**	**32,418**
Public and publicly guaranteed sector	14,867	9,001	11,704	28,382	17,513	14,906
Public Sector	14,865	9,001	11,704	28,382	17,513	14,906
of which: General Government	6,574	3,084	6,479	12,933	4,769	1,498
Private sector guaranteed by Public Sector	2	..	..	0	0	0
Private sector not guaranteed	9,735	20,393	20,052	30,747	20,550	17,512
Interest payments (long-term)	**9,975**	**15,294**	**18,789**	**17,302**	**24,909**	**22,874**
Public and publicly guaranteed sector	7,176	10,277	14,474	12,297	18,562	15,726
Public Sector	7,176	10,277	14,474	12,297	18,561	15,720
of which: General Government	4,127	7,555	11,533	8,885	14,347	10,923
Private sector guaranteed by Public Sector	0	..	..	0	2	6
Private sector not guaranteed	2,799	5,017	4,315	5,005	6,347	7,148
Summary external debt stock by creditor type						
Long-term External debt stocks	**173,047**	**346,355**	**352,699**	**364,970**	**385,081**	**387,931**
Public and publicly guaranteed debt from:	128,375	247,441	259,350	266,767	286,638	295,042
Official creditors	12,426	32,074	31,604	31,152	32,718	32,489
Multilateral	10,658	28,003	28,068	27,923	29,302	29,680
of which: World Bank	5,867	14,874	14,748	14,656	14,887	14,611
Bilateral	1,768	4,071	3,536	3,230	3,416	2,809
Private creditors	115,949	215,367	227,746	235,615	253,920	262,554
Bondholders	92,655	184,210	195,362	208,310	225,580	237,164
Commercial banks and others	23,294	31,157	32,383	27,304	28,341	25,390
Private nonguaranteed debt from:	44,672	98,914	93,349	98,203	98,443	92,888
Bondholders	19,848	84,752	77,863	78,753	80,120	74,589
Commercial banks and others	24,824	14,163	15,486	19,450	18,323	18,299
Use of IMF Credit	447	4,131	3,951	3,833	4,060	3,965
Net financial inflows						
Net debt inflows						
Use of IMF Credit	..	0	..	..	..	..
Long-term	9,102	37,756	18,041	1,712	21,231	5,105
Official creditors	1,299	1,130	244	-39	1,326	-271
Multilateral	1,490	982	679	236	1,300	273
of which: World Bank	1,343	-73	15	27	178	-278
Bilateral	-191	148	-435	-275	26	-544
Private creditors	7,803	36,626	17,797	1,751	19,905	5,376
Bondholders	5,230	38,605	16,804	15,653	20,058	7,974
Banks and other private	2,573	-1,979	993	-13,902	-153	-2,598
Short-term	-3,184	-584	-21,672	-16,457	-1,363	8,660
Net equity inflows						
Foreign direct investment	22,314	23,526	25,905	20,962	22,662	23,635
Portfolio equity	-3,492	4,834	3,601	9,477	10,320	2,421
Debt ratios						
External debt stocks to exports (%)	62	103	104	104	99	92
External debt stocks to GNI (%)	18	34	37	40	39	38
Debt service to exports (%)	11	12	13	19	15	12
Short-term to external debt stocks (%)	12	21	16	13	12	13
Multilateral to external debt stocks (%)	5	6	7	7	7	7
Reserves to external debt stocks (%)	48	43	41	41	39	38
Gross national income (GNI)	1,094,332	1,284,076	1,141,656	1,050,035	1,130,782	1,191,532

MOLDOVA

(US$ million, unless otherwise indicated)

	2008	2014	2015	2016	2017	2018
Summary external debt data by debtor type						
Total External debt stocks	**3,724**	**5,851**	**6,107**	**6,235**	**6,988**	**7,296**
Use of IMF Credit	347	699	628	574	562	496
Long-term external debt	2,019	3,677	4,255	4,313	4,756	4,891
Public and publicly guaranteed sector	805	1,027	1,072	1,212	1,442	1,450
Public Sector	805	1,027	1,072	1,212	1,442	1,450
of which: General Government	786	1,015	1,066	1,209	1,437	1,442
Private sector guaranteed by Public Sector	..	..	..	..	..	..
Private sector not guaranteed	1,214	2,650	3,183	3,101	3,315	3,441
Short-term external debt	1,358	1,475	1,224	1,348	1,670	1,910
Disbursements (long-term)	**484**	**440**	**312**	**381**	**596**	**551**
Public and publicly guaranteed sector	53	165	139	207	183	138
Public Sector	53	165	139	207	183	138
of which: General Government	43	162	139	207	180	134
Private sector guaranteed by Public Sector	..	..	..	..	..	..
Private sector not guaranteed	432	276	173	174	413	413
Principal repayments (long-term)	**391**	**456**	**312**	**265**	**249**	**375**
Public and publicly guaranteed sector	44	61	41	37	50	89
Public Sector	44	61	41	37	50	89
of which: General Government	41	54	35	34	48	88
Private sector guaranteed by Public Sector	..	..	..	..	..	..
Private sector not guaranteed	347	394	271	229	200	286
Interest payments (long-term)	**56**	**64**	**43**	**61**	**55**	**67**
Public and publicly guaranteed sector	17	17	15	15	20	22
Public Sector	17	17	15	15	20	22
of which: General Government	16	16	14	15	20	22
Private sector guaranteed by Public Sector	..	..	..	..	..	..
Private sector not guaranteed	39	47	28	45	35	44
Summary external debt stock by creditor type						
Long-term External debt stocks	**2,019**	**3,677**	**4,255**	**4,313**	**4,756**	**4,891**
Public and publicly guaranteed debt from:	805	1,027	1,072	1,212	1,442	1,450
Official creditors	790	1,001	1,050	1,189	1,417	1,425
Multilateral	504	847	876	960	1,086	1,152
of which: World Bank	440	564	570	634	696	712
Bilateral	286	154	173	229	331	273
Private creditors	15	26	22	23	25	25
Bondholders	6	..	..	..	..	..
Commercial banks and others	8	26	22	23	25	25
Private nonguaranteed debt from:	1,214	2,650	3,183	3,101	3,315	3,441
Bondholders	..	..	..	..	..	..
Commercial banks and others	1,214	2,650	3,183	3,101	3,315	3,441
Use of IMF Credit	347	699	628	574	562	496
Net financial inflows						
Net debt inflows						
Use of IMF Credit	11	-29	-41	-37	-44	-54
Long-term	94	-15	1	116	347	175
Official creditors	18	104	100	169	134	48
Multilateral	30	110	79	111	51	100
of which: World Bank	5	30	29	81	28	31
Bilateral	-13	-6	22	58	83	-52
Private creditors	76	-119	-100	-53	213	127
Bondholders	-6	..	..	..	..	..
Banks and other private	83	-119	-100	-53	213	127
Short-term	277	-358	-272	130	342	237
Net equity inflows						
Foreign direct investment	540	171	167	135	66	133
Portfolio equity	11	6	4	0	0	-1
Debt ratios						
External debt stocks to exports (%)	122	144	185	186	175	165
External debt stocks to GNI (%)	56	57	75	73	68	61
Debt service to exports (%)	17	14	13	13	11	13
Short-term to external debt stocks (%)	36	25	20	22	24	26
Multilateral to external debt stocks (%)	14	14	14	15	16	16
Reserves to external debt stocks (%)	45	37	29	35	40	41
Gross national income (GNI)	6,649	10,333	8,195	8,526	10,226	11,899

MONGOLIA

(US$ million, unless otherwise indicated)

	2008	2014	2015	2016	2017	2018
Summary external debt data by debtor type						
Total External debt stocks	**2,184**	**21,191**	**21,940**	**25,740**	**28,773**	**29,377**
Use of IMF Credit	95	73	68	66	189	287
Long-term external debt	2,019	18,743	19,437	23,086	25,422	25,992
Public and publicly guaranteed sector	1,657	3,863	3,993	5,120	7,492	7,856
Public Sector	1,657	3,863	3,993	5,120	7,492	7,856
of which: General Government	1,564	3,855	3,986	5,114	7,486	7,850
Private sector guaranteed by Public Sector	..	..	..	..	..	..
Private sector not guaranteed	362	14,881	15,444	17,965	17,929	18,135
Short-term external debt	70	2,374	2,435	2,589	3,163	3,098
Disbursements (long-term)	**435**	**2,128**	**2,066**	**5,102**	**3,976**	**8,107**
Public and publicly guaranteed sector	75	249	258	1,186	2,327	1,058
Public Sector	75	249	258	1,186	2,327	1,058
of which: General Government	75	249	258	1,186	2,327	1,058
Private sector guaranteed by Public Sector	..	..	..	..	..	..
Private sector not guaranteed	360	1,879	1,808	3,916	1,649	7,048
Principal repayments (long-term)	**41**	**872**	**1,323**	**939**	**2,928**	**6,919**
Public and publicly guaranteed sector	40	63	61	84	68	675
Public Sector	40	63	61	84	68	675
of which: General Government	40	62	61	83	68	674
Private sector guaranteed by Public Sector	..	..	..	..	..	..
Private sector not guaranteed	1	809	1,262	855	2,860	6,244
Interest payments (long-term)	**30**	**385**	**464**	**471**	**862**	**1,026**
Public and publicly guaranteed sector	24	98	95	112	217	244
Public Sector	24	98	95	112	217	244
of which: General Government	18	98	95	112	217	244
Private sector guaranteed by Public Sector	..	..	..	..	..	..
Private sector not guaranteed	6	287	369	358	644	782
Summary external debt stock by creditor type						
Long-term External debt stocks	**2,019**	**18,743**	**19,437**	**23,086**	**25,422**	**25,992**
Public and publicly guaranteed debt from:	1,657	3,863	3,993	5,120	7,492	7,856
Official creditors	1,571	2,360	2,480	2,846	3,801	4,214
Multilateral	964	1,094	1,152	1,205	1,644	1,875
of which: World Bank	338	450	434	423	579	570
Bilateral	607	1,266	1,328	1,641	2,157	2,339
Private creditors	86	1,503	1,513	2,275	3,691	3,642
Bondholders	75	1,500	1,500	2,000	3,400	3,400
Commercial banks and others	11	3	13	275	291	242
Private nonguaranteed debt from:	362	14,881	15,444	17,965	17,929	18,135
Bondholders	..	919	1,119	1,119	1,100	500
Commercial banks and others	362	13,962	14,325	16,846	16,829	17,635
Use of IMF Credit	95	73	68	66	189	287
Net financial inflows						
Net debt inflows						
Use of IMF Credit	-5	-61	-3	..	116	104
Long-term	394	1,256	743	4,163	1,049	1,188
Official creditors	38	189	186	339	848	430
Multilateral	28	23	106	85	377	260
of which: World Bank	10	6	4	2	130	5
Bilateral	10	166	80	254	472	170
Private creditors	357	1,067	557	3,824	201	757
Bondholders	..	19	200	500	781	0
Banks and other private	357	1,048	357	3,324	-581	757
Short-term	12	815	61	154	574	-64
Net equity inflows						
Foreign direct investment	828	-26	95	-399	828	799
Portfolio equity	13	-3	0	4	-10	-7
Debt ratios						
External debt stocks to exports (%)	72	345	422	454	418	370
External debt stocks to GNI (%)	40	189	203	251	293	254
Debt service to exports (%)	3	22	35	26	56	102
Short-term to external debt stocks (%)	3	11	11	10	11	11
Multilateral to external debt stocks (%)	44	5	5	5	6	6
Reserves to external debt stocks (%)	26	7	6	5	10	9
Gross national income (GNI)	5,450	11,233	10,786	10,265	9,825	11,571

MONTENEGRO

(US$ million, unless otherwise indicated)

	2008	2014	2015	2016	2017	2018
Summary external debt data by debtor type						
Total External debt stocks	**1,502**	**6,575**	**6,219**	**6,253**	**7,510**	**7,860**
Use of IMF Credit	40	37	36	35	37	36
Long-term external debt	860	6,257	5,948	6,075	7,327	7,708
Public and publicly guaranteed sector	851	2,360	2,549	2,420	2,970	3,422
Public Sector	851	2,273	2,486	2,372	2,927	3,396
of which: General Government	619	1,923	2,182	2,081	2,637	3,142
Private sector guaranteed by Public Sector	..	87	63	49	44	26
Private sector not guaranteed	9	3,897	3,399	3,655	4,356	4,286
Short-term external debt	602	280	235	143	146	116
Disbursements (long-term)	**64**	**1,012**	**1,051**	**1,391**	**1,935**	**1,958**
Public and publicly guaranteed sector	60	509	805	414	456	1,164
Public Sector	60	509	805	414	456	1,164
of which: General Government	39	457	796	384	438	1,144
Private sector guaranteed by Public Sector	..	..	..	..	..	..
Private sector not guaranteed	4	503	246	977	1,479	794
Principal repayments (long-term)	**28**	**988**	**1,125**	**1,093**	**992**	**1,449**
Public and publicly guaranteed sector	25	176	388	375	197	591
Public Sector	25	161	373	362	186	575
of which: General Government	17	124	340	327	142	527
Private sector guaranteed by Public Sector	..	15	15	13	11	17
Private sector not guaranteed	3	812	737	718	795	858
Interest payments (long-term)	**28**	**148**	**150**	**172**	**219**	**267**
Public and publicly guaranteed sector	27	94	87	88	97	104
Public Sector	27	91	85	86	95	102
of which: General Government	21	80	77	78	87	94
Private sector guaranteed by Public Sector	..	4	2	2	2	1
Private sector not guaranteed	0	53	63	84	122	163
Summary external debt stock by creditor type						
Long-term External debt stocks	**860**	**6,257**	**5,948**	**6,075**	**7,327**	**7,708**
Public and publicly guaranteed debt from:	851	2,360	2,549	2,420	2,970	3,422
Official creditors	836	1,079	1,131	1,092	1,324	1,445
Multilateral	556	728	627	593	626	567
of which: World Bank	340	354	306	280	290	261
Bilateral	281	351	504	500	698	878
Private creditors	15	1,281	1,418	1,328	1,646	1,976
Bondholders	..	786	1,043	1,138	1,295	1,394
Commercial banks and others	15	495	375	190	351	582
Private nonguaranteed debt from:	9	3,897	3,399	3,655	4,356	4,286
Bondholders	..	..	..	..	..	..
Commercial banks and others	9	3,897	3,399	3,655	4,356	4,286
Use of IMF Credit	40	37	36	35	37	36
Net financial inflows						
Net debt inflows						
Use of IMF Credit	..	..	..	..	..	..
Long-term	36	24	-73	298	943	509
Official creditors	36	-3	144	-12	132	156
Multilateral	23	-17	-32	-14	-44	-33
of which: World Bank	5	-12	-15	-17	-26	-18
Bilateral	13	14	176	2	175	188
Private creditors	0	27	-217	310	811	353
Bondholders	..	360	344	135	0	163
Banks and other private	0	-333	-561	175	811	191
Short-term	197	-236	-45	-92	2	-30
Net equity inflows						
Foreign direct investment	623	272	465	91	386	343
Portfolio equity	-6	16	10	17	14	0
Debt ratios						
External debt stocks to exports (%)	73	307	313	302	322	291
External debt stocks to GNI (%)	33	141	150	142	152	142
Debt service to exports (%)	3	53	64	61	52	64
Short-term to external debt stocks (%)	40	4	4	2	2	1
Multilateral to external debt stocks (%)	37	11	10	9	8	7
Reserves to external debt stocks (%)	29	10	12	14	14	16
Gross national income (GNI)	4,613	4,649	4,142	4,412	4,943	5,518

MOROCCO

(US$ million, unless otherwise indicated)

	2008	2014	2015	2016	2017	2018
Summary external debt data by debtor type						
Total External debt stocks	**21,005**	**42,875**	**43,070**	**46,375**	**49,796**	**49,029**
Use of IMF Credit	132	813	778	755	800	781
Long-term external debt	19,242	34,455	35,425	36,698	41,469	40,803
Public and publicly guaranteed sector	16,586	29,883	29,810	30,209	33,358	32,103
Public Sector	16,577	29,883	29,810	30,209	33,358	32,103
of which: General Government	9,537	18,644	17,893	18,540	20,451	19,536
Private sector guaranteed by Public Sector	9	..	..	..	..	..
Private sector not guaranteed	2,656	4,572	5,615	6,489	8,111	8,700
Short-term external debt	1,631	7,607	6,867	8,923	7,527	7,446
Disbursements (long-term)	**4,554**	**8,327**	**6,080**	**4,633**	**4,482**	**3,117**
Public and publicly guaranteed sector	3,093	6,239	3,730	3,040	2,969	1,655
Public Sector	3,093	6,239	3,730	3,040	2,969	1,655
of which: General Government	1,832	2,998	1,722	2,119	1,831	880
Private sector guaranteed by Public Sector	0	..	..	..	..	..
Private sector not guaranteed	1,461	2,087	2,350	1,593	1,513	1,462
Principal repayments (long-term)	**3,456**	**3,711**	**2,456**	**2,623**	**2,760**	**2,693**
Public and publicly guaranteed sector	1,800	1,871	1,652	2,067	2,352	2,010
Public Sector	1,797	1,871	1,652	2,067	2,352	2,010
of which: General Government	1,277	1,138	1,035	1,076	1,610	1,197
Private sector guaranteed by Public Sector	3	..	..	..	..	..
Private sector not guaranteed	1,656	1,841	804	557	408	682
Interest payments (long-term)	**710**	**966**	**981**	**964**	**958**	**1,031**
Public and publicly guaranteed sector	656	904	872	870	870	876
Public Sector	655	904	872	870	870	876
of which: General Government	406	559	470	461	470	464
Private sector guaranteed by Public Sector	1	..	..	..	..	..
Private sector not guaranteed	54	62	110	94	88	155
Summary external debt stock by creditor type						
Long-term External debt stocks	**19,242**	**34,455**	**35,425**	**36,698**	**41,469**	**40,803**
Public and publicly guaranteed debt from:	16,586	29,883	29,810	30,209	33,358	32,103
Official creditors	14,591	20,818	20,105	20,831	24,122	23,075
Multilateral	8,624	13,402	12,965	13,392	15,956	15,483
of which: World Bank	2,604	4,026	4,155	4,565	5,560	5,529
Bilateral	5,967	7,416	7,140	7,439	8,167	7,592
Private creditors	1,994	9,065	9,704	9,378	9,236	9,028
Bondholders	0	5,314	5,189	5,154	5,299	5,245
Commercial banks and others	1,994	3,751	4,516	4,224	3,937	3,783
Private nonguaranteed debt from:	2,656	4,572	5,615	6,489	8,111	8,700
Bondholders	..	..	..	..	..	..
Commercial banks and others	2,656	4,572	5,615	6,489	8,111	8,700
Use of IMF Credit	132	813	778	755	800	781
Net financial inflows						
Net debt inflows						
Use of IMF Credit	..	0	..	..	..	..
Long-term	1,098	4,615	3,624	2,009	1,722	425
Official creditors	1,753	1,101	929	1,164	1,299	-332
Multilateral	937	630	717	751	1,208	38
of which: World Bank	-25	277	529	521	532	146
Bilateral	817	472	212	413	91	-370
Private creditors	-656	3,514	2,695	845	423	757
Bondholders	-589	1,850	0	0	0	0
Banks and other private	-67	1,664	2,695	845	423	757
Short-term	-288	2,256	-740	2,055	-1,395	-82
Net equity inflows						
Foreign direct investment	2,423	3,134	2,240	1,626	1,952	3,008
Portfolio equity	148	..	..	-26	-33	-184
Debt ratios						
External debt stocks to exports (%)	66	117	127	132	126	112
External debt stocks to GNI (%)	23	40	43	46	46	42
Debt service to exports (%)	13	13	10	11	10	9
Short-term to external debt stocks (%)	8	18	16	19	15	15
Multilateral to external debt stocks (%)	41	31	30	29	32	32
Reserves to external debt stocks (%)	105	45	51	52	51	48
Gross national income (GNI)	92,311	107,503	99,245	101,427	107,331	116,111

MOZAMBIQUE

(US$ million, unless otherwise indicated)

	2008	2014	2015	2016	2017	2018
Summary external debt data by debtor type						
Total External debt stocks	**5,580**	**13,051**	**13,863**	**13,851**	**15,198**	**15,218**
Use of IMF Credit	183	327	399	355	343	303
Long-term external debt	4,816	12,285	12,665	12,919	13,765	13,683
Public and publicly guaranteed sector	2,874	9,614	9,940	10,131	10,924	11,058
Public Sector	2,874	9,614	9,940	10,131	10,924	11,058
of which: General Government	2,783	7,547	7,986	8,411	9,309	9,562
Private sector guaranteed by Public Sector	..	..	..	..	..	..
Private sector not guaranteed	1,942	2,671	2,725	2,788	2,840	2,626
Short-term external debt	581	439	799	577	1,090	1,231
Disbursements (long-term)	**661**	**2,661**	**1,066**	**891**	**1,653**	**2,336**
Public and publicly guaranteed sector	405	1,782	890	771	733	668
Public Sector	405	1,782	890	771	733	668
of which: General Government	395	1,257	890	771	733	668
Private sector guaranteed by Public Sector	..	..	..	..	..	..
Private sector not guaranteed	256	879	176	120	920	1,668
Principal repayments (long-term)	**373**	**428**	**391**	**351**	**1,169**	**582**
Public and publicly guaranteed sector	14	139	269	295	300	368
Public Sector	14	139	269	295	300	368
of which: General Government	14	114	160	186	191	250
Private sector guaranteed by Public Sector	..	..	..	..	..	..
Private sector not guaranteed	359	290	122	57	868	214
Interest payments (long-term)	**227**	**195**	**207**	**155**	**140**	**170**
Public and publicly guaranteed sector	20	132	156	112	121	157
Public Sector	20	132	156	112	121	157
of which: General Government	20	87	98	107	118	153
Private sector guaranteed by Public Sector	..	..	..	..	..	..
Private sector not guaranteed	207	62	51	43	20	13
Summary external debt stock by creditor type						
Long-term External debt stocks	**4,816**	**12,285**	**12,665**	**12,919**	**13,765**	**13,683**
Public and publicly guaranteed debt from:	2,874	9,614	9,940	10,131	10,924	11,058
Official creditors	2,867	7,347	7,735	8,148	9,019	9,238
Multilateral	1,664	3,377	3,591	3,725	4,085	4,224
of which: World Bank	1,149	2,285	2,461	2,555	2,822	2,904
Bilateral	1,203	3,970	4,145	4,423	4,935	5,013
Private creditors	7	2,267	2,205	1,983	1,905	1,820
Bondholders	..	850	850	727	727	727
Commercial banks and others	7	1,417	1,355	1,256	1,178	1,094
Private nonguaranteed debt from:	1,942	2,671	2,725	2,788	2,840	2,626
Bondholders	..	..	..	..	..	..
Commercial banks and others	1,942	2,671	2,725	2,788	2,840	2,626
Use of IMF Credit	183	327	399	355	343	303
Net financial inflows						
Net debt inflows						
Use of IMF Credit	0	-3	87	-33	-32	-32
Long-term	288	2,232	675	540	484	1,753
Official creditors	392	1,099	660	569	536	373
Multilateral	342	298	349	226	162	231
of which: World Bank	254	240	280	174	113	153
Bilateral	50	801	312	343	374	142
Private creditors	-103	1,133	14	-29	-52	1,380
Bondholders	..	..	..	..	..	..
Banks and other private	-103	1,133	14	-29	-52	1,380
Short-term	2	-84	280	-223	445	77
Net equity inflows						
Foreign direct investment	254	553	1,128	805	668	491
Portfolio equity	0	0	0	0	-5	0
Debt ratios						
External debt stocks to exports (%)	166	274	326	358	274	244
External debt stocks to GNI (%)	51	78	96	130	124	108
Debt service to exports (%)	18	13	15	14	25	13
Short-term to external debt stocks (%)	10	3	6	4	7	8
Multilateral to external debt stocks (%)	30	26	26	27	27	28
Reserves to external debt stocks (%)	28	23	17	15	21	20
Gross national income (GNI)	10,853	16,759	14,502	10,638	12,258	14,147

MYANMAR

(US$ million, unless otherwise indicated)

	2008	2014	2015	2016	2017	2018
Summary external debt data by debtor type						
Total External debt stocks	**8,950**	**14,349**	**14,291**	**14,149**	**15,012**	**14,936**
Use of IMF Credit	67	356	341	330	350	342
Long-term external debt	7,827	13,159	13,130	12,998	13,789	13,715
Public and publicly guaranteed sector	7,827	13,159	13,064	12,951	13,761	13,701
Public Sector	7,697	13,061	12,966	12,849	13,656	13,594
of which: General Government	1,789	4,803	4,767	5,019	5,711	6,156
Private sector guaranteed by Public Sector	131	98	98	101	105	107
Private sector not guaranteed	..	..	66	47	28	14
Short-term external debt	1,055	834	820	820	873	879
Disbursements (long-term)	**213**	**1,224**	**689**	**452**	**406**	**749**
Public and publicly guaranteed sector	213	1,224	604	452	406	749
Public Sector	213	1,224	604	452	406	749
of which: General Government	32	133	151	373	388	685
Private sector guaranteed by Public Sector	0	0	0	0	0	0
Private sector not guaranteed	..	..	85	..	..	..
Principal repayments (long-term)	**63**	**327**	**260**	**517**	**455**	**534**
Public and publicly guaranteed sector	63	327	241	498	436	519
Public Sector	63	327	241	498	436	519
of which: General Government	23	83	78	103	49	73
Private sector guaranteed by Public Sector	..	..	..	..	..	..
Private sector not guaranteed	..	..	19	19	19	14
Interest payments (long-term)	**25**	**316**	**263**	**281**	**227**	**309**
Public and publicly guaranteed sector	25	316	263	281	226	309
Public Sector	25	316	263	281	226	309
of which: General Government	3	102	98	113	53	149
Private sector guaranteed by Public Sector	..	..	..	..	..	..
Private sector not guaranteed	..	..	0	1	1	..
Summary external debt stock by creditor type						
Long-term External debt stocks	**7,827**	**13,159**	**13,130**	**12,998**	**13,789**	**13,715**
Public and publicly guaranteed debt from:	7,827	13,159	13,064	12,951	13,761	13,701
Official creditors	6,694	12,535	12,456	12,356	13,150	13,124
Multilateral	1,339	1,310	1,381	1,462	1,788	1,859
of which: World Bank	770	767	833	914	1,192	1,266
Bilateral	5,354	11,226	11,075	10,893	11,363	11,265
Private creditors	1,134	623	608	595	610	577
Bondholders	..	..	..	..	..	..
Commercial banks and others	1,134	623	608	595	610	577
Private nonguaranteed debt from:	..	..	66	47	28	14
Bondholders	..	..	..	..	..	..
Commercial banks and others	..	..	66	47	28	14
Use of IMF Credit	67	356	341	330	350	342
Net financial inflows						
Net debt inflows						
Use of IMF Credit	..	..	..	..	..	..
Long-term	150	896	429	-65	-48	216
Official creditors	150	811	362	-37	-25	258
Multilateral	3	-33	47	120	226	207
of which: World Bank	..	-8	53	108	214	181
Bilateral	146	844	316	-157	-250	51
Private creditors	0	85	66	-28	-24	-42
Bondholders	..	..	..	..	..	..
Banks and other private	0	85	66	-28	-24	-42
Short-term	..	..	..	..	..	..
Net equity inflows						
Foreign direct investment	864	2,173	4,053	3,319	3,094	3,554
Portfolio equity	..	0	0	0	0	..
Debt ratios						
External debt stocks to exports (%)	139	103	98	101	101	87
External debt stocks to GNI (%)	28	23	25	23	23	22
Debt service to exports (%)	1	5	4	6	5	5
Short-term to external debt stocks (%)	12	6	6	6	6	6
Multilateral to external debt stocks (%)	15	9	10	10	12	12
Reserves to external debt stocks (%)	42	29	30	33	33	36
Gross national income (GNI)	31,851	62,822	57,704	61,657	64,733	69,314

NEPAL

(US$ million, unless otherwise indicated)

	2008	2014	2015	2016	2017	2018
Summary external debt data by debtor type						
Total External debt stocks	**3,698**	**3,986**	**4,151**	**4,304**	**4,963**	**5,478**
Use of IMF Credit	89	165	194	171	168	156
Long-term external debt	3,551	3,488	3,608	3,755	4,374	5,070
Public and publicly guaranteed sector	3,551	3,445	3,551	3,672	4,299	4,941
Public Sector	3,551	3,445	3,551	3,672	4,299	4,941
of which: General Government	3,534	3,436	3,544	3,666	4,294	4,936
Private sector guaranteed by Public Sector	..	..	..	..	..	..
Private sector not guaranteed	..	43	57	83	75	129
Short-term external debt	57	333	349	379	421	252
Disbursements (long-term)	**103**	**255**	**428**	**430**	**599**	**920**
Public and publicly guaranteed sector	103	251	411	396	584	920
Public Sector	103	251	411	396	584	920
of which: General Government	103	251	411	396	584	920
Private sector guaranteed by Public Sector	..	..	..	..	..	..
Private sector not guaranteed	..	3	17	34	15	..
Principal repayments (long-term)	**127**	**172**	**169**	**177**	**196**	**180**
Public and publicly guaranteed sector	127	172	165	170	172	173
Public Sector	127	172	165	170	172	173
of which: General Government	125	170	164	169	172	172
Private sector guaranteed by Public Sector	..	..	..	..	..	..
Private sector not guaranteed	..	..	4	8	23	8
Interest payments (long-term)	**34**	**35**	**34**	**37**	**38**	**45**
Public and publicly guaranteed sector	34	35	33	36	36	42
Public Sector	34	35	33	36	36	42
of which: General Government	34	35	33	36	36	42
Private sector guaranteed by Public Sector	..	..	..	..	..	..
Private sector not guaranteed	..	..	1	1	2	4
Summary external debt stock by creditor type						
Long-term External debt stocks	**3,551**	**3,488**	**3,608**	**3,755**	**4,374**	**5,070**
Public and publicly guaranteed debt from:	3,551	3,445	3,551	3,672	4,299	4,941
Official creditors	3,547	3,444	3,551	3,672	4,299	4,941
Multilateral	3,187	3,103	3,213	3,313	3,888	4,435
of which: World Bank	1,507	1,517	1,640	1,708	2,022	2,477
Bilateral	360	340	337	359	411	506
Private creditors	4	1	0	0	0	0
Bondholders	..	..	..	..	..	..
Commercial banks and others	4	1	0	0	0	0
Private nonguaranteed debt from:	..	43	57	83	75	129
Bondholders	..	..	..	..	..	..
Commercial banks and others	..	43	57	83	75	129
Use of IMF Credit	89	165	194	171	168	156
Net financial inflows						
Net debt inflows						
Use of IMF Credit	0	-13	36	-18	-12	-8
Long-term	-23	83	259	253	404	740
Official creditors	-23	80	246	226	412	747
Multilateral	8	60	238	200	378	647
of which: World Bank	-8	53	185	120	211	512
Bilateral	-31	20	8	27	34	100
Private creditors	-1	3	13	26	-8	-8
Bondholders	..	..	..	..	..	..
Banks and other private	-1	3	13	26	-8	-8
Short-term	2	83	17	29	43	-170
Net equity inflows						
Foreign direct investment	-5	30	52	106	196	161
Portfolio equity	..	..	..	..	..	..
Debt ratios						
External debt stocks to exports (%)	190	142	155	167	166	..
External debt stocks to GNI (%)	29	20	19	20	20	19
Debt service to exports (%)	8	8	8	9	8	..
Short-term to external debt stocks (%)	2	8	8	9	8	5
Multilateral to external debt stocks (%)	86	78	77	77	78	81
Reserves to external debt stocks (%)	66	151	191	197	185	147
Gross national income (GNI)	12,668	20,336	21,755	21,506	25,172	29,044

NICARAGUA

(US$ million, unless otherwise indicated)

	2008	2014	2015	2016	2017	2018
Summary external debt data by debtor type						
Total External debt stocks	**4,718**	**10,078**	**10,509**	**10,985**	**11,461**	**11,618**
Use of IMF Credit	141	303	264	228	219	195
Long-term external debt	3,427	8,274	8,976	9,351	9,810	10,059
Public and publicly guaranteed sector	2,259	3,571	3,949	4,205	4,696	5,094
Public Sector	2,259	3,571	3,949	4,205	4,696	5,094
of which: General Government	1,543	2,850	3,125	3,397	3,912	4,136
Private sector guaranteed by Public Sector	0	..	..	..	..	..
Private sector not guaranteed	1,168	4,703	5,027	5,145	5,114	4,966
Short-term external debt	1,150	1,501	1,269	1,407	1,432	1,363
Disbursements (long-term)	**947**	**1,208**	**1,147**	**967**	**1,225**	**1,056**
Public and publicly guaranteed sector	184	401	385	373	539	572
Public Sector	184	401	385	373	539	572
of which: General Government	174	348	385	373	539	372
Private sector guaranteed by Public Sector	0	..	..	..	..	..
Private sector not guaranteed	763	806	763	594	685	484
Principal repayments (long-term)	**309**	**513**	**567**	**575**	**849**	**772**
Public and publicly guaranteed sector	52	63	72	89	122	136
Public Sector	52	63	72	89	122	136
of which: General Government	35	52	58	74	96	110
Private sector guaranteed by Public Sector	0	..	..	..	..	..
Private sector not guaranteed	257	449	495	486	727	636
Interest payments (long-term)	**98**	**157**	**189**	**211**	**260**	**262**
Public and publicly guaranteed sector	39	56	61	74	83	94
Public Sector	39	56	61	74	83	94
of which: General Government	29	49	57	70	79	89
Private sector guaranteed by Public Sector	0	..	..	..	..	..
Private sector not guaranteed	59	102	128	137	177	169
Summary external debt stock by creditor type						
Long-term External debt stocks	**3,427**	**8,274**	**8,976**	**9,351**	**9,810**	**10,059**
Public and publicly guaranteed debt from:	2,259	3,571	3,949	4,205	4,696	5,094
Official creditors	2,256	3,568	3,946	4,196	4,682	5,068
Multilateral	1,227	2,552	2,834	3,076	3,523	3,908
of which: World Bank	347	523	532	531	595	624
Bilateral	1,029	1,016	1,112	1,120	1,159	1,161
Private creditors	4	3	3	9	14	25
Bondholders	..	..	..	..	..	..
Commercial banks and others	4	3	3	9	14	25
Private nonguaranteed debt from:	1,168	4,703	5,027	5,145	5,114	4,966
Bondholders	..	..	..	..	..	..
Commercial banks and others	1,168	4,703	5,027	5,145	5,114	4,966
Use of IMF Credit	141	303	264	228	219	195
Net financial inflows						
Net debt inflows						
Use of IMF Credit	29	-22	-27	-29	-22	-19
Long-term	638	695	581	392	376	284
Official creditors	132	338	313	277	415	424
Multilateral	106	282	318	261	405	411
of which: World Bank	28	23	32	15	33	44
Bilateral	26	56	-5	16	10	13
Private creditors	506	357	268	115	-38	-140
Bondholders	..	..	..	..	..	..
Banks and other private	506	357	268	115	-38	-140
Short-term	-8	-197	-243	129	15	-105
Net equity inflows						
Foreign direct investment	627	884	950	899	772	359
Portfolio equity	..	..	..	..	..	..
Debt ratios						
External debt stocks to exports (%)	159	188	205	211	199	207
External debt stocks to GNI (%)	57	87	85	85	85	91
Debt service to exports (%)	14	13	15	16	20	19
Short-term to external debt stocks (%)	24	15	12	13	12	12
Multilateral to external debt stocks (%)	26	25	27	28	31	34
Reserves to external debt stocks (%)	24	23	24	22	24	19
Gross national income (GNI)	8,275	11,567	12,411	12,929	13,479	12,808

NIGER

(US$ million, unless otherwise indicated)

	2008	2014	2015	2016	2017	2018
Summary external debt data by debtor type						
Total External debt stocks	**962.3**	**2,023.3**	**2,239.5**	**2,535.0**	**3,058.9**	**3,260.0**
Use of IMF Credit	65.2	201.6	236.5	239.4	286.9	311.4
Long-term external debt	804.2	1,752.0	1,977.0	2,252.0	2,700.3	2,878.5
Public and publicly guaranteed sector	791.2	1,752.0	1,977.0	2,252.0	2,700.3	2,878.5
Public Sector	791.2	1,752.0	1,977.0	2,252.0	2,700.3	2,878.5
of which: General Government	790.7	1,752.0	1,977.0	2,252.0	2,700.3	2,878.5
Private sector guaranteed by Public Sector	..	..	..	..	..	..
Private sector not guaranteed	13.0	..	..	..	..	..
Short-term external debt	92.9	69.7	25.9	43.6	71.7	70.1
Disbursements (long-term)	**94.1**	**159.8**	**401.5**	**405.7**	**359.4**	**334.9**
Public and publicly guaranteed sector	94.1	159.8	401.5	405.7	359.4	334.9
Public Sector	94.1	159.8	401.5	405.7	359.4	334.9
of which: General Government	94.1	159.8	401.5	405.7	359.4	334.9
Private sector guaranteed by Public Sector	..	..	..	..	..	..
Private sector not guaranteed	..	..	..	..	..	..
Principal repayments (long-term)	**15.9**	**75.5**	**53.5**	**73.1**	**85.9**	**70.7**
Public and publicly guaranteed sector	9.4	75.5	53.5	73.1	85.9	70.7
Public Sector	9.4	75.5	53.5	73.1	85.9	70.7
of which: General Government	9.4	75.5	53.5	73.1	85.9	70.7
Private sector guaranteed by Public Sector	..	..	..	..	..	..
Private sector not guaranteed	6.5	..	..	..	..	..
Interest payments (long-term)	**6.9**	**29.2**	**24.1**	**31.9**	**37.5**	**43.7**
Public and publicly guaranteed sector	6.2	29.2	24.1	31.9	37.5	43.7
Public Sector	6.2	29.2	24.1	31.9	37.5	43.7
of which: General Government	6.2	29.2	24.1	31.9	37.5	43.7
Private sector guaranteed by Public Sector	..	..	..	..	..	..
Private sector not guaranteed	0.8	..	..	..	..	..
Summary external debt stock by creditor type						
Long-term External debt stocks	**804.2**	**1,752.0**	**1,977.0**	**2,252.0**	**2,700.3**	**2,878.5**
Public and publicly guaranteed debt from:	791.2	1,752.0	1,977.0	2,252.0	2,700.3	2,878.5
Official creditors	791.2	1,752.0	1,977.0	2,252.0	2,700.3	2,878.5
Multilateral	591.4	1,123.5	1,419.2	1,635.4	2,024.9	2,141.6
of which: World Bank	248.1	576.0	626.2	772.6	987.9	1,098.4
Bilateral	199.8	628.5	557.8	616.6	675.4	736.9
Private creditors	..	..	..	..	..	..
Bondholders	..	..	..	..	..	..
Commercial banks and others	..	..	..	..	..	..
Private nonguaranteed debt from:	13.0	..	..	..	..	..
Bondholders	..	..	..	..	..	..
Commercial banks and others	13.0	..	..	..	..	..
Use of IMF Credit	65.2	201.6	236.5	239.4	286.9	311.4
Net financial inflows						
Net debt inflows						
Use of IMF Credit	11.9	40.9	44.1	10.3	32.4	31.7
Long-term	78.2	84.3	348.0	332.6	273.5	264.2
Official creditors	84.7	84.3	348.0	332.6	273.5	264.2
Multilateral	67.4	119.0	361.0	264.8	240.0	184.9
of which: World Bank	15.0	61.1	76.0	170.3	159.4	140.7
Bilateral	17.3	-34.7	-13.0	67.8	33.5	79.3
Private creditors	-6.5	..	..	..	..	..
Bondholders	..	..	..	..	..	..
Banks and other private	-6.5	..	..	..	..	..
Short-term	-149.0	-9.0	-31.5	9.2	20.7	-10.8
Net equity inflows						
Foreign direct investment	-47.8	409.5	228.2	146.0	128.1	460.1
Portfolio equity	1.5	14.4	12.4	17.7	16.3	..
Debt ratios						
External debt stocks to exports (%)	85.6	109.5	157.4	189.4	198.0	..
External debt stocks to GNI (%)	18.0	25.0	31.7	34.4	38.5	36.1
Debt service to exports (%)	2.4	6.3	6.2	8.4	8.5	..
Short-term to external debt stocks (%)	9.7	3.4	1.2	1.7	2.3	2.2
Multilateral to external debt stocks (%)	61.5	55.5	63.4	64.5	66.2	65.7
Reserves to external debt stocks (%)	73.3	63.3	46.4	..	..	..
Gross national income (GNI)	5,360.3	8,078.0	7,064.7	7,365.2	7,942.0	9,040.1

NIGERIA

(US$ million, unless otherwise indicated)

	2008	2014	2015	2016	2017	2018
Summary external debt data by debtor type						
Total External debt stocks	**13,129**	**24,756**	**28,730**	**30,688**	**39,770**	**46,238**
Use of IMF Credit	242	2,427	2,322	2,252	2,386	2,330
Long-term external debt	12,887	22,328	26,408	28,436	37,384	43,907
Public and publicly guaranteed sector	3,902	9,133	10,133	10,756	18,117	24,422
Public Sector	3,888	9,133	10,133	10,756	18,117	24,422
of which: General Government	3,837	9,058	9,920	10,498	17,792	24,031
Private sector guaranteed by Public Sector	14	..	..	..	..	..
Private sector not guaranteed	8,985	13,195	16,275	17,680	19,267	19,485
Short-term external debt	0	0	0	0	0	0
Disbursements (long-term)	**1,369**	**8,433**	**5,476**	**4,199**	**11,172**	**11,200**
Public and publicly guaranteed sector	409	1,375	1,426	1,117	6,985	7,256
Public Sector	409	1,375	1,426	1,117	6,985	7,256
of which: General Government	409	1,295	1,283	1,064	6,934	7,182
Private sector guaranteed by Public Sector	0	..	..	..	..	..
Private sector not guaranteed	960	7,058	4,051	3,082	4,187	3,944
Principal repayments (long-term)	**597**	**4,278**	**1,132**	**1,858**	**2,736**	**4,461**
Public and publicly guaranteed sector	340	139	115	180	136	736
Public Sector	334	139	115	180	136	736
of which: General Government	303	139	115	180	136	736
Private sector guaranteed by Public Sector	6	..	..	..	..	..
Private sector not guaranteed	257	4,140	1,016	1,677	2,600	3,725
Interest payments (long-term)	**87**	**267**	**481**	**649**	**830**	**1,321**
Public and publicly guaranteed sector	87	126	280	174	204	593
Public Sector	86	126	280	174	204	593
of which: General Government	81	126	279	172	202	591
Private sector guaranteed by Public Sector	1	..	..	..	..	..
Private sector not guaranteed	..	141	200	475	625	727
Summary external debt stock by creditor type						
Long-term External debt stocks	**12,887**	**22,328**	**26,408**	**28,436**	**37,384**	**43,907**
Public and publicly guaranteed debt from:	3,902	9,133	10,133	10,756	18,117	24,422
Official creditors	3,789	8,133	9,133	9,756	12,317	13,754
Multilateral	3,024	6,734	7,489	7,867	10,070	10,872
of which: World Bank	2,455	5,779	6,226	6,640	7,913	8,557
Bilateral	765	1,400	1,645	1,889	2,247	2,881
Private creditors	112	1,000	1,000	1,000	5,800	10,668
Bondholders	..	1,000	1,000	1,000	5,800	10,668
Commercial banks and others	112	..	..	..	..	..
Private nonguaranteed debt from:	8,985	13,195	16,275	17,680	19,267	19,485
Bondholders	..	4,475	5,275	5,942	6,942	6,017
Commercial banks and others	8,985	8,720	11,000	11,737	12,324	13,468
Use of IMF Credit	242	2,427	2,322	2,252	2,386	2,330
Net financial inflows						
Net debt inflows						
Use of IMF Credit	..	0	..	..	..	..
Long-term	772	4,154	4,344	2,341	8,436	6,739
Official creditors	53	1,236	1,310	936	2,049	1,652
Multilateral	88	883	1,065	694	1,693	1,019
of which: World Bank	144	858	726	650	858	851
Bilateral	-35	353	245	242	356	633
Private creditors	719	2,918	3,034	1,405	6,387	5,087
Bondholders	..	2,350	800	667	5,800	3,943
Banks and other private	719	568	2,234	738	587	1,144
Short-term	0	0	0	0	0	0
Net equity inflows						
Foreign direct investment	8,132	4,639	3,133	4,444	3,495	1,997
Portfolio equity	-954	1,041	-540	325	2,919	2,206
Debt ratios						
External debt stocks to exports (%)	15	29	56	77	76	66
External debt stocks to GNI (%)	4	5	6	8	11	12
Debt service to exports (%)	1	5	3	6	7	8
Short-term to external debt stocks (%)	0	0	0	0	0	0
Multilateral to external debt stocks (%)	23	27	26	26	25	24
Reserves to external debt stocks (%)	404	148	98	89	100	93
Gross national income (GNI)	321,881	549,528	481,571	395,951	364,253	378,946

NORTH MACEDONIA

(US$ million, unless otherwise indicated)

	2008	2014	2015	2016	2017	2018
Summary external debt data by debtor type						
Total External debt stocks	**4,337**	**7,233**	**6,767**	**7,513**	**8,544**	**8,744**
Use of IMF Credit	13	273	91	88	93	91
Long-term external debt	3,013	5,741	5,662	6,320	7,133	7,309
Public and publicly guaranteed sector	1,574	3,140	3,109	3,473	3,829	4,061
Public Sector	1,574	3,140	3,109	3,473	3,829	4,061
of which: General Government	1,422	2,464	2,375	2,655	2,920	3,142
Private sector guaranteed by Public Sector	1	..	..	..	..	..
Private sector not guaranteed	1,438	2,602	2,553	2,847	3,304	3,248
Short-term external debt	1,312	1,218	1,014	1,105	1,318	1,344
Disbursements (long-term)	**789**	**1,520**	**1,094**	**1,465**	**1,020**	**1,422**
Public and publicly guaranteed sector	174	1,106	583	777	221	794
Public Sector	174	1,106	583	777	221	794
of which: General Government	104	836	395	604	110	672
Private sector guaranteed by Public Sector	..	..	..	..	..	..
Private sector not guaranteed	615	415	512	688	798	629
Principal repayments (long-term)	**293**	**662**	**699**	**702**	**645**	**1,077**
Public and publicly guaranteed sector	78	187	327	309	262	406
Public Sector	78	187	327	309	262	406
of which: General Government	63	106	255	235	177	317
Private sector guaranteed by Public Sector	0	..	..	..	..	..
Private sector not guaranteed	215	475	373	394	383	671
Interest payments (long-term)	**104**	**151**	**128**	**124**	**177**	**159**
Public and publicly guaranteed sector	54	62	78	86	112	105
Public Sector	54	62	78	86	112	105
of which: General Government	48	51	67	75	100	92
Private sector guaranteed by Public Sector	0	..	..	..	..	..
Private sector not guaranteed	50	89	51	38	65	54

	2008	2014	2015	2016	2017	2018
Summary external debt stock by creditor type						
Long-term External debt stocks	**3,013**	**5,741**	**5,662**	**6,320**	**7,133**	**7,309**
Public and publicly guaranteed debt from:	1,574	3,140	3,109	3,473	3,829	4,061
Official creditors	1,277	1,691	1,680	1,737	1,921	1,865
Multilateral	1,047	1,331	1,282	1,232	1,336	1,245
of which: World Bank	623	717	656	620	658	614
Bilateral	230	360	397	505	585	620
Private creditors	297	1,449	1,429	1,736	1,907	2,196
Bondholders	209	789	838	1,286	1,463	1,864
Commercial banks and others	89	660	591	450	444	332
Private nonguaranteed debt from:	1,438	2,602	2,553	2,847	3,304	3,248
Bondholders	..	..	..	..	..	..
Commercial banks and others	1,438	2,602	2,553	2,847	3,304	3,248
Use of IMF Credit	13	273	91	88	93	91

	2008	2014	2015	2016	2017	2018
Net financial inflows						
Net debt inflows						
Use of IMF Credit	..	-112	-172	..	..	..
Long-term	496	859	395	763	375	346
Official creditors	64	275	125	99	22	1
Multilateral	33	135	69	-10	-40	-39
of which: World Bank	38	38	-6	-16	-24	-21
Bilateral	31	140	55	109	62	39
Private creditors	432	584	271	664	352	345
Bondholders	..	664	133	498	0	482
Banks and other private	432	-81	137	166	352	-137
Short-term	-287	-170	-210	68	230	14
Net equity inflows						
Foreign direct investment	324	-141	89	325	246	479
Portfolio equity	-49	-4	-9	-8	-12	-34

	2008	2014	2015	2016	2017	2018
Debt ratios						
External debt stocks to exports (%)	96	129	133	134	133	112
External debt stocks to GNI (%)	44	65	69	73	79	72
Debt service to exports (%)	10	17	21	16	14	17
Short-term to external debt stocks (%)	30	17	15	15	15	15
Multilateral to external debt stocks (%)	24	18	19	16	16	14
Reserves to external debt stocks (%)	44	37	33	33	29	34
Gross national income (GNI)	9,790	11,150	9,747	10,248	10,832	12,140

PAKISTAN

(US$ million, unless otherwise indicated)

	2008	2014	2015	2016	2017	2018
Summary external debt data by debtor type						
Total External debt stocks	**49,682**	**62,232**	**66,712**	**73,093**	**86,070**	**90,957**
Use of IMF Credit	4,614	5,001	6,359	7,235	7,664	7,276
Long-term external debt	43,698	51,744	53,880	58,738	69,697	75,379
Public and publicly guaranteed sector	40,514	47,017	49,141	52,613	61,106	64,493
Public Sector	40,466	46,984	49,111	52,584	61,077	64,466
of which: General Government	39,914	46,528	48,560	52,047	60,460	64,072
Private sector guaranteed by Public Sector	48	33	30	29	29	26
Private sector not guaranteed	3,184	4,727	4,739	6,125	8,591	10,887
Short-term external debt	1,370	5,487	6,474	7,121	8,709	8,302
Disbursements (long-term)	**3,597**	**7,740**	**5,875**	**8,687**	**13,671**	**9,359**
Public and publicly guaranteed sector	2,685	7,597	5,502	6,394	11,145	6,844
Public Sector	2,685	7,597	5,502	6,394	11,145	6,844
of which: General Government	2,685	7,457	5,261	6,264	10,865	6,844
Private sector guaranteed by Public Sector	0	0	0	0	0	0
Private sector not guaranteed	912	143	373	2,294	2,526	2,515
Principal repayments (long-term)	**1,769**	**2,007**	**2,566**	**2,970**	**4,989**	**3,295**
Public and publicly guaranteed sector	1,312	1,777	2,205	2,588	4,562	2,834
Public Sector	1,311	1,776	2,204	2,586	4,560	2,832
of which: General Government	1,249	1,682	2,059	2,436	4,353	2,608
Private sector guaranteed by Public Sector	2	2	1	1	1	2
Private sector not guaranteed	456	229	361	382	427	460
Interest payments (long-term)	**1,033**	**756**	**1,010**	**1,233**	**1,570**	**2,195**
Public and publicly guaranteed sector	885	692	943	1,113	1,324	1,755
Public Sector	885	692	943	1,113	1,324	1,755
of which: General Government	871	685	933	1,103	1,311	1,742
Private sector guaranteed by Public Sector	0	0	0	0	0	0
Private sector not guaranteed	147	64	66	120	246	440
Summary external debt stock by creditor type						
Long-term External debt stocks	**43,698**	**51,744**	**53,880**	**58,738**	**69,697**	**75,379**
Public and publicly guaranteed debt from:	40,514	47,017	49,141	52,613	61,106	64,493
Official creditors	37,428	41,763	42,882	45,312	51,220	55,065
Multilateral	22,109	23,944	24,709	25,479	27,780	27,822
of which: World Bank	10,999	13,012	13,784	14,049	15,300	15,162
Bilateral	15,319	17,819	18,173	19,833	23,440	27,243
Private creditors	3,086	5,254	6,259	7,301	9,886	9,428
Bondholders	2,650	4,550	5,050	5,550	7,300	7,300
Commercial banks and others	436	704	1,209	1,751	2,586	2,128
Private nonguaranteed debt from:	3,184	4,727	4,739	6,125	8,591	10,887
Bondholders	850	12	12	12	12	12
Commercial banks and others	2,334	4,715	4,727	6,113	8,579	10,875
Use of IMF Credit	4,614	5,001	6,359	7,235	7,664	7,276
Net financial inflows						
Net debt inflows						
Use of IMF Credit	3,084	200	1,591	1,102	0	-212
Long-term	1,828	5,733	3,309	5,718	8,682	6,064
Official creditors	1,281	2,385	2,292	2,763	3,998	4,468
Multilateral	1,123	1,394	1,421	1,074	1,171	480
of which: World Bank	-205	1,134	1,285	654	491	183
Bilateral	158	992	871	1,690	2,827	3,988
Private creditors	547	3,348	1,017	2,954	4,684	1,596
Bondholders	0	3,000	500	500	1,750	0
Banks and other private	547	348	517	2,454	2,934	1,596
Short-term	-858	835	987	647	1,588	-407
Net equity inflows						
Foreign direct investment	5,438	1,917	1,571	2,396	2,798	2,487
Portfolio equity	-270	762	529	-339	-390	-529
Debt ratios						
External debt stocks to exports (%)	186	200	228	266	291	295
External debt stocks to GNI (%)	29	24	23	25	27	28
Debt service to exports (%)	11	15	14	16	23	20
Short-term to external debt stocks (%)	3	9	10	10	10	9
Multilateral to external debt stocks (%)	45	38	37	35	32	31
Reserves to external debt stocks (%)	14	19	27	27	18	10
Gross national income (GNI)	173,418	258,227	287,068	295,741	321,597	329,084

PAPUA NEW GUINEA

(US$ million, unless otherwise indicated)

	2008	2014	2015	2016	2017	2018
Summary external debt data by debtor type						
Total External debt stocks	**1,436**	**20,429**	**20,387**	**19,245**	**17,221**	**17,718**
Use of IMF Credit	14	182	174	169	179	175
Long-term external debt	1,412	19,439	19,902	18,414	16,966	17,082
Public and publicly guaranteed sector	1,067	1,369	1,501	1,919	2,303	3,408
Public Sector	1,067	1,369	1,501	1,919	2,303	3,408
of which: General Government	1,062	1,366	1,498	1,916	2,300	3,405
Private sector guaranteed by Public Sector	..	..	..	..	..	..
Private sector not guaranteed	345	18,070	18,400	16,494	14,663	13,674
Short-term external debt	10	808	311	663	77	462
Disbursements (long-term)	**951**	**1,027**	**562**	**1,538**	**1,320**	**3,046**
Public and publicly guaranteed sector	26	244	242	534	394	1,234
Public Sector	26	244	242	534	394	1,234
of which: General Government	26	244	242	534	394	1,234
Private sector guaranteed by Public Sector	..	..	..	..	..	..
Private sector not guaranteed	925	784	320	1,004	926	1,812
Principal repayments (long-term)	**932**	**822**	**519**	**2,662**	**2,111**	**2,030**
Public and publicly guaranteed sector	163	74	67	76	84	93
Public Sector	163	74	67	76	84	93
of which: General Government	163	74	66	75	84	93
Private sector guaranteed by Public Sector	..	..	..	..	..	..
Private sector not guaranteed	769	748	452	2,586	2,027	1,937
Interest payments (long-term)	**40**	**337**	**575**	**651**	**673**	**741**
Public and publicly guaranteed sector	32	20	21	25	51	88
Public Sector	32	20	21	25	51	88
of which: General Government	32	20	21	25	51	88
Private sector guaranteed by Public Sector	..	..	..	..	..	..
Private sector not guaranteed	8	317	555	626	622	653
Summary external debt stock by creditor type						
Long-term External debt stocks	**1,412**	**19,439**	**19,902**	**18,414**	**16,966**	**17,082**
Public and publicly guaranteed debt from:	1,067	1,369	1,501	1,919	2,303	3,408
Official creditors	1,023	1,368	1,500	1,703	1,954	2,371
Multilateral	721	1,012	1,087	1,168	1,278	1,633
of which: World Bank	229	252	250	262	277	446
Bilateral	303	356	413	535	676	739
Private creditors	44	1	1	216	349	1,037
Bondholders	..	..	..	..	..	500
Commercial banks and others	44	1	1	216	349	537
Private nonguaranteed debt from:	345	18,070	18,400	16,494	14,663	13,674
Bondholders	..	..	..	..	..	..
Commercial banks and others	345	18,070	18,400	16,494	14,663	13,674
Use of IMF Credit	14	182	174	169	179	175
Net financial inflows						
Net debt inflows						
Use of IMF Credit	..	0	..	..	..	..
Long-term	19	205	43	-1,124	-791	1,017
Official creditors	-131	176	176	242	181	452
Multilateral	-34	102	103	101	68	373
of which: World Bank	-27	14	5	17	4	174
Bilateral	-97	74	73	141	114	79
Private creditors	149	30	-133	-1,366	-972	565
Bondholders	..	..	..	..	..	500
Banks and other private	149	30	-133	-1,366	-972	65
Short-term	-164	494	-497	144	-383	235
Net equity inflows						
Foreign direct investment	-26	-30	204	-40	-242	335
Portfolio equity	..	-6	-1	-1	0	..
Debt ratios						
External debt stocks to exports (%)	23	227	237	231	168	166
External debt stocks to GNI (%)	13	90	96	95	80	78
Debt service to exports (%)	16	13	13	40	27	26
Short-term to external debt stocks (%)	1	4	2	3	0	3
Multilateral to external debt stocks (%)	50	5	5	6	7	9
Reserves to external debt stocks (%)	136	11	8	8	10	12
Gross national income (GNI)	11,025	22,621	21,258	20,288	21,611	22,602

PARAGUAY

(US$ million, unless otherwise indicated)

	2008	2014	2015	2016	2017	2018
Summary external debt data by debtor type						
Total External debt stocks	**12,520**	**16,467**	**16,125**	**16,224**	**15,925**	**15,806**
Use of IMF Credit	21	138	132	128	136	132
Long-term external debt	8,431	11,516	11,218	11,499	11,169	11,033
Public and publicly guaranteed sector	2,272	3,722	4,024	4,824	5,605	6,399
Public Sector	2,272	3,722	4,024	4,821	5,601	6,380
of which: General Government	1,992	3,591	3,883	4,658	5,417	6,194
Private sector guaranteed by Public Sector	..	..	0	4	4	19
Private sector not guaranteed	6,159	7,794	7,194	6,675	5,564	4,635
Short-term external debt	4,068	4,814	4,775	4,596	4,620	4,640
Disbursements (long-term)	**1,480**	**3,499**	**1,471**	**1,213**	**996**	**1,532**
Public and publicly guaranteed sector	196	1,261	496	1,037	978	1,003
Public Sector	196	1,261	496	1,033	978	988
of which: General Government	196	1,243	468	998	945	969
Private sector guaranteed by Public Sector	..	..	0	4	0	15
Private sector not guaranteed	1,284	2,238	975	176	18	530
Principal repayments (long-term)	**297**	**2,779**	**1,592**	**914**	**1,338**	**1,667**
Public and publicly guaranteed sector	238	196	183	234	209	208
Public Sector	238	196	183	234	209	208
of which: General Government	208	177	166	218	194	193
Private sector guaranteed by Public Sector	..	..	0	0	0	0
Private sector not guaranteed	59	2,583	1,409	681	1,129	1,459
Interest payments (long-term)	**136**	**227**	**312**	**371**	**356**	**553**
Public and publicly guaranteed sector	96	77	135	178	211	254
Public Sector	96	77	135	178	211	254
of which: General Government	87	73	131	174	206	249
Private sector guaranteed by Public Sector	..	..	0	0	0	0
Private sector not guaranteed	40	149	177	194	145	299
Summary external debt stock by creditor type						
Long-term External debt stocks	**8,431**	**11,516**	**11,218**	**11,499**	**11,169**	**11,033**
Public and publicly guaranteed debt from:	2,272	3,722	4,024	4,824	5,605	6,399
Official creditors	1,949	2,106	2,140	2,380	2,686	2,976
Multilateral	1,304	1,787	1,869	2,163	2,497	2,787
of which: World Bank	230	380	431	544	605	636
Bilateral	645	318	272	217	189	189
Private creditors	323	1,616	1,883	2,445	2,919	3,423
Bondholders	..	1,500	1,780	2,380	2,880	3,410
Commercial banks and others	323	116	103	65	39	13
Private nonguaranteed debt from:	6,159	7,794	7,194	6,675	5,564	4,635
Bondholders	..	800	800	800	600	600
Commercial banks and others	6,159	6,994	6,394	5,875	4,964	4,035
Use of IMF Credit	21	138	132	128	136	132
Net financial inflows						
Net debt inflows						
Use of IMF Credit	..	0	..	..	..	..
Long-term	1,183	720	-121	299	-342	-135
Official creditors	-13	104	45	242	295	290
Multilateral	-33	122	90	302	330	293
of which: World Bank	-22	38	51	113	62	31
Bilateral	20	-19	-44	-60	-35	-2
Private creditors	1,195	616	-167	57	-637	-425
Bondholders	..	1,300	280	600	300	530
Banks and other private	1,195	-684	-447	-543	-937	-955
Short-term	478	106	-39	-178	24	20
Net equity inflows						
Foreign direct investment	190	872	451	451	385	383
Portfolio equity	..	..	..	..	..	..
Debt ratios						
External debt stocks to exports (%)	122	118	136	127	112	108
External debt stocks to GNI (%)	53	42	46	47	42	40
Debt service to exports (%)	4	22	17	11	12	16
Short-term to external debt stocks (%)	32	29	30	28	29	29
Multilateral to external debt stocks (%)	10	11	12	13	16	18
Reserves to external debt stocks (%)	23	40	35	41	47	47
Gross national income (GNI)	23,492	38,813	34,808	34,592	37,805	39,663

PERU

(US$ million, unless otherwise indicated)

	2008	2014	2015	2016	2017	2018
Summary external debt data by debtor type						
Total External debt stocks	**34,720**	**67,906**	**67,185**	**69,611**	**67,558**	**66,697**
Use of IMF Credit	141	884	845	820	869	848
Long-term external debt	29,159	60,044	59,265	61,027	57,995	55,851
Public and publicly guaranteed sector	19,415	15,903	19,409	19,732	18,933	18,073
Public Sector	18,742	15,903	19,409	19,732	18,933	18,073
of which: General Government	18,722	15,897	19,403	19,726	16,778	15,918
Private sector guaranteed by Public Sector	672	0	..	..	..	..
Private sector not guaranteed	9,744	44,141	39,855	41,295	39,062	37,778
Short-term external debt	5,420	6,978	7,075	7,765	8,695	9,998
Disbursements (long-term)	**4,630**	**8,015**	**10,450**	**7,981**	**5,327**	**3,513**
Public and publicly guaranteed sector	1,165	450	4,865	1,977	2,587	569
Public Sector	1,165	450	4,865	1,977	2,587	569
of which: General Government	1,165	445	4,865	1,977	437	569
Private sector guaranteed by Public Sector	0	0	..	..	..	..
Private sector not guaranteed	3,466	7,565	5,585	6,004	2,740	2,945
Principal repayments (long-term)	**3,265**	**3,403**	**3,220**	**5,545**	**8,718**	**4,577**
Public and publicly guaranteed sector	2,618	1,021	907	980	3,746	1,257
Public Sector	2,516	1,010	907	980	3,746	1,257
of which: General Government	2,511	1,009	906	979	3,745	1,257
Private sector guaranteed by Public Sector	102	11	..	..	..	..
Private sector not guaranteed	647	2,382	2,313	4,565	4,973	3,320
Interest payments (long-term)	**1,808**	**2,021**	**2,204**	**2,090**	**2,151**	**2,328**
Public and publicly guaranteed sector	1,185	866	811	876	969	982
Public Sector	1,135	865	811	876	969	982
of which: General Government	1,134	865	811	876	914	873
Private sector guaranteed by Public Sector	50	0	..	..	..	..
Private sector not guaranteed	623	1,155	1,393	1,214	1,182	1,346
Summary external debt stock by creditor type						
Long-term External debt stocks	**29,159**	**60,044**	**59,265**	**61,027**	**57,995**	**55,851**
Public and publicly guaranteed debt from:	19,415	15,903	19,409	19,732	18,933	18,073
Official creditors	12,493	7,276	7,912	8,128	4,874	4,375
Multilateral	8,008	5,641	6,411	6,729	3,823	3,355
of which: World Bank	2,712	1,838	2,714	2,610	1,093	1,145
Bilateral	4,485	1,635	1,501	1,399	1,051	1,020
Private creditors	6,921	8,627	11,497	11,604	14,059	13,698
Bondholders	6,879	8,625	11,496	11,604	14,059	13,698
Commercial banks and others	42	2	1	0	..	..
Private nonguaranteed debt from:	9,744	44,141	39,855	41,295	39,062	37,778
Bondholders	3,599	20,207	15,250	13,875	16,340	15,510
Commercial banks and others	6,145	23,934	24,606	27,420	22,723	22,268
Use of IMF Credit	141	884	845	820	869	848
Net financial inflows						
Net debt inflows						
Use of IMF Credit	..	0	..	..	..	..
Long-term	1,366	4,612	7,230	2,437	-3,391	-1,064
Official creditors	-101	-183	716	190	-3,309	-442
Multilateral	32	-28	802	315	-2,866	-426
of which: World Bank	63	17	877	-104	-1,516	51
Bilateral	-133	-156	-86	-125	-443	-16
Private creditors	1,467	4,796	6,514	2,247	-83	-622
Bondholders	-1,488	3,193	4,722	-567	4,615	-1,077
Banks and other private	2,956	1,603	1,792	2,814	-4,698	455
Short-term	81	528	97	690	930	1,304
Net equity inflows						
Foreign direct investment	6,267	2,451	7,043	6,179	7,571	6,257
Portfolio equity	85	-79	-60	-307	-172	-442
Debt ratios						
External debt stocks to exports (%)	96	147	162	157	125	115
External debt stocks to GNI (%)	31	35	37	38	34	31
Debt service to exports (%)	15	12	13	18	21	12
Short-term to external debt stocks (%)	16	10	11	11	13	15
Multilateral to external debt stocks (%)	23	8	10	10	6	5
Reserves to external debt stocks (%)	87	90	90	87	92	88
Gross national income (GNI)	112,245	191,893	183,260	183,950	200,975	213,209

PHILIPPINES

(US$ million, unless otherwise indicated)

	2008	2014	2015	2016	2017	2018
Summary external debt data by debtor type						
Total External debt stocks	**58,270**	**77,170**	**76,495**	**72,931**	**74,382**	**78,824**
Use of IMF Credit	180	1,214	1,161	1,127	1,193	1,165
Long-term external debt	51,089	59,708	60,234	57,278	58,914	61,591
Public and publicly guaranteed sector	39,258	38,950	39,089	33,948	35,517	36,346
Public Sector	39,182	38,868	39,014	33,911	35,482	36,313
of which: General Government	30,430	33,011	33,592	28,892	30,726	31,777
Private sector guaranteed by Public Sector	76	83	75	37	35	33
Private sector not guaranteed	11,831	20,758	21,145	23,330	23,397	25,245
Short-term external debt	7,001	16,248	15,099	14,526	14,275	16,068
Disbursements (long-term)	**4,291**	**16,507**	**12,243**	**4,069**	**8,758**	**10,119**
Public and publicly guaranteed sector	2,128	3,283	6,529	1,512	3,472	5,693
Public Sector	2,128	3,273	6,529	1,512	3,472	5,693
of which: General Government	1,725	3,188	6,303	1,171	3,420	5,635
Private sector guaranteed by Public Sector	0	10	0	0	0	0
Private sector not guaranteed	2,163	13,224	5,714	2,557	5,286	4,426
Principal repayments (long-term)	**6,995**	**4,476**	**7,411**	**7,811**	**8,244**	**6,225**
Public and publicly guaranteed sector	3,592	2,600	3,152	4,079	3,026	2,370
Public Sector	3,589	2,594	3,144	4,040	3,023	2,367
of which: General Government	2,303	2,086	2,615	3,290	2,829	2,189
Private sector guaranteed by Public Sector	3	6	8	39	3	3
Private sector not guaranteed	3,402	1,876	4,259	3,732	5,219	3,855
Interest payments (long-term)	**3,376**	**3,056**	**3,161**	**3,137**	**2,878**	**2,536**
Public and publicly guaranteed sector	2,865	2,549	2,431	2,393	2,162	2,200
Public Sector	2,863	2,547	2,429	2,390	2,162	2,200
of which: General Government	2,338	2,178	2,061	2,039	1,857	1,912
Private sector guaranteed by Public Sector	2	2	2	2	1	1
Private sector not guaranteed	511	506	729	744	716	336
Summary external debt stock by creditor type						
Long-term External debt stocks	**51,089**	**59,708**	**60,234**	**57,278**	**58,914**	**61,591**
Public and publicly guaranteed debt from:	39,258	38,950	39,089	33,948	35,517	36,346
Official creditors	21,597	17,506	18,286	18,568	19,069	19,892
Multilateral	7,414	8,999	10,166	10,487	11,015	12,073
of which: World Bank	2,720	3,966	4,661	4,672	5,132	5,842
Bilateral	14,183	8,507	8,120	8,082	8,054	7,819
Private creditors	17,661	21,444	20,803	15,380	16,448	16,454
Bondholders	16,209	20,732	20,218	14,656	15,735	15,775
Commercial banks and others	1,452	712	585	724	713	678
Private nonguaranteed debt from:	11,831	20,758	21,145	23,330	23,397	25,245
Bondholders	1,314	5,900	5,362	5,262	5,962	6,687
Commercial banks and others	10,517	14,858	15,783	18,067	17,434	18,558
Use of IMF Credit	180	1,214	1,161	1,127	1,193	1,165
Net financial inflows						
Net debt inflows						
Use of IMF Credit	..	0	..	..	..	..
Long-term	-2,704	12,031	4,832	-3,742	513	3,894
Official creditors	-870	188	880	-35	120	735
Multilateral	-112	548	1,199	321	481	1,059
of which: World Bank	-287	237	700	10	443	709
Bilateral	-758	-360	-320	-356	-361	-324
Private creditors	-1,834	11,844	3,953	-3,707	393	3,159
Bondholders	-839	258	2,057	-2,766	1,071	3,344
Banks and other private	-994	11,586	1,895	-941	-678	-185
Short-term	-83	-661	-1,149	-573	-252	1,793
Net equity inflows						
Foreign direct investment	1,288	2,476	2,563	3,302	4,261	3,126
Portfolio equity	-462	1,196	-743	131	496	-1,031
Debt ratios						
External debt stocks to exports (%)	106	92	94	87	77	78
External debt stocks to GNI (%)	28	22	22	20	20	20
Debt service to exports (%)	19	9	13	13	11	9
Short-term to external debt stocks (%)	12	21	20	20	19	20
Multilateral to external debt stocks (%)	13	12	13	14	15	15
Reserves to external debt stocks (%)	57	93	97	101	98	90
Gross national income (GNI)	204,478	344,879	354,141	367,021	377,083	397,063

ROMANIA

(US$ million, unless otherwise indicated)

	2008	2014	2015	2016	2017	2018
Summary external debt data by debtor type						
Total External debt stocks	**99,447**	**111,824**	**96,448**	**96,117**	**114,007**	**112,116**
Use of IMF Credit	117	3,352	1,498	1,324	1,402	1,370
Long-term external debt	73,761	96,190	82,515	82,458	97,657	94,884
Public and publicly guaranteed sector	15,256	36,792	32,598	32,719	37,965	37,954
Public Sector	15,011	36,404	32,594	32,712	37,957	37,947
of which: General Government	12,658	35,397	31,798	32,048	37,344	37,476
Private sector guaranteed by Public Sector	245	389	4	7	8	7
Private sector not guaranteed	58,505	59,398	49,916	49,739	59,692	56,930
Short-term external debt	25,569	12,282	12,436	12,335	14,948	15,863
Disbursements (long-term)	**32,747**	**19,369**	**15,490**	**14,593**	**25,501**	**19,724**
Public and publicly guaranteed sector	3,059	6,382	3,594	3,694	3,888	5,932
Public Sector	3,059	6,382	3,590	3,691	3,888	5,932
of which: General Government	2,910	6,354	3,544	3,674	3,882	5,932
Private sector guaranteed by Public Sector	0	0	4	3	..	0
Private sector not guaranteed	29,688	12,986	11,896	10,898	21,613	13,793
Principal repayments (long-term)	**14,475**	**16,167**	**19,789**	**16,634**	**18,394**	**19,176**
Public and publicly guaranteed sector	2,543	1,206	4,726	2,735	2,285	4,516
Public Sector	2,427	1,206	4,371	2,735	2,284	4,516
of which: General Government	1,826	991	4,207	2,597	2,162	4,396
Private sector guaranteed by Public Sector	116	0	355	..	0	1
Private sector not guaranteed	11,932	14,961	15,064	13,898	16,110	14,659
Interest payments (long-term)	**2,926**	**2,274**	**1,978**	**1,845**	**1,895**	**2,091**
Public and publicly guaranteed sector	901	1,355	1,318	1,286	1,284	1,447
Public Sector	890	1,343	1,316	1,286	1,283	1,447
of which: General Government	733	1,329	1,307	1,280	1,278	1,442
Private sector guaranteed by Public Sector	10	11	3	0	0	0
Private sector not guaranteed	2,025	919	660	559	611	644
Summary external debt stock by creditor type						
Long-term External debt stocks	**73,761**	**96,190**	**82,515**	**82,458**	**97,657**	**94,884**
Public and publicly guaranteed debt from:	15,256	36,792	32,598	32,719	37,965	37,954
Official creditors	8,042	16,863	13,819	12,733	12,909	10,355
Multilateral	7,331	16,312	13,299	12,224	12,413	9,893
of which: World Bank	2,572	4,172	4,367	4,009	4,952	4,677
Bilateral	710	551	520	508	496	462
Private creditors	7,214	19,929	18,779	19,986	25,056	27,599
Bondholders	2,714	18,802	17,998	19,453	24,639	27,329
Commercial banks and others	4,500	1,127	782	533	417	270
Private nonguaranteed debt from:	58,505	59,398	49,916	49,739	59,692	56,930
Bondholders	0	328	233	164	207	634
Commercial banks and others	58,505	59,070	49,684	49,575	59,485	56,297
Use of IMF Credit	117	3,352	1,498	1,324	1,402	1,370
Net financial inflows						
Net debt inflows						
Use of IMF Credit	..	-5,897	-1,725	-134	..	..
Long-term	18,272	3,202	-4,299	-2,041	7,107	549
Official creditors	857	-137	-1,452	-732	-1,338	-2,078
Multilateral	839	-108	-1,424	-704	-1,306	-2,036
of which: World Bank	-48	199	572	-247	457	-65
Bilateral	18	-29	-28	-28	-32	-42
Private creditors	17,415	3,339	-2,847	-1,309	8,445	2,627
Bondholders	221	5,672	516	1,917	3,135	4,158
Banks and other private	17,194	-2,333	-3,363	-3,226	5,311	-1,531
Short-term	-3,753	-3,262	154	-101	2,613	914
Net equity inflows						
Foreign direct investment	7,459	3,754	3,971	4,778	4,462	5,888
Portfolio equity	21	535	362	-459	-61	-280
Debt ratios						
External debt stocks to exports (%)	166	131	128	119	124	108
External debt stocks to GNI (%)	48	57	56	52	55	48
Debt service to exports (%)	30	29	31	23	22	21
Short-term to external debt stocks (%)	26	11	13	13	13	14
Multilateral to external debt stocks (%)	7	15	14	13	11	9
Reserves to external debt stocks (%)	37	35	36	38	35	34
Gross national income (GNI)	208,929	197,100	173,746	183,552	206,179	233,697

RUSSIAN FEDERATION

(US$ million, unless otherwise indicated)

	2008	2014	2015	2016	2017	2018
Summary external debt data by debtor type						
Total External debt stocks	**419,281**	**549,603**	**467,699**	**533,204**	**518,191**	**453,938**
Use of IMF Credit	8,736	8,217	7,860	7,625	8,077	7,888
Long-term external debt	336,337	479,685	417,740	480,479	459,079	397,750
Public and publicly guaranteed sector	125,254	228,373	194,185	189,423	220,079	177,150
Public Sector	125,254	228,373	194,185	189,423	220,079	177,150
of which: General Government	28,523	40,243	30,807	39,035	55,179	43,550
Private sector guaranteed by Public Sector	..	..	..	..	..	..
Private sector not guaranteed	211,083	251,313	223,555	291,056	239,000	220,600
Short-term external debt	74,208	61,700	42,100	45,100	51,035	48,300
Disbursements (long-term)	**85,467**	**9,749**	**12,163**	**89,772**	**83,354**	**29,785**
Public and publicly guaranteed sector	29,549	591	5,579	20,007	50,928	10,406
Public Sector	29,549	591	5,579	20,007	50,928	10,406
of which: General Government	3,530	67	81	9,925	17,045	5,205
Private sector guaranteed by Public Sector	..	..	..	..	..	..
Private sector not guaranteed	55,918	9,158	6,584	69,765	32,427	19,378
Principal repayments (long-term)	**64,012**	**68,699**	**81,729**	**51,103**	**61,790**	**90,407**
Public and publicly guaranteed sector	29,212	45,811	40,610	24,728	20,552	53,040
Public Sector	29,212	45,811	40,610	24,728	20,552	53,040
of which: General Government	11,712	20,201	10,378	1,660	1,051	16,741
Private sector guaranteed by Public Sector	..	..	..	..	..	..
Private sector not guaranteed	34,800	22,888	41,120	26,374	41,238	37,367
Interest payments (long-term)	**15,119**	**19,678**	**19,036**	**20,121**	**19,008**	**19,039**
Public and publicly guaranteed sector	3,749	4,212	3,548	5,643	6,554	8,928
Public Sector	3,749	4,212	3,548	5,643	6,554	8,928
of which: General Government	1,924	2,840	2,349	1,249	1,657	2,761
Private sector guaranteed by Public Sector	..	..	..	..	..	..
Private sector not guaranteed	11,370	15,466	15,488	14,478	12,454	10,111
Summary external debt stock by creditor type						
Long-term External debt stocks	**336,337**	**479,685**	**417,740**	**480,479**	**459,079**	**397,750**
Public and publicly guaranteed debt from:	125,254	228,373	194,185	189,423	220,079	177,150
Official creditors	8,396	2,868	2,472	2,135	1,149	950
Multilateral	4,477	1,074	873	733	589	460
of which: World Bank	3,851	876	731	646	551	428
Bilateral	3,919	1,794	1,599	1,402	559	489
Private creditors	116,858	225,504	191,714	187,289	218,930	176,200
Bondholders	24,248	38,997	30,567	40,124	62,020	53,534
Commercial banks and others	92,610	186,507	161,147	147,165	156,910	122,666
Private nonguaranteed debt from:	211,083	251,313	223,555	291,056	239,000	220,600
Bondholders	10,320	11,492	11,639	18,156	16,879	19,890
Commercial banks and others	200,762	239,821	211,915	272,900	222,121	200,710
Use of IMF Credit	8,736	8,217	7,860	7,625	8,077	7,888
Net financial inflows						
Net debt inflows						
Use of IMF Credit	..	0	..	..	..	..
Long-term	21,455	-58,949	-69,567	38,669	21,565	-60,622
Official creditors	-1,237	-661	-388	-336	-986	-199
Multilateral	-687	-382	-198	-139	-144	-129
of which: World Bank	-485	-328	-145	-85	-95	-123
Bilateral	-550	-279	-189	-197	-842	-70
Private creditors	22,691	-58,288	-69,179	39,005	22,551	-60,423
Bondholders	-23,042	-23,103	-9,155	16,109	20,325	-4,659
Banks and other private	45,733	-35,186	-60,024	22,895	2,226	-55,764
Short-term	-26,104	-22,300	-19,600	3,000	5,935	-2,735
Net equity inflows						
Foreign direct investment	68,842	23,099	10,719	35,715	26,601	9,913
Portfolio equity	-15,383	-12,966	-5,538	-1,788	-7,940	-4,164
Debt ratios						
External debt stocks to exports (%)	72	90	109	143	113	81
External debt stocks to GNI (%)	26	28	35	43	34	28
Debt service to exports (%)	14	15	23	19	18	20
Short-term to external debt stocks (%)	18	11	9	8	10	11
Multilateral to external debt stocks (%)	1	0	0	0	0	0
Reserves to external debt stocks (%)	98	62	68	60	69	84
Gross national income (GNI)	1,614,364	1,992,022	1,325,846	1,247,227	1,536,571	1,616,242

RWANDA

(US$ million, unless otherwise indicated)

	2008	2014	2015	2016	2017	2018
Summary external debt data by debtor type						
Total External debt stocks	**928.9**	**2,909.9**	**3,452.0**	**4,318.7**	**4,825.3**	**5,488.4**
Use of IMF Credit	32.5	119.4	111.6	203.3	290.7	307.9
Long-term external debt	889.7	2,765.4	3,329.1	3,888.8	4,466.3	5,075.8
Public and publicly guaranteed sector	649.7	1,755.4	2,057.3	2,353.3	2,820.9	3,306.4
Public Sector	649.7	1,755.4	2,057.3	2,353.3	2,820.9	3,306.4
of which: General Government	648.7	1,754.6	2,056.6	2,352.6	2,820.2	3,305.7
Private sector guaranteed by Public Sector	..	..	..	..	..	..
Private sector not guaranteed	240.0	1,010.0	1,271.7	1,535.5	1,645.4	1,769.5
Short-term external debt	6.7	25.0	11.3	226.6	68.2	104.7
Disbursements (long-term)	**378.5**	**776.8**	**659.4**	**774.9**	**705.7**	**918.1**
Public and publicly guaranteed sector	114.5	286.8	375.7	368.1	399.4	563.0
Public Sector	114.5	286.8	375.7	368.1	399.4	563.0
of which: General Government	114.5	286.8	375.7	368.1	399.4	563.0
Private sector guaranteed by Public Sector	..	..	..	..	..	..
Private sector not guaranteed	264.0	490.0	283.8	406.8	306.3	355.1
Principal repayments (long-term)	**32.6**	**116.2**	**125.7**	**148.2**	**155.4**	**151.8**
Public and publicly guaranteed sector	8.6	15.2	17.4	23.0	27.7	25.5
Public Sector	8.6	15.2	17.4	23.0	27.7	25.5
of which: General Government	8.6	15.2	17.4	22.9	27.6	25.5
Private sector guaranteed by Public Sector	..	..	..	..	..	..
Private sector not guaranteed	24.0	101.0	108.4	125.2	127.8	126.3
Interest payments (long-term)	**14.9**	**50.1**	**56.1**	**68.8**	**83.3**	**102.5**
Public and publicly guaranteed sector	5.5	37.7	39.2	41.8	45.7	52.4
Public Sector	5.5	37.7	39.2	41.8	45.7	52.4
of which: General Government	5.5	37.7	39.2	41.8	45.7	52.4
Private sector guaranteed by Public Sector	..	..	..	..	..	..
Private sector not guaranteed	9.4	12.5	16.9	27.0	37.6	50.2
Summary external debt stock by creditor type						
Long-term External debt stocks	**889.7**	**2,765.4**	**3,329.1**	**3,888.8**	**4,466.3**	**5,075.8**
Public and publicly guaranteed debt from:	649.7	1,755.4	2,057.3	2,353.3	2,820.9	3,306.4
Official creditors	649.7	1,355.4	1,657.3	1,953.3	2,420.9	2,906.4
Multilateral	562.0	1,101.9	1,362.8	1,645.5	2,076.2	2,458.9
of which: World Bank	241.7	605.3	861.9	1,048.5	1,403.5	1,610.5
Bilateral	87.7	253.6	294.6	307.8	344.8	447.5
Private creditors	..	400.0	400.0	400.0	400.0	400.0
Bondholders	..	400.0	400.0	400.0	400.0	400.0
Commercial banks and others	..	..	..	..	..	..
Private nonguaranteed debt from:	240.0	1,010.0	1,271.7	1,535.5	1,645.4	1,769.5
Bondholders	..	..	..	..	..	..
Commercial banks and others	240.0	1,010.0	1,271.7	1,535.5	1,645.4	1,769.5
Use of IMF Credit	32.5	119.4	111.6	203.3	290.7	307.9
Net financial inflows						
Net debt inflows						
Use of IMF Credit	3.6	-2.8	-2.6	98.2	73.4	24.4
Long-term	345.9	660.6	533.7	626.8	550.3	766.3
Official creditors	105.9	271.6	358.3	345.1	371.8	537.5
Multilateral	93.2	233.4	309.0	322.8	345.1	425.3
of which: World Bank	40.5	167.0	284.5	216.6	287.8	241.2
Bilateral	12.7	38.2	49.3	22.4	26.7	112.2
Private creditors	240.0	389.0	175.4	281.6	178.5	228.8
Bondholders	..	..	..	..	..	0.0
Banks and other private	240.0	389.0	175.4	281.6	178.5	228.8
Short-term	-7.0	13.9	-13.7	215.3	-158.4	36.5
Net equity inflows						
Foreign direct investment	102.3	147.1	88.3	171.0	176.9	167.0
Portfolio equity	..	1.4	2.5	3.0	0.3	0.4
Debt ratios						
External debt stocks to exports (%)	128.9	219.0	232.9	279.8	241.3	266.7
External debt stocks to GNI (%)	19.2	37.1	42.7	52.3	54.0	59.0
Debt service to exports (%)	6.6	12.8	12.5	14.4	12.1	12.5
Short-term to external debt stocks (%)	0.7	0.9	0.3	5.2	1.4	1.9
Multilateral to external debt stocks (%)	60.5	37.9	39.5	38.1	43.0	44.8
Reserves to external debt stocks (%)	82.8	28.9	23.6	18.7	18.4	16.6
Gross national income (GNI)	4,832.8	7,837.7	8,077.9	8,264.8	8,934.6	9,308.1

SAMOA

(US$ million, unless otherwise indicated)

	2008	2014	2015	2016	2017	2018
Summary external debt data by debtor type						
Total External debt stocks	**207.4**	**450.2**	**437.4**	**417.5**	**443.1**	**427.5**
Use of IMF Credit	1.8	32.9	29.8	27.4	27.4	24.3
Long-term external debt	205.6	417.3	407.6	390.1	415.7	403.2
Public and publicly guaranteed sector	205.6	417.3	407.6	390.1	415.7	403.2
Public Sector	205.6	417.3	407.6	390.1	415.7	403.2
of which: General Government	203.5	416.5	407.0	389.7	415.5	403.1
Private sector guaranteed by Public Sector	..	..	..	..	..	..
Private sector not guaranteed	..	..	..	..	..	..
Short-term external debt	0.0	0.0	0.0	0.0	0.0	0.0
Disbursements (long-term)	**25.5**	**36.5**	**23.3**	**14.3**	**21.0**	**22.0**
Public and publicly guaranteed sector	25.5	36.5	23.3	14.3	21.0	22.0
Public Sector	25.5	36.5	23.3	14.3	21.0	22.0
of which: General Government	25.5	36.5	23.3	14.3	21.0	22.0
Private sector guaranteed by Public Sector	..	..	..	..	..	..
Private sector not guaranteed	..	..	..	..	..	..
Principal repayments (long-term)	**6.0**	**13.4**	**13.7**	**15.6**	**18.3**	**21.9**
Public and publicly guaranteed sector	6.0	13.4	13.7	15.6	18.3	21.9
Public Sector	6.0	13.4	13.7	15.6	18.3	21.9
of which: General Government	5.8	13.2	13.6	15.4	18.1	21.7
Private sector guaranteed by Public Sector	..	..	..	..	..	..
Private sector not guaranteed	..	..	..	..	..	..
Interest payments (long-term)	**2.1**	**5.7**	**5.6**	**5.8**	**5.7**	**6.1**
Public and publicly guaranteed sector	2.1	5.7	5.6	5.8	5.7	6.1
Public Sector	2.1	5.7	5.6	5.8	5.7	6.1
of which: General Government	2.1	5.7	5.6	5.7	5.7	6.1
Private sector guaranteed by Public Sector	..	..	..	..	..	..
Private sector not guaranteed	..	..	..	..	..	..
Summary external debt stock by creditor type						
Long-term External debt stocks	**205.6**	**417.3**	**407.6**	**390.1**	**415.7**	**403.2**
Public and publicly guaranteed debt from:	205.6	417.3	407.6	390.1	415.7	403.2
Official creditors	205.6	417.3	407.6	390.1	415.7	403.2
Multilateral	176.0	221.6	214.0	203.7	215.0	208.1
of which: World Bank	79.0	95.6	96.1	92.8	103.4	104.9
Bilateral	29.6	195.7	193.6	186.4	200.7	195.1
Private creditors	..	..	..	..	..	..
Bondholders	..	..	..	..	..	..
Commercial banks and others	..	..	..	..	..	..
Private nonguaranteed debt from:	..	..	..	..	..	..
Bondholders	..	..	..	..	..	..
Commercial banks and others	..	..	..	..	..	..
Use of IMF Credit	1.8	32.9	29.8	27.4	27.4	24.3
Net financial inflows						
Net debt inflows						
Use of IMF Credit	..	0.0	-1.6	-1.6	-1.6	-2.5
Long-term	19.6	23.1	9.5	-1.3	2.8	0.1
Official creditors	19.6	23.1	9.5	-1.3	2.8	0.1
Multilateral	0.0	-4.7	1.6	-4.3	-0.1	-2.0
of which: World Bank	1.9	-1.9	4.5	-0.6	5.2	4.0
Bilateral	19.5	27.8	7.9	3.0	2.9	2.1
Private creditors	..	..	..	..	..	..
Bondholders	..	..	..	..	..	..
Banks and other private	..	..	..	..	..	..
Short-term	0.0	0.0	0.0	0.0	0.0	0.0
Net equity inflows						
Foreign direct investment	45.9	22.6	26.9	2.5	9.1	16.7
Portfolio equity	..	0.0	-0.1	0.0	0.0	..
Debt ratios						
External debt stocks to exports (%)	107.2	184.4	182.6	162.7	154.5	137.2
External debt stocks to GNI (%)	34.5	58.1	55.5	54.4	54.4	51.3
Debt service to exports (%)	4.2	7.8	8.8	9.0	8.9	9.8
Short-term to external debt stocks (%)	0.0	0.0	0.0	0.0	0.0	0.0
Multilateral to external debt stocks (%)	84.9	49.2	48.9	48.8	48.5	48.7
Reserves to external debt stocks (%)	39.5	26.9	28.0	23.8	29.6	39.8
Gross national income (GNI)	601.9	775.4	788.0	768.1	814.7	832.6

SÃO TOMÉ AND PRÍNCIPE

(US$ million, unless otherwise indicated)

	2008	2014	2015	2016	2017	2018
Summary external debt data by debtor type						
Total External debt stocks	**131.7**	**229.0**	**243.2**	**248.2**	**266.3**	**249.6**
Use of IMF Credit	4.8	14.9	14.2	14.7	16.8	16.8
Long-term external debt	108.7	202.5	220.4	224.2	242.0	223.1
Public and publicly guaranteed sector	108.7	202.5	220.4	224.2	242.0	223.1
Public Sector	108.7	198.2	216.2	220.0	237.8	218.8
of which: General Government	108.7	198.2	216.2	220.0	237.8	218.8
Private sector guaranteed by Public Sector	0.0	4.2	4.2	4.2	4.2	4.2
Private sector not guaranteed	..	..	..	..	..	..
Short-term external debt	18.2	11.6	8.6	9.3	7.5	9.8
Disbursements (long-term)	**5.2**	**40.4**	**25.3**	**8.2**	**9.5**	**5.6**
Public and publicly guaranteed sector	5.2	40.4	25.3	8.2	9.5	5.6
Public Sector	5.2	40.4	25.3	8.2	9.5	5.6
of which: General Government	5.2	40.4	25.3	8.2	9.5	5.6
Private sector guaranteed by Public Sector	..	..	..	..	..	..
Private sector not guaranteed	..	..	..	..	..	..
Principal repayments (long-term)	**1.7**	**11.5**	**0.8**	**0.9**	**2.1**	**2.7**
Public and publicly guaranteed sector	1.7	11.5	0.8	0.9	2.1	2.7
Public Sector	1.7	11.5	0.8	0.9	2.1	2.7
of which: General Government	1.7	11.5	0.8	0.9	2.1	2.7
Private sector guaranteed by Public Sector	..	..	..	..	..	..
Private sector not guaranteed	..	..	..	..	..	..
Interest payments (long-term)	**0.3**	**1.1**	**1.0**	**1.1**	**1.1**	**1.3**
Public and publicly guaranteed sector	0.3	1.1	1.0	1.1	1.1	1.3
Public Sector	0.3	1.1	1.0	1.1	1.1	1.3
of which: General Government	0.3	1.1	1.0	1.1	1.1	1.3
Private sector guaranteed by Public Sector	..	..	..	..	..	..
Private sector not guaranteed	..	..	..	..	..	..
Summary external debt stock by creditor type						
Long-term External debt stocks	**108.7**	**202.5**	**220.4**	**224.2**	**242.0**	**223.1**
Public and publicly guaranteed debt from:	108.7	202.5	220.4	224.2	242.0	223.1
Official creditors	108.7	202.5	220.4	224.2	242.0	223.1
Multilateral	35.9	37.7	37.9	40.1	44.9	46.9
of which: World Bank	13.3	13.0	12.2	11.6	12.0	11.5
Bilateral	72.9	164.7	182.6	184.1	197.2	176.2
Private creditors	..	..	..	..	..	..
Bondholders	..	..	..	..	..	..
Commercial banks and others	..	..	..	..	..	..
Private nonguaranteed debt from:	..	..	..	..	..	..
Bondholders	..	..	..	..	..	..
Commercial banks and others	..	..	..	..	..	..
Use of IMF Credit	4.8	14.9	14.2	14.7	16.8	16.8
Net financial inflows						
Net debt inflows						
Use of IMF Credit	1.3	-1.1	-0.1	1.0	1.2	0.4
Long-term	3.5	28.9	24.6	7.2	7.4	2.9
Official creditors	3.5	28.8	24.6	7.2	7.4	2.9
Multilateral	3.5	0.8	1.4	2.9	2.9	2.9
of which: World Bank	2.7	-0.2	-0.3	-0.3	-0.3	-0.3
Bilateral	..	28.0	23.2	4.3	4.5	0.0
Private creditors	..	..	..	..	..	..
Bondholders	..	..	..	..	..	..
Banks and other private	..	..	..	..	..	..
Short-term	-1.0	-1.1	-3.0	0.9	-2.1	2.4
Net equity inflows						
Foreign direct investment	79.1	16.5	24.8	23.3	32.9	30.2
Portfolio equity	0.0	0.0	0.0	-0.1	0.1	0.0
Debt ratios						
External debt stocks to exports (%)	677.3	229.9	250.9	241.4	281.0	242.9
External debt stocks to GNI (%)	70.1	64.6	76.7	71.2	71.2	58.8
Debt service to exports (%)	12.0	13.9	2.9	2.8	4.1	4.5
Short-term to external debt stocks (%)	13.8	5.1	3.5	3.8	2.8	3.9
Multilateral to external debt stocks (%)	27.2	16.5	15.6	16.2	16.9	18.8
Reserves to external debt stocks (%)	46.5	27.7	30.0	25.5	22.1	17.5
Gross national income (GNI)	187.9	354.6	317.2	348.5	373.9	424.8

SENEGAL

(US$ million, unless otherwise indicated)

Summary external debt data by debtor type

	2008	2014	2015	2016	2017	2018
Total External debt stocks	**2,851**	**5,631**	**5,903**	**6,688**	**8,896**	**12,485**
Use of IMF Credit	102	395	344	299	283	242
Long-term external debt	2,552	5,236	5,559	6,388	8,613	12,243
Public and publicly guaranteed sector	2,372	4,964	5,330	6,149	8,363	11,800
Public Sector	2,372	4,964	5,330	6,149	8,363	11,800
of which: General Government	2,365	4,963	5,330	6,149	8,363	11,800
Private sector guaranteed by Public Sector	..	..	..	..	..	..
Private sector not guaranteed	180	272	229	239	250	442
Short-term external debt	197	0	0	0	0	0
Disbursements (long-term)	**522**	**996**	**643**	**1,228**	**2,083**	**4,396**
Public and publicly guaranteed sector	518	875	595	1,096	1,919	4,000
Public Sector	518	875	595	1,096	1,919	4,000
of which: General Government	518	875	595	1,096	1,919	4,000
Private sector guaranteed by Public Sector	..	..	..	..	..	..
Private sector not guaranteed	4	122	49	133	165	396
Principal repayments (long-term)	**126**	**214**	**193**	**207**	**329**	**475**
Public and publicly guaranteed sector	87	117	101	121	149	308
Public Sector	87	117	101	121	149	308
of which: General Government	86	116	101	121	149	308
Private sector guaranteed by Public Sector	..	..	..	..	..	..
Private sector not guaranteed	39	97	92	86	180	167
Interest payments (long-term)	**49**	**128**	**150**	**155**	**230**	**320**
Public and publicly guaranteed sector	36	111	138	145	224	309
Public Sector	36	111	138	145	224	309
of which: General Government	36	111	138	145	224	309
Private sector guaranteed by Public Sector	..	..	..	..	..	..
Private sector not guaranteed	13	17	12	10	6	11

Summary external debt stock by creditor type

	2008	2014	2015	2016	2017	2018
Long-term External debt stocks	**2,552**	**5,236**	**5,559**	**6,388**	**8,613**	**12,243**
Public and publicly guaranteed debt from:	2,372	4,964	5,330	6,149	8,363	11,800
Official creditors	2,367	4,022	4,271	5,105	6,139	7,283
Multilateral	1,551	2,755	2,778	3,054	3,618	3,920
of which: World Bank	786	1,504	1,598	1,670	1,999	2,070
Bilateral	817	1,267	1,493	2,051	2,521	3,362
Private creditors	4	942	1,060	1,044	2,224	4,517
Bondholders	..	931	886	874	2,025	4,031
Commercial banks and others	4	11	174	170	199	487
Private nonguaranteed debt from:	180	272	229	239	250	442
Bondholders	..	..	..	..	..	..
Commercial banks and others	180	272	229	239	250	442
Use of IMF Credit	102	395	344	299	283	242

Net financial inflows

	2008	2014	2015	2016	2017	2018
Net debt inflows						
Use of IMF Credit	38	-18	-34	-36	-34	-34
Long-term	396	782	450	1,021	1,754	3,922
Official creditors	433	258	493	972	665	1,337
Multilateral	197	159	189	368	314	417
of which: World Bank	133	138	162	124	224	123
Bilateral	236	98	305	605	350	920
Private creditors	-37	524	-43	49	1,090	2,585
Bondholders	..	489	..	..	1,100	2,051
Banks and other private	-37	35	-43	49	-10	534
Short-term	-135	0	0	0	0	0
Net equity inflows						
Foreign direct investment	442	351	259	271	367	629
Portfolio equity	-93	11	20	25	13	..

Debt ratios

	2008	2014	2015	2016	2017	2018
External debt stocks to exports (%)	75	123	137	152	181	..
External debt stocks to GNI (%)	17	29	34	36	43	53
Debt service to exports (%)	5	8	9	9	12	..
Short-term to external debt stocks (%)	7	0	0	0	0	0
Multilateral to external debt stocks (%)	54	49	47	46	41	31
Reserves to external debt stocks (%)	56	36	34	..	..	..
Gross national income (GNI)	16,902	19,394	17,376	18,529	20,496	23,435

SERBIA

(US$ million, unless otherwise indicated)

	2008	2014	2015	2016	2017	2018
Summary external debt data by debtor type						
Total External debt stocks	**30,493**	**32,999**	**31,301**	**29,537**	**34,333**	**34,339**
Use of IMF Credit	87	830	633	598	634	619
Long-term external debt	26,719	31,631	29,780	27,811	32,120	31,607
Public and publicly guaranteed sector	8,399	16,489	16,276	16,215	16,422	15,088
Public Sector	8,396	16,325	16,137	16,084	16,308	15,088
of which: General Government	6,752	14,882	14,823	14,879	15,140	14,183
Private sector guaranteed by Public Sector	3	164	139	131	114	0
Private sector not guaranteed	18,320	15,142	13,505	11,595	15,698	16,519
Short-term external debt	3,687	539	888	1,128	1,579	2,113
Disbursements (long-term)	**6,996**	**4,893**	**3,112**	**3,698**	**7,337**	**4,709**
Public and publicly guaranteed sector	294	1,810	1,378	1,207	1,439	1,502
Public Sector	294	1,810	1,378	1,207	1,439	1,502
of which: General Government	185	1,664	1,182	934	1,294	1,394
Private sector guaranteed by Public Sector	..	0	0	..	..	..
Private sector not guaranteed	6,703	3,083	1,734	2,492	5,898	3,207
Principal repayments (long-term)	**3,486**	**6,340**	**2,980**	**5,016**	**4,086**	**4,813**
Public and publicly guaranteed sector	181	923	827	1,030	2,195	2,501
Public Sector	180	923	819	1,027	2,161	2,389
of which: General Government	137	622	588	677	1,862	2,056
Private sector guaranteed by Public Sector	1	0	8	3	34	112
Private sector not guaranteed	3,305	5,417	2,153	3,986	1,891	2,312
Interest payments (long-term)	**1,136**	**1,241**	**1,117**	**917**	**869**	**908**
Public and publicly guaranteed sector	354	622	594	588	576	547
Public Sector	354	615	586	582	571	543
of which: General Government	308	546	532	536	542	523
Private sector guaranteed by Public Sector	0	7	8	6	5	4
Private sector not guaranteed	782	619	523	330	292	361
Summary external debt stock by creditor type						
Long-term External debt stocks	**26,719**	**31,631**	**29,780**	**27,811**	**32,120**	**31,607**
Public and publicly guaranteed debt from:	8,399	16,489	16,276	16,215	16,422	15,088
Official creditors	7,206	10,246	10,200	10,366	11,721	11,578
Multilateral	4,554	5,444	5,373	5,313	6,246	5,861
of which: World Bank	2,931	2,463	2,515	2,384	2,939	2,799
Bilateral	2,652	4,802	4,827	5,053	5,475	5,716
Private creditors	1,193	6,242	6,075	5,849	4,701	3,511
Bondholders	..	5,250	5,250	5,250	4,500	3,500
Commercial banks and others	1,193	992	825	599	201	11
Private nonguaranteed debt from:	18,320	15,142	13,505	11,595	15,698	16,519
Bondholders	165	878	1,041	1,206	2,825	2,752
Commercial banks and others	18,155	14,263	12,464	10,389	12,872	13,767
Use of IMF Credit	87	830	633	598	634	619
Net financial inflows						
Net debt inflows						
Use of IMF Credit	..	-755	-162	-16	..	..
Long-term	3,511	-1,447	132	-1,318	3,252	-105
Official creditors	111	1,091	656	391	421	191
Multilateral	160	-47	453	114	206	-117
of which: World Bank	12	68	274	-56	226	-17
Bilateral	-49	1,137	203	277	216	307
Private creditors	3,400	-2,538	-524	-1,709	2,830	-295
Bondholders	..	237	162	166	774	-1,000
Banks and other private	3,400	-2,775	-686	-1,874	2,056	705
Short-term	1,437	-151	211	382	350	633
Net equity inflows						
Foreign direct investment	2,762	1,879	2,107	1,521	1,657	3,119
Portfolio equity	-55	-22	-90	-14	-7	-28
Debt ratios						
External debt stocks to exports (%)	204	165	172	148	153	134
External debt stocks to GNI (%)	60	73	83	77	83	72
Debt service to exports (%)	32	42	23	30	22	22
Short-term to external debt stocks (%)	12	2	3	4	5	6
Multilateral to external debt stocks (%)	15	16	17	18	18	17
Reserves to external debt stocks (%)	36	34	34	34	32	35
Gross national income (GNI)	50,839	45,280	37,789	38,393	41,227	47,903

SIERRA LEONE

(US$ million, unless otherwise indicated)

	2008	2014	2015	2016	2017	2018
Summary external debt data by debtor type						
Total External debt stocks	**633.8**	**1,426.9**	**1,551.2**	**1,598.3**	**1,715.6**	**1,712.9**
Use of IMF Credit	80.0	303.2	391.0	443.9	509.5	501.1
Long-term external debt	544.8	910.1	946.3	953.4	1,011.1	1,023.3
Public and publicly guaranteed sector	544.8	910.1	946.3	953.4	1,011.1	1,023.3
Public Sector	544.8	910.1	946.3	953.4	1,011.1	1,023.3
of which: General Government	544.8	910.1	946.3	953.4	1,011.1	1,023.3
Private sector guaranteed by Public Sector	..	..	..	..	..	..
Private sector not guaranteed	..	..	..	..	..	..
Short-term external debt	9.0	213.6	213.9	201.0	195.1	188.5
Disbursements (long-term)	**68.9**	**52.7**	**80.0**	**42.7**	**68.0**	**57.0**
Public and publicly guaranteed sector	68.9	52.7	80.0	42.7	68.0	57.0
Public Sector	68.9	52.7	80.0	42.7	68.0	57.0
of which: General Government	68.9	52.7	80.0	42.7	68.0	57.0
Private sector guaranteed by Public Sector	..	..	..	..	..	..
Private sector not guaranteed	..	..	..	..	..	..
Principal repayments (long-term)	**2.4**	**14.2**	**14.6**	**21.0**	**24.7**	**28.5**
Public and publicly guaranteed sector	2.4	14.2	14.6	21.0	24.7	28.5
Public Sector	2.4	14.2	14.6	21.0	24.7	28.5
of which: General Government	2.4	14.2	14.6	21.0	24.7	28.5
Private sector guaranteed by Public Sector	..	..	..	..	..	..
Private sector not guaranteed	..	..	..	..	..	..
Interest payments (long-term)	**2.9**	**8.1**	**7.5**	**11.9**	**12.7**	**4.7**
Public and publicly guaranteed sector	2.9	8.1	7.5	11.9	12.7	4.7
Public Sector	2.9	8.1	7.5	11.9	12.7	4.7
of which: General Government	2.9	8.1	7.5	11.9	12.7	4.7
Private sector guaranteed by Public Sector	..	..	..	..	..	..
Private sector not guaranteed	..	..	..	..	..	..
Summary external debt stock by creditor type						
Long-term External debt stocks	**544.8**	**910.1**	**946.3**	**953.4**	**1,011.1**	**1,023.3**
Public and publicly guaranteed debt from:	544.8	910.1	946.3	953.4	1,011.1	1,023.3
Official creditors	333.7	714.6	752.8	760.0	817.7	833.0
Multilateral	273.0	564.0	591.7	602.5	670.1	680.9
of which: World Bank	108.4	236.7	225.7	224.3	275.7	284.3
Bilateral	60.6	150.6	161.2	157.5	147.6	152.1
Private creditors	211.1	195.4	193.4	193.4	193.4	190.3
Bondholders	..	..	..	..	..	..
Commercial banks and others	211.1	195.4	193.4	193.4	193.4	190.3
Private nonguaranteed debt from:	..	..	..	..	..	..
Bondholders	..	..	..	..	..	..
Commercial banks and others	..	..	..	..	..	..
Use of IMF Credit	80.0	303.2	391.0	443.9	509.5	501.1
Net financial inflows						
Net debt inflows						
Use of IMF Credit	18.0	40.6	102.0	66.8	38.1	3.6
Long-term	66.5	38.5	65.5	21.7	43.3	28.4
Official creditors	66.5	38.5	65.5	21.7	43.3	28.4
Multilateral	54.3	39.8	51.0	21.9	43.1	21.6
of which: World Bank	25.6	9.8	5.3	5.6	37.2	15.7
Bilateral	12.2	-1.3	14.4	-0.2	0.2	6.9
Private creditors	..	..	..	..	..	..
Bondholders	..	..	..	..	..	..
Banks and other private	..	..	..	..	..	..
Short-term	4.0	-0.5	0.7	-12.9	-5.9	-6.6
Net equity inflows						
Foreign direct investment	73.8	360.4	231.9	121.5	729.9	599.0
Portfolio equity	0.0	..	..	..	..	..
Debt ratios						
External debt stocks to exports (%)	182.1	94.5	196.9	170.3	209.9	..
External debt stocks to GNI (%)	23.5	29.1	37.3	48.8	47.3	45.1
Debt service to exports (%)	1.7	2.3	6.6	4.1	7.2	..
Short-term to external debt stocks (%)	1.4	15.0	13.8	12.6	11.4	11.0
Multilateral to external debt stocks (%)	43.1	39.5	38.1	37.7	39.1	39.8
Reserves to external debt stocks (%)	34.7	42.1	37.3	31.1	32.0	29.3
Gross national income (GNI)	2,700.6	4,896.1	4,162.1	3,277.0	3,629.6	3,798.5

SOLOMON ISLANDS

(US$ million, unless otherwise indicated)

	2008	2014	2015	2016	2017	2018
Summary external debt data by debtor type						
Total External debt stocks	**166.9**	**187.5**	**207.5**	**263.8**	**376.7**	**388.5**
Use of IMF Credit	1.0	31.8	27.7	23.6	21.0	17.1
Long-term external debt	162.8	140.8	158.0	205.6	327.8	328.4
Public and publicly guaranteed sector	137.1	89.6	81.2	86.7	96.5	96.0
Public Sector	137.1	89.6	81.2	86.7	96.5	96.0
of which: General Government	137.1	89.6	81.2	86.7	96.5	96.0
Private sector guaranteed by Public Sector	..	..	..	..	..	..
Private sector not guaranteed	25.8	51.1	76.8	118.9	231.3	232.3
Short-term external debt	3.1	15.0	21.7	34.7	27.9	43.0
Disbursements (long-term)	**1.1**	**13.4**	**32.6**	**38.4**	**177.0**	**36.8**
Public and publicly guaranteed sector	0.1	0.0	0.0	13.1	11.1	6.1
Public Sector	0.1	0.0	0.0	13.1	11.1	6.1
of which: General Government	0.1	0.0	0.0	13.1	11.1	6.1
Private sector guaranteed by Public Sector	..	..	..	..	..	..
Private sector not guaranteed	1.0	13.4	32.5	25.2	165.9	30.7
Principal repayments (long-term)	**10.8**	**13.5**	**8.5**	**13.2**	**17.1**	**29.5**
Public and publicly guaranteed sector	10.8	6.5	5.3	6.5	5.2	4.8
Public Sector	10.8	6.5	5.3	6.5	5.2	4.8
of which: General Government	10.8	6.5	5.3	6.5	5.2	4.8
Private sector guaranteed by Public Sector	..	..	..	..	..	..
Private sector not guaranteed	..	7.0	3.2	6.7	11.9	24.7
Interest payments (long-term)	**4.3**	**2.2**	**2.2**	**5.1**	**4.0**	**6.0**
Public and publicly guaranteed sector	4.3	1.4	1.1	1.1	1.1	1.1
Public Sector	4.3	1.4	1.1	1.1	1.1	1.1
of which: General Government	4.3	1.4	1.1	1.1	1.1	1.1
Private sector guaranteed by Public Sector	..	..	..	..	..	..
Private sector not guaranteed	0.0	0.8	1.1	4.0	3.0	4.9
Summary external debt stock by creditor type						
Long-term External debt stocks	**162.8**	**140.8**	**158.0**	**205.6**	**327.8**	**328.4**
Public and publicly guaranteed debt from:	137.1	89.6	81.2	86.7	96.5	96.0
Official creditors	136.6	89.6	81.2	86.7	96.5	96.0
Multilateral	113.7	76.5	69.3	75.9	86.8	87.5
of which: World Bank	44.5	34.1	31.2	33.6	36.1	36.6
Bilateral	23.0	13.1	11.9	10.8	9.7	8.5
Private creditors	0.4	..	..	..	..	..
Bondholders	..	..	..	..	..	..
Commercial banks and others	0.4	..	..	..	..	..
Private nonguaranteed debt from:	25.8	51.1	76.8	118.9	231.3	232.3
Bondholders	..	..	..	..	..	..
Commercial banks and others	25.8	51.1	76.8	118.9	231.3	232.3
Use of IMF Credit	1.0	31.8	27.7	23.6	21.0	17.1
Net financial inflows						
Net debt inflows						
Use of IMF Credit	..	-1.1	-2.7	-3.4	-3.8	-3.5
Long-term	-9.7	-0.1	24.0	25.1	159.9	7.3
Official creditors	-10.6	-6.5	-5.3	6.6	6.0	1.3
Multilateral	-7.8	-4.9	-4.2	7.7	7.1	2.4
of which: World Bank	-1.0	-1.6	-1.5	3.5	0.5	1.4
Bilateral	-2.8	-1.6	-1.1	-1.1	-1.1	-1.1
Private creditors	0.9	6.4	29.3	18.5	154.0	6.0
Bondholders	..	..	..	..	..	..
Banks and other private	0.9	6.4	29.3	18.5	154.0	6.0
Short-term	0.0	12.0	6.8	13.0	-6.8	15.2
Net equity inflows						
Foreign direct investment	57.7	1.2	6.9	28.6	29.9	19.3
Portfolio equity	..	..	..	..	0.0	0.0
Debt ratios						
External debt stocks to exports (%)	59.7	30.6	35.9	44.2	57.7	53.8
External debt stocks to GNI (%)	32.5	17.1	18.5	22.7	30.8	29.1
Debt service to exports (%)	5.4	2.8	2.4	3.8	3.9	5.6
Short-term to external debt stocks (%)	1.8	8.0	10.5	13.2	7.4	11.1
Multilateral to external debt stocks (%)	68.1	40.8	33.4	28.8	23.1	22.5
Reserves to external debt stocks (%)	53.2	249.0	238.2	184.4	144.2	150.9
Gross national income (GNI)	514.0	1,099.6	1,121.1	1,160.9	1,223.7	1,336.1

SOMALIA

(US$ million, unless otherwise indicated)

	2008	2014	2015	2016	2017	2018
Summary external debt data by debtor type						
Total External debt stocks	**2,984**	**2,960**	**2,894**	**2,865**	**2,958**	**2,932**
Use of IMF Credit	194	229	219	212	225	220
Long-term external debt	1,992	1,918	1,877	1,859	1,907	1,889
Public and publicly guaranteed sector	1,992	1,918	1,877	1,859	1,907	1,889
Public Sector	1,992	1,918	1,877	1,859	1,907	1,889
of which: General Government	1,968	1,895	1,854	1,836	1,884	1,866
Private sector guaranteed by Public Sector	..	..	..	..	..	..
Private sector not guaranteed	..	..	..	..	..	..
Short-term external debt	798	814	798	793	826	823
Disbursements (long-term)	**0**	**0**	**0**	**0**	**0**	**0**
Public and publicly guaranteed sector	0	0	0	0	0	0
Public Sector	0	0	0	0	0	0
of which: General Government	0	0	0	0	0	0
Private sector guaranteed by Public Sector	..	..	..	..	..	..
Private sector not guaranteed	..	..	..	..	..	..
Principal repayments (long-term)	**0**	**0**	**0**	**0**	**0**	**0**
Public and publicly guaranteed sector	0	0	0	0	0	0
Public Sector	0	0	0	0	0	0
of which: General Government	0	0	0	0	0	0
Private sector guaranteed by Public Sector	..	..	..	..	..	..
Private sector not guaranteed	..	..	..	..	..	..
Interest payments (long-term)	**0**	**0**	**0**	**0**	**0**	**0**
Public and publicly guaranteed sector	0	0	0	0	0	0
Public Sector	0	0	0	0	0	0
of which: General Government	0	0	0	0	0	0
Private sector guaranteed by Public Sector	..	..	..	..	..	..
Private sector not guaranteed	..	..	..	..	..	..
Summary external debt stock by creditor type						
Long-term External debt stocks	**1,992**	**1,918**	**1,877**	**1,859**	**1,907**	**1,889**
Public and publicly guaranteed debt from:	1,992	1,918	1,877	1,859	1,907	1,889
Official creditors	1,955	1,883	1,843	1,825	1,872	1,855
Multilateral	812	769	745	732	760	749
of which: World Bank	446	424	412	404	420	413
Bilateral	1,143	1,113	1,098	1,093	1,112	1,106
Private creditors	37	35	34	34	35	34
Bondholders	..	..	..	..	..	..
Commercial banks and others	37	35	34	34	35	34
Private nonguaranteed debt from:	..	..	..	..	..	..
Bondholders	..	..	..	..	..	..
Commercial banks and others	..	..	..	..	..	..
Use of IMF Credit	194	229	219	212	225	220
Net financial inflows						
Net debt inflows						
Use of IMF Credit	..	0	..	..	..	..
Long-term	0	0	0	0	0	0
Official creditors	0	0	0	0	0	0
Multilateral	0	0	0	0	0	0
of which: World Bank	0	0	0	0	0	0
Bilateral	0	..	0	0	0	0
Private creditors	0	..	0	0	0	0
Bondholders	..	..	..	..	..	..
Banks and other private	0	..	0	0	0	0
Short-term	0	0	0	0	0	0
Net equity inflows						
Foreign direct investment	87	261	303	334	384	409
Portfolio equity	..	..	..	..	..	..
Debt ratios						
External debt stocks to exports (%)	..	..	..	..	..	..
External debt stocks to GNI (%)	..	45	44	42	42	39
Debt service to exports (%)	..	..	..	..	..	..
Short-term to external debt stocks (%)	27	27	28	28	28	28
Multilateral to external debt stocks (%)	27	26	26	26	26	26
Reserves to external debt stocks (%)	..	..	..	..	..	..
Gross national income (GNI)	..	6,532	6,640	6,810	7,096	7,450

SOUTH AFRICA

(US$ million, unless otherwise indicated)

	2008	2014	2015	2016	2017	2018
Summary external debt data by debtor type						
Total External debt stocks	**69,960**	**141,599**	**138,078**	**146,041**	**180,497**	**179,306**
Use of IMF Credit	339	2,587	2,474	2,400	2,543	2,483
Long-term external debt	44,159	110,970	106,528	113,850	141,324	140,193
Public and publicly guaranteed sector	19,280	57,137	57,788	62,195	81,592	77,029
Public Sector	19,280	57,137	57,788	62,195	81,592	77,029
of which: General Government	14,430	53,558	53,149	56,451	74,754	69,512
Private sector guaranteed by Public Sector	..	..	..	..	..	..
Private sector not guaranteed	24,879	53,832	48,740	51,655	59,732	63,165
Short-term external debt	25,462	28,042	29,075	29,791	36,630	36,630
Disbursements (long-term)	**1,871**	**7,993**	**14,614**	**12,421**	**35,231**	**16,150**
Public and publicly guaranteed sector	1,219	3,559	1,935	5,433	20,292	3,747
Public Sector	1,219	3,559	1,935	5,433	20,292	3,747
of which: General Government	3	2,750	133	4,331	18,930	2,055
Private sector guaranteed by Public Sector	..	..	..	..	..	..
Private sector not guaranteed	652	4,435	12,679	6,988	14,939	12,403
Principal repayments (long-term)	**4,892**	**3,153**	**2,687**	**7,420**	**8,119**	**16,674**
Public and publicly guaranteed sector	2,753	1,048	221	1,355	1,242	7,708
Public Sector	2,753	1,048	221	1,355	1,242	7,708
of which: General Government	1,059	1,022	120	1,110	804	7,156
Private sector guaranteed by Public Sector	..	..	..	..	..	..
Private sector not guaranteed	2,139	2,104	2,465	6,065	6,877	8,967
Interest payments (long-term)	**1,931**	**3,706**	**5,612**	**5,721**	**5,725**	**6,706**
Public and publicly guaranteed sector	1,192	2,411	2,951	3,041	3,225	4,229
Public Sector	1,192	2,411	2,951	3,041	3,225	4,229
of which: General Government	948	2,308	2,712	2,737	2,862	3,807
Private sector guaranteed by Public Sector	..	..	..	..	..	..
Private sector not guaranteed	739	1,294	2,661	2,680	2,500	2,478
Summary external debt stock by creditor type						
Long-term External debt stocks	**44,159**	**110,970**	**106,528**	**113,850**	**141,324**	**140,193**
Public and publicly guaranteed debt from:	19,280	57,137	57,788	62,195	81,592	77,029
Official creditors	259	4,097	3,495	4,076	5,003	4,256
Multilateral	259	4,097	3,495	4,076	5,003	4,256
of which: World Bank	26	1,967	1,785	2,343	2,686	2,277
Bilateral	..	..	..	..	..	..
Private creditors	19,021	53,040	54,293	58,119	76,588	72,772
Bondholders	13,663	52,522	52,409	55,678	73,815	70,615
Commercial banks and others	5,358	518	1,884	2,441	2,774	2,158
Private nonguaranteed debt from:	24,879	53,832	48,740	51,655	59,732	63,165
Bondholders	8,322	10,366	10,309	9,878	10,116	11,187
Commercial banks and others	16,557	43,467	38,431	41,776	49,616	51,977
Use of IMF Credit	339	2,587	2,474	2,400	2,543	2,483
Net financial inflows						
Net debt inflows						
Use of IMF Credit	..	0	..	..	..	..
Long-term	-3,021	4,841	11,927	5,001	27,111	-525
Official creditors	-23	850	340	266	601	-168
Multilateral	-23	850	340	266	601	-168
of which: World Bank	0	745	357	324	230	-46
Bilateral	..	..	..	..	..	..
Private creditors	-2,998	3,991	11,587	4,735	26,510	-356
Bondholders	-2,401	534	1,620	2,831	18,359	-2,125
Banks and other private	-597	3,457	9,968	1,904	8,152	1,769
Short-term	1,418	793	1,033	716	6,839	0
Net equity inflows						
Foreign direct investment	6,729	1,292	-596	364	-265	1,377
Portfolio equity	-4,707	9,338	8,499	1,640	7,576	2,945
Debt ratios						
External debt stocks to exports (%)	64	120	133	151	165	153
External debt stocks to GNI (%)	25	41	45	51	53	51
Debt service to exports (%)	7	7	9	14	13	20
Short-term to external debt stocks (%)	36	20	21	20	20	20
Multilateral to external debt stocks (%)	0	3	3	3	3	2
Reserves to external debt stocks (%)	44	31	30	29	25	26
Gross national income (GNI)	277,827	341,280	309,671	287,557	338,405	354,663

SRI LANKA

(US$ million, unless otherwise indicated)

	2008	2014	2015	2016	2017	2018
Summary external debt data by debtor type						
Total External debt stocks	**16,321**	**42,263**	**43,925**	**46,646**	**50,760**	**52,626**
Use of IMF Credit	278	1,821	1,240	1,086	1,329	1,545
Long-term external debt	13,318	33,117	35,097	38,148	41,421	42,900
Public and publicly guaranteed sector	12,584	25,825	27,453	30,099	32,619	34,319
Public Sector	12,584	25,825	27,453	30,099	32,619	34,319
of which: General Government	12,483	22,973	24,820	27,426	30,842	33,751
Private sector guaranteed by Public Sector	..	..	..	..	..	..
Private sector not guaranteed	734	7,292	7,645	8,049	8,802	8,581
Short-term external debt	2,725	7,325	7,588	7,413	8,011	8,181
Disbursements (long-term)	**1,238**	**7,325**	**4,509**	**4,605**	**5,338**	**7,231**
Public and publicly guaranteed sector	1,083	4,093	3,760	3,985	4,357	5,073
Public Sector	1,083	4,093	3,760	3,985	4,357	5,073
of which: General Government	1,081	3,763	3,680	3,806	4,247	4,991
Private sector guaranteed by Public Sector	..	..	..	..	..	..
Private sector not guaranteed	156	3,232	750	620	981	2,158
Principal repayments (long-term)	**816**	**4,913**	**2,115**	**1,702**	**2,713**	**5,521**
Public and publicly guaranteed sector	755	2,702	1,718	1,186	2,486	3,189
Public Sector	755	2,702	1,718	1,186	2,486	3,189
of which: General Government	681	831	1,421	1,048	1,477	1,901
Private sector guaranteed by Public Sector	..	..	..	..	..	..
Private sector not guaranteed	61	2,211	397	516	227	2,333
Interest payments (long-term)	**286**	**705**	**779**	**990**	**1,029**	**1,547**
Public and publicly guaranteed sector	252	656	731	925	970	1,247
Public Sector	252	656	731	925	970	1,247
of which: General Government	245	557	644	787	851	1,153
Private sector guaranteed by Public Sector	..	..	..	..	..	..
Private sector not guaranteed	35	50	48	65	59	300

	2008	2014	2015	2016	2017	2018
Summary external debt stock by creditor type						
Long-term External debt stocks	**13,318**	**33,117**	**35,097**	**38,148**	**41,421**	**42,900**
Public and publicly guaranteed debt from:	12,584	25,825	27,453	30,099	32,619	34,319
Official creditors	11,285	17,030	17,219	17,710	18,924	20,045
Multilateral	5,559	6,876	6,901	7,186	7,853	8,050
of which: World Bank	2,381	2,843	2,784	2,970	3,244	3,210
Bilateral	5,725	10,154	10,317	10,524	11,071	11,995
Private creditors	1,300	8,795	10,234	12,389	13,695	14,274
Bondholders	500	7,000	8,650	10,150	11,150	12,400
Commercial banks and others	800	1,795	1,584	2,239	2,545	1,874
Private nonguaranteed debt from:	734	7,292	7,645	8,049	8,802	8,581
Bondholders	100	437	305	362	362	262
Commercial banks and others	634	6,855	7,340	7,687	8,440	8,319
Use of IMF Credit	278	1,821	1,240	1,086	1,329	1,545

	2008	2014	2015	2016	2017	2018
Net financial inflows						
Net debt inflows						
Use of IMF Credit	-78	-720	-506	-122	174	252
Long-term	422	2,413	2,394	2,903	2,625	1,710
Official creditors	270	1,301	547	618	641	1,274
Multilateral	228	322	273	452	340	333
of which: World Bank	40	125	60	270	118	34
Bilateral	43	979	275	165	300	941
Private creditors	152	1,112	1,846	2,286	1,984	436
Bondholders	-65	1,984	1,517	1,558	1,000	1,150
Banks and other private	217	-872	329	728	984	-714
Short-term	1,388	492	314	-234	490	166
Net equity inflows						
Foreign direct investment	542	469	439	710	535	463
Portfolio equity	-488	178	-60	24	359	-4

	2008	2014	2015	2016	2017	2018
Debt ratios						
External debt stocks to exports (%)	158	250	257	265	263	256
External debt stocks to GNI (%)	41	54	56	58	59	61
Debt service to exports (%)	12	38	21	19	22	36
Short-term to external debt stocks (%)	17	17	17	16	16	16
Multilateral to external debt stocks (%)	34	16	16	15	15	15
Reserves to external debt stocks (%)	15	17	15	11	14	..
Gross national income (GNI)	39,744	77,548	78,582	80,205	85,705	86,489

ST. LUCIA

(US$ million, unless otherwise indicated)

	2008	2014	2015	2016	2017	2018
Summary external debt data by debtor type						
Total External debt stocks	**832.2**	**527.0**	**530.2**	**542.2**	**622.1**	**615.8**
Use of IMF Credit	1.1	38.0	33.4	29.8	28.5	24.8
Long-term external debt	316.2	371.3	420.0	430.9	489.8	499.8
Public and publicly guaranteed sector	316.2	371.3	420.0	430.9	489.8	499.8
Public Sector	299.4	362.9	399.8	410.9	467.5	475.8
of which: General Government	287.5	359.3	396.7	408.4	462.0	469.8
Private sector guaranteed by Public Sector	16.8	8.4	20.2	20.0	22.3	24.0
Private sector not guaranteed	..	..	..	..	..	..
Short-term external debt	514.9	117.7	76.8	81.5	103.8	91.1
Disbursements (long-term)	**13.0**	**25.2**	**21.4**	**7.3**	**13.5**	**6.5**
Public and publicly guaranteed sector	13.0	25.2	21.4	7.3	13.5	6.5
Public Sector	12.9	25.2	21.4	7.3	13.5	6.5
of which: General Government	12.9	25.2	21.3	7.3	10.0	5.6
Private sector guaranteed by Public Sector	0.1	0.0	0.0	0.0	0.0	0.0
Private sector not guaranteed	..	..	..	..	..	..
Principal repayments (long-term)	**32.4**	**17.0**	**46.7**	**23.8**	**18.0**	**17.8**
Public and publicly guaranteed sector	32.4	17.0	46.7	23.8	18.0	17.8
Public Sector	31.1	14.8	44.5	21.7	16.6	16.5
of which: General Government	25.9	14.2	43.9	21.1	16.0	16.0
Private sector guaranteed by Public Sector	1.4	2.2	2.2	2.1	1.4	1.3
Private sector not guaranteed	..	..	..	..	..	..
Interest payments (long-term)	**15.1**	**16.7**	**18.9**	**19.9**	**23.5**	**25.0**
Public and publicly guaranteed sector	15.1	16.7	18.9	19.9	23.5	25.0
Public Sector	14.3	16.3	18.1	19.1	22.7	24.1
of which: General Government	13.8	16.2	18.0	19.0	22.5	23.9
Private sector guaranteed by Public Sector	0.8	0.4	0.8	0.8	0.8	0.9
Private sector not guaranteed	..	..	..	..	..	..
Summary external debt stock by creditor type						
Long-term External debt stocks	**316.2**	**371.3**	**420.0**	**430.9**	**489.8**	**499.8**
Public and publicly guaranteed debt from:	316.2	371.3	420.0	430.9	489.8	499.8
Official creditors	232.5	249.4	259.8	248.0	253.2	242.9
Multilateral	205.4	215.3	219.7	211.0	218.4	211.5
of which: World Bank	67.4	84.5	81.3	79.5	85.6	85.6
Bilateral	27.1	34.1	40.2	37.0	34.7	31.3
Private creditors	83.6	121.8	160.2	182.9	236.6	256.9
Bondholders	83.6	121.8	160.2	182.9	236.6	256.9
Commercial banks and others	0.0	..	..	..	..	..
Private nonguaranteed debt from:	..	..	..	..	..	..
Bondholders	..	..	..	..	..	..
Commercial banks and others	..	..	..	..	..	..
Use of IMF Credit	1.1	38.0	33.4	29.8	28.5	24.8
Net financial inflows						
Net debt inflows						
Use of IMF Credit	..	-0.9	-3.0	-2.7	-3.0	-3.0
Long-term	-19.4	8.2	-25.3	-16.5	-4.4	-11.3
Official creditors	-4.5	9.2	0.9	-11.1	-3.8	-11.1
Multilateral	-1.0	-4.0	-6.3	-8.1	-0.8	-7.9
of which: World Bank	3.7	2.6	0.0	0.4	1.7	2.0
Bilateral	-3.5	13.2	7.2	-3.0	-3.0	-3.2
Private creditors	-15.0	-1.0	-26.1	-5.4	-0.6	-0.2
Bondholders	-11.9	-1.0	-26.1	-5.4	-0.6	-0.2
Banks and other private	-3.1	..	..	..	..	..
Short-term	341.0	45.4	-40.9	4.8	22.3	-12.7
Net equity inflows						
Foreign direct investment	108.5	62.2	110.8	138.1	142.7	135.1
Portfolio equity	..	0.0	0.6	0.5	0.8	..
Debt ratios						
External debt stocks to exports (%)	152.9	53.7	51.3	55.7	61.5	49.1
External debt stocks to GNI (%)	68.5	36.7	35.7	34.5	36.5	35.1
Debt service to exports (%)	10.6	3.7	6.7	4.9	4.6	3.9
Short-term to external debt stocks (%)	61.9	22.3	14.5	15.0	16.7	14.8
Multilateral to external debt stocks (%)	24.7	40.9	41.4	38.9	35.1	34.4
Reserves to external debt stocks (%)	17.2	48.9	59.9	56.4	51.7	46.4
Gross national income (GNI)	1,214.8	1,435.5	1,486.5	1,572.9	1,702.3	1,752.3

ST. VINCENT AND THE GRENADINES

(US$ million, unless otherwise indicated)

	2008	2014	2015	2016	2017	2018
Summary external debt data by debtor type						
Total External debt stocks	**232.2**	**340.9**	**343.9**	**333.5**	**337.1**	**328.2**
Use of IMF Credit	0.5	27.2	24.9	22.9	21.9	18.0
Long-term external debt	231.5	313.7	318.9	306.5	314.8	310.2
Public and publicly guaranteed sector	231.5	313.7	318.9	306.5	314.8	310.2
Public Sector	231.5	313.7	318.9	306.5	314.8	310.2
of which: General Government	212.4	303.1	310.2	299.2	308.3	303.8
Private sector guaranteed by Public Sector	..	..	..	..	..	..
Private sector not guaranteed	..	..	..	..	..	..
Short-term external debt	0.2	0.0	0.1	4.1	0.3	0.0
Disbursements (long-term)	**52.1**	**49.4**	**28.9**	**13.3**	**31.0**	**25.3**
Public and publicly guaranteed sector	52.1	49.4	28.9	13.3	31.0	25.3
Public Sector	52.1	49.4	28.9	13.3	31.0	25.3
of which: General Government	50.1	49.4	28.8	12.7	29.7	22.9
Private sector guaranteed by Public Sector	..	..	..	..	..	..
Private sector not guaranteed	..	..	..	..	..	..
Principal repayments (long-term)	**19.8**	**22.1**	**24.8**	**24.6**	**24.7**	**29.1**
Public and publicly guaranteed sector	19.8	22.1	24.8	24.6	24.7	29.1
Public Sector	19.8	22.1	24.8	24.6	24.7	29.1
of which: General Government	19.4	20.1	22.9	22.7	22.7	26.5
Private sector guaranteed by Public Sector	..	..	..	..	..	..
Private sector not guaranteed	..	..	..	..	..	..
Interest payments (long-term)	**10.9**	**7.7**	**7.7**	**6.0**	**6.2**	**7.1**
Public and publicly guaranteed sector	10.9	7.7	7.7	6.0	6.2	7.1
Public Sector	10.9	7.7	7.7	6.0	6.2	7.1
of which: General Government	9.8	7.2	7.2	5.7	6.0	6.7
Private sector guaranteed by Public Sector	..	..	..	..	..	..
Private sector not guaranteed	..	..	..	..	..	..
Summary external debt stock by creditor type						
Long-term External debt stocks	**231.5**	**313.7**	**318.9**	**306.5**	**314.8**	**310.2**
Public and publicly guaranteed debt from:	231.5	313.7	318.9	306.5	314.8	310.2
Official creditors	160.9	296.6	308.2	299.2	300.6	299.8
Multilateral	135.4	252.2	255.6	251.7	245.8	240.7
of which: World Bank	22.3	33.0	32.0	31.5	32.7	31.8
Bilateral	25.5	44.4	52.6	47.5	54.7	59.0
Private creditors	70.6	17.1	10.7	7.3	14.3	10.5
Bondholders	..	..	..	..	10.4	9.1
Commercial banks and others	70.6	17.1	10.7	7.3	3.9	1.3
Private nonguaranteed debt from:	..	..	..	..	..	..
Bondholders	..	..	..	..	..	..
Commercial banks and others	..	..	..	..	..	..
Use of IMF Credit	0.5	27.2	24.9	22.9	21.9	18.0
Net financial inflows						
Net debt inflows						
Use of IMF Credit	..	5.7	-1.0	-1.3	-2.3	-3.5
Long-term	32.3	27.2	4.1	-11.4	6.3	-3.8
Official creditors	26.4	27.6	10.5	-8.0	-0.7	0.0
Multilateral	29.7	15.8	2.2	-3.0	-7.7	-4.3
of which: World Bank	1.1	2.1	0.2	0.5	-0.5	-0.2
Bilateral	-3.3	11.9	8.3	-5.0	7.0	4.3
Private creditors	5.9	-0.4	-6.4	-3.4	7.0	-3.8
Bondholders	..	..	..	..	10.4	-1.2
Banks and other private	5.9	-0.4	-6.4	-3.4	-3.4	-2.6
Short-term	0.0	0.0	0.0	0.0	0.0	0.0
Net equity inflows						
Foreign direct investment	75.2	109.9	53.6	154.7	99.8	100.3
Portfolio equity	..	0.7	-0.4	-0.8	-0.8	-0.1
Debt ratios						
External debt stocks to exports (%)	105.4	130.0	119.3	112.0	117.0	101.6
External debt stocks to GNI (%)	34.5	46.1	41.5	40.6	40.5	37.6
Debt service to exports (%)	13.9	11.6	11.6	10.8	11.6	12.3
Short-term to external debt stocks (%)	0.1	0.0	0.0	1.2	0.1	0.0
Multilateral to external debt stocks (%)	58.3	74.0	74.3	75.5	72.9	73.4
Reserves to external debt stocks (%)	36.0	46.2	48.3	57.6	54.0	51.7
Gross national income (GNI)	672.6	739.9	829.4	820.6	831.3	873.0

SUDAN

(US$ million, unless otherwise indicated)

	2008	2014	2015	2016	2017	2018
Summary external debt data by debtor type						
Total External debt stocks	**20,335**	**21,782**	**21,426**	**21,114**	**21,745**	**21,596**
Use of IMF Credit	486	591	557	531	555	542
Long-term external debt	13,163	15,945	15,797	15,546	15,875	15,672
Public and publicly guaranteed sector	13,163	15,945	15,797	15,546	15,875	15,672
Public Sector	13,163	15,945	15,797	15,546	15,875	15,672
of which: General Government	13,143	15,924	15,777	15,525	15,855	15,652
Private sector guaranteed by Public Sector	..	..	..	..	..	..
Private sector not guaranteed	..	..	..	..	..	..
Short-term external debt	6,685	5,247	5,072	5,037	5,315	5,382
Disbursements (long-term)	**673**	**291**	**558**	**151**	**116**	**88**
Public and publicly guaranteed sector	673	291	558	151	116	88
Public Sector	673	291	558	151	116	88
of which: General Government	673	291	558	151	116	88
Private sector guaranteed by Public Sector	..	..	..	..	..	..
Private sector not guaranteed	..	..	..	..	..	..
Principal repayments (long-term)	**219**	**180**	**414**	**224**	**139**	**159**
Public and publicly guaranteed sector	219	180	414	224	139	159
Public Sector	219	180	414	224	139	159
of which: General Government	219	180	414	224	139	159
Private sector guaranteed by Public Sector	..	..	..	..	..	..
Private sector not guaranteed	..	..	..	..	..	..
Interest payments (long-term)	**69**	**69**	**100**	**59**	**87**	**51**
Public and publicly guaranteed sector	69	69	100	59	87	51
Public Sector	69	69	100	59	87	51
of which: General Government	69	69	100	59	87	51
Private sector guaranteed by Public Sector	..	..	..	..	..	..
Private sector not guaranteed	..	..	..	..	..	..
Summary external debt stock by creditor type						
Long-term External debt stocks	**13,163**	**15,945**	**15,797**	**15,546**	**15,875**	**15,672**
Public and publicly guaranteed debt from:	13,163	15,945	15,797	15,546	15,875	15,672
Official creditors	10,773	11,373	11,231	11,025	11,276	11,092
Multilateral	3,323	3,498	3,376	3,378	3,525	3,504
of which: World Bank	1,300	1,246	1,228	1,219	1,283	1,283
Bilateral	7,450	7,875	7,855	7,648	7,751	7,587
Private creditors	2,390	4,572	4,566	4,520	4,599	4,580
Bondholders	..	..	..	..	..	..
Commercial banks and others	2,390	4,572	4,566	4,520	4,599	4,580
Private nonguaranteed debt from:	..	..	..	..	..	..
Bondholders	..	..	..	..	..	..
Commercial banks and others	..	..	..	..	..	..
Use of IMF Credit	486	591	557	531	555	542
Net financial inflows						
Net debt inflows						
Use of IMF Credit	-66	-11	-8	-10	-7	..
Long-term	454	112	145	-73	-24	-71
Official creditors	454	112	145	-73	-24	-71
Multilateral	154	56	-3	55	29	27
of which: World Bank	-1	8	18	17	16	20
Bilateral	299	55	147	-128	-52	-98
Private creditors	..	..	..	..	0	0
Bondholders	..	..	..	..	..	..
Banks and other private	..	..	..	..	0	0
Short-term	104	-103	-43	-21	60	51
Net equity inflows						
Foreign direct investment	-947	1,251	1,728	1,064	1,065	1,136
Portfolio equity	72	2	..	..	..	..
Debt ratios						
External debt stocks to exports (%)	167	359	436	455	370	422
External debt stocks to GNI (%)	40	29	24	24	19	57
Debt service to exports (%)	3	4	11	6	4	4
Short-term to external debt stocks (%)	33	24	24	24	24	25
Multilateral to external debt stocks (%)	16	16	16	16	16	16
Reserves to external debt stocks (%)	7	1	1	1	1	..
Gross national income (GNI)	50,828	74,214	87,965	86,576	112,471	37,949

SYRIAN ARAB REPUBLIC

(US$ million, unless otherwise indicated)

	2008	2014	2015	2016	2017	2018
Summary external debt data by debtor type						
Total External debt stocks	**5,389**	**4,609**	**4,420**	**4,368**	**4,605**	**4,589**
Use of IMF Credit	56	404	387	375	398	388
Long-term external debt	4,747	3,672	3,529	3,498	3,654	3,652
Public and publicly guaranteed sector	4,747	3,672	3,529	3,498	3,654	3,652
Public Sector	4,747	3,672	3,529	3,498	3,654	3,652
of which: General Government	4,071	3,156	3,035	3,013	3,144	3,153
Private sector guaranteed by Public Sector	..	..	..	..	..	..
Private sector not guaranteed	..	..	..	..	..	..
Short-term external debt	585	533	504	496	553	549
Disbursements (long-term)	**285**	**0**	**0**	**0**	**0**	**63**
Public and publicly guaranteed sector	285	0	0	0	0	63
Public Sector	285	0	0	0	0	63
of which: General Government	221	0	0	0	0	63
Private sector guaranteed by Public Sector	..	..	..	..	..	..
Private sector not guaranteed	..	..	..	..	..	..
Principal repayments (long-term)	**560**	**..**	**0**	**0**	**0**	**17**
Public and publicly guaranteed sector	560	..	0	0	0	17
Public Sector	560	..	0	0	0	17
of which: General Government	444	..	0	0	0	17
Private sector guaranteed by Public Sector	..	..	..	..	..	..
Private sector not guaranteed	..	..	..	..	..	..
Interest payments (long-term)	**125**	**..**	**0**	**0**	**0**	**1**
Public and publicly guaranteed sector	125	..	0	0	0	1
Public Sector	125	..	0	0	0	1
of which: General Government	104	..	0	0	0	1
Private sector guaranteed by Public Sector	..	..	..	..	..	..
Private sector not guaranteed	..	..	..	..	..	..
Summary external debt stock by creditor type						
Long-term External debt stocks	**4,747**	**3,672**	**3,529**	**3,498**	**3,654**	**3,652**
Public and publicly guaranteed debt from:	4,747	3,672	3,529	3,498	3,654	3,652
Official creditors	4,747	3,672	3,529	3,498	3,654	3,652
Multilateral	1,548	1,542	1,434	1,403	1,512	1,472
of which: World Bank	18	14	14	14	14	14
Bilateral	3,200	2,130	2,095	2,095	2,142	2,180
Private creditors	..	..	..	..	..	..
Bondholders	..	..	..	..	..	..
Commercial banks and others	..	..	..	..	..	..
Private nonguaranteed debt from:	..	..	..	..	..	..
Bondholders	..	..	..	..	..	..
Commercial banks and others	..	..	..	..	..	..
Use of IMF Credit	56	404	387	375	398	388
Net financial inflows						
Net debt inflows						
Use of IMF Credit	..	0	..	..	..	..
Long-term	-275	0	0	0	0	46
Official creditors	-275	0	0	0	0	46
Multilateral	85	0	0	0	0	1
of which: World Bank	-1	0	0	0	0	0
Bilateral	-360	0	0	0	0	44
Private creditors	..	..	..	..	..	..
Bondholders	..	..	..	..	..	..
Banks and other private	..	..	..	..	..	..
Short-term	-71	47	-46	-25	0	1
Net equity inflows						
Foreign direct investment	1,466	..	..	..	..	..
Portfolio equity	0	..	..	..	..	..
Debt ratios						
External debt stocks to exports (%)	27	..	..	..	..	..
External debt stocks to GNI (%)	..	..	..	..	..	..
Debt service to exports (%)	3	..	..	..	..	..
Short-term to external debt stocks (%)	11	12	11	11	12	12
Multilateral to external debt stocks (%)	29	33	32	32	33	32
Reserves to external debt stocks (%)	317	..	..	..	..	..
Gross national income (GNI)	..	..	..	..	..	..

TAJIKISTAN

(US$ million, unless otherwise indicated)

	2008	2014	2015	2016	2017	2018
Summary external debt data by debtor type						
Total External debt stocks	**2,497**	**5,123**	**5,142**	**5,166**	**6,098**	**5,977**
Use of IMF Credit	142	266	244	217	204	170
Long-term external debt	2,265	3,692	3,938	4,135	5,149	4,933
Public and publicly guaranteed sector	1,379	1,983	2,091	2,154	2,894	2,857
Public Sector	1,379	1,983	2,091	2,154	2,894	2,857
of which: General Government	1,366	1,979	2,087	2,149	2,890	2,851
Private sector guaranteed by Public Sector	..	..	..	..	..	..
Private sector not guaranteed	887	1,709	1,847	1,981	2,254	2,076
Short-term external debt	90	1,164	961	814	745	874
Disbursements (long-term)	**379**	**615**	**643**	**716**	**1,061**	**481**
Public and publicly guaranteed sector	356	128	251	211	790	127
Public Sector	356	128	251	211	790	127
of which: General Government	356	128	249	209	790	125
Private sector guaranteed by Public Sector	..	..	..	..	..	..
Private sector not guaranteed	24	487	392	505	271	354
Principal repayments (long-term)	**63**	**314**	**197**	**486**	**604**	**402**
Public and publicly guaranteed sector	51	101	96	112	113	129
Public Sector	51	101	96	112	113	129
of which: General Government	43	95	94	111	113	128
Private sector guaranteed by Public Sector	..	..	..	..	..	..
Private sector not guaranteed	12	213	101	374	490	273
Interest payments (long-term)	**29**	**92**	**89**	**108**	**60**	**120**
Public and publicly guaranteed sector	27	32	30	35	37	72
Public Sector	27	32	30	35	37	72
of which: General Government	23	32	30	35	37	71
Private sector guaranteed by Public Sector	..	..	..	..	..	..
Private sector not guaranteed	2	60	59	73	23	48
Summary external debt stock by creditor type						
Long-term External debt stocks	**2,265**	**3,692**	**3,938**	**4,135**	**5,149**	**4,933**
Public and publicly guaranteed debt from:	1,379	1,983	2,091	2,154	2,894	2,857
Official creditors	1,376	1,982	2,090	2,154	2,394	2,357
Multilateral	735	931	905	866	955	997
of which: World Bank	365	337	316	305	326	333
Bilateral	641	1,051	1,186	1,288	1,440	1,360
Private creditors	3	1	0	0	500	500
Bondholders	..	..	..	..	500	500
Commercial banks and others	3	1	0	0	0	0
Private nonguaranteed debt from:	887	1,709	1,847	1,981	2,254	2,076
Bondholders	..	..	..	..	..	..
Commercial banks and others	887	1,709	1,847	1,981	2,254	2,076
Use of IMF Credit	142	266	244	217	204	170
Net financial inflows						
Net debt inflows						
Use of IMF Credit	-31	-4	-11	-20	-25	-30
Long-term	316	301	446	229	458	80
Official creditors	305	28	155	99	177	-2
Multilateral	60	20	8	-17	47	61
of which: World Bank	7	-7	-7	-1	3	15
Bilateral	245	8	148	116	130	-63
Private creditors	11	274	291	130	281	81
Bondholders	..	..	..	..	500	0
Banks and other private	11	274	291	130	-219	81
Short-term	18	35	-204	-147	-69	129
Net equity inflows						
Foreign direct investment	376	134	201	108	68	142
Portfolio equity	0	1	0	0	0	0
Debt ratios						
External debt stocks to exports (%)	117	161	201	230	226	225
External debt stocks to GNI (%)	49	45	55	63	74	68
Debt service to exports (%)	6	13	12	28	26	22
Short-term to external debt stocks (%)	4	23	19	16	12	15
Multilateral to external debt stocks (%)	29	18	18	17	16	17
Reserves to external debt stocks (%)	4	3	1	2	11	6
Gross national income (GNI)	5,108	11,420	9,381	8,165	8,244	8,834

TANZANIA

(US$ million, unless otherwise indicated)

	2008	2014	2015	2016	2017	2018
Summary external debt data by debtor type						
Total External debt stocks	**6,010**	**14,503**	**15,278**	**16,189**	**18,397**	**18,585**
Use of IMF Credit	66	682	592	515	459	364
Long-term external debt	4,601	11,742	12,827	13,637	15,878	16,409
Public and publicly guaranteed sector	3,712	9,884	10,630	10,963	12,659	12,792
Public Sector	3,712	9,884	10,630	10,963	12,659	12,792
of which: General Government	3,667	9,848	10,597	10,930	12,623	12,758
Private sector guaranteed by Public Sector	0	..	..	..	..	..
Private sector not guaranteed	889	1,859	2,197	2,674	3,219	3,617
Short-term external debt	1,344	2,078	1,859	2,037	2,060	1,812
Disbursements (long-term)	**523**	**1,580**	**1,558**	**1,330**	**2,152**	**1,494**
Public and publicly guaranteed sector	523	1,296	1,142	854	1,593	1,026
Public Sector	523	1,296	1,142	854	1,593	1,026
of which: General Government	523	1,296	1,142	854	1,593	1,026
Private sector guaranteed by Public Sector	..	..	..	..	..	..
Private sector not guaranteed	..	284	416	476	558	468
Principal repayments (long-term)	**23**	**142**	**172**	**433**	**462**	**757**
Public and publicly guaranteed sector	14	78	93	296	331	687
Public Sector	14	78	93	296	331	687
of which: General Government	14	78	93	296	331	687
Private sector guaranteed by Public Sector	..	..	..	..	..	..
Private sector not guaranteed	9	64	78	138	130	70
Interest payments (long-term)	**27**	**81**	**107**	**181**	**180**	**218**
Public and publicly guaranteed sector	21	74	97	165	165	203
Public Sector	21	74	97	165	165	203
of which: General Government	21	74	97	165	165	203
Private sector guaranteed by Public Sector	0	..	..	..	..	..
Private sector not guaranteed	6	7	10	16	15	16
Summary external debt stock by creditor type						
Long-term External debt stocks	**4,601**	**11,742**	**12,827**	**13,637**	**15,878**	**16,409**
Public and publicly guaranteed debt from:	3,712	9,884	10,630	10,963	12,659	12,792
Official creditors	3,612	8,535	9,335	9,852	11,234	11,795
Multilateral	2,677	6,813	7,356	7,653	8,751	9,254
of which: World Bank	1,971	5,045	5,399	5,621	6,467	6,815
Bilateral	935	1,723	1,979	2,199	2,483	2,541
Private creditors	100	1,349	1,295	1,111	1,424	997
Bondholders	..	..	..	..	..	..
Commercial banks and others	100	1,349	1,295	1,111	1,424	997
Private nonguaranteed debt from:	889	1,859	2,197	2,674	3,219	3,617
Bondholders	..	..	..	..	..	..
Commercial banks and others	889	1,859	2,197	2,674	3,219	3,617
Use of IMF Credit	66	682	592	515	459	364
Net financial inflows						
Net debt inflows						
Use of IMF Credit	..	-28	-61	-62	-84	-85
Long-term	500	1,439	1,387	897	1,690	737
Official creditors	509	1,219	1,086	738	966	761
Multilateral	510	797	804	502	730	690
of which: World Bank	393	614	581	398	519	517
Bilateral	-1	422	282	236	236	71
Private creditors	-9	219	301	159	724	-24
Bondholders	..	..	..	..	..	..
Banks and other private	-9	219	301	159	724	-24
Short-term	172	304	-211	193	-17	-237
Net equity inflows						
Foreign direct investment	398	1,004	1,061	888	976	1,105
Portfolio equity	3	4	4	4	4	..
Debt ratios						
External debt stocks to exports (%)	105	167	171	173	207	..
External debt stocks to GNI (%)	22	30	33	33	35	33
Debt service to exports (%)	1	3	4	7	8	..
Short-term to external debt stocks (%)	22	14	12	13	11	10
Multilateral to external debt stocks (%)	45	47	48	47	48	50
Reserves to external debt stocks (%)	48	30	27	27	32	27
Gross national income (GNI)	27,627	49,140	46,478	48,664	52,107	56,211

THAILAND

(US$ million, unless otherwise indicated)

	2008	2014	2015	2016	2017	2018
Summary external debt data by debtor type						
Total External debt stocks	**66,619**	**146,057**	**131,819**	**137,571**	**157,583**	**169,241**
Use of IMF Credit	130	1,406	1,345	1,304	1,382	1,349
Long-term external debt	46,033	88,603	78,289	83,477	91,551	107,586
Public and publicly guaranteed sector	9,859	25,228	22,420	23,192	29,544	35,606
Public Sector	9,859	25,228	22,420	23,192	29,544	35,606
of which: General Government	4,380	21,871	19,415	20,363	26,552	32,835
Private sector guaranteed by Public Sector	..	..	..	..	..	..
Private sector not guaranteed	36,174	63,375	55,869	60,285	62,007	71,980
Short-term external debt	20,455	56,048	52,186	52,790	64,650	60,305
Disbursements (long-term)	**13,526**	**19,437**	**13,723**	**16,799**	**21,092**	**40,237**
Public and publicly guaranteed sector	1,638	479	184	1,133	6,600	6,889
Public Sector	1,638	479	184	1,133	6,600	6,889
of which: General Government	1,617	299	143	1,113	6,324	6,886
Private sector guaranteed by Public Sector	..	..	..	..	..	..
Private sector not guaranteed	11,888	18,958	13,539	15,666	14,492	33,348
Principal repayments (long-term)	**15,417**	**24,236**	**17,304**	**12,332**	**13,452**	**16,768**
Public and publicly guaranteed sector	2,184	454	1,154	482	396	908
Public Sector	2,184	454	1,154	482	396	908
of which: General Government	1,369	159	769	196	194	641
Private sector guaranteed by Public Sector	..	..	..	..	..	..
Private sector not guaranteed	13,233	23,782	16,149	11,850	13,056	15,861
Interest payments (long-term)	**1,092**	**793**	**786**	**1,531**	**819**	**1,164**
Public and publicly guaranteed sector	226	241	235	309	390	697
Public Sector	226	241	235	309	390	697
of which: General Government	63	175	176	250	340	640
Private sector guaranteed by Public Sector	..	..	..	..	..	..
Private sector not guaranteed	866	552	551	1,221	429	467
Summary external debt stock by creditor type						
Long-term External debt stocks	**46,033**	**88,603**	**78,289**	**83,477**	**91,551**	**107,586**
Public and publicly guaranteed debt from:	9,859	25,228	22,420	23,192	29,544	35,606
Official creditors	6,984	5,558	5,392	5,483	5,592	5,099
Multilateral	264	1,364	1,344	1,304	1,261	1,313
of which: World Bank	128	1,046	1,039	1,032	1,025	1,018
Bilateral	6,720	4,195	4,048	4,179	4,331	3,786
Private creditors	2,875	19,670	17,028	17,709	23,952	30,507
Bondholders	2,304	19,554	17,000	17,685	23,929	30,483
Commercial banks and others	571	116	28	24	23	23
Private nonguaranteed debt from:	36,174	63,375	55,869	60,285	62,007	71,980
Bondholders	5,068	11,920	8,888	9,188	10,043	12,841
Commercial banks and others	31,107	51,455	46,981	51,097	51,964	59,139
Use of IMF Credit	130	1,406	1,345	1,304	1,382	1,349
Net financial inflows						
Net debt inflows						
Use of IMF Credit	..	0	..	..	..	..
Long-term	-1,891	-4,800	-3,581	4,467	7,640	23,469
Official creditors	-744	131	-160	-31	-39	-574
Multilateral	-28	-10	-20	-40	-43	52
of which: World Bank	-2	-7	-7	-7	-7	-7
Bilateral	-716	141	-140	9	4	-625
Private creditors	-1,147	-4,931	-3,421	4,498	7,679	24,042
Bondholders	709	3,645	-1,956	985	7,099	9,356
Banks and other private	-1,855	-8,576	-1,465	3,513	580	14,686
Short-term	2,156	-5,848	-3,862	604	11,860	-4,345
Net equity inflows						
Foreign direct investment	8,256	10,934	9,874	4,327	8,875	13,292
Portfolio equity	-9,442	-5,811	-8,969	-786	598	-7,100
Debt ratios						
External debt stocks to exports (%)	31	50	47	48	49	49
External debt stocks to GNI (%)	24	38	35	35	36	35
Debt service to exports (%)	8	9	7	5	5	5
Short-term to external debt stocks (%)	31	38	40	38	41	36
Multilateral to external debt stocks (%)	0	1	1	1	1	1
Reserves to external debt stocks (%)	163	104	115	121	124	118
Gross national income (GNI)	280,757	386,382	380,595	392,935	434,950	482,317

TIMOR-LESTE

(US$ million, unless otherwise indicated)

	2008	2014	2015	2016	2017	2018
Summary external debt data by debtor type						
Total External debt stocks	..	**104.3**	**116.7**	**80.9**	**124.5**	**158.1**
Use of IMF Credit	..	11.2	10.7	10.4	11.0	10.7
Long-term external debt	..	21.8	45.7	70.5	110.5	144.7
Public and publicly guaranteed sector	..	21.8	45.7	70.5	110.5	144.7
Public Sector	..	21.8	45.7	70.5	110.5	144.7
of which: General Government	..	21.8	45.7	70.5	110.5	144.7
Private sector guaranteed by Public Sector	..	..	..	..	..	..
Private sector not guaranteed	..	..	..	..	..	..
Short-term external debt	..	71.3	60.3	0.0	3.0	2.6
Disbursements (long-term)	..	**15.0**	**24.0**	**25.1**	**35.7**	**40.0**
Public and publicly guaranteed sector	..	15.0	24.0	25.1	35.7	40.0
Public Sector	..	15.0	24.0	25.1	35.7	40.0
of which: General Government	..	15.0	24.0	25.1	35.7	40.0
Private sector guaranteed by Public Sector	..	..	..	..	..	..
Private sector not guaranteed	..	..	..	..	..	..
Principal repayments (long-term)	..	**0.0**	**0.0**	**0.0**	**0.3**	**0.7**
Public and publicly guaranteed sector	..	0.0	0.0	0.0	0.3	0.7
Public Sector	..	0.0	0.0	0.0	0.3	0.7
of which: General Government	..	0.0	0.0	0.0	0.3	0.7
Private sector guaranteed by Public Sector	..	..	..	..	..	..
Private sector not guaranteed	..	..	..	..	..	..
Interest payments (long-term)	..	**0.2**	**0.3**	**0.8**	**1.5**	**2.5**
Public and publicly guaranteed sector	..	0.2	0.3	0.8	1.5	2.5
Public Sector	..	0.2	0.3	0.8	1.5	2.5
of which: General Government	..	0.2	0.3	0.8	1.5	2.5
Private sector guaranteed by Public Sector	..	..	..	..	..	..
Private sector not guaranteed	..	..	..	..	..	..
Summary external debt stock by creditor type						
Long-term External debt stocks	..	**21.8**	**45.7**	**70.5**	**110.5**	**144.7**
Public and publicly guaranteed debt from:	..	21.8	45.7	70.5	110.5	144.7
Official creditors	..	21.8	45.7	70.5	110.5	144.7
Multilateral	..	19.5	43.4	68.1	101.4	131.5
of which: World Bank	..	2.9	10.0	15.6	27.0	33.5
Bilateral	..	2.3	2.3	2.4	9.1	13.2
Private creditors	..	..	..	..	..	..
Bondholders	..	..	..	..	..	..
Commercial banks and others	..	..	..	..	..	..
Private nonguaranteed debt from:	..	..	..	..	..	..
Bondholders	..	..	..	..	..	..
Commercial banks and others	..	..	..	..	..	..
Use of IMF Credit	..	11.2	10.7	10.4	11.0	10.7
Net financial inflows						
Net debt inflows						
Use of IMF Credit	..	..	..	..	..	..
Long-term	..	15.0	24.0	25.1	35.5	39.3
Official creditors	..	15.0	24.0	25.1	35.5	39.3
Multilateral	..	15.0	24.0	25.1	28.7	35.4
of which: World Bank	..	2.9	7.1	5.6	11.4	7.5
Bilateral	..	..	..	..	6.7	3.9
Private creditors	..	..	..	..	..	..
Bondholders	..	..	..	..	..	..
Banks and other private	..	..	..	..	..	..
Short-term	..	1.0	-11.0	-60.3	3.0	-0.4
Net equity inflows						
Foreign direct investment	39.7	33.9	43.0	5.5	6.7	47.9
Portfolio equity	..	0.0	..	..	0.0	..
Debt ratios						
External debt stocks to exports (%)	..	4.6	8.3	12.3	14.2	15.7
External debt stocks to GNI (%)	..	3.1	4.2	3.6	5.5	6.7
Debt service to exports (%)	..	0.0	0.1	0.1	0.2	0.3
Short-term to external debt stocks (%)	0.0	68.3	51.7	0.0	2.4	1.6
Multilateral to external debt stocks (%)	0.0	18.7	37.2	84.2	81.4	83.2
Reserves to external debt stocks (%)	..	298.6	375.0	347.3	437.2	426.4
Gross national income (GNI)	3,283.7	3,340.8	2,795.1	2,264.0	2,265.3	2,361.0

TOGO

(US$ million, unless otherwise indicated)

	2008	2014	2015	2016	2017	2018
Summary external debt data by debtor type						
Total External debt stocks	**1,641.7**	**986.3**	**1,064.2**	**1,170.4**	**1,634.1**	**1,760.7**
Use of IMF Credit	65.0	226.6	200.6	171.3	226.0	266.0
Long-term external debt	1,468.8	670.4	799.7	940.3	1,139.6	1,215.8
Public and publicly guaranteed sector	1,468.8	670.4	799.7	940.3	1,139.6	1,215.8
Public Sector	1,468.8	670.4	799.7	940.3	1,139.6	1,215.8
of which: General Government	1,443.9	665.2	795.0	936.3	1,135.6	1,212.1
Private sector guaranteed by Public Sector	..	..	..	..	..	..
Private sector not guaranteed	..	..	..	..	..	..
Short-term external debt	107.8	89.3	63.9	58.7	268.5	278.9
Disbursements (long-term)	**2.2**	**176.0**	**187.5**	**205.9**	**177.1**	**168.0**
Public and publicly guaranteed sector	2.2	176.0	187.5	205.9	177.1	168.0
Public Sector	2.2	176.0	187.5	205.9	177.1	168.0
of which: General Government	2.2	176.0	187.5	205.9	177.1	168.0
Private sector guaranteed by Public Sector	..	..	..	..	..	..
Private sector not guaranteed	..	..	..	..	..	..
Principal repayments (long-term)	**140.1**	**30.6**	**23.9**	**41.0**	**40.0**	**57.9**
Public and publicly guaranteed sector	140.1	30.6	23.9	41.0	40.0	57.9
Public Sector	140.1	30.6	23.9	41.0	40.0	57.9
of which: General Government	139.5	30.6	23.7	40.4	39.7	57.6
Private sector guaranteed by Public Sector	..	..	..	..	..	..
Private sector not guaranteed	..	..	..	..	..	..
Interest payments (long-term)	**51.3**	**15.7**	**18.6**	**22.6**	**19.4**	**26.4**
Public and publicly guaranteed sector	51.3	15.7	18.6	22.6	19.4	26.4
Public Sector	51.3	15.7	18.6	22.6	19.4	26.4
of which: General Government	51.2	15.6	18.6	22.6	19.4	26.4
Private sector guaranteed by Public Sector	..	..	..	..	..	..
Private sector not guaranteed	..	..	..	..	..	..
Summary external debt stock by creditor type						
Long-term External debt stocks	**1,468.8**	**670.4**	**799.7**	**940.3**	**1,139.6**	**1,215.8**
Public and publicly guaranteed debt from:	1,468.8	670.4	799.7	940.3	1,139.6	1,215.8
Official creditors	1,468.8	637.7	768.8	920.8	1,128.5	1,209.7
Multilateral	847.0	283.4	324.7	399.6	512.6	581.6
of which: World Bank	604.2	27.9	30.8	38.7	50.5	66.0
Bilateral	621.9	354.3	444.1	521.2	615.9	628.1
Private creditors	..	32.8	31.0	19.5	11.1	6.1
Bondholders	..	..	..	..	..	..
Commercial banks and others	..	32.8	31.0	19.5	11.1	6.1
Private nonguaranteed debt from:	..	..	..	..	..	..
Bondholders	..	..	..	..	..	..
Commercial banks and others	..	..	..	..	..	..
Use of IMF Credit	65.0	226.6	200.6	171.3	226.0	266.0
Net financial inflows						
Net debt inflows						
Use of IMF Credit	47.7	-12.2	-16.2	-24.1	43.3	46.1
Long-term	-137.9	145.4	163.6	164.9	137.1	110.2
Official creditors	-137.9	157.3	162.0	175.8	147.5	114.8
Multilateral	-137.2	60.9	61.4	85.2	69.3	89.0
of which: World Bank	-117.0	14.9	4.2	9.2	9.1	17.3
Bilateral	-0.7	96.4	100.6	90.6	78.2	25.9
Private creditors	..	-12.0	1.6	-11.0	-10.4	-4.7
Bondholders	..	..	..	..	..	..
Banks and other private	..	-12.0	1.6	-11.0	-10.4	-4.7
Short-term	8.0	4.0	-25.5	-4.9	210.2	10.4
Net equity inflows						
Foreign direct investment	19.6	97.2	88.0	28.4	-86.8	102.0
Portfolio equity	1.4	..	-0.2	-3.3	-89.0	..
Debt ratios						
External debt stocks to exports (%)	134.9	46.1	57.3	63.1	88.3	..
External debt stocks to GNI (%)	49.8	21.4	24.6	26.3	34.3	33.3
Debt service to exports (%)	16.0	2.8	3.2	4.8	5.0	..
Short-term to external debt stocks (%)	6.6	9.1	6.0	5.0	16.4	15.8
Multilateral to external debt stocks (%)	51.6	28.7	30.5	34.1	31.4	33.0
Reserves to external debt stocks (%)	35.4	51.4	53.9	..	..	..
Gross national income (GNI)	3,295.2	4,615.0	4,319.8	4,458.4	4,770.8	5,292.8

TONGA

(US$ million, unless otherwise indicated)

	2008	2014	2015	2016	2017	2018
Summary external debt data by debtor type						
Total External debt stocks	**99.0**	**195.8**	**184.3**	**178.0**	**196.9**	**188.7**
Use of IMF Credit	10.1	9.5	9.1	8.8	9.4	9.2
Long-term external debt	88.8	186.3	175.2	169.1	187.5	179.5
Public and publicly guaranteed sector	88.8	186.3	175.2	169.1	187.5	179.5
Public Sector	88.8	186.3	175.2	169.1	187.5	179.5
of which: General Government	88.7	186.3	175.2	169.1	187.5	179.5
Private sector guaranteed by Public Sector	..	..	..	..	..	..
Private sector not guaranteed	..	..	..	..	..	..
Short-term external debt	0.0	0.0	0.0	0.0	0.0	0.0
Disbursements (long-term)	**8.5**	**5.1**	**2.2**	**7.1**	**10.1**	**6.9**
Public and publicly guaranteed sector	8.5	5.1	2.2	7.1	10.1	6.9
Public Sector	8.5	5.1	2.2	7.1	10.1	6.9
of which: General Government	8.5	5.1	2.2	7.1	10.1	6.9
Private sector guaranteed by Public Sector	..	..	..	..	..	..
Private sector not guaranteed	..	..	..	..	..	..
Principal repayments (long-term)	**3.7**	**4.0**	**3.5**	**3.5**	**2.9**	**7.5**
Public and publicly guaranteed sector	3.7	4.0	3.5	3.5	2.9	7.5
Public Sector	3.7	4.0	3.5	3.5	2.9	7.5
of which: General Government	2.9	4.0	3.5	3.5	2.9	7.5
Private sector guaranteed by Public Sector	..	..	..	..	..	..
Private sector not guaranteed	..	..	..	..	..	..
Interest payments (long-term)	**1.7**	**3.0**	**2.9**	**2.7**	**2.7**	**3.6**
Public and publicly guaranteed sector	1.7	3.0	2.9	2.7	2.7	3.6
Public Sector	1.7	3.0	2.9	2.7	2.7	3.6
of which: General Government	1.6	3.0	2.9	2.7	2.7	3.6
Private sector guaranteed by Public Sector	..	..	..	..	..	..
Private sector not guaranteed	..	..	..	..	..	..
Summary external debt stock by creditor type						
Long-term External debt stocks	**88.8**	**186.3**	**175.2**	**169.1**	**187.5**	**179.5**
Public and publicly guaranteed debt from:	88.8	186.3	175.2	169.1	187.5	179.5
Official creditors	88.8	186.1	175.1	169.0	187.4	179.5
Multilateral	72.2	61.2	58.0	60.3	71.3	73.6
of which: World Bank	21.6	25.9	26.5	29.1	37.2	39.1
Bilateral	16.6	124.9	117.1	108.8	116.1	105.9
Private creditors	..	0.1	0.1	0.1	0.1	0.0
Bondholders	..	..	..	..	..	..
Commercial banks and others	..	0.1	0.1	0.1	0.1	0.0
Private nonguaranteed debt from:	..	..	..	..	..	..
Bondholders	..	..	..	..	..	..
Commercial banks and others	..	..	..	..	..	..
Use of IMF Credit	10.1	9.5	9.1	8.8	9.4	9.2
Net financial inflows						
Net debt inflows						
Use of IMF Credit	..	0.0	..	..	..	..
Long-term	4.8	1.1	-1.3	3.6	7.2	-0.6
Official creditors	4.8	1.5	-1.3	3.6	7.3	-0.6
Multilateral	-1.6	2.2	-0.6	4.2	7.3	4.0
of which: World Bank	0.6	4.6	1.7	3.5	6.2	2.8
Bilateral	6.4	-0.7	-0.7	-0.6	..	-4.6
Private creditors	..	-0.4	0.0	0.0	0.0	0.0
Bondholders	..	..	..	..	..	..
Banks and other private	..	-0.4	0.0	0.0	0.0	0.0
Short-term	..	0.0	0.0	0.0	0.0	0.0
Net equity inflows						
Foreign direct investment	1.4	13.2	12.5	6.8	-2.6	14.2
Portfolio equity	..	..	..	0.0	0.0	0.0
Debt ratios						
External debt stocks to exports (%)	156.4	201.4	145.9	145.7	141.1	122.5
External debt stocks to GNI (%)	27.8	43.8	41.9	44.1	45.1	41.3
Debt service to exports (%)	8.7	7.3	5.0	5.1	4.0	7.2
Short-term to external debt stocks (%)	0.0	0.0	0.0	0.0	0.0	0.0
Multilateral to external debt stocks (%)	72.9	31.3	31.5	33.9	36.2	39.0
Reserves to external debt stocks (%)	70.5	81.1	84.7	99.2	100.8	120.4
Gross national income (GNI)	356.5	447.1	440.0	403.6	436.9	457.2

TUNISIA

(US$ million, unless otherwise indicated)

	2008	2014	2015	2016	2017	2018
Summary external debt data by debtor type						
Total External debt stocks	**21,476**	**26,474**	**27,245**	**28,364**	**33,468**	**34,663**
Use of IMF Credit	53	1,537	1,768	1,987	2,105	2,280
Long-term external debt	17,093	18,091	18,903	19,682	23,904	24,289
Public and publicly guaranteed sector	14,546	16,577	17,720	18,190	21,832	22,153
Public Sector	14,363	16,214	17,437	17,922	21,534	21,911
of which: General Government	11,717	12,161	13,367	14,046	14,861	15,464
Private sector guaranteed by Public Sector	183	363	283	268	298	242
Private sector not guaranteed	2,547	1,514	1,182	1,493	2,072	2,136
Short-term external debt	4,330	6,846	6,575	6,694	7,458	8,093
Disbursements (long-term)	**1,251**	**2,427**	**3,349**	**1,949**	**3,910**	**2,166**
Public and publicly guaranteed sector	941	2,427	3,349	1,949	3,910	2,166
Public Sector	904	2,427	3,346	1,916	3,862	2,166
of which: General Government	709	1,454	2,524	1,515	1,130	1,746
Private sector guaranteed by Public Sector	37	..	3	33	47	..
Private sector not guaranteed	310	..	..	..	..	..
Principal repayments (long-term)	**1,184**	**1,347**	**1,495**	**1,312**	**1,939**	**1,403**
Public and publicly guaranteed sector	1,072	1,223	1,162	1,210	1,797	1,257
Public Sector	1,056	1,167	1,115	1,170	1,745	1,213
of which: General Government	788	803	667	673	1,292	785
Private sector guaranteed by Public Sector	16	56	47	40	52	44
Private sector not guaranteed	112	124	332	102	142	146
Interest payments (long-term)	**747**	**462**	**441**	**553**	**581**	**677**
Public and publicly guaranteed sector	633	462	441	457	448	540
Public Sector	626	452	433	452	443	535
of which: General Government	509	326	324	350	327	346
Private sector guaranteed by Public Sector	7	10	7	6	5	4
Private sector not guaranteed	115	..	..	96	133	137
Summary external debt stock by creditor type						
Long-term External debt stocks	**17,093**	**18,091**	**18,903**	**19,682**	**23,904**	**24,289**
Public and publicly guaranteed debt from:	14,546	16,577	17,720	18,190	21,832	22,153
Official creditors	9,381	12,783	12,769	12,790	14,909	14,786
Multilateral	6,075	8,930	9,131	9,201	10,751	10,805
of which: World Bank	1,375	2,062	2,399	2,343	3,160	3,515
Bilateral	3,306	3,853	3,638	3,589	4,158	3,981
Private creditors	5,165	3,793	4,952	5,400	6,923	7,367
Bondholders	4,050	3,364	4,315	4,840	6,263	6,789
Commercial banks and others	1,115	430	637	559	660	578
Private nonguaranteed debt from:	2,547	1,514	1,182	1,493	2,072	2,136
Bondholders	..	..	..	..	..	..
Commercial banks and others	2,547	1,514	1,182	1,493	2,072	2,136
Use of IMF Credit	53	1,537	1,768	1,987	2,105	2,280
Net financial inflows						
Net debt inflows						
Use of IMF Credit	..	1,047	301	282	0	228
Long-term	67	1,081	1,854	637	1,971	763
Official creditors	-115	651	946	308	817	381
Multilateral	-77	241	903	304	577	450
of which: World Bank	-205	106	495	-1	569	481
Bilateral	-38	410	43	4	240	-69
Private creditors	182	430	908	329	1,154	382
Bondholders	..	500	1,000	500	1,259	591
Banks and other private	182	-71	-92	-171	-105	-208
Short-term	345	274	-271	119	764	635
Net equity inflows						
Foreign direct investment	2,609	1,027	971	631	814	1,036
Portfolio equity	-39	72	153	-57	-64	-41
Debt ratios						
External debt stocks to exports (%)	84	120	152	163	185	174
External debt stocks to GNI (%)	51	58	65	70	87	90
Debt service to exports (%)	8	9	11	12	17	14
Short-term to external debt stocks (%)	20	26	24	24	22	23
Multilateral to external debt stocks (%)	28	34	34	32	32	31
Reserves to external debt stocks (%)	41	27	27	21	18	16
Gross national income (GNI)	42,244	45,928	41,813	40,631	38,688	38,498

TURKEY

(US$ million, unless otherwise indicated)

	2008	2014	2015	2016	2017	2018
Summary external debt data by debtor type						
Total External debt stocks	**290,572**	**406,062**	**399,949**	**409,421**	**456,174**	**445,139**
Use of IMF Credit	8,697	1,552	1,485	1,440	1,526	1,490
Long-term external debt	229,362	269,434	293,333	306,738	335,417	328,228
Public and publicly guaranteed sector	83,917	105,469	103,283	107,727	117,895	121,361
Public Sector	83,754	104,987	102,876	107,375	117,549	121,075
of which: General Government	65,875	86,594	82,798	84,350	92,237	93,215
Private sector guaranteed by Public Sector	162	482	407	352	346	286
Private sector not guaranteed	145,446	163,965	190,050	199,011	217,522	206,867
Short-term external debt	52,512	135,076	105,131	101,243	119,232	115,421
Disbursements (long-term)	**65,160**	**74,895**	**37,296**	**81,759**	**88,315**	**68,568**
Public and publicly guaranteed sector	10,690	14,067	9,066	14,323	17,576	15,844
Public Sector	10,631	14,067	9,066	14,323	17,576	15,844
of which: General Government	9,059	9,600	4,750	7,142	12,044	9,467
Private sector guaranteed by Public Sector	59	..	..	..	0	0
Private sector not guaranteed	54,470	60,828	28,230	67,436	70,739	52,725
Principal repayments (long-term)	**40,168**	**41,472**	**41,977**	**61,603**	**69,142**	**67,875**
Public and publicly guaranteed sector	7,735	7,135	6,531	8,437	11,284	10,723
Public Sector	7,735	7,105	6,502	8,392	11,233	10,677
of which: General Government	7,209	6,326	5,674	5,010	7,591	7,376
Private sector guaranteed by Public Sector	..	30	29	45	51	45
Private sector not guaranteed	32,433	34,337	35,446	53,166	57,858	57,152
Interest payments (long-term)	**11,564**	**9,937**	**10,194**	**10,934**	**12,099**	**11,509**
Public and publicly guaranteed sector	5,337	4,611	4,396	4,499	4,874	4,876
Public Sector	5,331	4,606	4,392	4,495	4,870	4,872
of which: General Government	4,489	4,143	3,963	4,000	4,283	4,290
Private sector guaranteed by Public Sector	6	5	4	4	4	4
Private sector not guaranteed	6,227	5,326	5,798	6,435	7,224	6,633
Summary external debt stock by creditor type						
Long-term External debt stocks	**229,362**	**269,434**	**293,333**	**306,738**	**335,417**	**328,228**
Public and publicly guaranteed debt from:	83,917	105,469	103,283	107,727	117,895	121,361
Official creditors	19,963	32,348	31,005	31,146	34,844	34,708
Multilateral	13,829	26,441	25,398	25,819	28,722	28,441
of which: World Bank	8,100	12,927	11,731	10,860	12,039	11,685
Bilateral	6,135	5,907	5,607	5,326	6,122	6,267
Private creditors	63,953	73,122	72,278	76,582	83,051	86,653
Bondholders	40,612	62,694	64,243	67,141	74,486	77,420
Commercial banks and others	23,342	10,427	8,035	9,441	8,565	9,233
Private nonguaranteed debt from:	145,446	163,965	190,050	199,011	217,522	206,867
Bondholders	6,759	29,836	29,666	34,475	41,793	38,983
Commercial banks and others	138,687	134,128	160,384	164,536	175,729	167,884
Use of IMF Credit	8,697	1,552	1,485	1,440	1,526	1,490
Net financial inflows						
Net debt inflows						
Use of IMF Credit	1,588	0	..	..	..	..
Long-term	24,992	33,423	-4,681	20,156	19,173	694
Official creditors	2,314	2,129	899	746	887	905
Multilateral	1,787	1,712	985	1,056	433	707
of which: World Bank	564	26	-265	-644	185	5
Bilateral	527	418	-87	-310	454	199
Private creditors	22,678	31,294	-5,580	19,411	18,286	-212
Bondholders	360	13,099	3,016	4,307	9,517	1,798
Banks and other private	22,318	18,195	-8,596	15,104	8,769	-2,009
Short-term	9,370	4,785	-29,944	-3,889	17,989	-3,810
Net equity inflows						
Foreign direct investment	17,650	12,692	15,885	10,794	10,175	11,985
Portfolio equity	716	2,559	-2,395	823	3,192	-908
Debt ratios						
External debt stocks to exports (%)	156	180	197	212	212	194
External debt stocks to GNI (%)	38	44	47	48	54	59
Debt service to exports (%)	30	26	27	39	40	37
Short-term to external debt stocks (%)	18	33	26	25	26	26
Multilateral to external debt stocks (%)	5	7	6	6	6	6
Reserves to external debt stocks (%)	24	26	23	22	18	16
Gross national income (GNI)	756,734	925,981	850,110	854,539	840,505	754,813

TURKMENISTAN

(US$ million, unless otherwise indicated)

	2008	2014	2015	2016	2017	2018
Summary external debt data by debtor type						
Total External debt stocks	**742.5**	**409.9**	**367.0**	**507.7**	**783.7**	**907.3**
Use of IMF Credit	107.5	101.2	96.7	93.9	99.4	97.1
Long-term external debt	591.1	307.9	269.5	259.9	267.3	503.6
Public and publicly guaranteed sector	590.5	261.9	231.4	231.4	220.6	468.9
Public Sector	590.5	261.9	231.4	231.4	220.6	468.9
of which: General Government	83.0	117.0	119.7	135.1	127.3	389.4
Private sector guaranteed by Public Sector	..	..	..	..	..	..
Private sector not guaranteed	0.6	46.0	38.1	28.5	46.8	34.6
Short-term external debt	43.8	0.8	0.8	153.9	417.0	306.7
Disbursements (long-term)	**29.5**	**43.7**	**22.0**	**29.4**	**29.3**	**276.2**
Public and publicly guaranteed sector	29.2	22.8	9.8	23.8	0.5	269.6
Public Sector	29.2	22.8	9.8	23.8	0.5	269.6
of which: General Government	0.0	16.7	6.3	21.3	0.1	269.6
Private sector guaranteed by Public Sector	..	..	..	..	..	..
Private sector not guaranteed	0.3	20.9	12.2	5.6	28.9	6.6
Principal repayments (long-term)	**140.8**	**49.5**	**49.5**	**33.9**	**32.6**	**39.9**
Public and publicly guaranteed sector	139.3	35.3	32.1	17.7	18.0	17.4
Public Sector	139.3	35.3	32.1	17.7	18.0	17.4
of which: General Government	14.9	3.8	3.7	6.7	8.7	7.8
Private sector guaranteed by Public Sector	..	..	..	..	..	..
Private sector not guaranteed	1.5	14.2	17.3	16.2	14.5	22.6
Interest payments (long-term)	**26.7**	**6.7**	**5.5**	**4.7**	**5.2**	**5.5**
Public and publicly guaranteed sector	26.6	6.0	4.6	4.3	4.6	4.8
Public Sector	26.6	6.0	4.6	4.3	4.6	4.8
of which: General Government	3.4	1.2	1.1	1.5	2.1	2.6
Private sector guaranteed by Public Sector	..	..	..	..	..	..
Private sector not guaranteed	0.1	0.7	0.9	0.4	0.7	0.7
Summary external debt stock by creditor type						
Long-term External debt stocks	**591.1**	**307.9**	**269.5**	**259.9**	**267.3**	**503.6**
Public and publicly guaranteed debt from:	590.5	261.9	231.4	231.4	220.6	468.9
Official creditors	504.0	261.9	231.4	231.4	220.6	199.3
Multilateral	20.1	93.5	97.9	114.5	107.9	102.0
of which: World Bank	14.2	4.9	3.0	1.0	0.0	..
Bilateral	483.9	168.4	133.5	116.9	112.7	97.3
Private creditors	86.5	..	..	..	..	269.6
Bondholders	..	..	..	..	..	..
Commercial banks and others	86.5	..	..	..	..	269.6
Private nonguaranteed debt from:	0.6	46.0	38.1	28.5	46.8	34.6
Bondholders	..	..	..	..	..	..
Commercial banks and others	0.6	46.0	38.1	28.5	46.8	34.6
Use of IMF Credit	107.5	101.2	96.7	93.9	99.4	97.1
Net financial inflows						
Net debt inflows						
Use of IMF Credit	..	0.0	..	..	..	..
Long-term	-111.3	-5.8	-27.4	-4.5	-3.2	236.3
Official creditors	-75.1	-12.5	-22.3	6.0	-17.6	-17.4
Multilateral	-2.8	14.9	4.4	16.6	-6.6	-5.8
of which: World Bank	-1.2	-1.8	-1.9	-2.0	-1.0	..
Bilateral	-72.3	-27.4	-26.7	-10.6	-10.9	-11.5
Private creditors	-36.2	6.7	-5.1	-10.6	14.4	253.7
Bondholders	..	..	..	..	..	..
Banks and other private	-36.2	6.7	-5.1	-10.6	14.4	253.7
Short-term	-45.0	-70.0	0.0	153.1	263.0	-110.3
Net equity inflows						
Foreign direct investment	1,277.0	3,830.1	3,043.0	2,243.2	2,085.9	1,985.1
Portfolio equity	..	..	..	..	..	..
Debt ratios						
External debt stocks to exports (%)	..	..	..	..	..	..
External debt stocks to GNI (%)	4.1	1.0	1.1	1.4	2.2	2.3
Debt service to exports (%)	..	..	..	..	..	..
Short-term to external debt stocks (%)	5.9	0.2	0.2	30.3	53.2	33.8
Multilateral to external debt stocks (%)	2.7	22.8	26.7	22.6	13.8	11.2
Reserves to external debt stocks (%)	..	..	..	..	..	..
Gross national income (GNI)	18,235.7	39,603.2	33,705.6	35,225.9	36,352.3	39,044.2

UGANDA

(US$ million, unless otherwise indicated)

	2008	2014	2015	2016	2017	2018
Summary external debt data by debtor type						
Total External debt stocks	**2,298**	**8,655**	**9,574**	**10,091**	**11,689**	**12,330**
Use of IMF Credit	55	252	240	233	246	241
Long-term external debt	1,785	7,869	8,779	9,356	10,969	11,581
Public and publicly guaranteed sector	1,785	4,216	4,872	5,450	6,906	7,716
Public Sector	1,784	4,212	4,868	5,446	6,903	7,713
of which: General Government	1,782	4,211	4,867	5,446	6,902	7,712
Private sector guaranteed by Public Sector	1	5	4	4	4	4
Private sector not guaranteed	..	3,653	3,907	3,906	4,063	3,865
Short-term external debt	458	533	554	502	473	509
Disbursements (long-term)	**277**	**462**	**1,135**	**938**	**1,965**	**1,167**
Public and publicly guaranteed sector	277	462	881	786	1,272	1,167
Public Sector	277	462	881	786	1,272	1,167
of which: General Government	277	462	881	786	1,272	1,167
Private sector guaranteed by Public Sector	0	..	..	..	..	..
Private sector not guaranteed	..	..	254	151	693	..
Principal repayments (long-term)	**53**	**155**	**46**	**779**	**98**	**463**
Public and publicly guaranteed sector	53	52	46	46	98	224
Public Sector	53	52	45	46	98	224
of which: General Government	53	52	45	46	98	224
Private sector guaranteed by Public Sector	..	0	0	0	0	..
Private sector not guaranteed	..	103	..	733	..	239
Interest payments (long-term)	**15**	**44**	**41**	**57**	**81**	**220**
Public and publicly guaranteed sector	15	44	41	55	81	98
Public Sector	15	44	41	55	81	98
of which: General Government	15	44	41	55	81	98
Private sector guaranteed by Public Sector	..	..	..	..	..	..
Private sector not guaranteed	..	..	..	1	..	122
Summary external debt stock by creditor type						
Long-term External debt stocks	**1,785**	**7,869**	**8,779**	**9,356**	**10,969**	**11,581**
Public and publicly guaranteed debt from:	1,785	4,216	4,872	5,450	6,906	7,716
Official creditors	1,760	4,216	4,872	5,450	6,906	7,676
Multilateral	1,565	3,651	3,887	4,080	4,887	5,059
of which: World Bank	1,004	2,407	2,510	2,576	2,980	3,095
Bilateral	195	565	985	1,370	2,019	2,617
Private creditors	25	..	..	..	0	41
Bondholders	..	..	..	..	..	..
Commercial banks and others	25	..	..	..	0	41
Private nonguaranteed debt from:	..	3,653	3,907	3,906	4,063	3,865
Bondholders	..	..	..	..	..	..
Commercial banks and others	..	3,653	3,907	3,906	4,063	3,865
Use of IMF Credit	55	252	240	233	246	241
Net financial inflows						
Net debt inflows						
Use of IMF Credit	0	-2	-1	0	..	..
Long-term	224	307	1,090	158	1,867	704
Official creditors	225	410	836	740	1,174	901
Multilateral	239	315	398	338	555	286
of which: World Bank	172	163	212	163	245	190
Bilateral	-14	95	438	402	619	615
Private creditors	-1	-103	254	-582	693	-197
Bondholders	..	..	..	..	..	..
Banks and other private	-1	-103	254	-582	693	-197
Short-term	432	64	22	-52	-29	36
Net equity inflows						
Foreign direct investment	578	741	552	396	708	1,264
Portfolio equity	13	5	10	16	15	49
Debt ratios						
External debt stocks to exports (%)	72	175	201	208	228	218
External debt stocks to GNI (%)	16	32	36	43	46	46
Debt service to exports (%)	2	4	2	17	4	12
Short-term to external debt stocks (%)	20	6	6	5	4	4
Multilateral to external debt stocks (%)	68	42	41	40	42	41
Reserves to external debt stocks (%)	100	38	30	31	32	27
Gross national income (GNI)	13,981	26,685	26,613	23,659	25,380	26,608

UKRAINE

(US$ million, unless otherwise indicated)

	2008	2014	2015	2016	2017	2018
Summary external debt data by debtor type						
Total External debt stocks	**99,523**	**126,817**	**117,456**	**115,006**	**115,435**	**114,512**
Use of IMF Credit	6,726	7,608	12,486	13,075	14,001	12,997
Long-term external debt	72,161	96,521	84,957	81,708	79,174	80,825
Public and publicly guaranteed sector	15,904	33,057	32,431	33,106	36,072	36,221
Public Sector	15,904	33,057	32,431	33,106	36,072	36,221
of which: General Government	14,777	31,075	30,432	31,051	33,723	35,484
Private sector guaranteed by Public Sector	..	..	..	..	..	..
Private sector not guaranteed	56,257	63,463	52,526	48,602	43,102	44,604
Short-term external debt	20,636	22,689	20,013	20,223	22,259	20,690
Disbursements (long-term)	**31,603**	**11,457**	**18,695**	**5,020**	**8,177**	**9,496**
Public and publicly guaranteed sector	1,109	4,807	15,518	2,752	5,759	4,060
Public Sector	1,109	4,807	15,518	2,752	5,759	4,060
of which: General Government	1,069	4,675	15,486	2,681	5,448	3,720
Private sector guaranteed by Public Sector	..	..	..	..	..	..
Private sector not guaranteed	30,493	6,650	3,176	2,268	2,418	5,437
Principal repayments (long-term)	**14,347**	**11,821**	**23,819**	**8,608**	**8,507**	**8,846**
Public and publicly guaranteed sector	1,234	2,323	13,580	1,898	3,455	3,603
Public Sector	1,234	2,323	13,580	1,898	3,455	3,603
of which: General Government	932	2,281	13,565	1,882	3,439	1,657
Private sector guaranteed by Public Sector	..	..	..	..	..	..
Private sector not guaranteed	13,113	9,499	10,239	6,710	5,051	5,243
Interest payments (long-term)	**3,347**	**5,049**	**4,012**	**3,116**	**2,975**	**2,809**
Public and publicly guaranteed sector	735	1,503	1,289	1,435	1,502	1,464
Public Sector	735	1,503	1,289	1,435	1,502	1,464
of which: General Government	603	1,355	1,142	1,286	1,347	1,437
Private sector guaranteed by Public Sector	..	..	..	..	..	..
Private sector not guaranteed	2,613	3,546	2,723	1,681	1,473	1,345
Summary external debt stock by creditor type						
Long-term External debt stocks	**72,161**	**96,521**	**84,957**	**81,708**	**79,174**	**80,825**
Public and publicly guaranteed debt from:	15,904	33,057	32,431	33,106	36,072	36,221
Official creditors	6,071	12,519	12,920	12,306	13,838	12,993
Multilateral	4,373	11,662	11,927	10,994	12,247	11,420
of which: World Bank	3,022	4,701	5,590	5,510	5,362	5,335
Bilateral	1,698	857	993	1,312	1,591	1,573
Private creditors	9,833	20,538	19,512	20,800	22,234	23,228
Bondholders	8,027	20,343	19,352	20,643	22,067	22,467
Commercial banks and others	1,805	195	159	156	167	761
Private nonguaranteed debt from:	56,257	63,463	52,526	48,602	43,102	44,604
Bondholders	4,964	7,380	4,495	3,831	4,419	5,344
Commercial banks and others	51,293	56,083	48,031	44,771	38,682	39,260
Use of IMF Credit	6,726	7,608	12,486	13,075	14,001	12,997
Net financial inflows						
Net debt inflows						
Use of IMF Credit	4,401	884	5,260	995	146	-689
Long-term	17,256	-364	-5,125	-3,588	-330	650
Official creditors	620	2,484	873	-429	880	-566
Multilateral	843	2,491	725	-760	645	-561
of which: World Bank	687	1,387	889	-80	-149	-27
Bilateral	-223	-6	147	330	235	-5
Private creditors	16,636	-2,848	-5,997	-3,158	-1,210	1,217
Bondholders	278	-2,554	-1,812	541	1,589	-275
Banks and other private	16,358	-294	-4,185	-3,699	-2,799	1,492
Short-term	-2,414	-14,483	-3,299	-974	1,114	-2,088
Net equity inflows						
Foreign direct investment	9,612	712	4,003	3,550	1,934	1,969
Portfolio equity	388	-391	177	69	110	-9
Debt ratios						
External debt stocks to exports (%)	113	179	219	217	183	161
External debt stocks to GNI (%)	56	96	131	124	106	90
Debt service to exports (%)	21	29	55	23	21	21
Short-term to external debt stocks (%)	21	18	17	18	19	18
Multilateral to external debt stocks (%)	4	9	10	10	11	10
Reserves to external debt stocks (%)	31	5	11	13	15	17
Gross national income (GNI)	178,277	131,945	89,920	92,420	109,177	127,764

UZBEKISTAN

(US$ million, unless otherwise indicated)

	2008	2014	2015	2016	2017	2018
Summary external debt data by debtor type						
Total External debt stocks	**5,070**	**12,556**	**14,059**	**15,801**	**16,866**	**17,630**
Use of IMF Credit	405	381	364	353	374	365
Long-term external debt	4,495	11,680	13,024	14,848	15,653	16,542
Public and publicly guaranteed sector	3,188	4,816	5,709	6,699	7,619	9,481
Public Sector	3,181	4,816	5,709	6,699	7,619	9,481
of which: General Government	2,279	3,369	4,004	4,408	5,162	6,838
Private sector guaranteed by Public Sector	7	..	..	..	..	..
Private sector not guaranteed	1,306	6,864	7,315	8,149	8,035	7,061
Short-term external debt	171	495	671	600	838	722
Disbursements (long-term)	**1,011**	**2,632**	**2,387**	**2,894**	**2,081**	**2,612**
Public and publicly guaranteed sector	317	923	1,258	1,393	1,100	2,282
Public Sector	317	923	1,258	1,393	1,100	2,282
of which: General Government	200	559	867	657	813	1,903
Private sector guaranteed by Public Sector	..	..	..	..	..	..
Private sector not guaranteed	694	1,709	1,130	1,501	981	330
Principal repayments (long-term)	**710**	**683**	**962**	**1,008**	**1,438**	**691**
Public and publicly guaranteed sector	460	307	285	343	343	382
Public Sector	447	307	285	343	343	382
of which: General Government	131	194	176	210	179	198
Private sector guaranteed by Public Sector	13	..	..	..	..	..
Private sector not guaranteed	250	376	677	665	1,095	309
Interest payments (long-term)	**141**	**199**	**281**	**354**	**449**	**284**
Public and publicly guaranteed sector	114	67	73	91	118	143
Public Sector	114	67	73	91	118	143
of which: General Government	71	38	37	49	68	96
Private sector guaranteed by Public Sector	0	..	..	..	..	..
Private sector not guaranteed	26	132	208	262	331	141
Summary external debt stock by creditor type						
Long-term External debt stocks	**4,495**	**11,680**	**13,024**	**14,848**	**15,653**	**16,542**
Public and publicly guaranteed debt from:	3,188	4,816	5,709	6,699	7,619	9,481
Official creditors	2,707	4,630	5,454	6,430	7,337	9,282
Multilateral	963	2,532	3,128	3,451	3,965	5,507
of which: World Bank	368	494	599	779	910	1,907
Bilateral	1,744	2,098	2,325	2,979	3,372	3,775
Private creditors	482	185	255	269	281	199
Bondholders	..	..	..	..	..	..
Commercial banks and others	482	185	255	269	281	199
Private nonguaranteed debt from:	1,306	6,864	7,315	8,149	8,035	7,061
Bondholders	..	..	..	..	..	..
Commercial banks and others	1,306	6,864	7,315	8,149	8,035	7,061
Use of IMF Credit	405	381	364	353	374	365
Net financial inflows						
Net debt inflows						
Use of IMF Credit	..	0	..	..	..	..
Long-term	300	1,950	1,425	1,885	643	1,921
Official creditors	38	537	884	1,026	781	1,972
Multilateral	45	380	629	356	448	1,575
of which: World Bank	-1	47	120	196	101	1,013
Bilateral	-7	157	255	671	333	397
Private creditors	263	1,413	541	859	-138	-51
Bondholders	..	..	..	..	..	..
Banks and other private	263	1,413	541	859	-138	-51
Short-term	-35	82	176	-71	238	-116
Net equity inflows						
Foreign direct investment	711	757	66	1,129	1,914	639
Portfolio equity	..	..	..	2	3	13
Debt ratios						
External debt stocks to exports (%)	..	..	..	124	112	102
External debt stocks to GNI (%)	16	16	17	19	28	34
Debt service to exports (%)	..	..	..	11	13	6
Short-term to external debt stocks (%)	3	4	5	4	5	4
Multilateral to external debt stocks (%)	19	20	22	22	24	31
Reserves to external debt stocks (%)	..	108	97	90	83	71
Gross national income (GNI)	31,271	79,585	83,307	82,713	60,375	52,023

VANUATU

(US$ million, unless otherwise indicated)

	2008	2014	2015	2016	2017	2018
Summary external debt data by debtor type						
Total External debt stocks	**148.9**	**203.3**	**256.8**	**293.4**	**401.4**	**402.2**
Use of IMF Credit	25.1	23.6	46.1	44.7	47.4	43.3
Long-term external debt	89.7	98.9	172.0	210.9	287.6	313.8
Public and publicly guaranteed sector	89.7	98.9	172.0	210.9	287.6	313.8
Public Sector	89.7	98.9	172.0	210.9	287.6	313.8
of which: General Government	89.2	98.6	171.7	210.7	287.4	313.8
Private sector guaranteed by Public Sector	..	..	..	..	..	..
Private sector not guaranteed	..	..	..	..	..	..
Short-term external debt	34.1	80.8	38.7	37.8	66.4	45.1
Disbursements (long-term)	**10.1**	**0.7**	**84.8**	**53.2**	**68.7**	**46.4**
Public and publicly guaranteed sector	10.1	0.7	84.8	53.2	68.7	46.4
Public Sector	10.1	0.7	84.8	53.2	68.7	46.4
of which: General Government	10.1	0.7	84.8	53.2	68.7	46.4
Private sector guaranteed by Public Sector	..	..	..	..	..	..
Private sector not guaranteed	..	..	..	..	..	..
Principal repayments (long-term)	**2.5**	**5.6**	**5.0**	**4.9**	**5.0**	**12.0**
Public and publicly guaranteed sector	2.5	5.6	5.0	4.9	5.0	12.0
Public Sector	2.5	5.6	5.0	4.9	5.0	12.0
of which: General Government	2.5	5.5	5.0	4.9	5.0	11.8
Private sector guaranteed by Public Sector	..	..	..	..	..	..
Private sector not guaranteed	..	..	..	..	..	..
Interest payments (long-term)	**1.1**	**1.4**	**1.3**	**3.2**	**3.5**	**4.2**
Public and publicly guaranteed sector	1.1	1.4	1.3	3.2	3.5	4.2
Public Sector	1.1	1.4	1.3	3.2	3.5	4.2
of which: General Government	1.1	1.4	1.3	3.2	3.5	4.2
Private sector guaranteed by Public Sector	..	..	..	..	..	..
Private sector not guaranteed	..	..	..	..	..	..
Summary external debt stock by creditor type						
Long-term External debt stocks	**89.7**	**98.9**	**172.0**	**210.9**	**287.6**	**313.8**
Public and publicly guaranteed debt from:	89.7	98.9	172.0	210.9	287.6	313.8
Official creditors	89.7	98.9	172.0	210.9	287.6	313.8
Multilateral	71.0	47.5	47.7	53.7	76.1	101.8
of which: World Bank	12.9	8.8	9.1	12.2	29.1	54.7
Bilateral	18.7	51.4	124.3	157.2	211.5	212.0
Private creditors	..	..	..	..	..	..
Bondholders	..	..	..	..	..	..
Commercial banks and others	..	..	..	..	..	..
Private nonguaranteed debt from:	..	..	..	..	..	..
Bondholders	..	..	..	..	..	..
Commercial banks and others	..	..	..	..	..	..
Use of IMF Credit	25.1	23.6	46.1	44.7	47.4	43.3
Net financial inflows						
Net debt inflows						
Use of IMF Credit	..	0.0	23.8	0.0	0.0	-3.0
Long-term	7.6	-4.9	79.8	48.3	63.7	34.4
Official creditors	7.6	-4.9	79.8	48.3	63.7	34.4
Multilateral	-2.1	-2.5	1.4	6.1	19.6	27.1
of which: World Bank	-0.4	-0.6	0.7	3.4	15.8	26.8
Bilateral	9.7	-2.4	78.4	42.1	44.0	7.2
Private creditors	..	..	..	..	..	..
Bondholders	..	..	..	..	..	..
Banks and other private	..	..	..	..	..	..
Short-term	10.0	57.1	-42.1	-0.9	28.6	-21.3
Net equity inflows						
Foreign direct investment	29.6	22.2	16.8	21.6	24.3	38.0
Portfolio equity	..	..	..	..	..	..
Debt ratios						
External debt stocks to exports (%)	47.5	46.9	71.7	69.9	..	..
External debt stocks to GNI (%)	24.5	24.9	35.6	37.6	47.7	45.9
Debt service to exports (%)	1.5	1.8	1.9	2.1	..	..
Short-term to external debt stocks (%)	22.9	39.7	15.1	12.9	16.6	11.2
Multilateral to external debt stocks (%)	47.7	23.4	18.6	18.3	19.0	25.3
Reserves to external debt stocks (%)	77.4	90.5	104.8	91.1	98.4	104.6
Gross national income (GNI)	608.1	815.2	721.5	780.6	840.9	875.4

VENEZUELA, RB

(US$ million, unless otherwise indicated)

	2008	2014	2015	2016	2017	2018
Summary external debt data by debtor type						
Total External debt stocks	**73,153**	**161,707**	**160,909**	**152,523**	**148,878**	**154,898**
Use of IMF Credit	488	3,685	3,524	3,419	3,622	3,537
Long-term external debt	52,391	127,435	116,287	107,406	104,016	105,140
Public and publicly guaranteed sector	36,111	70,093	69,000	67,212	69,713	70,837
Public Sector	36,111	70,093	69,000	67,212	69,713	70,837
of which: General Government	29,869	44,134	43,363	40,086	39,714	39,148
Private sector guaranteed by Public Sector	..	..	..	..	..	..
Private sector not guaranteed	16,279	57,342	47,286	40,193	34,303	34,303
Short-term external debt	20,274	30,587	41,098	41,698	41,240	46,221
Disbursements (long-term)	**14,790**	**17,180**	**21,359**	**2,637**	**4,009**	**3,738**
Public and publicly guaranteed sector	5,201	4,852	2,785	2,637	4,009	3,738
Public Sector	5,201	4,852	2,785	2,637	4,009	3,738
of which: General Government	4,840	1,237	1,706	638	1,136	823
Private sector guaranteed by Public Sector	..	..	..	..	..	..
Private sector not guaranteed	9,588	12,328	18,574	..	..	0
Principal repayments (long-term)	**7,336**	**15,027**	**17,560**	**11,499**	**7,526**	**2,551**
Public and publicly guaranteed sector	3,021	2,620	3,710	4,406	1,635	2,551
Public Sector	3,021	2,620	3,710	4,406	1,635	2,551
of which: General Government	2,435	2,620	2,309	3,896	1,635	1,326
Private sector guaranteed by Public Sector	..	..	..	..	..	..
Private sector not guaranteed	4,315	12,407	13,849	7,093	5,891	..
Interest payments (long-term)	**4,261**	**8,649**	**9,053**	**7,762**	**7,245**	**3,935**
Public and publicly guaranteed sector	3,017	5,762	5,849	5,324	5,172	3,935
Public Sector	3,017	5,762	5,849	5,324	5,172	3,935
of which: General Government	2,449	3,908	3,695	3,287	3,177	1,867
Private sector guaranteed by Public Sector	..	..	..	..	..	..
Private sector not guaranteed	1,243	2,887	3,204	2,438	2,073	..
Summary external debt stock by creditor type						
Long-term External debt stocks	**52,391**	**127,435**	**116,287**	**107,406**	**104,016**	**105,140**
Public and publicly guaranteed debt from:	36,111	70,093	69,000	67,212	69,713	70,837
Official creditors	3,550	9,726	10,025	8,754	7,922	8,360
Multilateral	2,701	5,830	6,118	6,032	6,136	6,453
of which: World Bank	..	..	..	..	..	..
Bilateral	849	3,897	3,906	2,721	1,786	1,907
Private creditors	32,561	60,367	58,976	58,459	61,791	62,477
Bondholders	30,063	59,535	56,828	54,318	55,199	52,721
Commercial banks and others	2,498	833	2,148	4,141	6,593	9,756
Private nonguaranteed debt from:	16,279	57,342	47,286	40,193	34,303	34,303
Bondholders	3,310	17,080	2,300	1,955	1,800	1,800
Commercial banks and others	12,969	40,261	44,986	38,238	32,503	32,503
Use of IMF Credit	488	3,685	3,524	3,419	3,622	3,537
Net financial inflows						
Net debt inflows						
Use of IMF Credit	..	0	..	..	..	..
Long-term	7,453	2,153	3,800	-8,862	-3,516	1,187
Official creditors	118	113	303	-1,276	-839	439
Multilateral	179	127	289	-86	102	318
of which: World Bank	..	..	..	..	..	..
Bilateral	-62	-14	14	-1,190	-941	121
Private creditors	7,336	2,041	3,497	-7,586	-2,677	748
Bondholders	2,479	2,117	-2,594	-2,855	726	-2,478
Banks and other private	4,857	-76	6,091	-4,731	-3,403	3,226
Short-term	621	746	10,511	600	-458	4,710
Net equity inflows						
Foreign direct investment	2,638	577	-282	446	-68	956
Portfolio equity	1	49	5	..	..	..
Debt ratios						
External debt stocks to exports (%)	69	206	405	521	..	..
External debt stocks to GNI (%)	23	34	..	..	..	..
Debt service to exports (%)	11	31	70	69	..	..
Short-term to external debt stocks (%)	28	19	26	27	28	30
Multilateral to external debt stocks (%)	4	4	4	4	4	4
Reserves to external debt stocks (%)	45	5	4	2	2	..
Gross national income (GNI)	316,633	476,934	..	..	..	..

VIETNAM

(US$ million, unless otherwise indicated)

	2008	2014	2015	2016	2017	2018
Summary external debt data by debtor type						
Total External debt stocks	**26,476**	**72,449**	**77,829**	**85,663**	**104,091**	**108,096**
Use of IMF Credit	195	456	436	423	448	438
Long-term external debt	22,077	58,389	65,402	72,519	81,744	88,074
Public and publicly guaranteed sector	22,077	44,830	46,363	48,036	51,790	53,321
Public Sector	22,077	44,602	46,144	47,840	51,620	53,176
of which: General Government	19,788	31,119	32,055	33,256	36,162	37,947
Private sector guaranteed by Public Sector	..	228	218	196	170	145
Private sector not guaranteed	..	13,559	19,039	24,484	29,954	34,752
Short-term external debt	4,204	13,604	11,991	12,720	21,898	19,585
Disbursements (long-term)	**2,799**	**13,807**	**12,952**	**13,112**	**18,661**	**21,535**
Public and publicly guaranteed sector	2,799	7,491	4,427	4,458	4,270	4,410
Public Sector	2,799	7,472	4,427	4,458	4,270	4,410
of which: General Government	2,031	4,597	2,771	2,846	2,748	3,347
Private sector guaranteed by Public Sector	..	19	0	0	0	0
Private sector not guaranteed	..	6,316	8,525	8,654	14,391	17,126
Principal repayments (long-term)	**772**	**5,317**	**4,928**	**5,734**	**11,247**	**14,909**
Public and publicly guaranteed sector	772	2,699	1,883	2,524	2,327	2,581
Public Sector	772	2,699	1,873	2,501	2,302	2,556
of which: General Government	563	1,947	1,046	1,514	1,271	1,402
Private sector guaranteed by Public Sector	..	..	10	23	25	25
Private sector not guaranteed	..	2,618	3,045	3,210	8,920	12,327
Interest payments (long-term)	**466**	**1,240**	**1,538**	**1,411**	**2,059**	**2,762**
Public and publicly guaranteed sector	466	811	822	879	940	1,043
Public Sector	466	807	818	874	935	1,038
of which: General Government	394	509	471	505	526	601
Private sector guaranteed by Public Sector	..	4	4	5	5	5
Private sector not guaranteed	..	429	717	532	1,119	1,718
Summary external debt stock by creditor type						
Long-term External debt stocks	**22,077**	**58,389**	**65,402**	**72,519**	**81,744**	**88,074**
Public and publicly guaranteed debt from:	22,077	44,830	46,363	48,036	51,790	53,321
Official creditors	19,407	35,910	37,744	40,338	44,773	47,070
Multilateral	8,082	19,077	20,174	21,166	23,286	23,723
of which: World Bank	5,110	12,090	12,638	13,110	14,683	14,968
Bilateral	11,325	16,834	17,570	19,172	21,488	23,346
Private creditors	2,670	8,920	8,618	7,698	7,017	6,251
Bondholders	1,059	1,900	1,877	1,521	1,516	1,511
Commercial banks and others	1,611	7,019	6,742	6,177	5,501	4,740
Private nonguaranteed debt from:	..	13,559	19,039	24,484	29,954	34,752
Bondholders	..	290	290	235	235	35
Commercial banks and others	..	13,269	18,749	24,248	29,718	34,717
Use of IMF Credit	195	456	436	423	448	438
Net financial inflows						
Net debt inflows						
Use of IMF Credit	-39	0	..	..	..	..
Long-term	2,027	8,490	8,024	7,378	7,413	6,627
Official creditors	1,613	3,948	2,770	2,844	2,689	2,576
Multilateral	836	2,048	1,800	1,443	1,146	845
of which: World Bank	553	1,338	1,054	830	885	592
Bilateral	777	1,900	971	1,401	1,543	1,731
Private creditors	414	4,542	5,253	4,535	4,724	4,051
Bondholders	-31	-685	-23	-411	-5	-205
Banks and other private	445	5,228	5,277	4,946	4,729	4,256
Short-term	-190	1,435	-1,613	729	9,178	-2,313
Net equity inflows						
Foreign direct investment	8,960	7,676	10,313	12,600	14,100	13,977
Portfolio equity	-578	252	134	..	..	..
Debt ratios						
External debt stocks to exports (%)	37	45	45	45	46	42
External debt stocks to GNI (%)	28	41	42	44	49	47
Debt service to exports (%)	2	4	4	4	6	7
Short-term to external debt stocks (%)	16	19	15	15	21	18
Multilateral to external debt stocks (%)	31	26	26	25	22	22
Reserves to external debt stocks (%)	90	47	36	43	47	51
Gross national income (GNI)	96,181	177,361	183,321	196,687	213,006	231,476

YEMEN, REPUBLIC OF

(US$ million, unless otherwise indicated)

	2008	2014	2015	2016	2017	2018
Summary external debt data by debtor type						
Total External debt stocks	**6,229**	**7,723**	**7,299**	**7,063**	**7,193**	**7,037**
Use of IMF Credit	140	546	522	497	508	469
Long-term external debt	5,696	6,862	6,477	6,322	6,317	6,205
Public and publicly guaranteed sector	5,696	6,862	6,477	6,322	6,317	6,205
Public Sector	5,696	6,862	6,477	6,322	6,317	6,205
of which: General Government	5,696	5,862	5,477	5,322	5,317	5,205
Private sector guaranteed by Public Sector	..	..	..	..	..	..
Private sector not guaranteed	..	..	..	..	..	..
Short-term external debt	393	316	300	243	368	362
Disbursements (long-term)	**285**	**455**	**60**	**24**	**4**	**19**
Public and publicly guaranteed sector	285	455	60	24	4	19
Public Sector	285	455	60	24	4	19
of which: General Government	285	455	60	24	4	19
Private sector guaranteed by Public Sector	..	..	..	..	..	..
Private sector not guaranteed	..	..	..	..	..	..
Principal repayments (long-term)	**134**	**283**	**282**	**98**	**66**	**71**
Public and publicly guaranteed sector	134	283	282	98	66	71
Public Sector	134	283	282	98	66	71
of which: General Government	134	283	282	98	66	71
Private sector guaranteed by Public Sector	..	..	..	..	..	..
Private sector not guaranteed	..	..	..	..	..	..
Interest payments (long-term)	**70**	**78**	**74**	**31**	**13**	**13**
Public and publicly guaranteed sector	70	78	74	31	13	13
Public Sector	70	78	74	31	13	13
of which: General Government	70	76	71	28	13	13
Private sector guaranteed by Public Sector	..	..	..	..	..	..
Private sector not guaranteed	..	..	..	..	..	..
Summary external debt stock by creditor type						
Long-term External debt stocks	**5,696**	**6,862**	**6,477**	**6,322**	**6,317**	**6,205**
Public and publicly guaranteed debt from:	5,696	6,862	6,477	6,322	6,317	6,205
Official creditors	5,690	6,862	6,477	6,322	6,317	6,205
Multilateral	3,036	3,484	3,182	3,039	3,110	3,004
of which: World Bank	2,113	1,910	1,780	1,668	1,695	1,586
Bilateral	2,654	3,378	3,295	3,283	3,207	3,201
Private creditors	6	0	..	..	..	..
Bondholders	..	..	..	..	..	..
Commercial banks and others	6	0	..	..	..	..
Private nonguaranteed debt from:	..	..	..	..	..	..
Bondholders	..	..	..	..	..	..
Commercial banks and others	..	..	..	..	..	..
Use of IMF Credit	140	546	522	497	508	469
Net financial inflows						
Net debt inflows						
Use of IMF Credit	-71	74	0	-10	-18	-27
Long-term	151	172	-222	-74	-62	-52
Official creditors	152	173	-222	-74	-62	-52
Multilateral	163	222	-166	-72	-62	-51
of which: World Bank	70	-46	-51	-64	-66	-71
Bilateral	-11	-49	-56	-2	0	0
Private creditors	-1	-1	..	..	..	..
Bondholders	..	..	..	..	..	..
Banks and other private	-1	-1	..	..	..	..
Short-term	-28	51	-23	-109	50	-82
Net equity inflows						
Foreign direct investment	40	-233	-15	-561	-270	-282
Portfolio equity	0	0	0	0	..	..
Debt ratios						
External debt stocks to exports (%)	59	82	386	738	..	..
External debt stocks to GNI (%)	25	19	18	23	27	26
Debt service to exports (%)	3	4	19	15	..	..
Short-term to external debt stocks (%)	6	4	4	3	5	5
Multilateral to external debt stocks (%)	49	45	44	43	43	43
Reserves to external debt stocks (%)	130	..	..	..	..	..
Gross national income (GNI)	24,996	40,608	41,283	30,904	26,784	26,913

ZAMBIA

(US$ million, unless otherwise indicated)

	2008	2014	2015	2016	2017	2018
Summary external debt data by debtor type						
Total External debt stocks	**3,080**	**9,339**	**11,917**	**15,359**	**17,520**	**19,116**
Use of IMF Credit	201	1,011	907	813	794	715
Long-term external debt	2,205	7,459	10,227	13,740	15,782	17,735
Public and publicly guaranteed sector	1,157	4,893	6,583	7,154	8,880	9,987
Public Sector	1,157	4,893	6,582	7,154	8,880	9,987
of which: General Government	1,087	4,861	6,557	7,133	8,859	9,970
Private sector guaranteed by Public Sector	0	0	0	0	0	0
Private sector not guaranteed	1,049	2,566	3,645	6,586	6,902	7,748
Short-term external debt	674	868	782	806	945	667
Disbursements (long-term)	**239**	**3,240**	**3,106**	**3,768**	**2,287**	**2,704**
Public and publicly guaranteed sector	118	1,590	1,909	798	1,756	1,473
Public Sector	118	1,590	1,909	798	1,756	1,473
of which: General Government	118	1,590	1,909	798	1,756	1,472
Private sector guaranteed by Public Sector	..	0	0	0	0	0
Private sector not guaranteed	121	1,650	1,197	2,970	531	1,231
Principal repayments (long-term)	**114**	**231**	**215**	**210**	**370**	**679**
Public and publicly guaranteed sector	61	90	97	146	155	295
Public Sector	61	90	97	146	155	295
of which: General Government	51	86	93	143	152	291
Private sector guaranteed by Public Sector	..	..	0	0	0	0
Private sector not guaranteed	53	141	118	63	215	385
Interest payments (long-term)	**39**	**123**	**259**	**448**	**386**	**702**
Public and publicly guaranteed sector	14	82	189	326	341	445
Public Sector	14	82	189	326	341	445
of which: General Government	13	82	189	325	341	445
Private sector guaranteed by Public Sector	..	..	..	..	..	..
Private sector not guaranteed	24	41	69	122	45	256
Summary external debt stock by creditor type						
Long-term External debt stocks	**2,205**	**7,459**	**10,227**	**13,740**	**15,782**	**17,735**
Public and publicly guaranteed debt from:	1,157	4,893	6,583	7,154	8,880	9,987
Official creditors	1,108	2,635	3,142	3,718	4,223	4,685
Multilateral	818	1,212	1,295	1,408	1,621	1,813
of which: World Bank	371	667	698	760	894	1,003
Bilateral	290	1,424	1,847	2,310	2,602	2,871
Private creditors	48	2,258	3,441	3,436	4,657	5,302
Bondholders	..	1,750	3,000	3,000	3,000	3,000
Commercial banks and others	48	508	441	436	1,657	2,302
Private nonguaranteed debt from:	1,049	2,566	3,645	6,586	6,902	7,748
Bondholders	..	..	..	..	..	..
Commercial banks and others	1,049	2,566	3,645	6,586	6,902	7,748
Use of IMF Credit	201	1,011	907	813	794	715
Net financial inflows						
Net debt inflows						
Use of IMF Credit	11	-35	-61	-69	-66	-61
Long-term	125	3,009	2,891	3,558	1,917	2,024
Official creditors	56	304	590	656	380	530
Multilateral	71	102	136	156	132	230
of which: World Bank	51	76	61	86	86	132
Bilateral	-16	202	454	500	248	300
Private creditors	70	2,704	2,301	2,902	1,537	1,495
Bondholders	..	1,000	1,250	0	0	0
Banks and other private	70	1,704	1,051	2,902	1,537	1,495
Short-term	96	78	-87	22	81	-225
Net equity inflows						
Foreign direct investment	603	727	309	267	456	-502
Portfolio equity	-6	6	0	3	-3	-5
Debt ratios						
External debt stocks to exports (%)	54	84	145	205	193	191
External debt stocks to GNI (%)	19	35	57	75	71	74
Debt service to exports (%)	3	4	7	10	9	15
Short-term to external debt stocks (%)	22	9	7	5	5	3
Multilateral to external debt stocks (%)	27	13	11	9	9	9
Reserves to external debt stocks (%)	36	33	25	15	12	8
Gross national income (GNI)	16,512	26,634	20,807	20,496	24,722	25,953

ZIMBABWE

(US$ million, unless otherwise indicated)

	2008	2014	2015	2016	2017	2018
Summary external debt data by debtor type						
Total External debt stocks	**5,841**	**8,372**	**9,380**	**11,223**	**12,115**	**12,286**
Use of IMF Credit	129	487	464	455	482	471
Long-term external debt	3,862	5,256	6,108	7,794	8,208	8,441
Public and publicly guaranteed sector	3,771	4,027	4,193	4,161	4,232	3,970
Public Sector	3,771	4,027	4,193	4,161	4,232	3,970
of which: General Government	3,142	3,455	3,488	3,531	3,611	3,412
Private sector guaranteed by Public Sector	..	..	..	..	..	..
Private sector not guaranteed	91	1,229	1,915	3,633	3,975	4,471
Short-term external debt	1,850	2,629	2,809	2,974	3,425	3,374
Disbursements (long-term)	**117**	**1,579**	**1,402**	**1,054**	**768**	**744**
Public and publicly guaranteed sector	51	211	461	167	107	44
Public Sector	51	211	461	167	107	44
of which: General Government	14	211	253	161	102	44
Private sector guaranteed by Public Sector	..	..	..	..	..	..
Private sector not guaranteed	66	1,368	941	887	662	700
Principal repayments (long-term)	**54**	**366**	**426**	**988**	**384**	**281**
Public and publicly guaranteed sector	2	111	116	108	111	76
Public Sector	2	111	116	108	111	76
of which: General Government	2	97	69	41	61	26
Private sector guaranteed by Public Sector	..	..	..	..	..	..
Private sector not guaranteed	52	255	310	880	273	205
Interest payments (long-term)	**10**	**125**	**202**	**121**	**267**	**251**
Public and publicly guaranteed sector	5	24	38	44	27	11
Public Sector	5	24	38	44	27	11
of which: General Government	5	23	24	23	24	10
Private sector guaranteed by Public Sector	..	..	..	..	..	..
Private sector not guaranteed	5	101	164	78	240	240
Summary external debt stock by creditor type						
Long-term External debt stocks	**3,862**	**5,256**	**6,108**	**7,794**	**8,208**	**8,441**
Public and publicly guaranteed debt from:	3,771	4,027	4,193	4,161	4,232	3,970
Official creditors	3,309	3,580	3,766	3,724	3,776	3,528
Multilateral	1,632	1,561	1,663	1,580	1,439	1,237
of which: World Bank	983	941	912	885	907	896
Bilateral	1,677	2,019	2,102	2,145	2,337	2,292
Private creditors	462	447	427	437	457	442
Bondholders	0	0	0	0	0	0
Commercial banks and others	462	447	427	437	457	442
Private nonguaranteed debt from:	91	1,229	1,915	3,633	3,975	4,471
Bondholders	..	..	..	..	..	..
Commercial banks and others	91	1,229	1,915	3,633	3,975	4,471
Use of IMF Credit	129	487	464	455	482	471
Net financial inflows						
Net debt inflows						
Use of IMF Credit	-2	-2	-2	-87	..	..
Long-term	63	1,213	976	66	385	463
Official creditors	35	99	341	23	7	-33
Multilateral	-2	-2	153	-69	-60	-41
of which: World Bank	0	-2	-7	-13	-5	0
Bilateral	37	101	187	91	67	8
Private creditors	28	1,114	635	43	378	496
Bondholders	0	0	0	0	0	..
Banks and other private	28	1,114	635	43	378	496
Short-term	-21	-88	134	93	320	-120
Net equity inflows						
Foreign direct investment	52	473	399	343	247	745
Portfolio equity	..	130	123	-80	-101	..
Debt ratios						
External debt stocks to exports (%)	..	197	225	262	245	239
External debt stocks to GNI (%)	147	47	52	60	58	40
Debt service to exports (%)	..	12	16	29	14	12
Short-term to external debt stocks (%)	32	31	30	27	28	27
Multilateral to external debt stocks (%)	28	19	18	14	12	10
Reserves to external debt stocks (%)	1	4	4	4	2	1
Gross national income (GNI)	3,972	17,643	17,981	18,773	20,852	30,864

APPENDIX
About the Data

User Guide to Tables

International Debt Statistics 2020 focuses on financial flows, trends in external debt, and other major financial indicators for low- and middle-income countries. This edition of *International Debt Statistics* (IDS) has been reconfigured to offer a more condensed presentation of the principal indicators. The longer version of the report will be found in the online tables.

Tables

Aggregate Tables

The aggregate tables are labeled by region name. Data are shown for all low- and middle-income countries and six regional groups (East Asia and Pacific, Europe and Central Asia, Latin America and the Caribbean, Middle East and North Africa, South Asia, and Sub-Saharan Africa).

Country Tables

Country tables are labeled by country name and ordered alphabetically. Data are shown for 122 low- and middle-income countries that report public and publicly guaranteed external debt to the World Bank's Debtor Reporting System (DRS). The tables also include key debt ratios and the composition of external debt stocks and flows for each country.

Each table shows a time series with the most recent five years, as well as 2008 as a comparison year. Full time series data are available for all countries in the World Bank's Open Data website (https://datacatalog.worldbank.org/dataset/international-debt-statistics).

Statistics

The general cutoff date for countries to report data for this publication was end-August 2019. The economic aggregates presented in the tables are prepared for the convenience of users. Although debt ratios can give useful information about developments in a debt-servicing capacity, conclusions drawn from them will not be valid unless accompanied by careful economic evaluation.

The macroeconomic data provided are collected from national statistical organizations, which in some cases may be subject to a considerable margin of error. The usual care must be taken in interpreting the ratios, particularly for the most recent years, because figures may be preliminary and subject to revision.

Specific country notes describing the sources of information that are not provided by the country are summarized in the "Data Documentation" section. Unless otherwise specified, data on long-term public and publicly guaranteed external debt for 2018 are based on reports provided by the country.

More detailed information on data sources, methodology, and compilation is provided in the appendix at the back of this book.

Aggregate Measures for Income Groups and Regions

Aggregate measures for income groups and regions include the 122 low- and middle-income countries that report public and publicly guaranteed external debt to the World Bank's DRS, whenever data are available. The aggregate "All low- and middle-income countries" is the sum of data for 122 countries.

Classification of Countries

For operational and analytical purposes, the World Bank's main criterion for classifying countries is gross national income (GNI) per capita (calculated by the *World Bank Atlas* method). Every country is classified as low-income, middle-income, or high-income. Low- and middle-income countries are sometimes referred to as developing countries. The term is used for convenience; it is not intended to imply that all countries in the group are experiencing similar development or that other countries have reached a preferred or final stage of development. Because GNI per capita changes over time, the country composition of income groups may change from one edition of *International Debt Statistics* to the next. Once the classification is fixed for an edition, based on GNI per capita in the most recent year for which data are available, all historical data presented are based on the same country grouping.

Symbols

0 or 0.0 means zero or small enough that the number would round to zero at the displayed number of decimal places.

.. means that data are not available or that aggregates cannot be calculated because of missing data in the years shown.

$ indicates current U.S. dollars unless otherwise specified.

User Guide to IDS Online Tables and Database

The country tables that were previously available in the *International Debt Statistics* print edition is now available online. Using an automated query process, these reference tables will be updated based on the revisions to the International Debt Statistics database.

Users can access all the online tables, download the PDF version of the publication, and view the report as an eBook on ISSUU, as well as access the database and download the archived editions of the publication by going to http://data.worldbank.org/products/ids.

How to Access IDS Online Country Tables

To access the IDS online tables, visit http://datatopics.worldbank.org/debt/ids and select from "Country," "Region," or "Topic" options. Click on "Analytical" to view the table with a select number of indicators as reported in the IDS publication, or "Standard" to view the tables with the full list of indicators available in the database.

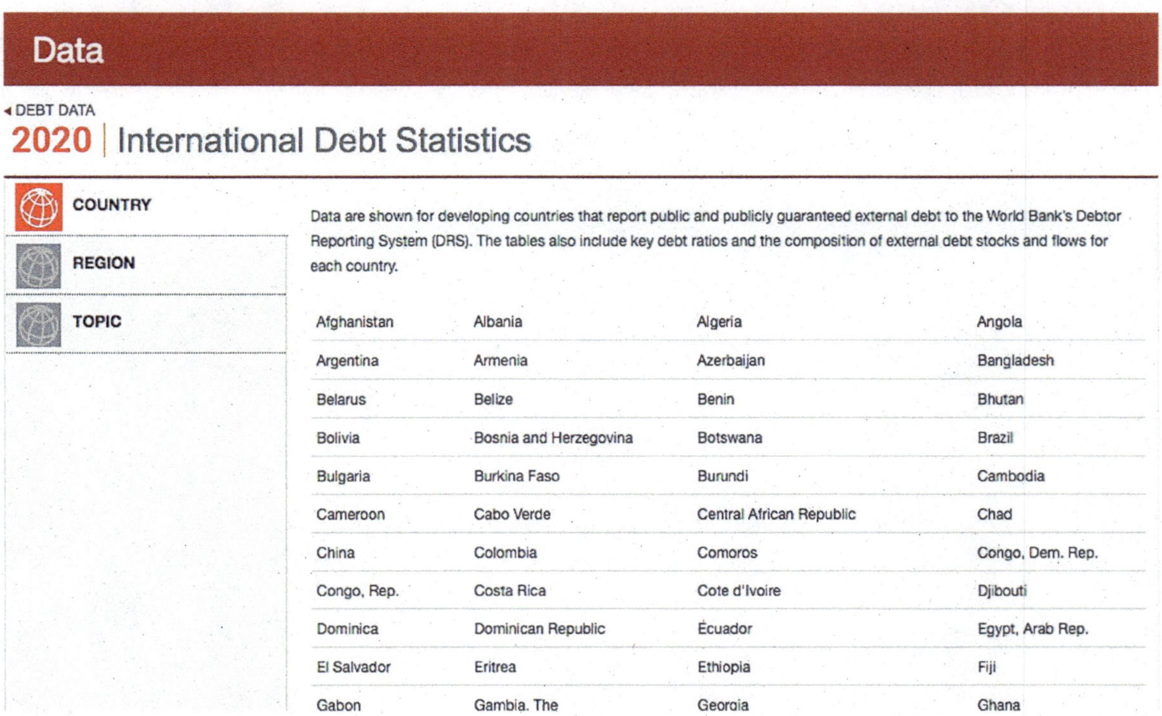
Data

◂ DEBT DATA

2020 | International Debt Statistics

COUNTRY

REGION

TOPIC

Data are shown for developing countries that report public and publicly guaranteed external debt to the World Bank's Debtor Reporting System (DRS). The tables also include key debt ratios and the composition of external debt stocks and flows for each country.

Afghanistan	Albania	Algeria	Angola
Argentina	Armenia	Azerbaijan	Bangladesh
Belarus	Belize	Benin	Bhutan
Bolivia	Bosnia and Herzegovina	Botswana	Brazil
Bulgaria	Burkina Faso	Burundi	Cambodia
Cameroon	Cabo Verde	Central African Republic	Chad
China	Colombia	Comoros	Congo, Dem. Rep.
Congo, Rep.	Costa Rica	Cote d'Ivoire	Djibouti
Dominica	Dominican Republic	Ecuador	Egypt, Arab Rep.
El Salvador	Eritrea	Ethiopia	Fiji
Gabon	Gambia, The	Georgia	Ghana

To access a specific country table directly without going through the above landing page, use the URL http://datatopics.worldbank.org/debt/ids/ and the country code (for example, http://datatopics.worldbank.org/debt/ids/country/DZA to view the table for Algeria). Similarly, to view the regional table, click on the "Region" tab and select one of the listed regions (for example http://datatopics.worldbank.org/debt/ids/region/SAS to view the table for South Asia).

2020 | International Debt Statistics

Data > Data Topics > Debt Data > Country Tables > Afghanistan

$ millions, unless otherwise indicated	2009	2010	2011	2012	2013	2014	2015
1. Summary external debt data							
External debt stocks	2,480.2	2,435.6	2,627.7	2,729.2	2,587.0	2,613.0	2,520.3
Long-term external debt	2,106.1	1,975.5	2,032.5	2,079.8	2,106.2	2,021.0	1,990.0
Public and publicly guaranteed	2,106.1	1,975.5	2,032.5	2,079.8	2,106.2	2,021.0	1,990.0
Private nonguaranteed	0.0	0.0	0.0	0.0	0.0	0.0	0.0
Use of IMF credit	352.8	355.2	372.6	387.6	375.6	334.8	300.2
Short-term external debt	21.4	104.8	222.7	261.7	105.1	257.2	230.2
of which interest arrears on long-term	21.4	67.8	210.7	219.6	86.1	205.4	188.5
Official creditors	21.3	67.8	210.7	219.6	86.1	205.4	188.5
Private creditors	0.0	0.0	0.0	0.0	0.0	0.0	0.0
Memo: principal arrears on LDOD	65.1	65.0	65.1	63.2	63.1	22.9	9.1
Official creditors	64.7	65.0	65.1	63.2	63.1	22.9	9.1
Private creditors	0.4	0.0	0.0	0.0	0.0	0.0	0.0
External debt flows							
Disbursements	126.2	84.6	81.2	70.4	36.7	31.7	26.0
Long-term external debt	108.8	76.0	62.2	52.1	36.7	31.7	26.0
IMF purchases	17.4	8.6	18.9	18.3	0.0	0.0	0.0
Principal repayments	3.1	1.0	0.9	5.4	16.8	31.6	39.0
Long-term external debt	3.1	1.0	0.9	1.6	4.2	12.1	18.7
IMF repurchases	0.0	0.0	0.0	3.7	12.6	19.5	20.3
Net flows	123.1	120.7	55.3	95.1	-3.2	33.0	-23.0
Long-term external debt	105.6	75.0	61.4	50.4	32.5	19.6	7.3
Short-term external debt	0.0	37.0	-25.0	30.1	-23.1	32.8	-10.1
Interest payments	7.6	9.5	9.5	9.5	8.3	10.6	9.9
Long-term external debt	6.5	7.7	8.9	8.3	7.5	9.1	8.7
IMF charges	1.1	0.8	0.3	0.1	0.3	0.1	0.1
Short-term external debt	0.0	1.0	0.3	1.1	0.5	1.4	1.1

Indicators

The indicator codes for each of the indicators online and in the publication are listed below. To view a specific indicator online, go to http://data.worldbank.org/indicator/ and add the indicator code at the end of the url; for example, to view a page for total debt stocks, this line should be in your browser: http://data.worldbank.org/indicator/DT.DOD.DECT.CD.

1. SUMMARY EXTERNAL DEBT DATA			
External debt stocks	DT.DOD.DECT.CD	**External debt flows**	
Long-term external debt	DT.DOD.DLXF.CD	**Disbursements**	DT.DIS.DLTF.CD
Public and publicly guaranteed	DT.DOD.DPPG.CD	Long-term external debt	DT.DIS.DLXF.CD
Private nonguaranteed	DT.DOD.DPNG.CD	IMF purchases	DT.DIS.DIMF.CD
Use of IMF credit	DT.DOD.DIMF.CD	**Principal repayments**	DT.AMT.DLTF.CD
Short-term debt	DT.DOD.DSTC.CD	Long-term external debt	DT.AMT.DLXF.CD
interest arrears on long-term	DT.IXA.DPPG.CD	IMF repurchases	DT.AMT.DIMF.CD
		Net flows	DT.NFL.DECT.CD
		Long-term external debt	DT.NFL.DLXF.CD
Memorandum items		Short-term external debt	DT.NFL.DSTC.CD
Principal arrears on long-term	DT.AXA.DPPG.CD	**Interest payments (INT)**	DT.INT.DECT.CD
Long-term public sector debt	DT.DOD.DPPG.CD	Long-term external debt	DT.INT.DLXF.CD
Long-term private sector debt	DT.DOD.PRVS.CD	IMF charges	DT.INT.DIMF.CD
Public & publicly guaranteed commitments	DT.COM.DPPG.CD	Short-term external debt	DT.INT.DSTC.CD

2. OTHER NON-DEBT RESOURCE FLOWS	
Foreign direct investment (net equity inflows)	BX.KLT.DINV.CD.WD
Portfolio equity flows	BX.PEF.TOTL.CD.WD

3. CURRENCY COMPOSITION OF PUBLIC AND PUBLICLY GUARANTEED DEBT (%)	
Euro	DT.CUR.EURO.ZS
Japanese yen	DT.CUR.JYEN.ZS
Pound sterling	DT.CUR.UKPS.ZS
Swiss franc	DT.CUR.SWFR.ZS
U.S. dollars	DT.CUR.USDL.ZS

4. AVERAGE TERMS OF NEW COMMITMENTS	
Official creditors	
Interest (%)	DT.INR.OFFT
Maturity (years)	DT.MAT.OFFT
Grace period (years)	DT.GPA.OFFT
Private creditors	
Interest (%)	DT.INR.PRVT
Maturity (years)	DT.MAT.PRVT
Grace period (years)	DT.GPA.PRVT

5. MAJOR ECONOMIC AGGREGATES	
Gross national income (GNI)	NY.GNP.MKTP.CD
Exports of goods, services, and primary income	BX.GSR.TOTL.CD
Personal transfers and compensation of employees	BX.TRF.PWKR.CD.DT
Imports of goods, services, and primary income	BM.GSR.TOTL.CD
Primary income on FDI (payments)	BX.KLT.DREM.CD.DT
International reserves	FI.RES.TOTL.CD

6. RATIOS	
External debt stocks to exports (%)	DT.DOD.DECT.EX.ZS
External debt stocks to GNI (%)	DT.DOD.DECT.GN.ZS
Debt service to exports (%)	DOD.DECT.GN.ZS
Short-term to external debt stocks (%)	DT.DOD.DSTC.ZS
Multilateral to external debt stocks (%)	DT.DOD.MLAT.ZS
Reserves to external debt stocks (%)	FI.RES.TOTL.DT.ZS
Current account balance	BN.CAB.XOKA.CD
Reserves to imports (months)	FI.RES.TOTL.MO

7. LONG-TERM EXTERNAL DEBT			
Debt outstanding and disbursed	DT.DOD.DLXF.CD	**Interest payments**	DT.INT.DLXF.CD
Public and publicly guaranteed	DT.DOD.DPPG.CD	**Public and publicly guaranteed**	DT.INT.DPPG.CD
Official creditors	DT.DOD.OFFT.CD	Official creditors	DT.INT.OFFT.CD
Multilateral	DT.DOD.MLAT.CD	Multilateral	DT.INT.MLAT.CD
of which: IBRD	DT.DOD.MIBR.CD	of which: IBRD	DT.INT.MIBR.CD
IDA	DT.DOD.MIDA.CD	IDA	DT.INT.MIDA.CD
Bilateral	DT.DOD.BLAT.CD	Bilateral	DT.INT.BLAT.CD
Private creditors	DT.DOD.PRVT.CD	Private creditors	DT.INT.PRVT.CD
of which: Bonds	DT.DOD.PBND.CD	of which: Bonds	DT.INT.PBND.CD
Commercial banks	DT.DOD.PCBK.CD	Commercial banks	DT.INT.PCBK.CD
Private nonguaranteed	DT.DOD.DPNG.CD	Private nonguaranteed	DT.INT.DPNG.CD
of which: Bonds	DT.DOD.PNGB.CD	of which: Bonds	DT.INT.PNGB.CD
Disbursements	DT.DIS.DLXF.CD	**Principal repayments**	DT.AMT.DLXF.CD
Public and publicly guaranteed	DT.DIS.DPPG.CD	Public and publicly guaranteed	DT.AMT.DPPG.CD
Official creditors	DT.DIS.OFFT.CD	Official creditors	DT.AMT.OFFT.CD
Multilateral	DT.DIS.MLAT.CD	Multilateral	DT.AMT.MLAT.CD
of which: IBRD	DT.DIS.MIBR.CD	of which: IBRD	DT.AMT.MIBR.CD
IDA	DT.DIS.MIDA.CD	IDA	DT.AMT.MIDA.CD
Bilateral	DT.DIS.BLAT.CD	Bilateral	DT.AMT.BLAT.CD
Private creditors	DT.DIS.PRVT.CD	Private creditors	DT.AMT.PRVT.CD
of which: Bonds	DT.DIS.PBND.CD	of which: Bonds	DT.AMT.PBND.CD
Commercial banks	DT.DIS.PCBK.CD	Commercial banks	DT.AMT.PCBK.CD
Private nonguaranteed	DT.DIS.DPNG.CD	**Private nonguaranteed**	DT.AMT.DPNG.CD
of which: Bonds	DT.DIS.PNGB.CD	of which: Bonds	DT.AMT.PNGB.CD

8. DEBT STOCK-FLOW RECONCILATION	
Total change in external debt stocks	DT.DOD.DECT.CD.CG
Net flows on external debt	DT.NFL.DECT.CD

9. DEBT STOCK-FLOW RECONCILATION	
Total amount rescheduled	DT.DXR.DPPG.CD
Total amount forgiven	DT.DFR.DPPG.CD
Debt buyback	DT.DSB.DPPG.CD

10. CONTRACTUAL OBLIGATIONS ON OUTSTANDING LONG-TERM EXTERNAL DEBT	
Official creditors	
Principal	DT.AMT.OFFT.CD
Interest	DT.INT.OFFT.CD
Private creditors	
Principal	DT.AMT.PRVT.CD
Interest	DT.INT.PRVT.CD

How to Access the Database

DataBank (http://databank.worldbank.org) is an online web resource that provides simple and quick access to collections of time series data. It has advanced functions for selecting and displaying data, performing customized queries, downloading data, and creating charts and maps. Users can create dynamic, custom reports based on their selection of countries, indicators, and years. All these reports can be easily edited, shared, and embedded as widgets on websites or blogs. For more information, see http://databank.worldbank.org/help.

Actions

Click to share the table using either the embed code or the URL

Click to edit and revise the table in DataBank

Click to export all metadata to Excel

Click to export the table to Excel

Click to export the table and corresponding indicator metadata to PDF

Click to print the table and corresponding indicator metadata

Click to access the IDS Online Tables Help file

Data Sources and Methodology

Data Sources

Debtor reporting system

The principal sources of information for the tables in *International Debt Statistics 2020* are reports to the World Bank through the World Bank's Debtor Reporting System (DRS) from member countries that have received either International Bank for Reconstruction and Development (IBRD) loans or International Development Association (IDA) credits. The DRS has its origin in the World Bank's need to monitor and assess the financial position of its borrowers. Since 1951, borrowers have been required to provide statistics on their public external debt and private sector debt that benefit from a public guarantee. Reporting countries submit reports on the annual status, transactions, and terms of the long-term external debt of public agencies and that of private ones guaranteed by a public agency in the debtor country. The DRS maintains these records on a loan-by-loan basis. In 1973, coverage of the DRS was expanded to include private sector nonguaranteed borrowing, but for this category of debt, data are provided by borrowers in aggregate rather than loan by loan.

Data submitted to the DRS are processed in the World Bank External Debt (WBXD) system, along with additional information received from the African Development Bank, the Asian Development Bank, the Inter-American Development Bank (IDB), the International Monetary Fund (IMF), institutions of the World Bank Group (IBRD and IDA), and the European Bank for Reconstruction and Development (EBRD). The WBXD is an internal system of the World Bank. Among its outputs is the International Debt Statistics (IDS) database, from which the tables in this publication and online database are produced.

Data on exports and imports (on a balance of payments basis), international reserves, current account balances, foreign direct investment (FDI) on equity, portfolio equity flows, and primary income of FDI are drawn mainly from the IMF, supplemented by United Nations Conference on Trade and Development (UNCTAD) reports and country data. Balance of payments data are presented according to the sixth edition of the IMF's *Balance of Payments Manual* (BPM6). Official aid flows come from data collected and published by the Development Assistance Committee (DAC) of the Organisation for Economic Co-operation and Development (OECD). Short-term external debt data are as reported by debtor countries or are estimates based on the Bank for International Settlements (BIS) quarterly series of commercial banks' claims on low- and middle-income countries. For some countries, estimates were prepared by pooling creditor and debtor information. Data on the gross national income of most low- and middle-income countries are collected from national statistical organizations or central banks by visiting and resident World Bank missions.

Every effort has been made to ensure the accuracy and completeness of the external debt statistics. Coverage has been improved through the efforts of the reporting agencies and close collaboration between the Bank and our partners, Commonwealth Secretariat (COMSEC) and UNCTAD, which provide debt recording and reporting systems across the globe, as well as through the work of the World Bank missions, which visit member countries to gather data and to provide technical assistance on debt issues. Nevertheless, quality and coverage vary among debtors and may also vary for the same debtor from year to year. Data on long-term external debt reported by member countries are checked against, and supplemented by, data from several other sources. Among these sources are the statements and reports of several regional development banks, government lending agencies, and official government websites.

Methodology

Aggregations

Total debt stock and other aggregate measures are derived from the summation of loan-level data on stocks and flows after conversion to a common currency. Other tabulations are compiled using terms and conditions reported in the loan-level data, such as currency composition, cancellations, rescheduling of other liabilities into long-term public and publicly guaranteed external debt, and debt buybacks.

Aggregates for regional and income groups are based on the World Bank's operational classifications, which may differ from common geographic usage or income groups used by other organizations. Country classifications of DRS reporting countries in 2018 are shown in the country groups section. The same classification is used for all historical data shown in *International Debt Statistics* and the online tables and online database.

Currency conversion

Data on external obligations are normally reported to the World Bank in the currency of repayment and are converted into a common currency (U.S. dollars) using official exchange rates published by the IMF.

Commitments, disbursements, and debt service payments (flows) are converted to U.S. dollars at the annual average exchange rate for the year. Debt outstanding (disbursed and undisbursed) at the end of a given year (stock) is converted at the exchange rate in effect at the end of the relevant year. Consequently, year-to-year changes in debt outstanding and disbursed may not be equal to net flows (disbursements less principal repayments); similarly, changes in debt outstanding (including undisbursed debt) may not equal commitments less repayments. Discrepancies will be particularly significant when exchange rates have moved sharply during the year. Projected debt service is converted to U.S. dollars at rates in effect at the end of December 2018.

Beginning with 1991, all ruble debt owed to the former Soviet Union has been converted at a rate of US$1 = 0.6 ruble, except in cases where a bilateral agreement specifying a different conversion rate is in place. Adoption of this methodology does not constitute an endorsement by the World Bank staff of the appropriateness or validity of the exchange rate used. That matter must be resolved bilaterally between the Russian Federation and its debtor countries.

Starting with the 1988–89 edition of *World Debt Tables* (a predecessor of IDS), all data pertaining to IBRD loans from 1985 onward are recorded at their current market value. Starting with the 1991–92 edition, all data pertaining to Asian Development Bank loans from 1989 onward are recorded at their current market value. Starting with the 1998 edition, all data pertaining to African Development Bank and African Development Fund loans from 1997 onward are recorded at their current market value.

Debt stock and flow reconciliation

Because of currency conversions and the timing of transactions, there may be differences between the change in aggregate stocks from one period to the next and flows during the relevant period; changes in debt outstanding, including undisbursed amounts, will therefore differ from commitments less repayments.

Changes in the stock of debt from one period to the next can be attributed to five factors: the net flow of debt, the net change in interest arrears, the capitalization of interest, a reduction in debt resulting from debt forgiveness or other debt reduction mechanisms, and cross-currency valuation effects. Any residual difference in the change in stock not explained by one of those five factors may indicate inconsistencies in the reported data or specific phenomena prevailing in an individual country (for example, an incomplete historical series for all categories of debt). Starting in 1989, the IDS includes the debt stock reconciliation, but not all components are shown in the IDS print edition and online tables.

External debt restructuring

Starting in 1985, the WBXD includes information on the restructuring of debt by official creditors in the context of the Paris Club, restructuring by commercial creditors, debt swap operations, buybacks, and bond exchanges. It attempts to capture accurately the effect of debt restructuring on both external debt stocks and external debt flows, consistent with the terms on which the restructuring takes place. In the compilation and presentation of external debt data, a distinction is made between cash flows and imputed flows. According to this criterion, restructured service payments and the shift in liabilities from one financial instrument to another as a result of debt restructuring are considered to be imputed flows. Both cash flows and imputed flows are recorded separately in WBXD.

The imputed flows and stock changes associated with debt restructuring are included in the IDS tables and online database to complement the cash-basis transactions recorded in the main body of the data. Such data encompass information on the debt stock and debt flows restructured each year, the amount of principal forgiven (interest forgiven is shown as a memorandum item), and the amount of external debt stock reduced either by forgiveness or by a debt buyback operation. Changes in creditors and debtors that result from debt restructuring are also reflected. For example, when insured commercial credits are rescheduled, the creditor classification shifts from private to official (bilateral), reflecting the assumption of the assets by the official credit insurance agencies in the creditor country. The IDS data will show a reduction in the external debt owed to the original private creditors equal or similar to the amount of debt restructured and a corresponding increase in the debt owed to the new official creditor. Similarly on the debtor side, when a government accepts responsibility for the payment of restructured debt previously owed by a private enterprise, the relevant change in the debtor category will be reflected. Likewise, if short-term external debt is restructured into a long-term obligation, the stock of short-term external debt will decline and the stock of long-term external debt will rise by the amount of short-term debt restructured. In the event of a debt swap of long-term external debt (external debt to equity, external debt for nature, or external debt for development), the face value of the external debt swapped will be recorded as a decline in long-term external debt stock, but no flow transaction (principal repayment) will be recorded.

Projections of future disbursements and debt service payments

The WBXD system projects future disbursements and future debt service payments on the assumption that every existing loan commitment will be fully used and repaid in full.

Future disbursements

Disbursement projections are made using one of the following methods:

- *Specific schedules.* Debtor countries are requested to submit a schedule of future disbursements, if available, at the time each new loan is first reported.
- *Standard schedules.* In the absence of specific schedules, the WBXD system projects the future disbursement schedule according to the undisbursed balance of each loan at the end of the most recent reporting period.

These projected schedules are based on profiles derived from the disbursement pattern of comparable loans that fully disbursed. Thirty different profiles have been compiled corresponding to each category of creditor and, in the case of official creditors, for concessional and nonconcessional loans. Each profile is derived by applying regression analysis techniques to a body of data on actual disbursements for each fully disbursed loan in the WBXD database. The profiles are periodically updated to take into account the evolving pattern of disbursements observed for fully disbursed loans.

Future principal payments are generated by the WBXD system according to the repayment terms of each loan. Principal repayments (amortization) are based on the amount of the loan commitment. If the amortization schedule follows a set pattern (for example, equal semiannual payments), the WBXD system calculates repayments automatically using the loan commitment amount, the first and final payment dates, and the frequency of the payments. If future payments are irregular, the WBXD system requires a schedule.

Future interest payments are generated by the WBXD system according to the disbursed and outstanding balance of the loan at the beginning of the period. Using the interest rate specified in the loan contract, the first and final interest payment dates, and the frequency of payments, the WBXD system calculates the stream of future interest payments due. If interest payments are irregular, the WBXD system requires a schedule.

Future debt service payments are the sum of future principal and interest payments due on existing commitments, including the undisbursed portion. They do not include debt service payments that may become due as a result of new loans contracted in subsequent years, nor do they take into account the effect of any change to future debt service obligations resulting from actions such as prepayment or rescheduling or from cancellations that occurred after the most recent year-end data reported to the DRS.

Both projected disbursements and future debt service payments are converted into U.S. dollars using end-December 2018 exchange rates. Likewise, future interest payments on loans with a variable interest rate (for example, loans from commercial banks tied to the London Interbank Offered Rate [LIBOR]) are based on the interest rate prevailing at end-December 2018.

Treatment of arrears

The DRS collects information on arrears of both principal and interest. Principal in arrears is included in the amount of long-term external debt outstanding and is shown separately. Interest in arrears on long-term external debt and interest in arrears on the use of IMF credit are included as part of short-term external debt outstanding and are shown separately. Clearance of interest in arrears by repayment will be recorded as an interest payment in the relevant creditor category of the loan (or loans) on which the arrears were incurred, as a corresponding reduction in the level of short-term debt outstanding, and as a net reduction in interest arrears. Clearance of interest arrears through debt restructuring or forgiveness will be recorded as a reduction in the level of short-term debt outstanding and a net reduction in interest arrears. When interests are rescheduled, they will be capitalized: This change will be recorded as an increase in long-term debt outstanding equal to the amount of interest capitalized and the reduction in short-term debt outstanding noted previously.

External Debt and Its Components

This section describes the compilation of the major components of external debt included in the IDS tables and database and the relationship between them, as shown in figure A.1. Information about general methods of compiling external debt data is discussed in the previous section titled "Methodology." For concise definitions, see the glossary.

Total external debt

Total external debt shown in the IDS is the sum of long-term external debt, short-term debt, and IMF credit. It represents the total debt owed to nonresident creditors and is repayable in both foreign and domestic currency.

Short-term debt

Short-term debt is defined as external debt with an original maturity of one year or less. The DRS requires debtor countries to report only on their long-term external debt. However, to gain a comprehensive picture of total external obligations, the World Bank encourages debtor countries to voluntarily provide information on their short-term external obligations.

By its nature, short-term external debt is difficult to monitor: Loan-by-loan registration is normally impractical, and monitoring systems typically rely on information requested periodically by the central bank from the banking sector. The World Bank regards the debtor country as the authoritative source of information on its short-term debt. Unless otherwise specified in the country tables, the data for short-term debt are derived from the data provided by the quarterly external debt statistics database (see QEDS). BIS data on international bank lending is the second source of the short-term debt. These data are reported on the basis of residual maturity, but an estimate of short-term external liabilities by original maturity can be derived by deducting from claims due in one year those that, 12 months earlier, had a maturity of between one and two years. However, not all commercial banks report to the BIS in a way that allows the full maturity distribution to be determined, and the BIS data include liabilities only to banks within the BIS reporting area. Consequently, the results should be interpreted with caution.

The flow of short-term debt may be derived from the change in claims (stock) data in the BIS quarterly series over consecutive periods, but valuation adjustments resulting from exchange rate

Figure A.1. **External Debt and Its Components**

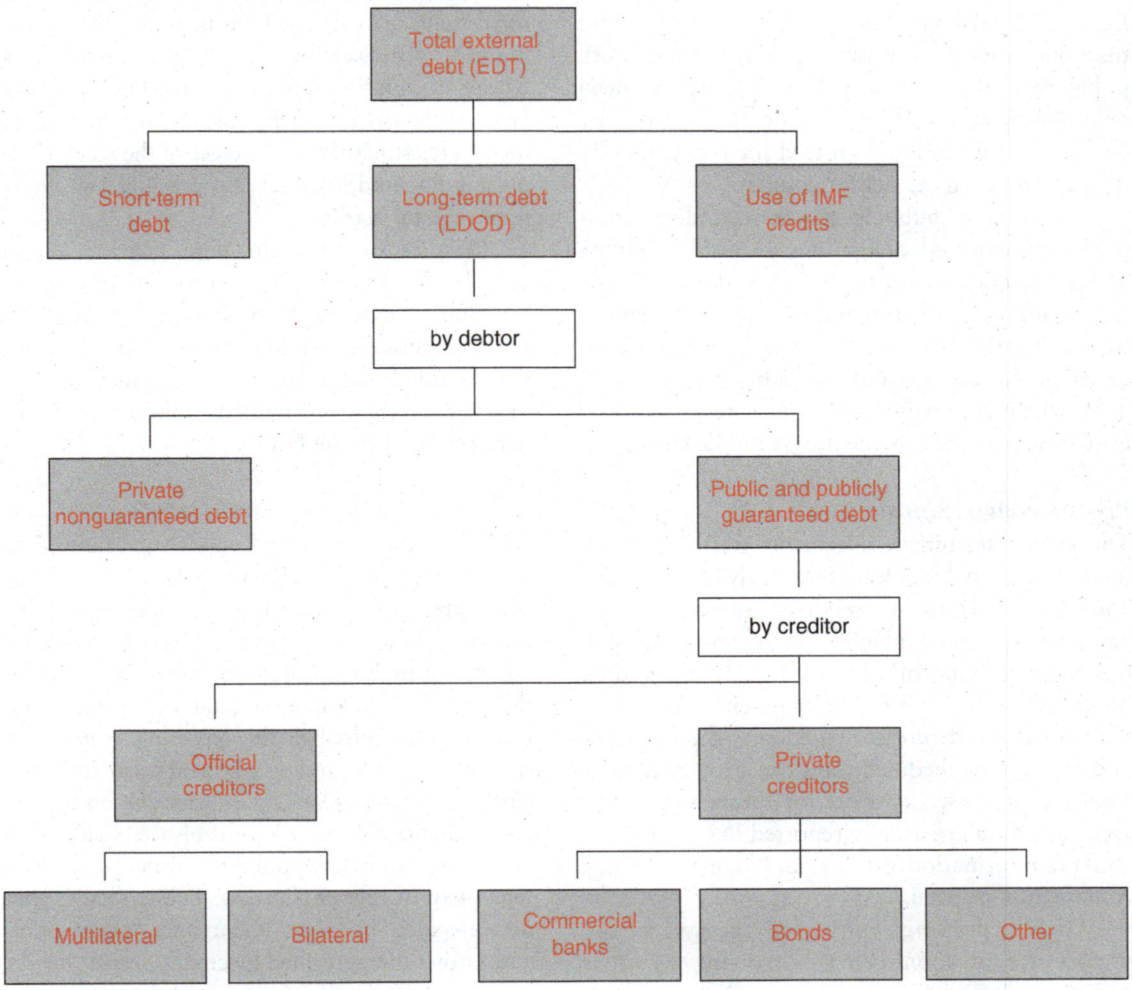

movements will affect the calculations, as will prepayment and refinancing of long-term maturities falling due. When short-term external debt has been rescheduled, lags in reporting and differences in the treatment of the rescheduled external debt by debtors and creditors may result in double counting.

Interest in arrears on long-term external debt and interest in arrears on the use of IMF credit are added to short-term debt and are separately identified.

Use of IMF credit

Data related to the operations of the IMF are provided by the IMF Treasurer's Department. They are converted from special drawing rights (SDR) into dollars using end-of-period exchange rates for stocks and average-over-the-period exchange rates for flows. IMF trust fund operations under the Enhanced Structural Adjustment Facility, Extended Fund Facility, Poverty Reduction and Growth Facility, and Structural Adjustment Facility (Enhanced Structural Adjustment Facility in 1999) are presented together with all of the IMF's special facilities (buffer stock, supplemental reserve, compensatory and contingency facilities, oil facilities, and other facilities). SDR allocations are also included in this category. According to the BPM6, SDR allocations are recorded as the incurrence of a debt liability of the member receiving them (because of a requirement to repay the allocation in certain circumstances, and also because interest accrues). This debt item was introduced for the first time in IDS 2013 with historical data starting in 1999.

Long-term debt

Long-term debt has an original maturity of more than one year. It comprises the obligations of both public and private debtors. Private nonguaranteed debt comprises the external obligations of private debtors that are not guaranteed for repayment by a public entity in the debtor country.

Public and publicly guaranteed debt comprises the external obligations of public debtors and has two components: (a) public debt, which is borrowing by the national government or agency, by a political subdivision or agency, or by autonomous public bodies, and (b) publicly guaranteed debt, which is borrowing by a private agency that is guaranteed for repayment by a public entity.

Private nonguaranteed debt

The DRS reporting requirements were expanded in 1973 to include long-term private nonguaranteed debt. Data are reported annually on an aggregate basis and include, for the reporting year, the total amount of disbursed and outstanding debt; the amount of disbursements, principal repayments, and interest payments; the principal and interest rescheduled; and the projected principal and interest payments for future years. The aggregate data are usually reported in U.S. dollars, and no information on the underlying currency composition is given.

DRS reporting countries recognize the importance of monitoring borrowing by their private sector, particularly when it constitutes a significant portion of total external debt, but many countries acknowledge the difficulty of this process. Detailed data are available only when countries have registration requirements for private nonguaranteed debt in place, most commonly in connection with exchange controls. When formal registration of private nonguaranteed debt is not mandatory, compilers must rely on balance of payments data and financial surveys.

The data on private nonguaranteed debt in this publication is as reported or as estimated for countries where this type of external debt is known to be significant. The estimation of private nonguaranteed debt is based on the national data on quarterly external debt statistics (QEDS) or IMF data. Flows are derived from the change in stock over consecutive periods and are adjusted for the effects of exchange rate movements (assuming the currency composition mirrors that of public and publicly guaranteed debt) and for any known debt restructuring. Principal repayments are estimated on the basis of the average maturity observed for loans to private sector borrowers in countries reporting to the DRS and on the basis of the stock of debt outstanding. Interest payments are estimated on the basis of the stock of debt outstanding and interest rates prevailing in international capital markets.

Balance of payments data provide a useful guideline in the estimation process: private nonguaranteed external debt may be derived as a residual between net long-term external borrowing recorded in the balance of payments and net long-term public and publicly guaranteed external debt reported to the DRS.

Public and publicly guaranteed debt

Data related to public and publicly guaranteed debt are reported to the DRS on a loan-by-loan basis. The data provide annual information on the disbursed and outstanding balance and the undisbursed balance of each loan, the cumulative disbursements, the principal and interest paid and principal and interest restructured in the reporting year, and the stock of any outstanding payment's arrears of principal and interest. Detailed information on the terms and conditions of each loan is also reported. Public debt and private debt publicly guaranteed are shown separately in this publication. Public sector debt is disaggregated by government and "other public" and further disaggregated by creditor type.

Official creditors

Official creditors include multilateral and bilateral lenders. In general, official creditors provide loans (and, in some cases, provide grants) to public bodies, although in some cases they may lend to other entities with a public guarantee.

Multilateral creditors are international financial institutions such as the World Bank, regional development banks, and other multilateral and intergovernmental agencies whose lending is administered on a multilateral basis. Funds administered by an international financial organization on behalf of a single donor government constitute bilateral loans (or grants). For lending by a number of multilateral creditors, the data presented in this publication are taken from the creditors' records. Such creditors include the African Development Bank, the Asian Development Bank, the IDB, IBRD, and IDA. (IBRD and IDA are institutions of the World Bank.)

Bilateral creditors are governments and their agencies, including central banks, aid agencies, official export credit agencies, and autonomous agencies such as the U.S. Department of Agriculture or the Federal Home Loan Bank. Member countries of the OECD Development Assistance Committee (DAC) and some other countries also report information on loans extended bilaterally or officially guaranteed to the Creditor Reporting System of the OECD.

Private creditors

Private creditors include commercial banks, bondholders, and other private creditors. This line includes only publicly guaranteed creditors. Nonguaranteed private creditors are shown separately.

Bonds include publicly issued or privately placed bonds.

Commercial bank loans are loans from private banks and other private financial institutions.

Credits of other private creditors include credits from manufacturers, exporters, and other suppliers of goods, plus bank credits covered by a guarantee of an export credit agency. This line is included in the online database but is not shown in the published tables. It can be obtained as the difference between (a) credits of total private creditors and (b) bonds and commercial bank loans.

Data Documentation

Country Specific Notes on Debt

Country	Country Notes
Afghanistan	Short-term debt before to 2015 is based on data from the BIS. Data include the effects of Paris Club debt restructuring agreements signed in 2010 and HIPC and MDRI debt relief.
Angola	Long-term private nonguaranteed debt data are estimates based on Central Bank data and are not available before 2009. Short-term debt before 2012 is based on data from the BIS.
Argentina	Long-term private nonguaranteed debt data before 2008 are World Bank staff estimates. Short-term debt before 2010 is based on data from the BIS.
Azerbaijan	Long-term private nonguaranteed debt data are World Bank staff estimates based on the market data. Short-term debt is based on data from the BIS.
Bangladesh	Short-term debt before 2012 is based on data from the BIS. Long-term private nonguaranteed debt data from 2007 are World Bank staff estimates based on reports provided by the country and are not available prior to 2007.
Belarus	Long-term private nonguaranteed debt data from 2014 are World Bank staff estimates based on reports provided by the country.
Belize	Long-term private nonguaranteed debt data from 2008 are based on Central Bank data.
Benin	Short-term debt is based on data from the BIS. Data include the effects of Paris Club debt restructuring agreement and HIPC and MDRI debt relief.
Bhutan	Short-term debt is based on data from the BIS.
Bolivia	Long-term private nonguaranteed debt data are World Bank staff estimates based on reports provided by the country.
Bosnia and Herzegovina	Long-term private nonguaranteed debt data from 2005 are World Bank staff estimates. Short-term debt is based on data from the BIS.
Botswana	Short-term debt is based on data from the BIS.
Bulgaria	Long-term private nonguaranteed debt data from 2008 are World Bank staff estimates based on reports provided by the country. Short-term debt before 2009 is World Bank staff estimates based on Central Bank data. The data may include long-term public and publicly guaranteed debt owed by the state-owned railway.
Burkina Faso	Data include HIPC and MDRI debt relief.
Burundi	Data include the effects of Paris Club debt restructuring agreement and HIPC and MDRI debt relief.
Cambodia	Long-term private nonguaranteed debt data are estimates based on Central Bank data. Data include MDRI debt relief.
Cameroon	Short-term debt is based on data from the BIS. Data include the effects of HIPC and MDRI debt relief.

Country	Country Notes
Central African Republic	Short-term debt is based on data from the BIS. Data include the effects of HIPC and MDRI debt relief.
Chad	Long-term public and publicly guaranteed debt data from 2016 are World Bank staff estimates based on the original terms of the loans. Short-term debt is based on data from the BIS. Data include the effects of HIPC debt relief.
China	Long-term public and publicly guaranteed and long-term private nonguaranteed are World Bank staff estimates based on the aggregate reports provided by the country and market data.
Comoros	Data include the effects of Paris Club debt restructuring agreements signed in 2010 and 2013, and the HIPC debt relief.
Congo, Republic of	Short-term debt is based on data from the BIS. Data include the effects of Paris Club debt restructuring agreement and HIPC and MDRI debt relief.
Congo, Democratic Republic of	Short-term debt is based on data from the BIS. Data include the effects of Paris Club debt restructuring agreement and HIPC and MDRI debt relief.
Costa Rica	Long-term private nonguaranteed debt data are World Bank staff estimates based on reports provided by the country. Short-term debt before 2005 is based on data from the BIS.
Côte d'Ivoire	Long-term private nonguaranteed debt data are World Bank staff estimates. Short-term debt is based on data from the BIS. Data include the effects of Paris Club agreement signed in 2011, 2012 and HIPC and MDRI debt relief.
Djibouti	Short-term debt before 2017 is based on data from the BIS. Data include the effects of Paris Club debt restructuring agreement signed in 2008.
Dominican Republic	Long-term private nonguaranteed debt data for 2018 are World Bank staff estimates, prior to 2018 is based on country reports. Short-term debt before 2009 and 2014 onward is based on data from the BIS. Data include the effects of Paris Club debt restructuring agreement signed in 2005.
El Salvador	Long-term private nonguaranteed debt data from 2005 to 2016 are World Bank staff estimates based on reports provided by the country.
Eritrea	Long-term public and publicly guaranteed debt from 2010 are World Bank staff estimates. Short-term debt is based on data from the BIS.
Eswatini	Short-term debt is based on data from the BIS.
Ethiopia	Short-term debt is based on data from the BIS. Data include the effects of HIPC and MDRI debt relief.
Fiji	Long-term private nonguaranteed debt data for 2012 are World Bank staff estimates. Short-term debt is based on data from the BIS.
Gabon	Long-term public and publicly guaranteed debt data before 2008 are World Bank staff estimates based on reports provided by the country. Short-term debt is based on data from the BIS. Data include the effects of Paris Club debt buyback agreement signed in 2007.
Gambia, The	Short-term debt is based on data from the BIS. Data include the effects of HIPC and MDRI debt relief.
Ghana	Long-term private nonguaranteed debt data only cover bonds. Short-term debt is based on data from the BIS. Data include the effects of MDRI debt relief.
Grenada	Short-term debt is based on data from the BIS.
Guatemala	Long-term private nonguaranteed debt data are World Bank staff estimates based on market data. Short-term debt before 2012 is based on data from the BIS.
Guinea	Long-term public and publicly guaranteed debt for 2016 are World Bank staff estimates. Short-term debt is based on data from the BIS. Data include the effects of Paris Club debt restructuring agreement signed in 2010, 2012 and HIPC debt relief.
Guinea-Bissau	Short-term debt is based on data from the BIS. Data include the effects of Paris Club debt restructuring agreement and HIPC and MDRI debt relief.
Guyana	Long-term private nonguaranteed debt data after 2014 are World Bank staff estimates based on market data. Short-term debt is based on data from the BIS. Principal payment shown from 2012 include rice for oil deal. Data include the effects of HIPC and MDRI debt relief.
Haiti	Long-term private nonguaranteed debt data only cover IDB loans. Short-term debt before 2007 is based on data from the BIS. Data include the effects of Paris Club restructuring agreements signed in 2006 and 2009 and HIPC and MDRI debt relief.

Country	Country Notes
Honduras	Data include the effects of HIPC and MDRI debt relief.
India	External debt data prior to 2003 are revised from fiscal year to calendar year. Long-term public and publicly guaranteed bonds include Foreign Institutional Investor debt (FII) as reported by the Reserve Bank of India.
Iran, Islamic Republic of	Short-term debt is based on Central Bank data.
Jamaica	Short-term debt before 2012 is based on data from the BIS.
Jordan	Long-term private nonguaranteed debt data from 2001 are based on reports provided by the country. Short-term debt before 1999 is based on data from the BIS.
Kenya	Long-term private nonguaranteed debt data are World Bank staff estimates based on market data. Short-term debt is based on data from the BIS.
Kyrgyz Republic	Long-term private nonguaranteed debt data are World Bank staff estimates based on reports provided by the country.
Lao People's Democratic Republic	Long-term private nonguaranteed debt data are World Bank staff estimates. Short-term debt is based on data from the BIS.
Lebanon	Long-term private nonguaranteed debt data from 2008 to 2012 are World Bank staff estimates based on the 2013-2017 debt stock. Short-term debt before 2013 is based on data from the BIS.
Lesotho	Large interest payment was made during 2007 to a creditor country to settle a long-standing claim.
Liberia	Long-term private nonguaranteed debt data are World Bank staff estimates based on market data. Data include the effects of Paris Club rescheduling agreement signed in 2008 and 2010, and HIPC and MDRI debt relief.
Madagascar	Long-term private nonguaranteed debt data for 2017 and 2018 are World Bank staff estimates based on market data. Short-term debt from 2017 is based on data from the BIS. Data include the effects of HIPC and MDRI debt relief.
Malawi	Short-term debt is based on data from the BIS. Data include the effects of Paris Club rescheduling agreement signed in 2006 and HIPC and MDRI debt relief.
Maldives	Long-term private nonguaranteed and short-term debt data from 2006 are World Bank staff estimates based on reports provided by the country. Short-term debt is based on data from the BIS.
Mali	Short-term debt is based on data from the BIS. Data include the effects of HIPC and MDRI debt relief.
Mauritania	Short-term debt is based on data from the BIS. Data include the effects of MDRI debt relief.
Mauritius	Long-term private nonguaranteed debt data from 2009 to 2010 are based on reports provided by the country and do not include offshore liabilities and 2011-2018 are World Bank staff estimates based on reports provided by the country. Short-term debt is based on reports provided by the country and includes offshore liabilities.
Mongolia	Long-term private nonguaranteed debt data before 2016 are World Bank staff estimates based on reports provided by the country. Short-term debt before 2008 is based on data from the BIS.
Montenegro	Long-term private nonguaranteed debt data for 2018 and 2017 are World Bank staff estimates, prior to 2017 is based on country reports. Short-term debt for 2018 are World Bank staff estimates, prior to 2018 is based on country reports
Morocco	Short-term debt before 2009 is based on data from the BIS.
Mozambique	Short-term debt is based on data from the BIS. Data include HIPC and MDRI debt relief.
Myanmar	Long-term public and publicly guaranteed before 2018 are World Bank staff estimates based on the original terms of the loans. Long-term private nonguaranteed debt data are World Bank staff estimates based on the market data.
Nepal	Long-term private nonguaranteed debt data are World Bank staff estimates based on reports provided by the country.
Nicaragua	Short-term debt before 2007 is based on data from the BIS. Data include the effects of HIPC and MDRI debt relief.
Niger	Short-term debt is based on data from the BIS. Data include the effects of HIPC and MDRI debt relief.
Nigeria	Long-term private nonguaranteed debt data from 2005 are estimates based on market data.

Country	Country Notes
Pakistan	Long-term private nonguaranteed debt data from 2006 to 2015 World Bank staff estimates based on the reports provided by the country. Short-term debt before 2010 is based on data from the BIS.
Papua New Guinea	Short-term debt is based on data from the BIS.
Peru	Long-term private nonguaranteed debt data are World Bank staff estimates based on reports provided by the country.
Philippines	Long-term private nonguaranteed debt data no longer include unregistered debt and are revised from 2005 based on the reports provided by the country.
Russia Federation	Long-term public and publicly guaranteed and long-term private nonguaranteed debt are World Bank staff estimates based on reports provided by the country.
Rwanda	Data include the effects of HIPC and MDRI debt relief.
Samoa	Short-term debt data are excluded since BIS data include debt liabilities of offshore centers located in the country. BIS short-term debt data for 2016, 2017 and 2018 are $3.9 billion, $4.2 billion and $4.4 billion, respectively.
São Tomé and Principe	Short-term debt is based on data from the BIS. Data include HIPC and MDRI debt relief.
Senegal	Short-term debt before 2009 is based on data from the BIS.
Serbia	Beginning 2006, the data for Serbia exclude Montenegro. Short-term debt before 2014 is World Bank staff estimates based on Central Bank data.
Sierra Leone	Short-term debt before 2016 is based on data from the BIS.
Somalia	Long-term public and publicly guaranteed debt data are World Bank staff estimates based on the original terms of the loans.
South Africa	Long-term public and publicly guaranteed and long-term private nonguaranteed debt data are World Bank staff estimates.
St. Lucia	Short-term debt before 2012 is based on data from the BIS.
St. Vincent and the Grenadines	Short-term debt data are excluded since BIS data include debt liabilities of offshore centers located in the country. BIS short-term debt data for 2014, 2015, 2016, 2017 and 2018 are $1239 million, $676 million, $806 million, $787 million and $532 million respectively.
Sudan	Data includes South Sudan. Long-term public and publicly guaranteed debt data exclude penalty interest. Short-term debt is based on data from the BIS.
Syrian Arab Republic	Long-term public and publicly guaranteed debt data are World Bank staff estimates. Short-term debt is based on data from the BIS.
Tajikistan	Short-term debt before 2015 is based on data from the BIS. Data include MDRI debt relief.
Tanzania	Long-term public and publicly guaranteed debt data include debt liabilities of Zanzibar. Long-term public, publicly guaranteed and private nonguaranteed debt data are World Bank staff estimates based on the original terms of the loans. Short-term debt is based on data from the BIS. Data include the effects of HIPC and MDRI debt relief.
Timor-Leste	Short-term debt is based on data from the BIS.
Togo	Short-term debt is based on data from the BIS. Data include the effects of Paris Club debt restructuring agreement and HIPC and MDRI debt relief.
Tunisia	Long-term private nonguaranteed debt data from 2008 are estimates based on reports provided by the country.
Turkey	Long-term public and publicly guaranteed debt data include nonresident deposits made under the Dresdner Bank scheme, amounting to $8.4 million at end-2018.
Turkmenistan	Long-term public and publicly guaranteed debt from 2010 are World Bank staff estimates. Long-term private nonguaranteed debt data (excluding bonds) only cover European Bank for Reconstruction and Development lending.
Uganda	Long-term private nonguaranteed debt data are World Bank staff estimates based on market data. Data include the effects of HIPC and MDRI debt relief.

Country	Country Notes
Uzbekistan	Short-term debt is based on data from the BIS.
Vanuatu	Short-term debt is based on data from the BIS.
Venezuela, República Bolivariana de	Long-term public and publicly guaranteed debt are World Bank staff estimates based on creditors data and estimates on the 2016 debt stocks. Long-term private nonguaranteed debt data and short-term debt are World Bank staff estimates based on country reports.
Vietnam	Short-term debt before 2016 is based on data from the BIS.
Yemen, Republic of	Short-term debt is based on data from the BIS.
Zambia	Long-term private nonguaranteed data before 2016 are World Bank staff estimates based on reports provided by the country. Short-term debt is based on data from the BIS. Data include the effects of HIPC and MDRI debt relief.
Zimbabwe	Long-term private nonguaranteed data are World Bank staff estimates based on reports provided by the country. Data from 2001 include late interest fee owed to Paris Club and Commercial Creditors. Short-term debt is based on data from the BIS.

Sources of the Macroeconomic Indicators

The macroeconomic data are prepared by The World Bank from a variety of sources. Data on Personal Transfers and Compensation of Employees are prepared by World Bank staff based on IMF balance of payments statistics. Data on foreign direct investments and current account balance are prepared by World Bank staff based on IMF balance of payments statistics and UNCTAD publication. Other macroeconomic data are from IMF balance of payments statistics.

Data on exports of goods, services, and primary income are based on countries' balance of payments statistics for the following countries:

Benin (2018)
Comoros (2013–17)
Eswatini (2018)
Grenada (2018)
Guinea (2018)
Kenya (2018)
Lebanon (2018)
Nigeria (2018)
Papua New Guinea (2018)
Samoa (2018)
Sri Lanka (2018)
St. Lucia (2018)
St. Vincent, and the Grenadines (2018)
Timor-Leste (2018)
Zimbabwe (2018)

Data on imports of goods, services, and primary income are based on countries' balance of payments statistics for the following countries:

Benin (2018)
Comoros (2013–17)
Eswatini (2018)
Grenada (2018)
Guinea (2018)
Kenya (2018)
Lebanon (2018)
Nigeria (2018)
Papua New Guinea (2018)
Samoa (2018)
Sri Lanka (2018)
St. Lucia (2018)
St. Vincent, and the Grenadines (2018)
Timor-Leste (2018)
Zimbabwe (2018)

Data on current account balance are based on countries' balance of payments statistics for the following countries:

Algeria (2018)	Guinea-Bissau (2018)	Samoa (2018)
Benin (2018)	Kenya (2018)	Senegal (2018)
Burkina Faso (2018)	Lebanon (2018)	St. Lucia (2018)
Burundi (2018)	Malawi (2018)	St. Vincent and the Grenadines (2018)
Comoros (2013–17)	Mali (2018)	Timor-Leste (2018)
Côte d'Ivoire (2018)	Niger (2018)	Togo (2018)
Dominica (2018)	Nigeria (2018)	Venezuela, RB (2018)
Eswatini (2018)	Papua New Guinea (2018)	Zimbabwe (from 2018)
Grenada (2018)		

Data on personal transfers and compensation of employees are based on countries' balance of payments statistics for the following countries:

Dominica (2018)	Lebanon (2018)	St. Lucia (2018)
Grenada (2018)	Nigeria (2018)	St. Vincent and the Grenadines (2018)
Guinea (2018)	Sri Lanka (2018)	Zimbabwe (2018)

Data on portfolio equity are based on countries' balance of payments statistics for the following countries:

Kenya (2018)	Sri Lanka (2018)	St. Vincent and the Grenadines (2018)
Nigeria (2018)	St. Lucia (2018)	Sierra Leone (from 2012)

Data on primary income on foreign direct investment are based on countries' balance of payment statistics for the following countries:

Dominica (2018)	Lebanon (2018)	St. Lucia (2018)
Grenada (2018)	Nigeria (2018)	

Data on foreign direct investment are based on countries' balance of payments statistics for the following countries:

Dominica (2018)	St. Lucia (2018)	St. Vincent and the Grenadines (2018)
Grenada (2018)		

Country Groups

Regional Groups

East Asia and Pacific

Cambodia (A)
China (P)
Fiji (A)
Indonesia (A)
Lao PDR (A)
Mongolia (A)
Myanmar (A)
Papua New Guinea (A)
Philippines (A)
Samoa (A)
Solomon Islands (A)
Thailand (A)
Timon-Leste (A)
Tonga (A)
Vanuatu (A)
Vietnam (A)

Europe and Central Asia

Albania (A)
Armenia (A)
Azerbaijan (A)
Belarus (A)
Bosnia and Herzegovina[a] (A)
Bulgaria (A)
Georgia (A)
Kazakhstan (A)
Kosovo (A)
Kyrgyz Republic (A)
Moldova (A)
Montenegro (A)
North Macedonia (A)
Romania (A)
Russian Federation (P)
Serbia[a,b] (A)
Tajikistan (A)
Turkey (A)
Turkmenistan (E)
Ukraine (A)
Uzbekistan (A)

Latin America and the Caribbean

Argentina (A)
Belize (A)
Bolivia (A)
Brazil (A)
Colombia (A)
Costa Rica (A)
Dominica (A)
Dominican Republic (A)
Ecuador (A)
El Salvador (A)
Grenada (A)
Guatemala (A)
Guyana (A)
Haiti (A)
Honduras (A)
Jamaica (A)
Mexico (A)
Nicaragua (A)
Paraguay (A)
Peru (A)
St. Lucia (A)
St. Vincent and the Grenadines (A)
Venezuela, RB (E)

Middle East and North Africa

Algeria (A)
Djibouti (A)
Egypt, Arab Rep. (A)
Iran, Islamic Rep. (A)
Jordan (A)
Lebanon (A)
Morocco (A)
Syrian Arab Republic (E)
Tunisia (A)
Yemen, Rep. (A)

South Asia

Afghanistan (A)
Bangladesh (A)
Bhutan (A)
India (A)
Maldives (A)
Nepal (A)
Pakistan (A)
Sri Lanka (A)

Sub-Saharan Africa

Angola (A)
Benin (A)
Botswana (A)
Burkina Faso (A)
Burundi (A)
Cabo Verde (A)
Cameroon (A)
Central African Republic (A)
Chad (E)
Comoros (A)
Congo, Dem. Rep. (A)
Congo, Rep. (A)
Côte d'Ivoire (A)
Eritrea (E)
Eswatini (A)
Ethiopia (A)
Gabon (A)
Gambia, The (A)
Ghana (A)
Guinea (A)
Guinea-Bissau (A)
Kenya (A)
Lesotho (A)
Liberia (A)
Madagascar (A)
Malawi (A)
Mali (A)
Mauritania (A)
Mauritius (A)
Mozambique (A)
Niger (A)
Nigeria (A)
Rwanda (A)
São Tomé and Príncipe (A)
Senegal (A)
Sierra Leone (A)
Somalia (E)
South Africa (E)
Sudan[c] (P)
Tanzania (E)
Togo (A)
Uganda (A)
Zambia (A)
Zimbabwe (A)

Note: Letters in parenthesis indicate DRS reporters' status: (A) as reported, (P) preliminary, and (E) estimated. The status "as reported" indicates that the country was fully current in its reporting under the DRS and that World Bank staff are satisfied that the reported data give an adequate and fair representation of the country's total public debt. "Preliminary" data are based on reported or collected information, but because of incompleteness or other reasons, an element of staff estimation is included. "Estimated" data indicate that countries are not current in their reporting and that a significant element of staff estimation has been necessary in producing the data tables.

a. For Bosnia and Herzegovina, total debt before 1999, excluding IBRD and IMF obligations and short-term debt, is included under Serbia.
b. Data prior to 2006 include Montenegro.
c. Data include South Sudan.

Income Groups

Low-income countries

Afghanistan
Benin
Burkina Faso
Burundi
Central African Republic
Chad
Congo, Dem. Rep.
Eritrea
Ethiopia
Gambia, The
Guinea
Guinea-Bissau
Haiti
Liberia
Madagascar
Malawi
Mali
Mozambique
Nepal
Niger
Rwanda
Sierra Leone
Somalia
Syrian Arab Republic
Tajikistan
Tanzania
Togo
Uganda
Yemen, Rep.

Middle-income countries

Albania
Algeria
Angola
Argentina
Armenia
Azerbaijan
Bangladesh
Belarus
Belize
Bhutan
Bolivia
Bosnia and Herzegovina
Botswana
Brazil
Bulgaria
Cabo Verde
Cambodia
Cameroon
China
Colombia
Comoros
Congo, Rep.
Costa Rica
Côte d'Ivoire
Djibouti
Dominica
Dominican Republic
Ecuador
Egypt, Arab Rep.
El Salvador
Eswatini
Fiji
Gabon
Georgia
Ghana
Grenada
Guatemala
Guyana
Honduras
India
Indonesia
Iran, Islamic Rep.
Jamaica
Jordan
Kazakhstan
Kenya
Kosovo
Kyrgyz Republic
Lao PDR
Lebanon
Lesotho
Maldives
Mauritania
Mauritius
Mexico
Moldova
Mongolia
Montenegro
Morocco
Myanmar
Nicaragua
Nigeria
North Macedonia
Pakistan
Papua New Guinea
Paraguay
Peru
Philippines
Romania
Russian Federation
Samoa
São Tomé and Príncipe
Senegal
Serbia
Solomon Islands
South Africa
Sri Lanka
St. Lucia
St. Vincent and the Grenadines
Sudan
Thailand
Timor-Leste
Tonga
Tunisia
Turkey
Turkmenistan
Ukraine
Uzbekistan
Vanuatu
Venezuela, RB
Vietnam
Zambia
Zimbabwe

Note: Low-income countries are those with a GNI per capita of $1,025 or less in 2018. Middle-income countries are those with a GNI per capita of more than $1,026 but less than $12,375. Italicized countries are IDA-only countries as of July 1, 2019; IDA-only excludes blend and IBRD countries.

Glossary

Debtor Reporting System (DRS)

Bilateral official creditors are official agencies that make loans on behalf of one government to another government or to public (and, in some cases, private) borrowers in another country.

Bonds are debt instruments issued by public and publicly guaranteed or private debtors with durations of one year or longer. Bonds usually give the holder the unconditional right to fixed money income or contractually determined, variable money income.

Commitments of public and publicly guaranteed debt constitute the total amount of new long-term loans to public sector borrowers or borrowers with a public sector guarantee extended by official and private lenders and for which contracts were signed in the year specified.

Concessional debt conveys information about the borrower's receipt of aid from official lenders at concessional terms as defined by the World Bank, that is, loans with an original grant element of 35 percent or more. Loans from major regional development banks—African Development Bank, Asian Development Bank, and the Inter-American Development Bank—are classified as concessional according the World Bank classification.

Contractual obligations on outstanding long-term external debt are the anticipated debt service payments on long-term external debt contracted up to December 31 of the reporting year.

Debt buyback is the repurchase by a debtor of its own debt, either at a discount price or at par value. In the event of a buyback of long-term debt, the face value of the debt bought back will be recorded as a decline in stock outstanding of long-term debt, and the cash amount received by creditors will be recorded as a principal repayment. For example, if a country buys back long-term external debt of face value B at a price P, then long-term external debt will decline by B, and principal repayment will increase by P. The difference between the price at which the debt was bought back and the face value is recorded as a debt stock write-off (the related transactions are not separately identified in the International Debt Statistics [IDS] publication but are available in the online database).

Debt forgiveness grants include both debts canceled by agreement between debtor and creditor and reductions in the net present value of official nonconcessional loans resulting from concessional rescheduling or refinancing. Data are recorded on a disbursement basis and include debt forgiveness from bilateral and multilateral creditors.

Debt outstanding and disbursed is the value at year's end of long-term external debt owed by public and publicly guaranteed debtors and private nonguaranteed debtors.

Debt restructurings are revisions to debt service obligations agreed on by creditors and debtors. Such agreements change the amount and timing of future principal and interest payments.

Debt service to exports is the ratio of the sum of principal repayments and interest paid on total long-term debt (public and publicly guaranteed debt and private nonguaranteed debt) to the value of exports of goods and services and receipts of primary income from abroad.

Debt stock-flow reconciliation shows the indicators that affect the change in debt stocks from one period to the next.

Disbursements are drawings during the year specified on loan commitments contracted by the borrower.

Exports of goods, services, and primary income constitute the total value of exports of goods and services, and primary income.

External debt flows are debt-related transactions during the year specified. They include disbursements, principal repayments, and interest payments.

External debt stocks comprise public and publicly guaranteed long-term external debt, private nonguaranteed long-term external debt, use of IMF credit, and short-term external debt, including interest arrears on long-term debt.

External debt stocks to exports is the ratio of outstanding external debt to the value of exports of goods and services and receipts of primary income from abroad.

External debt stocks to GNI is the ratio of outstanding external debt to gross national income.

Foreign direct investment refers to direct investment equity flows in the reporting economy. It is the sum of equity capital, reinvestment earnings, and other capital. Direct investment is a category of cross-border investment associated with a resident in one economy having control or a significant degree of influence on the management of an enterprise that is resident in another economy. Ownership of 10 percent or more of the ordinary shares or voting stock is the criterion for determining the existence of a direct investment relationship.

Government sector debt consists of all external debt obligations of all levels of the departments, branches, agencies, foundations, institutes, nonmarket and non-profit institutions controlled by the government, and other publicly controlled organizations engaging in non-market activities.

Grace period is the time between the date on which a loan is committed and the date on which the first principal payment is due. The information presented in International Debt Statistics is the average grace period on all public and publicly guaranteed debt committed during the specified period.

Grants are legally binding commitments that obligate a specific value of funds available for disbursement for which there is no payment requirement. They include debt forgiveness grants and grants from bilateral and multilateral agencies (such as the International Development Association).

Gross national income (GNI) is the sum of value added by all resident producers, plus any product taxes (less subsidies) not included in the valuation of output, plus net receipts of primary income compensation of employees and property income from abroad. Yearly average exchange rates are used to convert GNI from local currency to U.S. dollars.

Heavily Indebted Poor Country (HIPC) Initiative is a program of the World Bank and the International Monetary Fund (IMF) to provide debt relief to qualifying countries with unsustainable debt burdens.

Imports of goods, services, and primary income constitute the total value of goods and services imported and income payable to nonresidents. Interest arrears on long-term debt are interest payments due but not paid, shown on a cumulative basis.

Interest arrears are due and payable immediately and are therefore regarded as short-term obligations. Thus, an increase in interest arrears on long-term debt will be recorded as an increase in short-term debt. Interest in arrears on the use of IMF credit is also considered to be part of short-term external debt.

Interest payments are the amounts of interest paid in foreign currency, goods, or services in the year specified.

Interest rate is the interest rate applicable to a loan commitment as specified in the loan contract. The information presented in International Debt Statistics is the average interest on all public and publicly guaranteed debt committed during the specified period.

IMF charges are the amounts of interest paid in foreign currency in the year specified for transactions with the IMF.

IMF purchases are the total drawings on the general resources account of the IMF during the year specified, excluding drawings in the reserve tranche.

IMF repurchases are the amounts of principal (amortization) paid in foreign currency in the year specified for transactions with the IMF.

International reserves constitute the sum of a country's monetary authority's holdings of special drawing rights, its reserve position in the IMF, its holdings of foreign exchange, and its holdings of gold (valued at year-end London prices).

Long-term external debt is debt that has an original or extended maturity of more than one year and that is owed to nonresidents by residents of an economy and is repayable in foreign currency, goods, or services.

Maturity is the date on which the final principal repayment on a loan is due. It is the sum of the grace and repayment periods. The information presented in International Debt Statistics is the average maturity on all public and publicly guaranteed debt committed during the specified period.

Multilateral Debt Relief Initiative (MDRI) is a program of the World Bank, the IMF, the Inter-American Development Bank, and the African Development Bank that provides additional debt relief to countries that have completed the HIPC process.

Multilateral official creditors are official agencies owned or governed by more than one country that provide loan financing. They include international financial institutions such as the World Bank, regional development banks, and other intergovernmental agencies.

Multilateral to external debt stocks is the ratio of the stock of debt owed to multilateral creditors to total external debt.

Net flows on external debt are disbursements on long-term external debt and IMF purchases minus principal repayments on long-term external debt and IMF repurchases. Up to 1984, this calculation included only long-term external debt and IMF flows. Since 1985, the calculation includes the change in stock of short-term debt (excluding interest arrears on long-term external debt).

Official creditors are governments or other bilateral public entities, such as export-import agencies, development agencies, and multilateral financial institutions, such as the World Bank and regional development banks.

Personal transfers and compensation of employees is the sum of personal transfers and compensation of employees. Personal transfers consist of all current transfers in cash or in kind made or received by resident households to or from nonresident households. Personal transfers thus include all current transfers between resident and nonresident individuals. Compensation of employees refers to the income of border, seasonal, and other short-term workers who are employed in an economy where they are not resident and of residents employed by nonresident entities.

Portfolio equity is the category of international investment that covers investment in equity securities. Equity securities include shares, stocks, participation, or similar documents (such as American Depositary Receipts) that usually denote ownership of equity.

Present value of debt outstanding is the nominal value of all future debt service obligations on existing debt discounted at prevailing market rates of interest. The interest rates used in this calculation are the Commercial Interest Reference Rates (CIRR) for each relevant currency compiled and published by the Organisation for Economic Co-operation and Development.

Primary income on FDI are payments of direct investment income (debit side), which consist of income on equity (dividends, branch profits, and reinvested earnings) and income on the intercompany debt (interest).

Principal arrears on long-term debt are principal repayments due but not paid on long-term external debt, shown on a cumulative basis.

Principal repayments are the amounts of principal (amortization) paid in foreign currency, goods, or services in the year specified with respect to long-term external debt.

Private creditors are bondholders, commercial banks, and other trade-related lenders.

Private nonguaranteed debt is debt owed by private sector borrowers to external creditors on loans that do not benefit from a public sector guarantee by the debtor country.

Public and publicly guaranteed debt outstanding and disbursed is the value of debt at year's end of public sector borrowers, or borrowers with a public sector guarantee, owed to official and private lenders.

Public and publicly guaranteed external debt comprises public debt (an external obligation of a public debtor, such as the national government or agency, a political subdivision or agency, or an autonomous public body) and publicly guaranteed external debt (an external obligation of a private debtor that is guaranteed for repayment by a public entity).

Public debt is an external obligation of a public debtor, including all levels of government, state-owned enterprises, public corporations, development banks, and any other autonomous public bodies of government.

Publicly guaranteed debt is an external obligation of a private debtor that is guaranteed for repayment by a public entity.

Reserves to external debt stocks is the ratio of international reserves to outstanding external debt.

Reserves to imports (months) is the ratio of international reserves to the value of imports of goods, services, and primary income in the year shown and is expressed in months:

$$\frac{\text{Reserves}}{\text{Imports/12}}$$

Short-term external debt has an original maturity of one year or less. Available data permit no distinction among public, publicly guaranteed, and private nonguaranteed short-term external debt.

Short-term to external debt stock ratio is the ratio of short-term external debt to total outstanding external debt.

Special Drawing Rights (SDRs) refer to an international reserve asset that was created by the IMF in 1969 to supplement its member countries' official reserves. The value of SDRs is based on a basket of four key international currencies: the U.S. dollar, the pound sterling, the Japanese yen, and the euro. In addition to playing a role as a supplementary reserve asset, SDRs serve as the unit of account for the IMF and some other international organizations.

Technical cooperation grants include (a) free-standing technical cooperation grants, which are intended to finance the transfer of technical and managerial skills or of technology for the purpose of building up general national capacity without reference to any specific investment projects, and (b) investment-related technical cooperation grants, which are aimed at strengthening the capacity to execute specific investment projects.

Total amount forgiven is the total amount of principal and interest due, principal and interest in arrears, and debt stock forgiven in the year specified.

Total amount rescheduled is the total amount of external debt rescheduled, including principal and interest due, principal and interest in arrears, charges, penalties, and debt stock in the year specified.

Total change in external debt stocks is the difference in the external debt stock between two consecutive years.

Use of IMF credit denotes members' drawings on the IMF other than amounts drawn against the country's reserve tranche position. Use of IMF credit includes purchases and drawings under Stand-By, Extended, Structural Adjustment, Enhanced Structural Adjustment, and Systemic Transformation Facility Arrangements as well as trust fund loans. SDR allocations are also included in this category.